THE STATE OF THE WORLD'S CHILDREN 2017

Children in a Digital World

unicef

for every child

Contents

Adolescents in Bhutan and 25 other countries talked about what digital technology means to them in the State of the World's Children 2017 workshops. To hear what they had to say, look out for the "What do adolescents think about …" boxes in this report or read the companion report, Young and Online: Children's perspectives on life in the digital age. ©UNICEF BHUTAN/2017/SHERPA

Foreword

The State of the World's Children 2017 is about an extraordinary subject that increasingly affects almost every aspect of life for millions of children around the world and, indeed, for us all: digital technology.

As the influence of digital technology – and especially the internet – has increased, the debate about its impact has grown louder: Is it a boon to humankind, offering unlimited opportunity for communication and commerce, learning and free expression? Or is it a threat to our way of life, undermining the social fabric, even the political order, and threatening our well-being?

This is an interesting but essentially academic debate. Because for better and for worse, digital technology is a fact of our lives. Irreversibly.

For better:

The boy living with cerebral palsy, interacting online on an equal footing with his peers, for the first time in his life his *abilities* more 'visible' than his *disability*.

The girl who fled the violence in the Syrian Arab Republic with her family, recapturing her future guided by a teacher at the Za'atari refugee camp as she uses a digital tablet to learn.

The young blogger in the Democratic Republic of the Congo using the internet to report on the lack of safe water and sanitation and other serious issues in his community.

For worse:

The girl who is forbidden by the rules of her family or her society to go online, missing out on the chance to learn and connect with friends.

The teenager whose personal information is misused by marketers and shared online.

The boy whose video game habit has taken over his life, at least according to his parents.

And worse still:

A boy driven nearly to suicide by cyberbullying that follows him everywhere.

A 14-year-old girl whose ex-boyfriend created a social media profile featuring nude pictures he forced her to take of herself.

An eight-year-old girl in the Philippines forced to perform live-stream sex acts by a neighbour who operates a child sexual abuse website.

Beyond the harm to individual children that digital technology can enable or abet is its capacity to incite violence on a massive scale that affects the lives and futures of hundreds of thousands of children. We need look no further for confirmation of this grim potential than an insidious social media campaign in Myanmar this year that incited horrific violence against members of the Rohingya ethnic minority, which resulted in the killing and maiming of children and forced hundreds of thousands to flee towards uncertain futures.

The internet is all of these things, reflecting and amplifying the best and worst of human nature. It is a tool that will always be used for good and for ill. Our job is to mitigate the harms and expand the opportunities digital technology makes possible.

That's what this report is about. It surveys the landscape of digital opportunity as it relates to – and affects – children. It examines the digital divides that prevent millions of children from accessing through the internet new opportunities to learn and, someday, to participate in the digital economy, helping to break intergenerational cycles of poverty.

It also explores the undeniably dark side of the internet and digital technology, from cyberbullying to online child sexual abuse to Dark web transactions and currencies that can make it easier to conceal trafficking and other illegal activities that harm children. It reviews some of the debates about less obvious harms children may suffer from life in a digital age – from digital dependencies to the possible impact of digital technology on brain development and cognition. And it outlines a set of practical recommendations that can help guide more effective policymaking and more responsible business practices to benefit children in a digital age.

Equally important, this report includes the perspectives of children and young people on the impact of digital technology in their lives – telling their own stories about the issues that most affect them.

Their voices matter ever more – and are louder than ever before – in a digital world. A world they are not only inheriting, but helping to shape.

By protecting children from the worst digital technology has to offer, and expanding their access to the best, we can tip the balance for the better.

Anthony Lake
UNICEF Executive Director

© UNICEF/UN024828/Nesbitt

The State of the World's Children – Children in a Digital World

Key messages

Digital technology has already changed the world – and as more and more children go online around the world, it is increasingly changing childhood.

❯ Youth (ages 15–24) is the most connected age group. Worldwide, 71 per cent are online compared with 48 per cent of the total population.

❯ Children and adolescents under 18 account for an estimated one in three internet users around the world.

❯ A growing body of evidence indicates that children are accessing the internet at increasingly younger ages. In some countries, children under 15 are as likely to use the internet as adults over 25.

❯ Smartphones are fuelling a 'bedroom culture', with online access for many children becoming more personal, more private and less supervised.

Connectivity can be a game changer for some of the world's most marginalized children, helping them fulfil their potential and break intergenerational cycles of poverty.

❯ Digital technologies are bringing opportunities for learning and education to children, especially in remote regions and during humanitarian crises.

❯ Digital technologies also allow children to access information on issues that affect their communities and can give them a role in helping to solve them.

❯ Digital technologies can deliver economic opportunity by providing young people with training opportunities and job-matching services, and by creating new kinds of work.

❯ To accelerate learning, information and communication technology (ICT) in education needs to be backed by training for teachers and strong pedagogy.

But digital access is becoming the new dividing line, as millions of the children who could most benefit from digital technology are missing out.

❯ About 29 per cent of youth worldwide – around 346 million individuals – are *not* online.

❯ African youth are the least connected. Around 60 per cent are not online, compared with just 4 per cent in Europe.

❯ Digital divides go beyond the question of access. Children who rely on mobile phones rather than computers may get only a second-best online experience, and those who lack digital skills or speak minority languages often can't find relevant content online.

❯ Digital divides also mirror prevailing economic gaps, amplifying the advantages of children from wealthier backgrounds and failing to deliver opportunities to the poorest and most disadvantaged children.

❯ There is a digital gender gap as well. Globally, 12 per cent more men than women used the internet in 2017. In India, less than one third of internet users are female.

**DENNAR GARY
ALVAREZ MEJIA, 19
PLURINATIONAL STATE
OF BOLIVIA**

"One of the key challenges many young people are struggling with is the proper verification of sources. Even though technological innovations have accelerated the pace of life, it's important that we take our time to check the validity, credibility and overall quality of the sources of information that we use."

VOICES OF YOUTH
Young bloggers
speak out

Voices of Youth is UNICEF's digital platform for young people to learn more about issues affecting their lives. This vibrant community of youth bloggers from all over the world offers inspiring, original insights and opinions on a variety of topics.

Full articles by youth contributors featured in *The State of the World's Children 2017* can be found at: <www.voicesofyouth.org/ en/sections/content/pages/ sowc-2017>

Digital technology can also make children more susceptible to harm both online and off. Already-vulnerable children may be at greater risk of harm, including loss of privacy.

❯ ICTs are intensifying traditional childhood risks, such as bullying, and fuelling new forms of child abuse and exploitation, such as 'made-to-order' child sexual abuse material and live streaming of child sexual abuse.

❯ Predators can more easily make contact with unsuspecting children through anonymous and unprotected social media profiles and game forums.

❯ New technologies – like cryptocurrencies and the Dark web – are fuelling live streaming of child sexual abuse and other harmful content, and challenging the ability of law enforcement to keep up.

❯ Ninety-two per cent of all child sexual abuse URLs identified globally by the Internet Watch Foundation are hosted in just five countries: the Netherlands, the United States, Canada, France and the Russian Federation.

❯ Efforts to protect children need to focus particularly on vulnerable and disadvantaged children, who may be less likely to understand online risks – including loss of privacy – and more likely to suffer harms.

❯ While attitudes vary by culture, children often turn first to their peers when they experience risks and harms online, making it harder for parents to protect their children.

The potential impact of ICTs on children's health and happiness is a matter of growing public concern – and an area that is ripe for further research and data.

❯ Although most children who are online view it as a positive experience, many parents and teachers worry that immersion in screens is making children depressed, creating internet dependency and even contributing to obesity.

❯ Inconsistent advice can be confusing for caregivers and educators, underlining the need for more high-quality research on the impact of ICTs on well-being.

❯ Researchers acknowledge that excessive use of digital technology can contribute to childhood depression and anxiety. Conversely, children who struggle offline can sometimes develop friendships and receive social support online that they are not receiving elsewhere.

❯ For most children, underlying issues – such as depression or problems at home – have a greater impact on health and happiness than screen time.

❯ Taking a 'Goldilocks' approach to children's screen time – not too much, not too little – and focusing more on what children are doing online and less on how long they are online, can better protect them and help them make the most of their time online.

**DEVONNIE GARVEY, 19
JAMAICA**

"Without the ready availability of knowledge and the global network accessible through the internet, my economic prospects would seem grim. But that's not the case. Instead I find myself with more hope than many people employed in a bricks-and-mortar 9-to-5 job."

The private sector – especially in the technology and telecommunication industries – has a special responsibility and a unique ability to shape the impact of digital technology on children.

❯ The power and influence of the private sector should be leveraged to advance industry-wide ethical standards on data and privacy, as well as other practices that benefit and protect children online.

❯ Governments can promote market strategies and incentives that foster innovation and competition among service providers to help lower the cost of connecting to the internet, thereby expanding access for disadvantaged children and families.

❯ Technology and internet companies should take steps to prevent their networks and services from being used by offenders to collect and distribute child sexual abuse images or commit other violations against children.

❯ Media stories about the potential impact of connectivity on children's healthy development and well-being should be grounded in empirical research and data analysis.

❯ And internet companies should work with partners to create more locally developed and locally relevant content, especially content for children who speak minority languages, live in remote locations and belong to marginalized groups.

Digital technology has already changed the world – and as more and more children go online around the world, it is increasingly changing childhood.

❯ Youth (ages 15–24) is the most connected age group. Worldwide, 71 per cent are online compared with 48 per cent of the total population.

❯ Children and adolescents under 18 account for an estimated one in three internet users around the world.

❯ A growing body of evidence indicates that children are accessing the internet at increasingly younger ages. In some countries, children under 15 are as likely to use the internet as adults over 25.

❯ Smartphones are fuelling a 'bedroom culture', with online access for many children becoming more personal, more private and less supervised.

What do adolescents and youth think of life online?

As part of the research for *The State of the World's Children 2017*, U-Report – an innovative social messaging tool used by nearly 4 million young people around the world to share their views on a range of common concerns – sent four questions to U-Reporters worldwide. The poll garnered a total of 63,000 responses. Data highlighted here reflect the responses of adolescents and youth (ages 13–24) from 24 countries.*

How did you learn to use the internet?

Learned on their own

42%

69% of young people in Honduras said they learned on their own compared to 19% in the Central African Republic (CAR).

Learned from friends or siblings

39%

Reported more often by those in low-income countries.

What do you like about the internet?

Learning things for school or health

40%

Learning skills I can't learn at school

24%

Indonesia

Burundi

Brazil

"Learning skills that I can't learn at school" was especially important to those in Indonesia (47%), Burundi (35%) and Brazil (34%).

Read about politics and/or improving my community

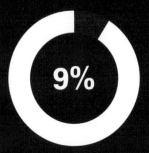

9%

More popular among older age groups.

What do you dislike about the internet?

Violence

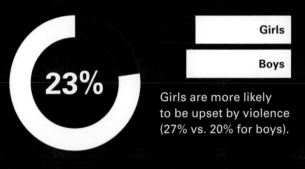

23%

Girls

Boys

Girls are more likely to be upset by violence (27% vs. 20% for boys).

Unwanted sexual content

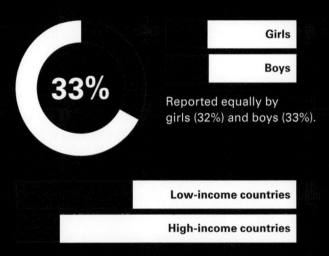

33%

Girls

Boys

Reported equally by girls (32%) and boys (33%).

Low-income countries

High-income countries

Young people in low-income countries are more likely to be upset by unwanted sexual content (42% vs. 16% in high-income countries).

"There is nothing I dislike about the internet."

13% Low-income countries

3% High-income countries

What would make the internet better for you?

Young people from low-income countries were 2.5 times more likely to ask for greater access to digital devices

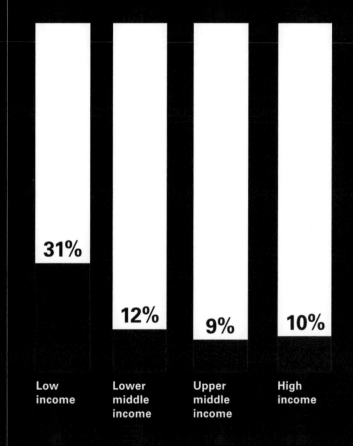

31%

12%

9%

10%

Low income

Lower middle income

Upper middle income

High income

* Only countries with a minimum of 100 respondents each were included in the 'country' category analysis, namely: Algeria, Bangladesh, Brazil, Burkina Faso, Burundi, Cameroon, Central African Republic, Chad, Chile, Côte d'Ivoire, El Salvador, Guatemala, Honduras, India, Indonesia, Liberia, Malaysia, Mexico, Mongolia, Pakistan, Peru, Philippines, Thailand and Ukraine.

Introduction: Children in a Digital World

The State of the World's Children 2017: Children in a Digital World examines the ways in which digital technology has already changed children's lives and life chances – and explores what the future may hold.

If leveraged in the right way and made universally accessible, digital technology can be a game changer for children being left behind – whether because of poverty, race, ethnicity, gender, disability, displacement or geographic isolation – connecting them to a world of opportunity and providing them with the skills they need to succeed in a digital world.

But unless we expand access, digital technology may create new divides that prevent children from fulfilling their potential. And if we don't act now to keep pace with rapid change, online risks may make vulnerable children more susceptible to exploitation, abuse and even trafficking – as well as more subtle threats to their well-being.

This report argues for faster action, focused investment and greater cooperation to protect children from the harms of a more connected world – while harnessing the opportunities of the digital age to benefit every child.

The constant churn of
new technologies, such as
virtual reality – enjoyed here
by 12-year-old Mansoor in
the Za'atari refugee camp,
Jordan – is making it hard
for policy to keep up.
© UNICEF/UN051295/HERWIG

Like globalization and urbanization, 'digitalization' has already changed the world. The rapid proliferation of information and communications technology (ICT) is an unstoppable force, touching virtually every sphere of modern life, from economies to societies to cultures … and shaping everyday life.

Childhood is no exception. From the moment hundreds of millions of children enter the world, they are steeped in a steady stream of digital communication and connection – from the way their medical care is managed and delivered to the online pictures of their first precious moments.

As children grow, the capacity of digitalization to shape their life experiences grows with them, offering seemingly limitless opportunities to learn and to socialize, to be counted and to be heard.

Especially for children living in remote locations, or those held back by poverty, exclusion and emergencies that force them to flee their homes, *digital technology and innovation can open a door to a better future*, offering greater access to learning, communities of interest, markets and services, and other benefits that can help them fulfil their potential, in turn breaking cycles of disadvantage.

But millions of children do not enjoy that access, or their access is *intermittent or of inferior quality* – and they are most often the children who are already most deprived. This only compounds their deprivation, effectively denying them the skills and knowledge that could help them fulfil their potential and helping *break intergenerational cycles of disadvantage and poverty*.

Digital technology and interactivity also pose significant risks to *children's safety, privacy and well-being*, magnifying threats and harms that many children already face offline and making already-vulnerable children even more vulnerable.

Even as ICT has made it *easier to share knowledge and collaborate, so, too, has it made it easier to produce, distribute and share sexually explicit material* and other illegal content that exploits and abuses children. Such technology has opened new channels for the *trafficking of children* and new means of concealing those transactions from law enforcement. It has also made it far easier for children to access inappropriate and potentially harmful content – and, more shockingly, to produce such content themselves.

Even as ICT has made it easier for children to connect to one another and share experiences online, it has also made it easier to use those *new channels of connectivity and communication for online bullying*, with a much greater reach – and thus potentially

Digital technology allows 17-year-old Gabriela Vlad (seen here with a neighbour) to keep in touch with her mother, who, like many Moldovan parents, works abroad to support her family. Learn more about Gabriela's story at <http://www.unicef.org/sowc2017>
© UNICEF/UN0139536/ GILBERTSON VII PHOTO

greater risk – than offline bullying. Similarly, it has increased opportunities for wider misuse and exploitation of children's privacy, and changed the way children regard their own private information.

Even as the internet and digital entertainment have spurred tremendous creativity and expanded children's access to a wealth of enriching and entertaining content, they have also raised questions of *digital dependency*, and 'screen addiction', among children. And even as such technologies have greatly enlarged platforms for the free expression of ideas, they have also broadened the distribution of hate speech and other negative content that can shape our children's view of the world – and of themselves.

Some of the impacts of digitalization on children's well-being are not universally agreed. Indeed, some are the subject of *growing public debate among policymakers and parents alike*. And while the potentially equalizing power of digitalization on children's chances in life cannot be denied, that promise has yet to be realized.

These challenges will only intensify as the reach and range of digitalization expands and its many opportunities continue to be exploited commercially and otherwise. More digital devices, online platforms and applications will be available for children's use. The Internet of Things, artificial intelligence and machine learning are here to stay, creating new opportunities but also new challenges.

What can governments, international organizations, civil society, communities, families and children themselves do to help limit the harms of a more connected world, while harnessing the opportunities of a digital world to benefit every child?

First and foremost, we need to *identify and close the gaps:* in access to quality online resources, in knowledge about how children use the internet and children's knowledge

of how to protect themselves online, and in both policymaking and regulatory frameworks that have not caught up with the pace of change.

Despite the rapid spread of access to digital and online experiences around the world, there are still wide gaps in children's access to digital and communications technology. Access to ICTs – and the quality of that access – has become a new dividing line. For example, children whose access is limited to a small range of local content services viewed via inferior devices with a slow connection are missing out on the full range of content and opportunities their better-connected peers enjoy. These disparities mirror and potentially exacerbate those already affecting disadvantaged children offline.

Gaps in our knowledge about children's lives online, including the impact of connectivity on a range of areas, such as cognition, learning and social emotional development, make it more difficult to develop dynamic policies that get ahead of issues by addressing risks and making the most of opportunities. Gaps in our understanding of how children feel about their experience of connectivity – including their perceptions of risks – further limit us.

There are also clear gaps in *children's* knowledge about risks online, and despite rapidly increasing usage among children and adolescents, many lack digital skills and the critical ability to gauge the safety and credibility of content and relationships they experience online. This reflects a need for much more widespread digital literacy opportunities that can both safeguard and empower children.

Finally, and crucially, all these gaps both reflect and produce lags in policymaking: Regulatory frameworks for digital protection, digital opportunity, digital governance and digital accountability are not keeping pace with the rapidly changing digital landscape, and are overlooking the unique impact digital technologies have on children. If left unclosed, those regulatory gaps will quickly be exploited. There is no shortage of principles and guidelines for digital policymaking; what is lacking is consistent coordination and a commitment to tackling common challenges with children's interests at the fore.

Especially now, as the world works to realize the Sustainable Development Goals (SDGs), ICTs and the internet can be powerful enablers, helping realize the promise of the SDGs to leave no one behind. But action – by governments, international organizations, civil society, academia, the private sector, and families, children and young people – must match the pace of change.

The State of the World's Children 2017: Children in a Digital World provides a timely review based on prevailing and new data sources of children's lives in a digital world – examining the evidence, discussing the issues and exploring some of the key controversies, as well as proposing principles and concrete recommendations.

Throughout, the report presents the perspectives of industry leaders and digital activists, and includes the views of children and young people, gleaned through adolescent workshops carried out in 26 countries, a specially commissioned U-Report poll presents opinions from adolescents in 24 countries about their digital experiences, commentary by youth bloggers from UNICEF's Voices of Youth, and analysis drawn from the pioneering Global Kids Online Survey.

Chapter One looks at the opportunities digitalization offers to children everywhere, but especially children disadvantaged by poverty, exclusion, conflicts and other crises. For example, ICTs are bringing education to children in remote parts of Brazil and Cameroon and to girls in Afghanistan who cannot leave their homes. ICTs are also enabling child bloggers and reporters in

the Democratic Republic of the Congo to advocate for their rights. They're increasingly supporting children and their families in emergencies. And they're literally giving a voice to children with disabilities: "The day I received an electronic notepad connected to the internet, my life literally changed," Ivan Bakaidov, an 18-year-old with cerebral palsy, writes in this report.

Chapter Two examines the data on who is being left behind and what it means to be unconnected in a digital world. The top-line numbers are striking: Nearly one third of all youth worldwide – around 346 million 15–24 year olds – are *not* online. In Africa, 3 out of 5 youth (aged 15 to 24) are offline; in Europe, the proportion is just 1 in 25. But digital divides go deeper than just connectivity. In a world where 56 per cent of websites are in English, many children cannot find content they understand or that's relevant to their lives. Many also lack the skills, as well as the access to devices like laptops, that would allow them to make the most of online opportunities. If these digital divides are not bridged, they will deepen existing socio-economic divisions.

Chapter Three delves into the digital dark side and the risks and harms of life online, including the internet's impact on children's right to privacy and expression. ICTs have amplified some of the traditional dangers of childhood: Once confined to the schoolyard, the bully can now follow victims into their homes. But they have also created new dangers, such as expanding the reach of predators, fostering the creation of made-to-order child sexual abuse material, and broadening the market for the broadcasting of live sex abuse. As one child victim of online streaming said, "When the foreigner says, 'get naked', then we undress." And then there are the dangers that many children and parents are unaware of – the threats to children's privacy and identity, for example, from the industrial-scale data processing that the internet has now made possible.

Chapter Four explores some of the ways digitalization is changing childhood, for better and for worse. ICTs have changed how children form and maintain their friendships, allowing them to maintain almost-constant contact with their peers. They have also transformed how many children spend their leisure time, providing them with a constant feed of videos, social media updates and highly immersive games. Many adults fear these changes are not all for the better, and worry that excessive screen time is isolating children from their families and surroundings, fuelling depression and even making children obese.

The report concludes with priority actions and practical recommendations for how society can harness the power of digitalization to benefit the most disadvantaged children and limit the harms to protect those children who are most vulnerable. These include:

1. Provide all children with affordable access to high-quality online resources.
Actions should include creating incentives to encourage telecom and technology companies to lower the costs of connectivity; taking the needs of the unconnected into account when developing infrastructure plans; investing in more public hotspots and the creation of more culturally and linguistically appropriate content; and confronting cultural and other barriers that prevent children – especially girls – from going online.

2. Protect children from harm online.
Actions should include coordinating more closely at the international and national levels and deepening collaboration between law enforcement and the technology industry to keep pace with digital technology that can enable and conceal illegal trafficking and other online child sexual abuse.

3. Safeguard children's privacy.
Actions should include urging a much greater commitment by the private sector and government to protect and not misuse children's data and to respect its encryption; enforcing the application of international standards in collecting and using data about children online; and teaching children how to protect themselves from threats to their own privacy.

4. Teach digital literacy to keep children informed, engaged and safe online.
Actions should include greater collaboration between governments and technologists to develop ICT platforms and curricula from primary school through high school, supporting online libraries and expanding the capacity of public libraries to teach digital skills; investing in teacher training in digital technology; teaching children how to recognize and protect themselves from online dangers; and making digital citizenship a core component of digital literacy instruction.

5. Leverage the power of the private sector to advance ethical standards and practices that protect and benefit children online.
Actions should include ethical product development and marketing that mitigates risks to children and a greater commitment to expanding children's access to connectivity and content online. The private sector – especially technology and telecom industries – has a special responsibility and a unique ability to shape the impact of digital technology on children.

6. Put children at the centre of digital policy.
Actions should include investing in better data about children's access and activities online; developing regulatory frameworks that recognize the distinct needs of children; strengthening coordination and knowledge sharing at the global level to address the challenges of a digital world; deepening collaboration with children's organizations; and engaging more systematically with policymakers and lawmakers.

01
Digital Opportunity: The promise of connectivity

JACK LIDDALL, 16
UNITED KINGDOM

"Nowadays, at the touch of a button, it is possible to contact a friend on the other side of the world, from Edinburgh to New York to Paris to Beijing. Anywhere is possible. With such power and the endless possibilities, it should come as no surprise that people, let alone the younger generation, are now more and more civically engaged."

Full articles by youth contributors featured in *The State of the World's Children 2017* can be found at:
<www.voicesofyouth.org/en/sections/content/pages/sowc-2017>

Digital technology is already the great game changer of our time – and it could be transformative for the world's most disadvantaged and vulnerable children, helping them learn, grow and fulfil their potential.

Digitalization allows children with disabilities to connect with friends and make decisions for themselves; provides access to education for children living in remote or marginalized areas; and, in humanitarian settings, helps children on the move find a safe route and connect with their families. Greater online connectivity has opened new avenues for civic engagement, social inclusion and other opportunities, with the potential to break cycles of poverty and disadvantage.

In Za'atari refugee camp in Jordan, a class of girls is learning English. Their classroom is rough and ready, its bare walls marked only by brown patches where the paint has peeled away. But the girls are smiling. At the head of the classroom, their young teacher calls out a question in English: "Where is the lamp?"

The girls carefully hold electronic tablets showing colourful images of the inside of a home. The girls search for the lamp. If they touch the right picture, the tablet calls out "good job"; if they get it wrong, it asks them to try again. "It's fun to learn with this," says 11-year-old Saha. "It's very useful for us. We can use it to learn things we didn't know before."[1]

In Kinshasa, 17-year-old Glodi is preparing to go on a reporting assignment. Three years ago, he was inspired to become a 'Young Reporter' following a presentation by a journalism network[2] in his school: "It was new to me," he says. "I had never heard of the right to participation, for example." After a week of training, Glodi began writing about issues in his community. "In my neighbourhood, many people do not have access to water, hygiene and sanitation, so it was logical for me to write about this subject." His articles appear on the Ponabana (For the Children) blog, which provides a voice for children in the Democratic Republic of the Congo (<www.ponabana.com>). "Writing for Ponabana allows me to reach a wide audience," says Glodi. "We are the most computerized generation, so we have to talk to people where they are: on the internet."

In the Russian Federation, Ivan is chatting online. But if his friends were to meet him in person, "they would not understand a word that I say," he writes (*see page 33*). That's because the 18-year-old has severe speech problems, a result of cerebral palsy. Being online, however, allows him to chat like any other teenager: "Some of my virtual friends don't even know that I have a disability." It's not just socializing where the internet is making a difference in Ivan's life: "Even though I am a student, I can't physically access my school. However, with the help of the internet and phones I am attending the classes and following the teachers' instructions."

In southern Chad, 17-year-old Oudah is dreaming of home. Like tens of thousands of others, he was forced to flee conflict in the Central African Republic. For the past few years he's been living in the Danamadja refugee camp, just across the border from his home country. Staying connected with his friends and family is a constant challenge, but digital technologies provide him with a lifeline. "I use the internet to stay in touch with my brothers who are still in the Central African Republic," he says. "It's been three years since I've been separated from my family and friends. It is important to stay in touch with them so I don't feel too lonely."

We are the most computerized generation, so we have to talk to people where they are: on the internet.

Technology needs to be supported by strong teachers, motivated learners and sound pedagogy.

Saha, Glodi, Ivan and Oudah live very different lives, but they are linked by one thing: In big ways and small, they are enjoying the opportunities brought by digital technologies and connectivity.

They are not alone: There are countless stories and examples of how children around the world are capturing opportunities to learn and enjoy themselves online and to shape their own paths into adulthood. Often without the help of adults, they are using online platforms to do their homework; learn how to play the guitar or make their mother's favourite soup; chat with friends; access health information; bring positive change to their communities; find out what's happening locally and globally; and design and write blogs to express their talents and opinions.

These opportunities must be considered alongside the reality that they are not available to millions of children (*see Chapter 2*), as well the risks of life online (*see Chapter 3*) and the potential impact of connectivity on children's well-being (*see Chapter 4*). But they provide an exciting window on what is already happening and a sense of what could happen in the future.

Education and learning in a digital world

The idea that digital connectivity could transform education has attracted global interest and opened up new possibilities, as development organizations, commercial software and hardware producers and educational institutions develop, pilot and try to scale up new digital products and services in the education sector. Information and communication technologies (ICTs) are already expanding access to high-quality educational content, including textbooks, video material and remote instruction, and at a much lower cost than in the past. They can potentially

increase student motivation by making learning more fun and relatable. And they create opportunities for personalized learning, helping students to learn at their own pace and helping educators with limited resources provide students with better learning opportunities.

How well are digital technologies fulfilling this promise? Without question, they have opened access to learning opportunities for children around the world, especially those in remote regions. They have allowed children to participate in e-learning and to access a wide range of educational and learning content that was unavailable to previous generations of children.

But when it comes to whether or not digital technologies are accelerating learning in the classroom, the picture has up to now been much more mixed. This paradox of the digital revolution in education was captured by the late Steve Jobs, founder and CEO of Apple. According to Jobs, while he "spearheaded giving away more computer equipment to schools than anybody on the planet," he concluded that "what's wrong with education cannot be fixed with technology."[3] Research increasingly supports Jobs's view. It shows that if such technologies are to have any chance of improving learning outcomes, they need to be supported by strong teachers, motivated learners and sound pedagogy.

How ICTs can expand access to learning

Digital tools and connectivity can provide children with access to education in places where few such opportunities exist. A sense of their promise was evident at a United Nations Educational, Scientific and Cultural Organization (UNESCO) gathering of education and development professionals in 2015 that looked at the role of ICTs in meeting the education aims of the Sustainable Development Goals. This gathering put forward the idea that innovations in ICTs could

help bridge the knowledge divide by creating both formal and informal learning pathways – through, for example, the distribution of education content and e-learning – and by fostering the development of job-related skills.[4]

Digital connectivity is already bringing educational content to children in rural and other marginalized areas. For example, in Brazil, the Amazonas state government's educational initiative, Centro de Mídias de Educação do Amazonas (Media Centre for Education), has been providing educational content since 2007 to children and youth living remotely. Using satellite television, classes are taught by teachers in the state capital of Manaus and beamed into classrooms in rural communities. The students are supported by professional face-to-face tutors and can ask teachers questions in real time. In addition to paper-based material, they also have access to digital textbooks and other educational resources via the internet.[5]

In Cameroon, a pilot project called Connect My School aims to provide access to educational content and digital tools to children living in remote areas of the country. Internet connectivity is provided by solar-powered equipment within a 500-metre range, allowing a whole school to be connected. And child-friendly tablets, with a parental control system, allow access to educational apps such as Wikipedia and learning games, as well as drawing, text and photo/video apps. About 2,000 fifth-year students have participated in this initiative, and teachers report that children are benefiting from the online content.

The Afghan Institute of Learning is reaching girls and women who cannot travel outside their home owing to social restrictions[6] with an SMS-based literacy programme. Results in reading skills show promise. Significantly, the programme is run in conjunction with teachers and physical classes operated by a devoted non-profit organization, underlining

"We are the most computerized generation," says Glodi, 17, a Ponabana blogger in Kinshasa, Democratic Republic of the Congo. "So we have to talk to people where they are: on the internet." © UNICEF/ DRC/2017/Wingi

Internet connectivity is provided by solar-powered equipment, allowing a whole school to be connected.

the importance of providing children with strong teaching and pedagogical support in their use of ICTs in education.

Virtual, or online, schools can bring specific programmes of instruction to children. The promise of this model for underserved or marginalized children is evident in such efforts as those of the Jaago Foundation, a small organization in Bangladesh founded in 2007. Using interactive video conferencing technology, the organization connects an online teacher in Dhaka with a rural or underserved urban classroom and two local teachers to provide instruction and follow-up. This project currently serves 2,500 students living in poverty in 13 schools.

According to UNESCO, the volume of open educational resources (OERs) – materials in the public domain or introduced with an open license and thus freely usable by anyone – has increased significantly in recent years, providing a strategic opportunity to improve the quality of education and facilitate policy dialogue, knowledge sharing and capacity-building.[7] But content quality can vary significantly,

underscoring the need for serious critical appraisal of materials to make sure they really will contribute to children's learning. The upside, however, is that once a satisfactory level of quality is attained, digital tools allow such resources to be easily scaled up and distributed, reaching areas of the world previously unreached by traditional information sharing and content distribution.

A second chance to learn

Skills and vocational training programmes are areas where digital connectivity is opening opportunities to learn. This is particularly true for disadvantaged children, who sometimes leave formal schooling to bring in income for their families[8] (*see section on economic participation*), and for underserved or marginalized children.

For example, in Kampala, Uganda, the Women in Technology Uganda organization offers digital vocational training for young women in underserved communities. The set-up enables students to go at their own pace, which may benefit those not accustomed to formal schooling. In addition to teaching young women digital skills, the training also focuses on building confidence, leadership and life skills. Girls attending the programme have reported learning ICT and entrepreneurship skills and going on to use the internet to identify their own business opportunities.

Similarly, the Youth for Technology Foundation in Nigeria is implementing an initiative to empower young people and create opportunities for income generation and access to new market services. The TechCommunities programme, for example, engages students in technology projects, field work and meaningful internships, setting them up to become leaders and innovators in their communities. According to the organization, 90 per cent of the programme graduates are engaged in entrepreneurship activities.[9]

The internet has greatly increased the supply of open educational resources, with the potential to increase children's learning opportunities. © UNICEF/UNI48335/Pirozzi

IT Girls – Bosnia and Herzegovina

Globally, there were 250 million fewer women online than men in 2016, according to the International Telecommunication Union. Women are also notably under-represented in STEM – science, technology, engineering and mathematics – jobs. Bridging this gender digital divide is a considerable challenge, but a number of initiatives point to how girls' digital access can be improved. One promising path is to promote ICT skills among girls, which also has the benefit of building up confidence and fundamental employment and entrepreneurship skills.

In Bosnia and Herzegovina, UNICEF, the United Nations Development Programme and UN Women have since 2016 been implementing an initiative called IT Girls, which aims to increase job opportunities for young women and girls by providing them with computer programming skills. The pilot organized six training programmes for 67 adolescent girls in both urban and rural locations. Currently, three additional training programmes are under way aiming to reach an additional 60 girls. The training, which covers basic web development skills, also enhances girls' knowledge of online safety and boosts their presentation skills. An important feature of IT Girls is its equity component: The training sessions are organized in parts of the country where children typically have less access to technology and information about ICTs, reaching girls from minorities, rural communities and other vulnerable groups.

According to the first-year evaluation, the initiative has successfully raised young girls' awareness of opportunities in the ICT sector, not only by promoting the ICT industry as exciting, diverse and lucrative, but also by bolstering their confidence and inspiring them to take on new challenges.[10]

Do ICTs improve learning outcomes in formal education?

Harnessing the power of digital technologies to improve student learning outcomes – and to give students the skills they need to transition to adulthood – seems natural in a connected world. Delivering on this potential has proved considerably more complicated, however. This is not to say that ICTs cannot be designed to improve student learning. But this will only happen if educators and technology designers learn the lessons of the past.

A first lesson is that it's not enough merely to provide children with access to digital technology, such as laptop computers and tablets, without also supporting them with trained teachers and software that complement school curricula. Simply giving students digital tools results in their using the technology, but appears to do little to enhance learning.[11]

As an example, take the One Laptop Per Child (OLPC) project, which launched to great fanfare in 2006 when the first prototypes were shipped. More than 3 million laptops had been distributed to primary schools around the world by 2016. Several countries, including Argentina, Mexico, Peru, Rwanda and Uruguay – which rolled out a national programme for every

What do adolescents think about ... how schools are preparing them for the digital age?

In mid-2017, almost 500 adolescents from 26 countries took part in workshops to discuss their experiences with information and communication technologies (ICTs) and their hopes and fears for the digital age. The events were organized with the support of UNICEF Country Offices and National Committees and Western Sydney University (WSU) in Australia. Findings from the workshops appear throughout this report and in a companion report from WSU.

Most participants in the *State of the World's Children 2017* workshops* said they believed digital technologies were vital to their futures ...
"If we do not use the computer, if we do not know computer, then we do not know anything, including ... good things for our lives." GIRL, 14, TIMOR-LESTE

and many had clear ideas about how they could use such technologies when they grew up.
"To produce music, get clients and send work done, make jingles for companies, run a free music download site and application." BOY, 19, NIGERIA

"To become a better person and get a degree to find a job." GIRL, 15, PORTUGAL

"To call or text people on the phone, do research on the internet, to listen to music, to do some presentations on the laptop, and play some games on the phone, laptop and computer." GIRL, 13, VANUATU

They thought digital technology skills mattered, but so did other skills.
"Critical thinking skills." GIRL, 16, MALAYSIA

"Coding!!! To create new programmes and games!!" GIRL, 17, MALAYSIA

About one in five participants said they had no access to digital technology at school.
"Zero technology is available to us." BOY, 15, CENTRAL AFRICAN REPUBLIC

Access for the rest varied greatly ...
"There is a computer, but it's located in the principal's office." GIRL, 15, PERU

"My school approves use of computer, it's mandatory. School provides Wi-Fi signal, but not much more. My computer or laptop is always in my backpack." GIRL, 15, PARAGUAY

but most could use computer labs ...
"We have computers and computer lab. We can use it whenever we want." GIRL, 16, BHUTAN

although the facilities were not always perfect.
"The school has a rather large number of computers in the computer lab, but unfortunately it can be difficult for students to use them due to problems such as regular electricity shortages." BOY, 16, DEMOCRATIC REPUBLIC OF THE CONGO

School computers were also sometimes underused.
"We have a computer lab in my college but the teachers don't allow [us] to use [it]." BOY, 16, BANGLADESH

Participants thought such underuse often reflected teachers' lack of technological confidence.
"My teacher takes good care about digital education, but other teachers in school don't. It's because they are not familiar with digital technology." BOY, 12, REPUBLIC OF KOREA

Half the participants said they had done some digital technology training outside school. Their motivations ranged from securing a better future ...
"I have attended a course at CEBRAC [an employment agency] where I learned to use Excel and spreadsheets. I participated because I could do it for free and I thought it would be important to have something like this in my CV." GIRL, 16, BRAZIL

to supporting their education …

"I attended [IT training outside school] because learning how to use computers will help me with the work I get at school." BOY, 17, PERU

to building their capacity for innovation and social entrepreneurship …

"I participated in the Technovation challenge and built an app that solves an issue in our community to learn coding and pitch my ideas." GIRL, 17, TUNISIA

to exploring the digital world …

"I went to online media literacy camp because I want to learn more about how to be safe online and how to use it in a constructive way." BOY, 15, THAILAND

to following their parents' orders.

"Honestly, I attended that class because my father forced me." GIRL, 16, BHUTAN

Some participants said they had also taught themselves digital skills.

"I learned coding through YouTube. I watched so many videos about coding and thus I have learned coding." GIRL, 17, BANGLADESH

Participants in the workshops said information technology (IT) education in schools focused mainly on 'traditional' skills, such as using software, saving files and typing. Some also learned about online safety or coding. Few were learning skills for more creative practices, such as building websites or apps or making videos.

"They could teach us not only more things related to 'the typical job', but also designing and programming [and] not only from the intellectual side, but also social and personal." GIRL, 14, URUGUAY

"The school programme has got old and doesn't correspond with modern world." GIRL, 16, BELARUS

Indeed, they had clear views on what schools needed to do to educate them about digital technology. They wanted training to begin earlier …

"[We] ask the authorities to go into every school so that children start learning computer science from primary school." GROUP RESPONSE, CENTRAL AFRICAN REPUBLIC

and they wanted better connectivity …

"Considering that we already have access to some devices at school, I would suggest that we are provided with free internet connection to allow us to complete our research and work." GIRL, 14, DEMOCRATIC REPUBLIC OF THE CONGO

as well as more highly skilled teachers.

"Hire young specialists." GIRL, 15, BELARUS

And they wanted more guidance on the positives and negatives of technology.

"School educators should make time for children to better understand and therefore make better use of technology, to know the advantages and the disadvantages." BOY, 16, DEMOCRATIC REPUBLIC OF THE CONGO

"Teachers should teach classes that help us to use digital technology appropriately." GIRL, 17, JAPAN

IN SUMMARY

Adolescents said technology use in schools generally lagged significantly behind their digital practices outside of school hours. They felt that digital technologies were compartmentalized in IT subjects and inadequately harnessed for broader learning at school.

* Participants' responses have been shortened and edited for clarity where necessary.

In Cameroon, 12-year-old Waibai Buka is benefiting from the Connect My School initiative. She recently had a chance to show the tablet to her mother: "I showed her what I was doing at school with my tablet. She was so proud of me." Learn more about Waibai's story at <http://www.unicef.org/sowc2017> © UNICEF/UN0143476/Prinsloo

child in Years 1–6 – made large purchases. According to a study conducted in 2009, the children in Uruguay seemed to find the computers easy and fun to use.[12] However, studies in Peru[13] (in 2012) found no evidence that the programme increased learning in mathematics or languages, nor that the laptops improved attendance, increased time spent on homework, influenced reading habits or raised motivation. Today, the One Laptop Per Child programme is no longer expanding. Key offices are closed, and only minimal support is provided to countries that previously purchased OLPC devices.[14]

Adult supervision

The vast majority of student-focused computer-delivery programmes, however, rely on adult guidance to help students, who use the technology as an additional tool. While most interventions that provide computer-assisted learning and materials may achieve modest learning gains, they are not always cost-effective,[15] even in high-income, high-connectivity settings. Implementation can also be an issue: Research suggests that blended learning – where students use digital tools under adult guidance in a traditional classroom setting – can boost learning outcomes, but only when well planned and if teachers are well supported.[16]

Some blended learning projects – curricula combining digital and traditional components overseen by a teacher – show promise: In one randomized controlled trial in 2007 involving 111 schools in India, for example, students in Year 4 who participated in a computer-aided mathematics-focused learning programme increased their scores compared to the control group.[17]

Also in India, a 2017 evaluation of a blended-approach after-school learning programme for middle school students showed increased test scores in mathematics and Hindi after approximately five months. The programme provided individually customized educational content to match each student's level and rate of progress.[18]

The work of the Avallain Foundation[19] in Kenya is also having a positive impact on student performance and motivation using a blended-learning approach. According to an impact study in 2017, learning outcomes have considerably improved for students using the organization's digital learning platform, a-ACADEMY. Students who benefited the most were those from slum areas.[20] During a group discussion in Nairobi's Mathare slum, some of the students (aged 11 to 12) told *The State of the World's Children 2017* report team that they felt more motivated to attend school and learn and, with the integration of digital tools such as a laptop in the classroom, saw a rise in their test scores.[21]

But it is important to note that many similar programmes have failed to show improved learning. These include the Computers in Education programme in Colombia, which a 2009 World Bank study said had "little impact on students' math and Spanish test scores … hours of study, perceptions of school, and relationships with their peers."[22] Similarly, a 2013 experimental study of 1,123 students in Years 6–12 in California found that, while distribution of computers had a great effect on computer ownership and total hours of computer use, there was no evidence that this affected education outcomes such as grades, standardized test scores, credits earned, attendance and disciplinary action.[23] The reasons why some programmes succeed while others fail is not always apparent – and more research and

analysis is needed to help bring the best of these programmes to scale, while learning from some of the 'fails'.

How can the performance of ICTs in education be improved?

Understanding the impact of ICTs on student learning is a challenge, in part because it is not always possible to determine precisely what's driving any change in student learning outcomes. Is it just the technology or are other factors at work?

For example, several key studies[24] showing strong learning outcomes had very capable implementing partners. Paradoxically, because it is difficult to conduct experimental trials without such a partner, the possibility that a capable organization itself is a prerequisite for an effective digital learning programme is difficult to see in field experiments.[25]

Nevertheless, some factors are clearly needed if ICTs are to work effectively in education. At the top of the list are well-trained teachers and appropriate teaching practices. The importance of these is underscored in a number of international studies. The Organisation for Economic Co-operation and Development (OECD), which has studied the impact of ICTs on learning outcomes in more than 60 countries through its Programme for International Student Assessment (PISA), suggests that without strong pedagogy, there is no benefit to having technology in the classroom.[26] Similarly, the World Bank's *World Development Report 2018: Learning to realize education's promise* also stresses that ICTs have the potential to increase learning, but only if they enhance the teacher-learner relationship.[27]

A second point is the need to understand students' starting points. Evidence shows that well-prepared students under good adult guidance may be able to take advantage of technology (or at least not be harmed by its distractions), but poorly prepared students without enough adult guidance are often distracted by technology.[28] Indeed, the risk that technology can distract children in the classroom, especially weaker students, is clear.

For example, a study carried out in 91 schools in England among children aged 11–16 found that banning mobile phones had a positive effect on their standardized test scores. What's more, the effect was strongest for low-performing students and absent for the best-performing, which suggests that technology in some cases can have a negative effect on low-achieving students.[29] The authors of this study conclude that restricting mobile phone use in schools could be a low-cost policy to reduce educational inequalities.

What about the future of ICTs in education? A number of technologies offer promising fields of exploration, including laptop content aligned with the curriculum, photo-based monitoring of teachers[30] and, in particular, computer-assisted personalized learning,[31] which is attracting growing interest in international development circles.

This sort of adaptive-learning approach, which is built around the idea of 'teaching at the right level',[32] is not new, but ICTs have increased their potential to boost learning, especially for children attending schools with limited resources. Instead of using the child's age or year as the trigger for what he or she should be taught next, ICT-based adaptive learning designs a course of instruction based on the child's actual abilities – as monitored by a digital interface that enables students to follow their own path through a subject based on their current level of understanding and at a pace that feels comfortable and manageable.

Given advances in artificial intelligence and neuroscience, further testing and experimentation may help unlock the potential of ICTs across a range of learning settings, particularly in under-resourced low-income communities. But to have a positive impact, technology in education should be focused on precise learning objectives.[33] In other words, discussion must begin with the educational goal – not the technology.

Giving children a voice in their communities

This generation of young people grew up in the era of digital activism – and digital 'slacktivism'. Children and adolescents are using social media and digital technology to amplify their voices and seek solutions to problems affecting their communities that affect them.

Organized efforts to encourage, cultivate and channel children's participation using digital tools are varied and growing in scope. For example, since 2009, a community-mapping initiative called Map Kibera – which uses digital open mapping techniques and GPS devices, along with digital information sharing – has helped young people in a Nairobi slum identify hazards in their communities and advocate for solutions to specific concerns.[34] This information, in turn, is being shared with and used by policymakers, helping drive real change.

U-Report, a free tool for community participation, is also playing an important role in providing young people with a new channel for participation. What started out as a local innovation to help young Ugandans engage on issues that affect their lives and futures has become a global network of nearly 4 million users who use it to voice their opinions, connect to their leaders and help change the conditions in their communities. Information from U-Reporters can be instantly mapped and analysed, yielding vital information and real-time insights about how young people see their world and what they think is most important. In turn, these aggregated views are used

Pupils at the Hanka Education Centre in Mathare, Nairobi, Kenya, say they feel more motivated to attend school since the arrival of laptops in the classroom.

In Port-au-Prince, Haiti, young people use mobile phones to make geotagged photographs of abandoned cars, as part of a project to map safe and unsafe zones in the city. © UNICEF/UNI128320/Dormino

by development partners in their advocacy with governments – and even shared directly with elected leaders.

Another such project is the Climate Change Digital Map, which involves children and young people from over 18 countries. This project empowers children and young people to look at what is happening in their communities, capture it on a digital map and use the results for advocacy. At the United Nations Framework Convention on Climate Change Conference of the Parties in 2015 and 2016, selected climate mappers spoke about climate change and its impact on children drawing on their experience and knowledge gained from the project.

Social media activism

For young people – digital natives – using social media for social activism is practically second nature. From the Ice Bucket Challenge in 2014 – where a stunt by young people trying to raise money for a terminally ill friend unleashed a global movement that raised millions of dollars for disease research – to pre-teens using the internet to launch local campaigns around personal concerns, digital technology has enabled a new age of digital participation.

The impact of social media has also been felt in political issues. In Brazil in 2013, for example, thousands of mostly young people used social media platforms to coordinate a protest against corruption and demand better public policies. One of the young people to give a face to this nationwide phenomenon was 17-year-old Jimmy Lima, who used social media to mobilize approximately 15,000 protesters in Brasilia alone.[35]

Children and young people are also making their voices heard through blogging. Perhaps the most well-known example is the story of Malala Yousafzai. Using a pseudonym, Malala began blogging for the BBC about girls' right to education in

Pakistan in 2009. Only 12, she used the reach of cyberspace to spotlight education under the restrictive Taliban regime. Once her identity was known, Malala was subject to a death threat issued by the Taliban and, in 2012, was shot and seriously wounded. Her recovery and fearless continuation of her advocacy for girls' education captured the attention of the world – and won her the 2014 Nobel Peace Prize.

In the Democratic Republic of the Congo, the digital platform Ponabana is offering children the chance to speak and be heard about what's happening in their communities. Through the active participation of child bloggers and reporters, Ponabana is helping to create awareness and advocate for children's rights among local decision-makers.

Challenges to participation

Digital connectivity has opened exciting opportunities for children's participation, but some significant obstacles to such participation cannot be ignored.

One is the political realities facing web users in much of the world. Malala and many others have brought attention to child rights violations by speaking out online. But their words have also created tensions, both in their communities and with their governments. Since 2011, the influence of social media on activism has been a major concern among governments. According to Freedom House, internet freedom has declined in recent years, as measured by the number of governments that have targeted social media and communication apps (WhatsApp and Telegram, for example) to stop information flows, especially during political protests. Two thirds of all internet users – adults and children – live in countries where criticism of the government, military or ruling family is censored.[36]

A second obstacle is that children often don't appreciate the possibilities of using

> "
>
> *2/3 of all internet users live in countries where criticism of the government, military or ruling family is censored.*

What do adolescents think about ... using ICTs to drive social change?

"When I grow up," they said ...

"I will use technology to spread advocacy on climate change and ending violence, and to help others in need." GIRL, 15, FIJI

"I will use technology to research ways to develop Third World countries and implement changes that would decrease poverty levels in the world." GIRL, 15, KIRIBATI

"I will use technology to advocate to people about health issues." GIRL, 15, NIGERIA

"I will use technology to change the world. Use it to design better stuff, create new things, make education more interesting through technology." BOY, 17, FIJI

They viewed digital technologies as powerful tools for raising their own awareness ...

"[To] inform myself and other people about what's happening in my country and in other places of the world." GIRL, 15, PARAGUAY

sharing knowledge and awareness in society ...

"[We would] make a survey, find out the organizations that work on it and spread awareness ... online."
GROUP RESPONSE, BANGLADESH

"[We would raise] online awareness: advertise youth programmes, produce educational clips, participate in online forums on ways of addressing the issues."
GROUP RESPONSE, SOLOMON ISLANDS

building support for social change ...

"[Digital technologies can change] the attitude of society to the people in need."
GROUP RESPONSE, REPUBLIC OF MOLDOVA

"[They can help us] to abandon the old ways of thinking and break stereotypes."
GROUP RESPONSE, REPUBLIC OF KOREA

and addressing specific social challenges, such as reducing violence and social inequalities.

"Child abuse needs to be stopped and children's rights respected by using social media sites ... to disseminate information and spread our message." GROUP RESPONSE, SENEGAL

"Children with special needs can't study on equal terms with other children. It is important to introduce inclusiveness in schools of the country. [We can design] online actions/info campaigns."
GROUP RESPONSE, BELARUS

But their ideas for using ICTs to promote social change were limited – for example, only a few highlighted how ICTs could be used to create and share content.

"We can make videos, groups to [make] people aware of child labour through internet."
GIRL, 15, BANGLADESH

"[To help solve delinquency] we can create a platform where young people can know and show their skills and talents so they can have more opportunities which they can invest their time." GROUP RESPONSE, GUATEMALA

That said, they had other ideas about how technology could help address social challenges. A key theme for many was the potential to put people in contact with services …

"Developing an app for drug addicts so that they can avail themselves of counselling services." GROUP RESPONSE, BHUTAN

"I want to use social media to spread information on disabled children and link them to organizations who work [with] disabled children." GIRL, 15, BANGLADESH

while others saw the potential of ICTs to give a voice to marginalized or vulnerable groups.

"Create discussion forums for girls to express themselves." GROUP RESPONSE, SENEGAL

Participants believed digital technologies could amplify their voice in debates and decision-making processes on issues that affect their lives …

"Do a campaign to have impact, and to make us understand that we have voices and votes." GROUP RESPONSE, GUATEMALA

"[They help] communication with society, with the representatives of the community, with influential people." GROUP RESPONSE, BELARUS

but there were barriers that could prevent this from happening, including limited online access and, especially, low levels of digital literacy. They had views on how this could be addressed.

"We should create a technological centre, sort of cyber centre, open to everyone and located in every province to give internet access to all of those who do not currently have access with staff ready to help everyone who comes in." GROUP RESPONSE, BURUNDI

They saw schools as having a key role to play in facilitating their engagement and participation in their communities …

"Schools can offer lectures about issues that are covered by the press and encourage the students to be interested in debating and be brave to show their ideals." GIRL, 19, BRAZIL

and in helping them deploy digital technologies to seek social change.

"I think school is the first and safest place to create a social platform … it prepares us to have better relationships with others, including communications skills. Maybe we can have more smart access to technology devices to facilitate our involvement and engagement in the community." GIRL, 19, TUNISIA

IN SUMMARY

A key goal of digital literacy is to help people understand the opportunities inherent in digital technologies, including their power to help meet the world's challenges. But without adequate online access, children and adolescents in many places find it hard to understand and grasp these opportunities.

* Participants' responses have been shortened and edited for clarity where necessary.

FIGURE 1.1 OLDER CHILDREN ARE MORE LIKELY TO BE CIVICALLY ENGAGED ONLINE
CIVIC AND PARTICIPATION PRACTISES, BY COUNTRY, BY AGE
(% OF CHILDREN WHO REPORT DOING THIS 'AT LEAST EVERY WEEK')

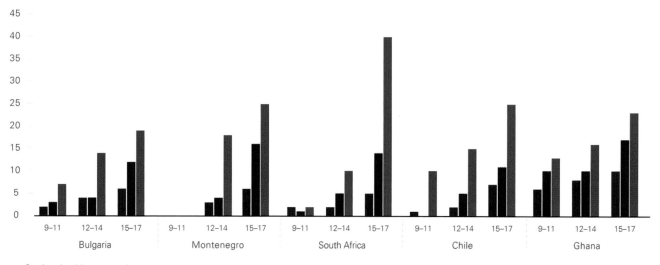

■ Got involved in a campaign or protest
■ Discussed political or social problems with other people
■ Looked for resources or events about my local neighbourhood

Source: Global Kids Online partner countries 2016–2017, aggregated by UNICEF Office of Research – Innocenti.

digital technologies for participation and, even if they do, may not know how to take advantage of them. As research from the EU Kids Online and Global Kids Online projects indicates (*see chart above*), while most young people are involved in sharing online content, and some have basic skills in creating videos, they often lack the digital skills and knowledge to move up the ladder towards civic participation.

Opportunities for economic participation: Preparing children for the digital workforce

Digital technology can be a pathway to expanding economic opportunity for young adults entering the workforce and for children and adolescents preparing themselves for the jobs of tomorrow in several important ways. These include providing digital skills that enhance employability; making access to existing job opportunities and training more efficient and more widely available; and providing a new jobs sphere (the 'digital economy') in which youth can seek employment.[37]

Digital skills to improve employability:
The proliferation of mobile phones all over the world has provided a clear avenue for programmes aimed to help youth develop their digital skills. For example, the Somalia Youth Livelihood Program, locally known as 'Shaqodoon', provides access to training, internships, work and entrepreneurial opportunities for at-risk youth (14–24 years old) via pre-recorded lessons – about financial literacy and workforce readiness – played on MP3 devices. Shaqodoon then links youth to work opportunities through an online database that is also accessible to employers. Use of mobile technology to connect youth with employers has proved more efficient than traditional methods and reaches rural and nomadic groups more effectively.[38]

Accessing job opportunities: Young people are also increasingly using mobile technology to look for employment; mobile job-matching services are growing, with more countries covered, more employers posting on them, and more young people searching through them.[39] It will be important to understand this dynamic to help prepare youth to enter the workforce of the future, and shape the workforce of the future so that it can best serve a youth population that is growing in many places *(see box on Connecting Africa's youth, Chapter 2).*

Networking is a common way to connect job seekers and employers, and it seems a natural fit for a generation that is heavily connected via social media. As of October 2017, the free digital platform *Oportunidades para Internacionalistas* connects more than 34,000 young people in Mexico.[40] Youth can market their skills online and reach potential employers efficiently.

'Digital economy' jobs: The digital economy has been criticized for eliminating some jobs, but it has also created new ones for which digitally literate young people may be particularly well suited. These include 'microwork', a sort of digital assembly line of discrete digital tasks that contribute towards a larger project, and

Skills for the twenty-first century

Today's children will enter a labour market that, for many, will be profoundly different from the one in which their parents worked. This transformation – often dubbed the Fourth Industrial Revolution – is built on a raft of developments in areas like machine learning, robotics, nanotechnology and biotechnology.[45] Once largely disconnected, these technologies are becoming increasingly integrated and, as a result, are driving economic change at a pace without historical precedent.[46]

Complicating this shift is that some of the poorest countries have yet to experience even the equivalent of the rapid industrialization wrought by the Second Industrial Revolution. But they, too, will be affected. Some will be able to take advantage of new technologies, allowing at least parts of their economies to leapfrog into the future; but others may suffer, as automation eats into their competitive advantage of low-cost, low-skilled labour.[47]

Are children acquiring the skills to thrive in the Fourth Industrial Revolution? There are reasons to be concerned. According to UNESCO, 250 million children worldwide are basically illiterate and innumerate, while 200 million young people will leave school lacking the skills they need to thrive.[48] And even for those who are acquiring basic reading and numeracy skills, the workplaces of the future increasingly require digital skills – and digital literacy.

Definitions vary, but, according to the World Economic Forum, these skills can be divided into three broad categories: Foundational Literacies, including traditional literacy and numeracy and also – among others – ICT, scientific and cultural literacies; Competencies, including critical thinking, creativity, communication and collaboration; and Character Qualities, including curiosity, adaptability and leadership.[49] The OECD also emphasizes that non-cognitive skills, such as communication, creativity, collaboration and empathy, will continue to determine career success.[50]

While acquiring a broader range of skills is clearly an advantage for any individual, there is much debate over whether even highly skilled workers – such as radiographers and economists – can expect to enjoy stable job prospects in the twenty-first century.[51] On the other hand, while previous industrial revolutions did indeed destroy jobs, over time, more jobs were created than were lost.[52] Whether that pattern will hold true in the Fourth Industrial Revolution remains to be seen.

work as an 'infomediary', or helping less digitally literate consumers use and access digital information.[41] The ITU also points to crowdsourcing (distribution of mostly skilled tasks by an online aggregator) as well as app and game development as new types of employment available in the digital age.[42]

While ICTs offer promising avenues for preparing young people to enter the workforce, there are still barriers that prevent them from realizing their full potential. In many parts of the world, for example, girls and women still face significant cultural barriers in digital access and skill development. Cost remains an obstacle to access for many children and young people, while the quality of educational instruction to build children's digital skills varies widely.[43] More broadly, traditional development challenges – among them improving education, access to health care, promoting good governance and improving the business climate – are "preventing the digital revolution from fulfilling its transformative potential."[44]

Opportunities for social inclusion

Digital tools and connectivity can be game changers for the most disadvantaged children, especially children on the move, children living with disabilities and children who experience exclusion and marginalization because of their ethnicity or sexual identity.

Children on the move

Around the world today, nearly 50 million children are on the move – 28 million of them driven from their homes by conflict and millions more migrating to escape crushing poverty and the growing impact of climate change.[53] These children increasingly rely on digital technology – especially mobile connectivity – throughout their journeys.

For example, in the Za'atari refugee camp for Syrian refugees in Jordan, 88 per cent of youth surveyed in 2015 owned a mobile phone and more than half used the internet either once or multiple times per day.[54]

Digital technology is especially important for children who are traveling unaccompanied by their families or caring adults.[55]

Plan International found that children and youth (up to 24 years) migrating without parents or other guardians used ICTs to plan and prepare for migration; facilitate the actual journey; stay in touch with their families; connect to support and work opportunities; and cope with integration and sometimes forced repatriation. Some of them also used social platforms such as Facebook to connect with people in other countries who were going through similar experiences, to share information and provide support.[56]

Despite this great promise for children on the move, most have low to no access. Overall, however, one third of refugee households have a basic phone; a little more than a third have an internet-capable phone; and just under a third have no phone. Even in areas with minimal connectivity, refugees have less than others: In rural areas, refugees are twice as likely as the rural population in general to have no 2G or 3G network available to them.[57]

Recognizing the growing role of digital technology in humanitarian situations, the United Nations High Commissioner for Refugees has called for all refugees and the communities that host them to be connected to the internet so that they can use these technologies to improve their lives.

The agency's Innovation Learn Lab has developed projects using various digital platforms with an eye to assessing what works, what doesn't and what can be brought to scale. In one Learn Lab example, children in the network of refugee camps in Dadaab, Kenya – the largest and most

In Danamadja, we are in a closed box. Without internet, the outside world moves forward but we are lagging behind.

Staying connected far from home

In Chad, the refugee camp of Danamadja stands in the midst of a vast forest. Here, for refugees from conflict in the Central African Republic, just across the border, staying connected represents a challenge. "Most of the young people who want to use the internet have to walk long distances to connect to the network," says Mahamat Djida, 25, who owns a phone-charging booth. "Service is really weak and unstable but we do not have many options."

"My parents stayed behind in Bangui. The only way for me to stay in touch with them is through WhatsApp and Messenger," explains Fatima, "I speak to them two to three times a week but it depends on what I can afford."

Beyond helping to stay in touch with families and friends, mobile phones and the internet have also offered young people opportunities to cope with life in the camp. Adam Souleymane, a 16-year-old refugee, is very proud of his new smartphone. "I bought a phone and now I use the internet to do research, especially in biology. There is no library in the camp," he says.

"I do not have a phone and I miss my Facebook" adds his friend Ali Amine, 18 years old, while playing with Adam's phone. "In Danamadja, we are in a closed box. Without internet, the outside world moves forward but we are lagging behind."

Being born on the wrong side of the digital divide has many implications for these children. In that context, it is vital to advocate for improved access to digital technologies and support for youth seeking to use them to solve the issues that affect their lives.

Forced to flee her home in Nigeria, Khadija, 15, now lives in the Dar es Salaam refugee camp in Chad. She hopes one day to work in IT and says the internet is "the best way to learn and to share knowledge." © UNICEF/ UN028860/Tremeau

protracted refugee agglomeration in the world – are benefiting from 13 Instant Network Schools. This type of digital 'school in a box' features tablet computers, internet access and educational content developed jointly with the local community. Initial reports indicate that the effort has increased teacher and student motivation.[58]

Excluded and marginalized children

Digital tools and connectivity have also helped minority groups feel more integrated in their communities[59] and opened new windows for expression, networking, political activism and social inclusion.

For indigenous people, such as the Aboriginal and Torres Strait Islander populations in Australia, social media use provides a sense of power and control over their identities and communities.[60]

Online resources and environments have also been important sources of information and socialization for lesbian, gay, bisexual and transgender (LGBT) youth, who use digital platforms to learn more about their community and find a sense of belonging.[61] According to a 2013 study by GLSEN, an organization dedicated to ending discrimination based on gender identity in schools, LGBT adolescents usually do not receive LGBT-relevant health information in schools or at home, and thus turn to online resources to find information on topics of health and sexuality.[62] Consequently, the digital age can help empower and bring together different groups, breaking cultural barriers and enhancing social cohesion.

Child helplines have historically helped children needing support find someone to talk to. Each year, millions of children reach out through helpline services; in 2015, such helplines received around 20 million contacts.[63] From Egypt to Sweden, digital technologies are transforming this sector of child aid by

introducing new communication tools for children whose preferred communication method may be by text/SMS messaging, email, chat rooms, online bulletin boards and other ways that have expanded the capacity to reach children in need.[64]

Children living with disabilities

Many of the world's children with disabilities are isolated and struggle with stigma, discrimination and a social environment that does not accommodate their needs or support realization of their rights. For example, they are often subject to more adult interventions than other children, which can limit their agency. Digital communication offers them a way to express themselves, make their own choices and participate in decisions affecting them. It also has the potential to facilitate communication with friends and reduce feelings of isolation.[65] Digital technologies can also provide access to education, skills training and employment.

Mobile applications can help children and young people with disabilities be more independent. They can be used for instant communication and activities that address unique sensory, physical and cognitive needs: iSign, for example, facilitates communication between deaf students, teachers and peers who do not know sign language.

Yuudee is an application that facilitates communication for children with autism, who can press an icon to 'speak' an idea or an answer or express a need. This app can also help teachers and parents teach children with autism communication and cognitive skills. Other digital platforms help children with special needs take tests on the same subject matter as their peers. The DAISY consortium of talking book libraries, which now has a global reach, makes text accessible to children who, because of visual impairment or for some other reason, cannot read print.

Children with autism can press an icon to 'speak' an idea or express a need.

Online, my wheelchair is invisible

IVAN BAKAIDOV, 18, RUSSIAN FEDERATION

Nowadays digital technologies are being developed with the speed of optical fibre, changing the lives of millions of people in this world. But especially for children with disabilities, modern technologies play a central role.

I am 18 years old and I have cerebral palsy, a physical disability that affects my movement and posture, which is why I am using a wheelchair. The day I received an electronic notepad connected to the internet, my life literally changed.

The notepad provides me with freedom of communication. Channels of communication have changed drastically over the past 300 years: from physical mail brought to you by a postman on a horse to real-time digital messengers. This progress has highly benefited persons with disabilities, as now communication requires less mobility. Today, children and young people with disabilities can communicate with family members and peers online. I have multiple friends online, from various parts of the world. If we were to meet in person, they would not understand a word that I say, as I have a speech impediment. However, due to the help of technology, I can seamlessly communicate with them. Some of my virtual friends don't even know that I have a disability.

In a similar way I can communicate with teachers. Education is another area in which modern technology is invaluable for children with disabilities. The opportunities for self-education are unlimited. Even though I am a student, I can't physically access my school. However, with the help of the internet and phones I am attending the classes and following the teachers' instructions, regardless of my physical condition. There are also online platforms that allow young people to obtain work diplomas without ever having to leave their wheelchairs.

This leads me to another field where digital technologies create more opportunities: employment. In the modern economy, where mental labour is more valued than physical labour, someone with a physical disability can find a job much more easily than a hundred years ago.

Today's employer doesn't care whether his programmer, journalist or SEO manager uses a wheelchair or not, as long as the employee does the work. Particularly in the world of coding, persons with disabilities might even have an advantage sometimes. For example, nowadays specialists in site accessibility are in high demand in Russia. In my case, I just recently consulted and supported a group of graphic designers in St. Petersburg on that issue.

The increased use of digital technologies has inspired me to develop my own programmes for alternative communication, helping people who are mute, have speech impediments or severe physical disabilities. For example, DisType is a software I developed that helped me to speak as an advocate at the World Humanitarian Summit, which took place in Istanbul in 2016.

DisQwerty allows searching for a word or expression with only one button, which can be tremendously helpful. Another programme I developed, DisTalk, allows someone to speak by using only images. All the programmes are free of charge and anyone can access them – you can learn more about the projects at <http://en.aacidov.ru>.

As you can see well from my example, digital technologies help to remove barriers and open opportunities for children and young people with disabilities.

Ivan Bakaidov, 18, is a young advocate from the Russian Federation who has cerebral palsy and cleft palate. Having had a speech impairment since childhood, Ivan wants to help other children and young people with disabilities solve communication problems and fulfil their right to be included.

Access to such services remains limited, so for most children with disabilities, especially those living in underserved or otherwise marginalized contexts, this type of assistive application remains out of reach.

The barriers preventing access for children with disabilities include the fact that they live in rural areas without access to the technology; they can't afford it; their parents are not aware of it; or appropriate devices for their particular needs are not yet available. Surveys from 2006 of people living with disabilities in developed countries have found that they are half as likely to have a computer at home as someone without a disability, even less likely to have internet access – and even less likely to go online when they do.[66] While these surveys did not look specifically at children, they point to the need to understand the barriers to access. When they do access the internet, children with disabilities, in particular those with learning disabilities or developmental delays, may face specific risks (*see Chapter 3*).

Pointing the way forward

There is no question that ICTs have already opened avenues for children to develop, learn, participate and improve themselves and their situation. As the next chapter shows, these benefits are far from equally shared – and the benefits and opportunities emerging for children do not necessarily look the same in all parts of the world. Countries are still in different phases of technological development and internet penetration, and many have significant social, economic and cultural barriers to connectivity. Most of the research is still concentrated in high-income countries, while a lot still needs to be done in other parts of the world. In addition, listening to children themselves is paramount when approaching issues that deal with their rights.[67]

But assessing the extent to which these opportunities can expand, and the actual benefits they bring for children, is challenging for several reasons. A key one is time: While they are indeed exciting and inspiring, many of the examples cited in this report and elsewhere are still too new to evaluate for impact. In such a fast-moving area, research has a hard time keeping up with what is happening right now. In addition, and except for formal education, rigorous studies that quantify or evaluate the gains stemming from children seizing these opportunities are rare. Even less documented and researched are the digital experiences of disadvantaged children, especially those in low- and middle-income countries.[68]

This underscores the need for more research and evaluation to better understand how children are availing themselves of opportunities in the digital age and, especially, to understand why some children benefit more than others.

To transform opportunities into real benefits for children in a digital age, especially for learning, participation and social inclusion, it is critical to understand the context of children's digital experiences and provide adequate guidance and support, especially for children on the move, excluded children and those living with disabilities.

Technology is still at the service of human capacities and human constraints. In education, these would include student motivation, teacher capability and sound pedagogy. Evidence suggests that technology has benefits where positive human forces for learning are already in place. A digital tool cannot fix dysfunctional bureaucracies or decrease educational inequality where these are not being addressed by the larger society.

To truly benefit children, especially the most disadvantaged, the design process for digital products must begin by considering children's specific needs – using the principles of Universal Design as a guiding reference, for example.

Connected children see digital connectivity as an overwhelmingly positive part of their lives.[69] Their enthusiasm, fascination and motivation to connect is a reflection of the clear power and potential these tools have to offer – not just to improve their everyday lives but also to expand their chances for a better future. This power and potential needs to be fully supported, in particular by bringing connectivity to as many children as possible and giving them the skills to maximize the benefits of life in the digital world.

Digital technology could be a game changer for children living in some of the lowest-income countries, such as Bangladesh.
© UNICEF/UNI157753/Mawa

PERSPECTIVE

Realizing Limitless Possibilities: Technology empowers people with disabilities

Kartik Sawhney

It was 2001 when I started out at a mainstream primary school in India. Having attended a special school for the blind until then, I found the new school challenging and daunting. I had no idea how to interact with my peers and teachers, or simply how to adapt to the new environment. I completed my homework in Braille, and every day my mother patiently transcribed it into print so that my teachers could understand it. None of them had expertise in teaching blind students, yet their support and encouragement, along with that of my parents, helped me to excel and have a great experience.

The next year, my life changed completely. I was exposed to a computer – an amazing computer that could speak to me. I would spend the entire day playing with it, only to be even more amazed with every new feature I found. My introduction to the Web and the prospect of getting whatever information I needed by pressing the Enter key was unbelievable and empowering.

As I grew fond of this new toy, I wanted to understand it more deeply. How could my computer in India get information from a computer at Google headquarters in the United States? How could I watch TV shows on my computer? How did it know what websites I'd be interested in without me necessarily typing them? These questions encouraged me to start reading textbooks on computer science and computer programming in the sixth grade, which allowed me to start developing an application that could help me be more efficient. While a lot of these were simple apps that helped me apply my knowledge, others were born of my frustration at not being able to have the same learning experience as my peers.

In the 11th grade, for example, I could not understand graphs and curves in my calculus class. Despite several attempts to visualize these based on their verbal descriptions, I was unable to picture them well. I almost gave up, until I was struck by an idea that combined my passion for music and tech. Thus was born Audio Graph Describer, software that converts a graph into its tonal representation. Visualizing a graph through variation in frequencies not only allowed me to understand the complicated graphs that once distressed me, but helped rekindle my interest in math and science. This is the power of technology!

As I continued with school, my interest in tech increased. I knew I wanted to study computer science in college in order to develop technology that can empower people to realize their potential. Once there, I met others who shared a similar vision. In the United States, I was pleasantly surprised to meet several developers with disabilities, since there are few in India. With firsthand experience about everyday challenges, I found them well equipped to brainstorm, conceptualize and implement transformative ideas to enhance accessibility for the disabled community.

I have been fortunate to try out several of these ideas – from a pair of augmented reality glasses that allow a volunteer to describe things a blind user sees in real time, to an app that uses computer vision to help with object and text recognition and scene descriptions; from a wheelchair that uses eye gaze to move around, to tremendous advances in real-time automated captioning.

As a young person passionate about technology and disability advocacy, these technologies excite me more than ever, and I can't wait for other revolutionary technologies in the near future that will reduce the word 'disability' to a mere nuisance.

While recent and upcoming technology has been very helpful, there are still concerns that need our attention. Most people with disabilities around the world are consumers of this technology, but not innovators. As is evident from several successful engineers with disabilities, disability is no barrier to

Digital technology is creating opportunities for children with disabilities, such as this blind boy in Kuala Lumpur, Malaysia, who uses text-to-speech software to take part in classes. © UNICEF/UNI182589/Pirozzi)

technical excellence. Thus, there is a dire need to encourage and, more importantly, provide necessary support and resources to help people with disabilities consider technology as a potential career avenue.

Similarly, several applications and websites fail to comply with accessibility standards, compelling more than 1 billion people with disabilities around the world to miss out. This is due not just to lack of accessibility training, but also disability awareness. It thus becomes important to intensify our efforts in this space. I look forward to all of us working in our own little ways to truly realize the limitless possibilities of technology.

Kartik Sawhney is pursuing a Master of Science in computer science at Stanford University with a focus on artificial intelligence. His technical interests lie in machine learning, natural language processing, accessibility and assistive technologies.

Disability is no barrier to technical excellence.

What do children need to know for the digitial world?

Based on research contributions from Petar Kanchev, Expert of the Safer Internet programme at the Applied Research and Communications Fund in Bulgaria; Sanjay Asthana, School of Journalism, Middle Tennessee State University; and The State of the World's Children report team.

It's increasingly recognized that children need to be better prepared for lives suffused in digital technologies. As one mother in Za'atari refugee camp in Jordan said, "In my time, someone who was illiterate could not read and write. Now, someone who is illiterate does not know how to use the internet. I don't want our children to be illiterate. It's really important. We want a better future for our kids."[70]

But what does it mean to be 'literate' in the digital era? More broadly, what skills and attributes do children need to avoid online risks and maximize opportunities? These questions have produced a host of responses from parents, teachers, policymakers and academics, most of which can be grouped into two broad concepts – 'digital (and media) literacy' and 'digital citizenship'. Definitions of both these concepts vary and often overlap, which may affect the design of educational programmes for children – for example, some skills or attributes may be overemphasized at the expense of others.

So how might these concepts be more clearly defined?

Digital literacy:

Work by Global Kids Online, UNESCO and others strongly emphasizes four sets of abilities. Children should be able to:

1. Access and operate in digital environments safely and effectively;

2. Critically evaluate information;

3. Communicate safely, responsibly and effectively through digital technology; and

4. Create digital content.

The value of digital literacy is widely recognized. During the 2014 Day of General Discussion on digital media and children's rights, the United Nations Committee on the Rights of the Child tasked Member States to include digital literacy in their school curricula.[71] Developing children's digital and media literacy from an early age has also been identified as a crucial prerequisite for an effective democratic society in the twenty-first century.

Digital citizenship:

Earlier definitions of digital citizenship were often quite broad, but more recent research supports a narrower definition for several reasons, including to improve the focus of teaching on the subject and to ensure that learning goals are well defined.[72] Two principles are put forward as being at the core of digital citizenship, namely:

1. Respectful and tolerant behaviour towards others; and

2. Online civic engagement.

Even if the definitions are sometimes fuzzy, the overall goal of teaching digital literacy and digital citizenship is clear: To equip children with a full portfolio of skills and knowledge that allows them to avoid online risks, maximize online opportunities and exercise their full rights in the digital world. This last point is significant: Findings from Global Kids Online suggest that while most young people share online content and many create videos, they often lack the required digital skills and knowledge to move up the 'ladder of opportunities' towards civic participation – a significant area of online opportunity.[73]

SPECIAL SECTION: How ICTs are supporting humanitarian action

For the past two years, drought has stricken much of Somalia, laying waste to the land and forcing families to leave their homes in the countryside in the hope of finding help in towns and cities. In this ancient landscape, some of the assistance is coming in the most modern form – digital cash straight to families' phones. The help is a lifesaver for parents and children: As one father told an Oxfam official, "We can decide [how to spend the money] and buy what food and how much water we need or whether to invest in hay for a lamb or education for a child."

Digital cash is just one example of how ICTs are being used increasingly to support children and their families living through humanitarian emergencies and other challenging situations. Their impact can be seen in many areas: For example, by improving communications, they're allowing humanitarian workers to better coordinate responses and keep affected populations informed during crises (*see box:* Staying connected far from home, *page 31).*

Big data in health emergencies

In health emergencies, digital technologies are being used to save millions of lives. During disease outbreaks, for example, mobile network platforms can provide infected individuals and affected households with life-saving information, essential commodities and financial support.[74] In Uganda, for example, the national Ebola task force operationalized an mHealth platform, mTrac, that enables real-time alerts and surveillance via SMS from communities and health workers. A similar tool, mHero, was used during the Ebola outbreak in Liberia, supporting updates to the national health worker registry, strengthening communications and providing real-time data on critical health services.[75]

The use of 'big data' to help manage health emergencies – as well as other humanitarian situations – is attracting growing interest. Big data – large data sets that can be used to analyse trends – from mobile phones, for example, can provide vital information during disease outbreaks, helping countries to respond more effectively or even prevent outbreaks from becoming epidemics.

During the dengue outbreak in Pakistan in 2013, anonymized call data from almost 40 million Telenor Pakistan subscribers were used to predict the spread and timing of the disease, contributing to better national response mechanisms.[76]

During the Zika outbreak, UNICEF and Amadeus – which provides technical support to the global travel industry – partnered and analysed global travel data to better understand patterns of the spread of Zika and potential outbreak zones.[77]

Similarly, a pilot UNICEF initiative, Magic Box, is being developed to work with real-time information and support life-saving humanitarian responses in emergency situations.[78] Magic Box collects real-time anonymized data, such as from mobile phone usage, to better understand human activity. An analysis of the data is then used

Mobile phone data are helping countries respond more effectively and prevent outbreaks altogether.

ICTs are playing an increasing role during humanitarian crises, such as the Ebola outbreak in Liberia in 2014. © UNICEF/ UNI176804/Ryeng

to improve the management of humanitarian disasters, providing alarms and supporting critical response and recovery.

Education, emergencies and ICTs

Around the world today, an estimated 27 million children living in conflict zones are out of school.[79] The absence of resources, such as books, adequate classrooms and trained teachers, is the main barrier to children's education in emergencies.

Digital technologies can help fill these gaps, by helping to create opportunities for distance learning for children and teachers, improving coordination of educational activities during emergencies, disseminating educational information and supporting the development and dissemination of digital curricula.

ICTs can also help governments and local authorities to better manage education systems in emergencies and chronic crises. For example, in the Central African Republic, where violence and unrest have forced many children out of school, the government is using EduTrac, a mobile-phone-based

data-collection system, to collect basic information including which schools are functioning and how many students are attending school, even in the most hard-to-reach areas.

Biometrics, refugees and social protection

One striking application of ICTs in recent humanitarian situations has been the use of biometrics to register the identity of refugees, which is then used to provide them with essential services. Biometrics uses an individual's physical characteristics, such as the face, iris or fingerprint, to create a unique identity record. In humanitarian work, iris scanning has already been used to repatriate Afghan refugees and to provide cash transfers to Syrian refugees in Jordan.[80]

Indeed, cash transfer systems – whether supported by biometrics or not – are another aspect of humanitarian assistance that is benefiting greatly from ICTs. Increasingly, these transfers are administered through mobile money systems, which is expanding their reach and improving their efficiency.

"

Digital payments are expanding the reach and efficiency of cash transfer programmes.

According to data from GSMA, a trade group of mobile network operators, in many of the countries hosting displaced populations, mobile money networks are more developed than the formal banking system.[81] Cash transfers in humanitarian settings improve children's lives in a range of ways, in part because households receiving payments prioritize spending on child-specific needs, such as food, housing, health and education.[82] By offering recipients a basic transaction account, digital payments can also foster longer-term financial inclusion.[83]

Ethics and privacy in data collection and sharing in emergencies

There are obvious benefits to using digital technologies for collecting and sharing data in emergencies. But these uses also raise important ethical issues, reflecting the ways in which the digital revolution is transforming who can generate, access and transmit this growing flood of data.[84]

Protection of affected populations – their rights, safety and dignity – is fundamental to humanitarian principles, as is assuring that risks are properly addressed with appropriate and timely interventions. Vulnerable groups such as children and adolescent girls are especially at risk of violence, abuse and exploitation in humanitarian situations. Technologies connecting data with individuals' identities inevitably raise the risk that data may be breached or misused in manners that cause harm, whether intended or inadvertent.

In the case of refugees and migrants, the consequences of data breaches can become matters of life and death. In the wrong hands, data could be used to identify and target people based on their ethnicity, immigration status or other identity signifier.

Without broader and coherent ethical frameworks for data science governance, children may suffer the consequences hardest and longest,[85] since the full impact of privacy violations later in life is still largely unpredictable. As United Nations Under-Secretary-General for Humanitarian Affairs Stephen O'Brien, has noted, "safeguarding privacy and ensuring sensitive data is handled appropriately, especially in conflict settings, are critical issues for our community as it becomes data-driven."[86]

Developing common standards for data collection, use and management is a task for the entire humanitarian sector. The literature suggests three critical areas where minimum standards should be developed to start building a solid framework in the area:

❯ **Rights, privacy and consent**. Common ethical standards are needed to govern the use of data and privacy protections.

❯ **Data sharing and retention.** Clear guidance is needed on who should share data and when, and there need to be protocols on what data should be retained, from what sources, for how long and for what purpose.

❯ **Protection of vulnerable populations.** There needs to be a shared understanding of how sharing or using certain types of data can increase the risks faced by certain groups.[87]

It is understandable that humanitarian organizations in the field are rightly more focused on responding to emergencies than working through legal details about data collection and sharing. However, to fully benefit from the potential of digital technologies in emergencies and other contexts, the international community must simultaneously address concerns on how to respect privacy and fundamental rights, particularly for the world's most vulnerable populations, including children and adolescents.

The consequences of data breaches can become matters of life and death.

02
Digital Divides: Missed opportunities

**EMMANUELLA AYIVI, 15
BENIN**

"In Benin, a lot of young people and children do not have access to digital technologies and the internet. This lack of access to the digital world puts young people at a grave disadvantage. I have been in numerous situations where the lack of internet access was a serious problem."

Full articles by youth contributors featured in
The State of the World's Children 2017 can be found at:
<www.voicesofyouth.org/en/sections/content/pages/sowc-2017>

To be unconnected in a digital world is to be deprived of new opportunities to learn, communicate and develop skills for the twenty-first century workplace. Unless these gaps in access and skills are identified and closed, rather than being an equalizer of opportunity, connectivity may deepen inequity, reinforcing intergenerational cycles of deprivation.

In a world where digital access and digital skills increasingly influence children's futures, the contours of global connectivity are troubling. Just over 29 per cent of the world's youth (15–24 years old) – or 346 million – do not use the internet.[1] Nearly 9 out of 10 of the young people currently not using the internet live in Africa, Asia or the Pacific. Africa has the highest share of non-users.

Disparities in access are particularly striking in low-income countries: Fewer than 5 per cent of children under 15 use the internet in Bangladesh and Zimbabwe.

These digital divides mirror broader socio-economic divides – between rich and poor, men and women,[2] cities and rural areas, and between those with education and those without.[3] For example, 81 per cent of people in developed countries use the internet, more than double the proportion in developing countries (40 per cent), which, in turn, is more than double the proportion in least developed countries (15 per cent).[4]

But digital divides do not merely separate the connected and the unconnected. They go deeper, concerning *how* people – including children – use information and communication technologies (ICT), as well as the *quality* of the online experience. Both of these can vary greatly, reflecting factors that include the level of users' skills and education, the types of device they use, family income and the availability of content in their own language. Some children going online for the first time find themselves in a digital space where their language, culture and concerns are notable by their absence.

Why does all this matter? Regardless of whether they are fully online, partly online or completely unconnected, every child today is growing up in a digital world powered by technology and information. In the immediate term, children who are unconnected are missing out on rich educational resources, access to global information and online opportunities for learning; they are also forgoing ways to explore new friendships and self-expression *(see Special Section: Connected children)*.[5]

For disadvantaged children, such as those living with disabilities, connectivity can mean the difference between social exclusion and equal opportunity. For children on the move, it can mean a safer journey, the chance to remain in touch with family members and a better chance to find work and educational opportunities in a foreign land.[6]

As children reach adulthood and enter the world of work, connectivity will increasingly mean the difference between their ability to earn a living or not. Those with access to digital technologies and the skills to make the best use of them will have the advantage over those who are unconnected and unskilled. Evidence from adult populations shows that the benefits of digital technology go to those with the skills to leverage it.[7]

According to Organisation for Economic Co-operation and Development (OECD)

Connectivity will increasingly mean the difference between the ability to earn a living or not.

data from the world's wealthiest countries, ICT experience has had a large impact on participation in the labour force and on wages in countries like Australia and the United States. Adults without ICT experience, even if employed, were likely to earn less than those with ICT skills.[8] Other studies of adult populations in countries such as India[9] and Tunisia[10] reflect similar findings.

The risk that connectivity can become a driver of inequity, not an equalizer of opportunity, is both real and immediate. Consider mobile technology, which has become embedded in every aspect of daily life – and at a singular pace. As the *World Bank's World Development Report 2016: Digital dividends* points out, "More households in developing countries own a mobile phone than have access to electricity or clean water, and nearly 70 per cent of the bottom fifth of the population in developing countries own a mobile phone." Connectivity via mobile may have a long way to go to shrink the divide. However, as smartphone adoption skyrockets in many countries, including emerging economies,[11] it is easy to imagine how central access will be or is already.

Digital connectivity is not only the "new necessity of our times";[12] it offers the potential to break intergenerational cycles of disadvantage from which the poorest children may not otherwise be able to break away.[13]

Who are the unconnected children?

Global data on children's access to, and use of, the internet are hard to find. Many countries do not collect relevant data and, even if they do, the age range used to estimate 'children' often varies, posing challenges to uniformity in data. What is clear, however, is that existing

socio-economic disparities are strongly reflected in which children are – and are not – online.

Nearly 9 out of 10 of the young people (aged 15–24) currently not using the internet live in Africa or Asia and the Pacific.[14] In 2017, Africa was also the region with the highest proportion of non-users among 15- to 24-year-olds – the population segment often considered to be highly connected *(see Figures 2.1 and 2.2)*.[15]

These disparities in access are particularly striking in some low-income countries. In Bangladesh and Zimbabwe, fewer than 1 in 20 children under 15 uses the internet *(see Figure 2.3)*.[16] For children in these countries, challenges of poor quality connectivity are likely compounded by high data costs – most of the countries with the least affordable mobile-broadband prices are also among the least developed countries in Africa and Asia and the Pacific.[17]

Although scarce, available data on the urban-rural digital divide for young people (15–24 years old) in countries such as Cameroon, Malawi and Zimbabwe also show marked disparities, with rural youth in these countries experiencing very low levels of connectivity *(see Figure 2.4)*.

But it is not only in low-income countries that children face barriers of access. Even in high-connectivity countries, family income does much to determine children's ability to meet their online needs.

In 2015, the OECD's Programme for International Student Assessment (PISA) revealed substantial discrepancies between advantaged students and disadvantaged students for both computer and internet access. Across countries and economies, on an average, 88 per cent of the advantaged students had two or more computers at home compared with only 55 per cent of the disadvantaged students. Variations in internet access were

Even in high-connectivity countries, family income does much to determine children's ability to meet their online needs.

FIGURE 2.1 YOUTH IN LOW-INCOME COUNTRIES ARE LEAST LIKELY TO CONNECT
PROPORTION OF YOUTH (15–24) WHO ARE NOT USING THE INTERNET (%)

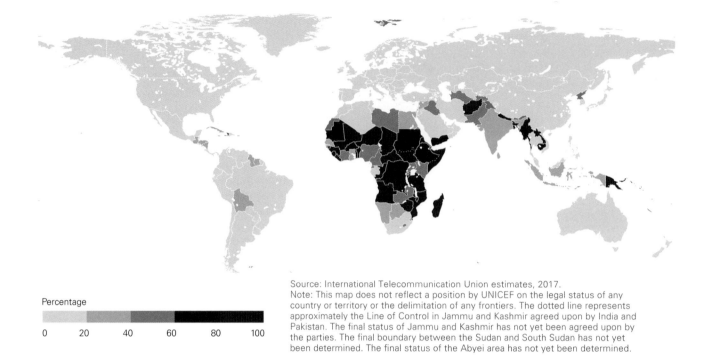

Percentage

0   20   40   60   80   100

Source: International Telecommunication Union estimates, 2017.
Note: This map does not reflect a position by UNICEF on the legal status of any country or territory or the delimitation of any frontiers. The dotted line represents approximately the Line of Control in Jammu and Kashmir agreed upon by India and Pakistan. The final status of Jammu and Kashmir has not yet been agreed upon by the parties. The final boundary between the Sudan and South Sudan has not yet been determined. The final status of the Abyei area has not yet been determined.

FIGURE 2.2 ABOUT THREE OUT OF FIVE YOUTH IN AFRICA ARE NOT ONLINE
PERCENTAGE OF 15–24-YEAR-OLDS WHO ARE NON-INTERNET USERS BY REGION, 2017

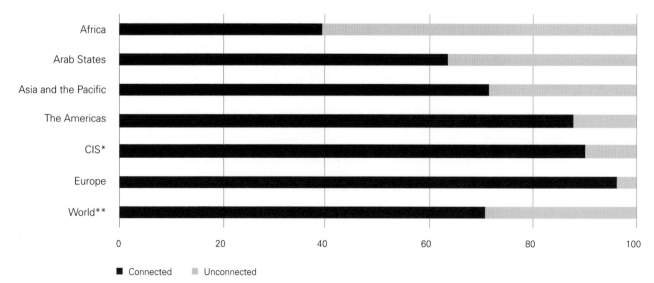

■ Connected   ■ Unconnected

*   Commonwealth of Independent States.
** Estimates for the 'World' figure include a few 'other economies' not included in any of the regions.
     Source: International Telecommunication Union (ITU) estimates, 2017.

FIGURE 2.3 CHILDREN FROM THE LOWEST-INCOME COUNTRIES USE THE INTERNET LEAST

PERCENTAGE OF UNDER-15 CHILDREN USING THE INTERNET, SELECTED COUNTRIES AND TERRITORIES, 2012–2016

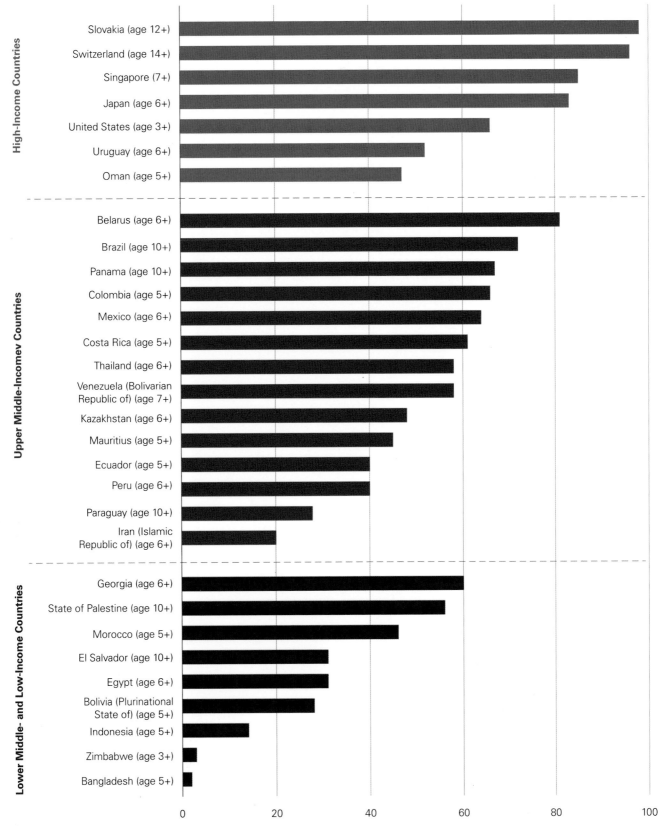

Source: Eurostat, ITU and UNICEF, 2012–2016.
Note: Income classification follows World Bank income classification as of August 2017.

also clear. In 40 countries and economies, virtually every student (99 per cent) in the top socio-economic quartile had home internet, but in 15 countries this was true for only one in two students in the bottom quartile.[18]

These inequalities in access *within* countries can reinforce existing inequities for children who cannot meet the demands of the digital age. The case of the homework gap in the United States, where the lack of home broadband access puts low-income schoolchildren at a disadvantage, is a telling example *(see box: Mind the homework gap).*

A persistent gender gap

The world over, more men than women use the internet; what's more this gap is not narrowing but widening. The global gap in internet use between men and women grew from 11 per cent in 2013 to 12 per cent in 2016.[19] The gap is particularly striking in some low-income countries *(see Figure 2.5).* From a global perspective, the gender digital divide is proving "incredibly difficult to overcome, reflecting broader social gender inequalities," according to the Broadband

FIGURE 2.4 YOUTH IN RURAL AREAS ARE LESS LIKELY TO GO ONLINE
PERCENTAGE OF 15–24-YEAR-OLDS WHO USED THE INTERNET OVER THE PAST YEAR IN SELECTED COUNTRIES, 2012–2016

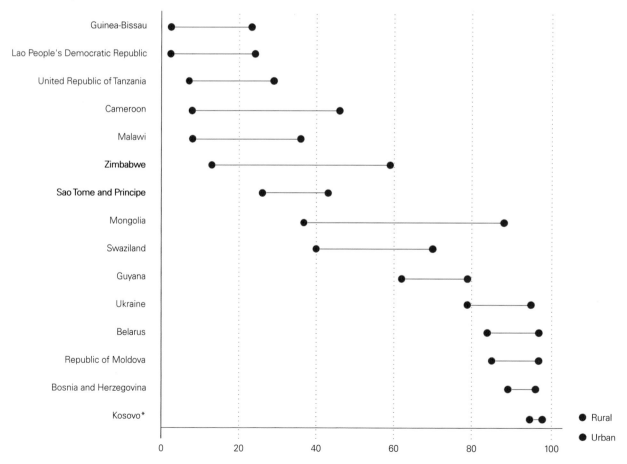

Source: UNICEF analysis based on Demographic and Health Surveys and Multiple Indicator Cluster Surveys.
* All references to Kosovo are made in the context of UN Security Council Resolution 1244 (1999).

Commission for Digital Development's 2015 report.[20]

What's behind this divide? A survey by the GSM Association (GSMA) of 22 low- and middle-income countries in 2015 found that various socio-economic and cultural barriers – among them social norms, education levels, lack of technical literacy and lack of confidence – tend to keep girls and women from using mobile phones.[21] Women used phones less frequently and less intensively than men, especially

for higher-level uses such as accessing the internet.[22]

Country-level examples give a sense of the kinds of barriers girls and women confront. In India, where only 29 per cent of all internet users are female, girls in rural areas often face restrictions on their use of ICTs solely because of their gender. One village governing body in rural Rajasthan stated that girls were not to use mobile phones or social media. Another village in Uttar Pradesh banned unmarried girls from using mobile phones (and from wearing jeans

"

In India, only 29% of all internet users are female.

FIG 2.5 GIRLS ARE LEAST LIKELY TO GO ONLINE IN LOW-CONNECTIVITY COUNTRIES
PERCENTAGE OF 15–19-YEAR-OLDS WHO USED THE INTERNET OVER THE PAST YEAR IN SELECTED COUNTRIES, 2012–2016

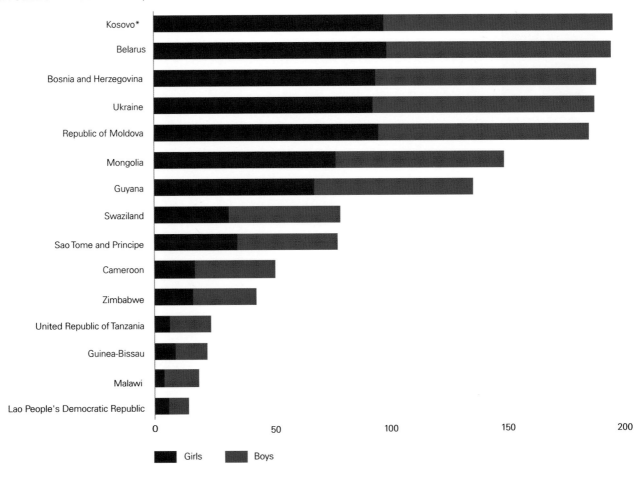

Source: UNICEF analysis based on Demographic and Health Surveys and Multiple Indicator Cluster Surveys conducted 2012–2016.
* All references to Kosovo are made in the context of UN Security Council Resolution 1244 (1999).

PERSPECTIVE

How digital technologies herald a bright future

Karim Sy and Laura Maclet

It goes without saying that digital technologies are invading every aspect of our lives. But transitioning to an inclusive information society that offers opportunities for all is a major global challenge. New technologies give us a different perspective on the world and help us address problems from a new angle. That is why they are so important.

People in Africa understand this all too well. The pace of technological progress there is faster than anywhere else in the world – between 2010 and 2015, mobile cellular subscriptions jumped 70 per cent and almost half of the people on the continent now have a mobile phone contract. Despite the uneven digital and technological landscape, these technologies are increasingly becoming part and parcel of everyday life – even in rural areas, where people have shown a readiness to embrace mobile technologies. New apps are appearing all the time, across areas such as agriculture, health and education. A prime example is Farmdrive – an initiative that connects small-scale farmers to lenders in rural areas of Kenya using mobile telephones.

Mobile internet is heralding new opportunities in many different areas, and the success of mobile banking, which has revolutionized the banking sector, is now prompting innovative approaches to education. By 2050, more than half of the world's population growth is expected to occur in Africa, while, by some estimates, 65 per cent of children starting primary school today will work in jobs that are yet to exist – jobs in artificial intelligence, machine learning, robotics, 3D printing and nanotechnologies. As these new occupations emerge, people will need to continue learning and acquiring skills throughout their lives. And we will have to learn to adapt. The internet is also opening up new opportunities for people in remote areas to earn an income from simple activities. Samasource, a project that aims to reduce poverty through creating digital jobs, is a prime example of how

empowerment and basic digital education can drive value creation.

So how can African children learn the skills they need to thrive in the future? How should we be educating people in today's world of technological advances and societal upheaval?

Technologies serve no purpose without a human dimension. So, if we want everyone to use digital devices, we need to spread knowledge widely and rethink the respective roles of both the technologies and educators. The internet is steadily breaking down barriers to accessing knowledge, which is no longer the preserve of the classroom. Technology and multimedia bring with them opportunities to learn in new ways and develop customized learning pathways. Yet as technology opens up access to knowledge, there is a real risk that people who cannot use these new tools will be left behind. The answer is to get everyone on board – teachers, entrepreneurs, parents, technology communities, charities and non-profits, and public policymakers. If children know how to use digital technologies and get the support they need, they will be able to access – and use – a whole new world of technical and personal skills. What's more, educators will be able to add these technologies to their arsenal of resources – doing away with the conventional model of centralized, top-down public education.

Right now, children lack the safe and secure learning opportunities they need to reach their full potential. The digital revolution is about more than learning to use new tools and technologies. It is about a major paradigm shift in people's mindsets and habits.

The Jokkokids project, supported by the Open Society Initiative for West Africa (OSIWA), organizes extra-curricular workshops where children learn about the connections between digital technologies and other areas, such as

manufacturing (do-it-yourself, recycling, etc.), self-expression and the arts. The idea is that learning stems first and foremost from great teaching, high-quality multidisciplinary content, and the teacher's relationship with technology. If we want children to gain confidence in their abilities and make steady progress towards their full potential, we should encourage them to learn digital skills alongside other subject areas. This is a long-term process of continuous improvement, based on feedback from the global educational community. The aim is to do something that, ultimately, benefits everyone.

At its training centre in Ziguinchor, NGO Futur au Présent works with girls aged 6–10 who have previously been engaged in child labour. The scheme began in 2014 and, by 2016, 60 young girls had stopped working and returned to school. After 18 months, 90 per cent of these girls were at the top of their class. Outside of lessons, the girls are enrolled in the Jokkokids scheme, as well as the Ideas Box project run by the NGO Libraries Without Borders, which fosters digital inclusion through cross-cutting sessions in which children learn about digital technologies, robotics and self-expression in a friendly and welcoming setting.

Programmes like these help children see the link between theory and practice. By revisiting what they have learned in the classroom during extra-curricular time, getting to grips with new tools and materials, and thinking about themselves and the people and world around them, children steadily build the resilience they need to cope in an ever-changing, complex, uncertain and ambiguous world. Never has there been a more urgent need to rethink the way we do things, especially in teaching and learning. But that change can only come about if we get everyone on board.

Karim Sy is a successful serial entrepreneur. In 2010, he founded Jokkolabs – an open innovation ecosystem that runs a network of 'creative spaces' in France and eight African countries. A member of Ashoka since 2012, Karim has kick-started a series of digital innovation projects, fuelling the entrepreneurial ecosystem in Africa and Europe. He was recently named as a member of the Presidential Council for Africa by French President Emmanuel Macron.

Laura Maclet coordinates Jokkolabs' Education & Training Cluster. She holds a degree in politics, linguistics and information science, and is a qualified secondary-level teacher. She specializes in educational programme design, deployment and dissemination.

Connectivity rates are very low in some countries. Fewer than 5 per cent of children under 15 use the internet in Zimbabwe.
© UNICEF/UN050415/MUKWAZHI

Never has there been a more urgent need to rethink the way we do things.

What do adolescents think about ... the barriers that stop them from going online?

Many participants in the *State of the World's Children 2017* workshops* said they faced barriers to going online. Limited connectivity was at the top of their list of challenges ...

"I want to search ... the internet but the signal is very bad." BOY, 16, TIMOR-LESTE

"Slow connection – it's always shutting down and all my tabs get lost." GIRL, 16, TUNISIA

while, in a third of the countries, participants cited unreliable power as a problem.
"No electricity." GIRL, 13, VANUATU

Connectivity issues were worse in rural areas.
"When I go to the countryside and there's no signal, I get desperate because I can't communicate." GIRL, 14, PARAGUAY

A lack of devices at home or at school was another barrier, with significant numbers saying they could not regularly access a desktop computer, laptop, tablet or mobile phone.
"We don't have a computer at home." GIRL, 15, BURUNDI

"No availability of technology." BOY, 15, JORDAN

Many said they had to share devices with other family members ...
"I need to share the iPad with all my family so I use it just a little bit." GIRL, 15, REPUBLIC OF MOLDOVA

or rely on old devices that were not powerful enough or had weak batteries – a source of frustration.
"I cannot use the mobile phone outside my home because the battery [life is] too short." BOY, 14, URUGUAY

Participants had a range of workarounds, including switching between devices to maximize their time online.
"My laptop becomes slow after using for some time so I use my smartphone for solving this issue." BOY, 17, BANGLADESH

Cost was another barrier, with 'running out of credit' being the challenge most often reported by participants.
"I had a phone but no credit to make calls." BOY, 14, CENTRAL AFRICAN REPUBLIC

"I want to call my mum to tell her that my little brother is sick but I have run out of credit." GIRL, 10, CENTRAL AFRICAN REPUBLIC

"There's no money to recharge." GIRL, 16, PERU

A number of participants thought the state should do more.
"The state should provide free internet." GIRL, 10, CENTRAL AFRICAN REPUBLIC

"Government should decrease the cost of internet." BOY, 17, BANGLADESH

Participants faced other barriers to going online, including concerns over loss of privacy ...
"Sometimes I am afraid to enter in some website for cybersecurity problems like hacking." BOY, 16, BANGLADESH

"Being worried about my privacy makes me reluctant to go online." GIRL, (AGE NOT GIVEN), THAILAND

and school rules – many noted that they were forbidden to bring personal devices to school or to use them during school hours.

"Bringing your own device is not allowed and devices can be confiscated, which is why students need to wait for the computer class to access [technology]." BOY, 16, DEMOCRATIC REPUBLIC OF THE CONGO

"I think it would be fine to use digital devices at school, but those are only allowed during the break time and lunch time." BOY, 15, REPUBLIC OF KOREA

Some participants responded by breaking the rules.

"The usage of devices are not allowed at school … [My solution is to] sneakily use it." GIRL, 18, THAILAND

Some also felt schools should be more open and responsive to students' wants and needs.

"[We need] spaces/moments in which we can use it at school." GIRL, 14, PARAGUAY

"[Schools should be] analysing the reason for which a student wants to use his mobile phone or computer." BOY, 17, PARAGUAY

Family rules were another barrier, with restrictions on when participants could use devices …

"Our parents switch off the Wi-Fi at night because of negative waves." GIRL, 16, TUNISIA

"I am not happy because my father gets angry at me if I spend a lot of time playing on my phone." BOY, 19, TIMOR-LESTE

and at what age.

"I don't have a smartphone because my family thinks I'm still young." GIRL, 17, BANGLADESH

Many participants believed that parents needed to ensure children were using technology appropriately, even if the rules were sometimes annoying or caused friction.

"[I can] accept why it's forbidden and think about it." BOY, 15, PARAGUAY

"[I will] wait until I am in Grade 7 [to get a smartphone]." BOY, 15, THAILAND

Some participants said their lack of digital literacy was a barrier …

"Sometimes I want to go online but there is no one to help me and show me." GIRL, 12, CENTRAL AFRICAN REPUBLIC

"Not knowing how to use social media [stops me going online]." GIRL, 15, BURUNDI

as was lack of time.

"Because we are at school and once we arrive home we should do other things first: to study, to wash dishes, etc." GIRL, 14, URUGUAY

"[I have a] lot of homework [or am] busy doing home chores." GIRL, 15, KIRIBATI

"Most of my time I use it for study or work so I only have the night to use the internet." BOY, 17, GUATEMALA

Finally, many participants reported experiencing multiple barriers to using digital technology.

"The obstacles that I face are mainly to find someone who can lend me his phone, secondly, it is to find money to buy units, finally, the lack of electricity." BOY, 17, BURUNDI

IN SUMMARY

Barriers preventing children from maximizing opportunity in the digital age are multifaceted – a complexity that needs to be reflected in efforts to improve children's online access. But these efforts can take novel approaches. For example, they may not have to replicate the 'one device per person' model common in wealthier countries. A final insight is that rules guiding technology use in schools and other settings should ideally be developed in conjunction with children to increase the likelihood of their abiding by them.

* Participants' responses have been shortened and edited for clarity where necessary.

Mind the Homework Gap: The divide facing the lowest-income children in the United States

The United States presents a particularly compelling case of the sort of digital inequality children can face in high-connectivity countries. While most American households with school-aged children (aged 6–17) had home broadband access in 2015, around 5 million did not.[23]

For some, this was because they lived in an area without a connection or with only a very slow connection. Cost was also an important factor – the unconnected households were likely to have an annual income below US$50,000. But the access fault line did not stop at income: Among the low-income households, black and Hispanic households trailed similar-income white families in broadband by 10 percentage points.[24]

What does this mean for schoolchildren? Across the country, students from households without high-speed home internet are facing what policymakers and educators call 'the homework gap'.[25] As school curricula increasingly incorporate internet-based learning and online testing, low-income students in areas with poor internet connectivity or those who cannot afford broadband are left at a marked disadvantage. High school students report being unable to complete school work or getting lower grades due to lack of home broadband access.[26]

The reality of the divide has been captured eloquently by the popular press: school buses equipped with Wi-Fi being parked overnight in underserved neighbourhoods so that children can connect for their studies;[27] children heading to local libraries and fast-food chains to access free hotspots;[28] and children hanging out on the sidewalks of the local elementary school well into the evening with the family's only phone, trying to download an assignment.[29]

and T-shirts).[30] This council believed that mobile phone use would increase crimes against girls and women. In Sri Lanka, a 2015 national study[31] of 11- to 18-year-olds found that girls accounted for only a third of adolescents using computers and mobile phones to go online. In focus group discussions, parents revealed that they often restricted girls from accessing the internet.[32]

A 2017 review of evidence from low- and middle-income countries revealed important patterns of gender-based discrepancies among adolescents: When parents or caregivers provide the technology, girls get access at an older age than boys; girls' access is also more curtailed or supervised; and the idea of ICT-related careers is associated more with boys than with girls.[33]

There are potentially serious consequences for girls excluded from the digital age. They may be unable to access online services and information, including about issues related to their health and sexuality, such as HIV and puberty; they may face barriers to furthering their education and to developing the skills necessary in the global economy of the twenty-first century; they may not be able to access social and political information that affects them; and they may be excluded from opportunities to make their voices heard.

Once connected, how do you use?

The digital divide is typically thought of in terms of access – the haves and have-nots of connectivity. But since the 1990s, researchers have paid more attention to a 'second level'[34] of divides that goes beyond access. The idea of second-level divides broadly covers differences in people's online skills and abilities, types of online activities pursued, patterns of internet use and the devices used to go online.[35] Put otherwise, people's personal circumstances – skills, education and so on – affect how they use the internet.

For example, internet users with higher levels of education appear to use more advanced online services, such as e-commerce and financial activities, than users with lower education levels, who tend to limit their online activities to communications and entertainment.[36] So, even though the primary digital divide of access is narrowing, digital divides could be shifting to second-level divides based on growing inequalities in digital skills and usage.[37]

Research on second-level divides among children is scarce, but there are exceptions. In 2011, EU Kids Online, a research network that interviewed 25,000 children and their parents in 25 European countries, found that children from wealthier households engaged in a wider 'repertoire' of activities than those from less wealthy households.[38] More recently, the 2015 OECD PISA study showed that across countries, students from higher socio-economic backgrounds were more likely to use the internet to obtain practical information or read the news. Their lower-income peers, on the other hand, tended to spend online time chatting and playing games.

The study noted that these differences were similar to those found in studies of adult populations, suggesting a strong correlation of second-level divides with wider social inequalities and cultural preferences.[39]

All this points to worrying prospects for the most excluded children and the world at large. The digital 'haves' will likely continue to have more, in terms of connectivity, access to a range of devices and advanced digital skills than the digital 'have-nots', and will have it earlier in life, perpetuating cycles of disadvantage and reinforcing privilege.[40]

Emerging second-level divides

There is increasing interest in how other digital divides may manifest themselves, and whether they may create new digital silos or lead to exclusion. Two divides in particular may have implications for children's lives: First, the leapfrogging of first-time internet users directly to mobile devices in low-income countries; and second, the relative lack of online content in minority languages and the absence of content concerning large swathes of the world, especially low- and middle-income countries.

Many users in middle- and low-income countries without consistent access to internet access on personal computers are using mobile phones to leapfrog into the information age *(see Figure 2.6)*. However, mobile phones are not "functionally equivalent substitutes" for personal computers, providing users with only a 'second-best' online experience.[41] The constraints of the mobile internet – particularly for tasks associated with producing information such as long-form writing, video editing and design[42] – may not always be apparent to new users in low-income countries. Many go online for the first time only through mobile phones and may be unaware "of the degree to which their online experience falls short of a PC-based online experience."[43]

While the gap in access is narrowing, digital divides could be shifting to second-level divides.

In the United States, research on smartphone adoption by adolescents showed that those from lower-income households were more likely to go online primarily through their mobile devices.[44] In addition, children in low-income households who had internet access only via mobile devices used it less frequently, and for a narrower set of activities.[45]

Findings from Global Kids Online (see box opposite) also suggest that the user experience of children who have internet access via mobile phone alone may differ

from that of others because "the small screen limits the amount and complexity of content that can be readily viewed." When searching for information online, for example, "mobile users tend to scan content rather than process and analyse it more deeply."[46]

Given the role of mobile technologies in connecting children in some of the world's least-connected regions (see box: Connecting Africa's youth), there are clear concerns that offering children only a second-best experience risks spurring new forms of inequity.

FIGURE 2.6 CHILDREN RELY HEAVILY ON SMARTPHONES TO GO ONLINE
PERCENTAGE OF CHILDREN USING EACH DEVICE AT LEAST ONCE A MONTH, 2016–2017

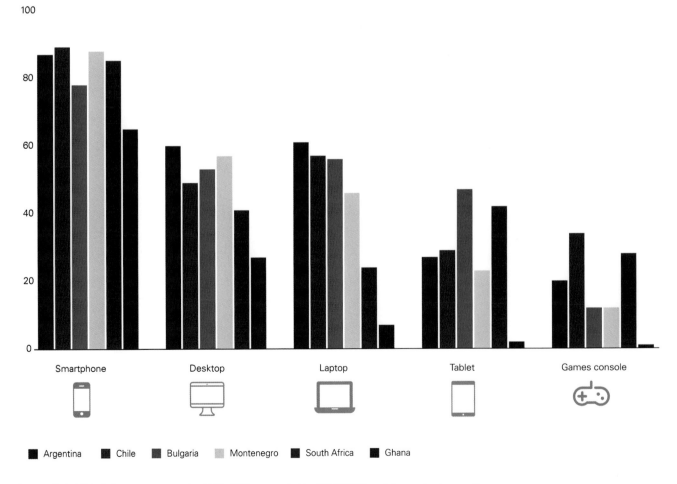

■ Argentina   ■ Chile   ■ Bulgaria   ■ Montenegro   ■ South Africa   ■ Ghana

Source: Global Kids Online partner countries 2016–2017, aggregated by UNICEF Office of Research – Innocenti.

In response to the access problems of some of the lowest-income and lowest-connectivity markets, some global content providers offer free or lower-priced data plans. Similar to generic 'zero rating' programmes that exempt certain sites from the customer's data limit,[47] these initiatives allow customers who find data costs prohibitive to access selected content for free or at low cost when they sign up with certain service providers. Examples include Facebook's Free Basics, Wikipedia Zero and Google Free Zone,[48] as well as UNICEF's Internet of Good Things (IoGT), which, in partnership with a group of mobile network operators and Free Basics, provides information to in-need populations in 60 countries and territories and 12 languages on issues such as children rights, internet safety, maternal health, hygiene, epidemics, HIV/AIDS and positive parenting. Such programmes bring affordable internet services and access to critical information to users who might otherwise go completely without.

But zero-rating programmes are not without their critics. Some raise concerns that the next billion internet users, both adults and children, may be led not to an inclusive, participatory internet to which they can contribute but rather to an internet where "they will have little to do but post on social networks and consume media using the apps, services and platforms developed by a few big players" from a few countries.[49]

The absence of relevant content and languages

Besides issues of affordability and accessibility, there is another barrier facing many of the billions of unconnected people in the digital space – namely, the lack of useful online content in their native language.[50] This may discourage potential users from trying to go online or prevent them from

Global Kids Online

Global Kids Online (GKO) is a research project and network that supports worldwide efforts to conduct rigorous, comparable research on children's use of digital technology. It is coordinated by the UNICEF Office of Research-Innocenti in partnership with the London School of Economics and the EU Kids Online network. GKO provides well-tested and robust research tools – a baseline survey, methodological guides and qualitative protocols – to support quality research on children's online experiences that can be used to influence policy or programming and inform campaigns and advocacy efforts.

Each GKO project is implemented by a local partner to ensure contextual relevance and national impact. Since 2016, nearly 10,000 children and 5,000 parents have been surveyed in 10 countries through the work of UNICEF country offices and research institutions in Argentina, Brazil, Bulgaria, Chile, Ghana, Montenegro, Philippines, Serbia, South Africa and Uruguay.

directly gauging the potential utility and relevance of the internet.[51] But it raises a bigger concern, too: namely, that the absence of content that speaks directly to children's diverse cultural contexts and experiences may widen knowledge gaps.

The internet of today is, of course, far more multilingual than it was at the beginning of the century. But the fact remains that, in 2016, just 10 languages accounted for the majority of websites, with 56 per cent of them in English.[52]

In 2016, 56% of websites were in English.

Artificial intelligence and its potential impact on children
By Sandra Cortesi and Urs Gasser

Over the past few years, technologies based on artificial intelligence (AI) have begun to change our daily lives as they are rolled out at an accelerated pace not only in professional working environments but also at home and in schools.

Hello Barbie and Green DIno are just two examples of AI-enabled toys that have already made their way into some children's homes, with many more under development across the globe – including internet-connected teddy bears with embedded mics, cameras, sensors and other networked technologies. These AI-enabled toys might be fun for children to play with and may foster language development and socio-emotional learning, but they also raise serious privacy and safety concerns, particularly when connected to the internet.

For older children, AI-based technologies play an increasingly important role in learning, whether they are studying in formal educational institutions or interacting with interactive online platforms, advanced games or the like in individual and social learning environments. Again, AI-fuelled 'ed tech' – including AI-powered digital tutors, learning assistants and personalized educational programmes – can offer wonderful opportunities to young learners and lead to better learning outcomes. At the same time, the complex interplay between data sets and algorithms that power these 'black box' AI systems give rise to pressing questions about bias and discrimination as well as concerns related to transparency and accountability. Moreover, and perhaps most fundamentally, absent appropriate safeguards, legal protections and sound policies, AI-based technologies may further exacerbate existing inequalities among children and young people, leading to an even deeper and arguably more decisive digital divide that shapes learning outcomes and future opportunities for young people to develop and flourish.

The stakes are high, in terms of both potential benefits and risks, and it is the shared responsibility of AI companies, caregivers, educators and policymakers to ensure that AI-based applications used by children are designed and deployed in such ways that they embrace the positive potential while avoiding the pitfalls.

Sandra Cortesi is Director of Youth and Media and Urs Gasser is Executive Director of the Berkman Klein Center for Internet & Society at Harvard University. Since 2010, the Berkman Klein Center and UNICEF have collaborated to promote a holistic understanding of the impact that digital technology has on children's lives. Learn more at <http://www.digitallyconnected.org/>

Translation tools such as Google Translate, which currently supports 103 languages, can help, but they still leave many people in the world uncovered,[53] particularly users in low-income countries.[54] However, Google's Neural Machine Translation system, aimed at increasing the fluency and accuracy of Google Translate, could set the standard for future machine translation. Not only does it provide better translation of spoken language into translated text, but it can translate languages rarely written down, such as Haitian Creole or Japanese Ainu. This will make a huge difference in humanitarian settings, for example, where relief workers can struggle to communicate with children and families in need.[55] Or, in the context of skills and learning, where the instant translation of Massive Open Online Courses (MOOCs), which provide a free and flexible way to learn new skills, could reach disadvantaged or remote populations.

Gaps in content reflect not just how users' lives and concerns are represented online but also who gets to *create* content.[56] Using the example of Wikipedia, the Oxford Internet Institute (OII) has shown the scale of these gaps in content and content creation. Wikipedia, "the world's

Young people living in many parts of Africa and Asia, such as these girls in Sudan, often struggle to find information online that's relevant to their own lives and in their own language. © UNICEF/UNI166091/NOORANI

Information poverty

Digital exclusion manifests itself in varied ways in a child's life, both in the short and long term. A child deprived of access to information – whether from a newspaper, television or the internet – is denied a fair chance to develop and better her or his situation. Imagine a girl living in a poor, rural household anywhere in the world. How will she compete with her advantaged counterparts in the classroom or, later, for a job, if she is not equipped with the same access to information about the world? What will be her job prospects without equal access to social networking sites, learning platforms and online job postings?

UNICEF's Office of Innovation is contributing to research on solutions to the very real problem of 'information poverty'. Its approach is built on the idea that access to information is a right – leading to opportunity and better outcomes for children and their communities. Denial of that right contributes to expanding and extending gaps in opportunity for children, making the most disadvantaged even worse off and fuelling intergenerational cycles of poverty.

But how is a child's information poverty measured? Hundreds of ever-changing variables must be taken into account and data are scarce. To start with, who and where are the children most deprived of information? What are the underlying causes and barriers to access? And why are some of those with access not using it? To date, dimensions of information poverty include availability, access, usage, resilience, social graph, content and skills.

Machine learning and the combination of new data sources – such as satellite imagery, mobile phone data, social media and online search analyses – with traditional ones could help to provide a measurement. Quantifying such poverty would be a valuable advocacy tool for programme development and influencing policy and resource allocation.

Information poverty pilot projects are under way in Brazil, Liberia and Mozambique. In Liberia, for example, building on lessons from the Ebola crisis – namely, how a lack of information about the disease contributed to its spread – UNICEF Innovation is working with partners to measure the impact of access to information across different sectors, with a special focus on health and resilience.

To better understand the needs of youth in vulnerable communities, the pilot in Mozambique is mapping how access to their main channels of information (TV, radio, family and phone) affects their decisions and outcomes around life-and-death issues such as malaria and child marriage.

A world without information poverty could be one with less spread of infectious disease; better insights on how digital education can improve and accelerate learning outcomes for the most disadvantaged children; reduced gender inequality; and improved financial inclusion – just to name a few benefits.

largest and most used repository of user-generated content,"[57] averages more than 18 billion page views per month.[58] It is a platform where, technically, anyone with internet access can write or make changes to content.

Notably, OII's mapping of Wikipedia articles shows marked geographical unevenness in content. In 2014, most of the articles in the 44 language versions mapped were found to focus mainly on places, events and people in North America, Europe, Australia and parts of Asia, such as India and Japan. Certain regions, such as Africa, were greatly under-represented. In fact, information about many countries in Africa and Asia was written up in a non-local language, predominantly English, but also French and German. The researchers argued that on Wikipedia, "the South is largely being defined and described by others."[59]

Wikipedia is just one small slice of the internet. But its content gaps underscore the point that increased connectivity may not necessarily reduce unequal access to and production of information.[60] They also highlight the need for policy on digital divides to go beyond the issue of access and for children to be given the skills, education and tools that would allow them to participate in the digital realm as creators, and not mere consumers, of content, with more to look forward to than being stuck in a whirlpool of social media and videos of "singing dogs [and] snoring camels."[61]

Pointing the way forward

For children to not only survive but also thrive in a digital world, they need a new set of tools. Whether they're called 'digital literacy' or 'digital citizenship', these tools go well beyond simple technical ability such as usage skills: They equip children to evaluate the information they find online; to understand what it means to socialize online; to behave responsibly and keep themselves safe online; to advocate for their interests or those of their communities;

Cuba's first online generation

Something has changed on the streets of Cuba. After school and on weekends, and in parks and on avenues, groups of children can be seen chatting away on video calls with relatives and friends or playing the sort of games that children almost everywhere play online. The sight is familiar in much of the world, but in Cuba it would have been unimaginable just two years ago.

That's because it was only in 2015 that the government launched paid Wi-Fi hotspots in public spaces across the island. By the end of 2016, more than 600 collective 'surfing spaces' and more than 300 public Wi-Fi hotspots had been set up. The initiative has transformed access to the internet for adults and children. According to official figures, some 250,000 connections are made from the Wi-Fi hotspots every day.[62]

The hotspots, which allow access to international sites, are proving popular with young Cubans: "Connecting to the internet is the coolest right now," says Diego, a 14-year-old from Havana. "Having the money for an internet card is better than a new T-shirt. If you don't go online, you're out, you are missing out."

This is not, however, the first encounter with the online world for Cuban children. Since 1987, the Joven Club (Youth Club) system has been providing young people with a gateway to the technology of the digital world in a country where personal computers and

internet access are not common. Currently, almost 4,000 children and adolescents[63] visit the more-than 600 clubs every day to attend courses, surf national sites featuring approved educational content with built-in child protection elements and access entertainment and educational content.

Jennifer, 17, is one of them: "Online, I can find information for school in EcuRed [the Cuban encyclopedia] and also chat with people. The internet opens up another world that we don't see. It's exciting."

Away from such official access points, and reflecting the island's make-do culture, many young Cubans also 'connect' offline, swapping content by Bluetooth or buying terabyte-sized 'Paquete' – packages of TV shows, films, video clips, magazines and apps stored on hard drives and USBs. Concerned at the sometimes-inappropriate content in these packages, the Joven Club distributes its own 'Mochila' package of information and entertainment. The packages feature safe content seeking to promote healthy lifestyles and spiritual development.

Cuba is just at the dawn of its own digital age – and the government is committed to continue increasing connectivity. Acting now to anticipate the opportunities for children to come, as well as the potential risks, is an important task for all in Cuba.

These girls attend computer classes in the West Bengal city of Howrah. Women and girls account for only 29 per cent of India's internet users.
© UNICEF/UN063162/ALTAF AHMAD

to improve their learning; and to develop new talents and skills. Children who have these tools will have the advantage in a knowledge-based society.

Policy action is also needed to improve education, raise literacy and otherwise strengthen children's non-digital foundations, so that they can make the most out of being connected. Both the *World Bank's World Development Report 2016: Digital dividends* and Facebook's *State of Connectivity 2015* emphasized the importance of foundational skills such as the quality of education, learning and teaching, to create conditions not only for greater adoption of the internet but also for better quality of its use.

Literacy, too, is key. As the OECD's 2015 PISA study stressed, ensuring that every child attains "a baseline level of proficiency in reading and mathematics will do more

to create equal opportunities in a digital world than can be achieved by expanding or subsidizing access to high-tech devices and services".[64]

But technology will certainly play a role, and state action is likely to be needed to plug the communications gaps. Bringing equitable online access to some of the least-connected communities will be challenging. For example, for those living on less than US$2 a day in countries like India and the United Republic of Tanzania, the average cost of a smartphone is 16 per cent of their annual income.[65] Even if mobile phones with internet capabilities were to become more affordable, the extreme poor would still have to contend with high airtime and data costs.[66] GSMA estimates that 90 per cent of the one billion new mobile subscribers expected by 2020 will come from "developing markets"

Without state-led commitment, children will be further left behind.

and acknowledges that affordable mobile services and extending network coverage for the rural poor are particular challenges on the way to universal, affordable access.[67]

As the World Bank's 2016 report on digital dividends points out, expanding communication networks in lower-income countries, which are primarily based on mobile networks built by the private sector, may leave gaps in the 'backbone infrastructure' of a country, especially in rural areas, for providing universal high-speed networks. This trajectory is different from that followed in most high-income countries, which was based on initial state led investments in telephone infrastructure, followed only later by private sector participation and mobile

and internet networks. Without state-led commitment to complement market-based and private sector solutions, children left behind in a digitally connected world will be at great risk of further exclusion and marginalization.

Finally, the need for more in-depth data to capture different aspects of children's lives in the digital age cannot be emphasized enough. There is a serious lack of comprehensive data collation at country, regional and global levels on how children access and use ICTs. Unless such evidence-based information is documented, stakeholders, including policymakers, will continue to be limited in their understanding of the digital inequalities facing children and, therefore, unable to take effective action.

Connecting Africa's youth

Africa will see its youth population almost double from 240 million in 2016 to 460 million in 2050[69] – a youth bulge that will meet a global connectivity revolution in full swing. What is the potential outcome of seizing this window of opportunity? The region's high proportion of youth (15–24 years old) could take advantage of broadband's expansion to work in the global digital economy.

But given current trends and evidence to date, how likely is this to happen?

This depends on whether youth will have the ability (and means) to connect to the internet, the digital skills to navigate their way around it and the educational foundation to take advantage of the opportunities they find there. The jobs themselves, or a climate that fosters entrepreneurship, must also be available.

First, connectivity: Today, only about 1 in 10 people in sub-Saharan Africa living in areas covered by 3G networks actually subscribes to mobile broadband.[70] And it is estimated that by 2020, only about two out of

five Africans will be connected to broadband, primarily through mobile devices. Only one African country (Nigeria) is among the 10 countries adding the most mobile subscribers by 2020.[71]

Rapid urbanization will likely exert a complex influence on young Africans' ability to connect. In 2013, two out of five people in Africa lived in cities;[72] by 2050, it will be three out of five.[73] Urban youth will be more likely to have access to 3G coverage, but may be less likely to have access to work or other means of enhancing their ability to afford the technology to connect. With many young Africans today working in the informal economy, using mobile devices to access job opportunities will require a shift in the current paradigm.

Digital connectivity, for those young Africans who have it, provides an outlet for urbanized, educated youth to make their voices heard and a platform for demanding that governments respond to their concerns. Equipping young Africans with the digital skills today to navigate their world of tomorrow is crucial to their future.

SPECIAL SECTION: What do connected children do online?

The world's connected children are digital pioneers: In countries with relatively high levels of connectivity, 15- to 24-year-olds typically outnumber the overall online population.[74] Data are scarce on users below age 15, but evidence from a number of countries indicates they often use the internet at a rate similar to, or even in excess of, adults aged 25 and over.[75]

Many are **always online**: In high-income contexts, it is becoming difficult "to draw the line between offline and online" in children's lives.[76] In the United States, for example, 92 per cent of 13- to 17-year-olds report going online daily. Mobile devices, particularly smartphones – and 73 per cent of this age group have smartphones – enable some to be online "almost constantly."[77] The picture is similar in Europe, where children access the internet from multiple locations and using multiple devices,[78] especially smartphones but also desktop and laptop computers, tablets and game consoles.

They are becoming **younger and more mobile**: Evidence from high-connectivity countries suggests children are going online at ever-younger ages. In Bulgaria, for example, the age at which children first used the internet was commonly 10 in 2010 but had dropped to 7 by 2016.[79] In China, children under 10 made up 2.9 per cent of all internet users in 2016, up from 2.7 per cent in 2015.[80] In Brazil, the proportion of 9- and 10-year-olds using the internet increased from 35 per cent in 2012 to 37 per cent in 2013.[81] It is not uncommon for children who are not yet even teenagers to own their own phones. A survey in Algeria, Egypt, Iraq and Saudi Arabia in 2013 found that age 10 or 12 was the most common age for receiving a first mobile phone.[82] In 2015, age 10 was found to be the common age for a child to first own a mobile

phone in the Philippines, while in Honduras it was age 12.[83]

They're increasingly part of a '**bedroom culture**': Devices like smartphones and tablets are changing how and where children go online. Mobile phones enable children to access the internet in the privacy of their bedrooms or from a friend's house.[84] The result is online access that is more personal, more private and less supervised.

They go online to strengthen **friendships and find new friends**: The role of social networking in expanding friendships can be seen in countries as diverse as Egypt, India, Indonesia, Iraq and Saudi Arabia, where more than 90 per cent of children using mobiles reported that social networking strengthens relationships with close friends. Children also reported that it helps them build relationships with friends to whom they are not so close and with friends of friends.[85] But these platforms can also be a venue where conflicts and drama among friends play out. For some, they can be a source of pressure, with adolescents feeling the need to post 'attractive' content about themselves, for example, or content that would be 'liked' by others (see box by Mizuko Ito).[86]

And they go online to **access information and learning**: Using the internet to do homework is increasingly common in high-income countries,[87] but it is also a primary online practice in some middle-income

For children living in high-connectivity countries, such as Ahmad Abdul-Halim in Germany, it's increasingly hard to "draw the line between offline and online". © UNICEF/UN043764/GILBERTSON VII PHOTO

countries. In Brazil in 2013, schoolwork ranked first among children's main activities on the internet.[88] In Argentina, around 80 per cent of adolescents reported searching on Wikipedia or Google, and using video tutorials on subjects such as mathematics and history. "I flunked math," said a boy in Argentina, "so I watched a couple of vids where they explained what I had to study."[89] Children value the information they can access online,[90] including information on a wide range of recreational activities[91] and health issues.[92] As an adolescent in South Africa put it, the

value-added of the internet was "just that you know more about things you do not know much about."[93]

But, overall, they have a **narrow range of online activities**: The conventional wisdom is that children and adolescents are well ahead of adults in how they navigate and take advantage of digital technologies. However, the range of what children do online appears often to be quite narrow.

Evidence for this comes from the Global Kids Online[94] (GKO) international research

Why do teens <3 mobile and social media? By Mizuko Ito

In the late nineties, my research focused on Tokyo teens who were at the forefront of the text messaging and mobile internet revolution. The mobile phone had just pivoted from being a status symbol of the business executive to a fashion item for high school girls. The grownup world was up in arms about teens using these mobile phones for their frivolous social banter, and dubbed them *oyayubizoku* (thumb tribe) and *nagarazoku* (multitasking tribe). The poster child for the *nagarazoku* was the teen texting while walking or riding a bike.

Researchers puzzled over why teens were such enthusiastic adopters of mobile communication. Many attributed this to a natural affinity to new technology and teen obsession with peer communication. After conducting extensive studies, we reached a different conclusion.[96] Teens take to mobile and social media so they can communicate with their peers in peace.

Unlike adults, teens lack spaces for private communication, particularly in urban environments like Tokyo. In their daily lives, they move between home, where they lack access to their peers, and school, where they are with their peers but can't communicate privately. The landline phone is shared with family,

so it is not truly private. The mobile phone was more revolutionary for teens than their elders because it was the first time they could easily communicate directly with a peer or romantic partner. When these same teens moved in with their romantic partner, the volume of text messaging decreased dramatically.

It's common to assign quirks of teen behaviour to their developmental stage or generational identity. Yet more often than not, teens behave like anyone would under the same circumstances. They have less resistance to new technology because they lack certain habits, but they often offer a preview of how other age groups will come to adopt a new technology. Now that people of all ages have flocked to texting and Facebook, I feel our early research has been validated. Teens take to mobile and social media for the same reasons that the rest of us do – because they want to be connected with people they care about.

Mizuko Ito is a cultural anthropologist, educational researcher, entrepreneur and advocate. She is director of the Connected Learning Lab at the University of California, Irvine, and a co-founder of Connected Camps, a non-profit organization offering online, project-based, social STEM learning for kids in all walks of life.

project. Figure 2.7 (*"What are children doing online?"*) presents data collected by GKO on 17 children's online practices, grouping them into three loose categories: social, entertainment and learning; information and exploration; and civic engagement and creativity.

In all three countries represented here – Bulgaria, Chile and South Africa – the highest number of children engaged in just five to nine online practices. And the practices of more than half of these children fell into just one category: social, entertainment and learning. At the other end of the scale, the smallest group of children were those engaging in 15 or more practices. Users in this group were more

engaged in creative practices, such as developing videos and creating blogs as well as activities related to civic engagement, such as discussing political issues online. Although not presented in the graphic, age was a factor, with older children more likely to engage in a greater number of practices.

The data from these three countries highlight the point that while connected children avail themselves of many online opportunities, their fuller engagement with the internet – doing more diverse or sophisticated activities – is not a given. A challenge for research and policy is to find ways to support children to engage in more creative and participatory activities.[95]

FIGURE 2.7 WHAT ARE CHILDREN DOING ONLINE?

PERCENTAGE OF CHILDREN AGED 9-17 REPORTING INVOLVEMENT IN ONLINE ACTIVITIES, 2016–2017

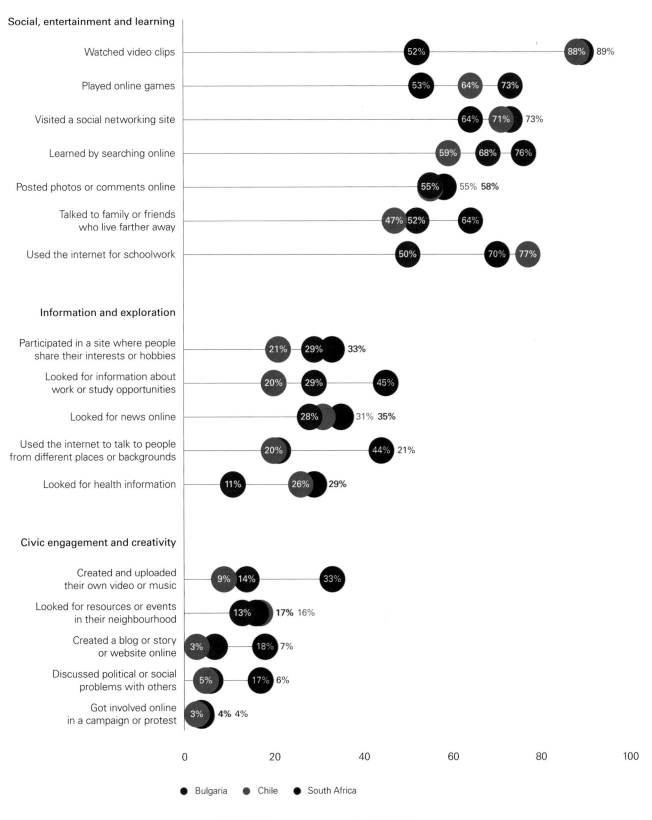

Source: Global Kids Online partner countries 2016–2017,
aggregated by UNICEF Office of Research – Innocenti.

PERSPECTIVE

A Vision for the Future: Reflections on children's rights in the digital age

Pony Ma

As a father, my wish is to see my child grow and strive, a wish shared by parents the world over. How can our children grow up happy and safe from harm and disease? Do they need fresh air, clean water, a beautiful environment, a harmonious family, a supportive society or a country that is rich and strong? I believe they need all of those, and more.

My child was born 'digital', into a generation whose members have been dubbed 'digital natives'. They are the happiest generation because they have convenient, fast and effective access to information and can enjoy their lives like no other before them.

Meanwhile, we are increasingly aware that not all children are realizing their rights. And we are seeing how the denial of child rights takes on a new meaning in the internet age. Regardless of their region, wealth or status, children have the right to develop; to fully participate in family, cultural and social life; and to have equal access to information, self-expression and education.

However, even with better technologies and improvements in productivity, the gap between those with and without access to computers and the internet is expanding. In December 2016, the number of 'netizens' under 19 years of age reached 171 million – in China alone. Yet, many children in China, and around the world, lack access for economic and social reasons. The internet, as a public property, can and should be leveraged to bridge this digital divide.

To connect people in rural parts of China, in 2015 we initiated a mobile internet programme called WeCountry. Two years later, while problems remain to be solved, we are pleasantly surprised to find that the programme has helped teach those new to the internet how to use it and has given many disadvantaged children access to information and learning opportunities.

But, implementing child rights in a digital age is not only about closing the digital gap. As one of China's largest comprehensive internet service providers, Tencent bears a considerable responsiblity: Millions of children are using our products to communicate, learn and entertain themselves every day. Children and parents need to understand there are risks behind these opportunities. False or malicious information and violent or pornographic material online put children at risk of harm. Data breaches releasing personal or private information, such as children's photos or identities, can be used to exploit them and lead to serious consequences. Cyber violence and bullying has become a global problem. Finally, internet fraud, organized crime and child trafficking threaten to translate online shadows into offline evils.

As a father, I am deeply worried by the online risks children face daily. As an internet entrepreneur, I am very aware of the responsibilities on my shoulders.

Tencent is accountable for protecting the online safety of every child. To this end, Tencent incorporates online child protection in all aspects of its business practices. For example, in November 2016, the company launched the 'Tencent for children – Child rights protection in a digital world' initiative and announced the Child Online Protection Project with UNICEF. The partnership will dive into a wide range of issues including cyber violence, cyberbullying, exposure to inappropriate content and online gaming. The aim is to form a balanced understanding of children's internet usage for the purposes of policy advocacy, raising public awareness and building an industry coalition. This project will help advance the agenda of online child protection across sectors – government, the information and communication technology (ICT) industry, academia and civil society organizations – and explore the positive impact of the internet on children.

The internet age is characterized by rapid, innovative changes in technology and human-computer interactions and has the

In Cebu, the Philippines, 16-year-old Jan (background centre) suffered cyberbullying and read posts about self-harm during a difficult time in her life. She now works to educate her peers about online safety.
© UNICEF/UN014975/ESTEY

potential to broaden children's experiences and development. It is easy to imagine how image recognition, artificial intelligence (AI), augmented reality, gene sequencing and even neural technology will improve children's lives.

At the same time, new technologies will demand our full attention in terms of potential risks. Take, for example, the debate around potential biases or discrimination by AI algorithms. It is still unclear whether algorithms are introducing gender or racial biases into decision-making.

As a driving force for technological innovation, the ICT industry is duty-bound to place child rights and protection at the heart of technology and product innovation efforts, where they will serve to influence legislation and policymaking, improve public awareness and develop industry standards to safeguard the global Child Online Protection Initiative.

Protecting every child from all forms of online harms is our common aspiration.

Each and every child also needs the patience and proper guidance of parents, which allows them to be curious about the world around them – real or virtual – so they can keep exploring and grow up healthy, happy and independent.

An old Chinese saying advises, "Take care of one's own children first and then extend the same care to the children of others." Protection of children's rights should cross the boundaries of industries, organizations and countries. Only cooperation can hold us accountable and allow us to protect children for the benefit of all humankind. Let's join our hands and forge ahead for the next generation and beyond.

Pony Ma is the co-founder of Tencent, one of the largest internet companies in China, and currently serves as its executive director, chairman of the board and chief executive officer. Pony oversees strategic development, overall direction and management of Tencent. He received his Bachelor of Science in Computer Science from Shenzhen University in 1993.

"

The ICT industry is duty-bound to place child rights and protection at the heart of technology and product innovation.

03
Digital Dangers:
The harms
of life online

**YOUSEF AL HEREK, 17
SYRIAN ARAB REPUBLIC**

"I started to dig deeper and read about hacking – what if someone illegally accessed my account and started reading my private messages? I decided that my privacy is priority, so I updated the operation systems of my phone and computer and added additional security layers to protect my accounts and myself."

Full articles by youth contributors featured in
The State of the World's Children 2017 can be found at:
<www.voicesofyouth.org/en/sections/content/pages/sowc-2017>

It has never been easier for bullies, sex offenders, traffickers and those who harm children to contact potential victims around the world, share images of their abuse and encourage each other to commit further crimes. Digital connectivity has made children more accessible through unprotected social media profiles and online game forums. It also allows offenders to be anonymous – reducing their risk of identification and prosecution – expand their networks, increase profits and pursue many victims at once.

Children's privacy is also at stake. Most children – and many parents – have very limited, if any, awareness of how much personal data they are feeding into the internet, much less how it might one day be used.

No child is safe from online risk, but the most vulnerable are those most likely to suffer the harms.

In Madagascar, a 17-year-old girl was asked by her teacher for the equivalent of about US$300.00 in exchange for a passing grade. Desperate to find the money, she reached out to a man she'd been in contact with online for six months. "He kidnapped me and kept me locked in his house for two months. He raped me repeatedly," she said. After her rescue by a new cybercrime police unit, she received medical attention, advice and psychological support at a One-Stop Service Centre managed by the government with support from UNICEF. The man and teacher were both arrested. "I'm doing OK now. I've gone back to school," she said. "I wish I had had some guidance. My parents didn't know I was talking to strangers."[1]

For most parents and caregivers, the girl's story represents their worst nightmare of what can happen when a child goes online. Although her experience represents an extreme example of online harms, it goes to the heart of widespread concerns about the threats facing children on the internet: Namely, that going online can dismantle the traditional protections most societies try to place around children, exposing them to unacceptable content,

unacceptable behaviour and potentially dangerous contacts with the outside world.

These risks are not entirely new – children have long bullied and been bullied, have often been exposed to, or sought out, violent and sexual material, and have always been at risk from sexual offenders. But most parents probably feel it was easier to protect previous generations from such risks. The front door was once a barrier to schoolyard bullies; now, social media allows them to follow their victims into their homes.

These risks must be seen in context, however. All children face the possibility of encountering harm as a result of internet technologies. But for most children, the possibility remains just that – a possibility. Understanding why risk translates into actual harm for certain children, and not for others, is crucial. It opens our eyes to the underlying vulnerabilities in the child's life that can place him or her at greater risk in the digital age. By better understanding and addressing these vulnerabilities, we can better protect children both online and offline, and better enable them to enjoy the opportunities that come from being connected in the digital age.

Going online can dismantle the traditional protections most societies try to place around children.

Winny Moreira, centre, used her experience of being cyberbullied to create the YouTube video shown on the screens, which aims to help other Brazilian girls protect themselves online.
© UNICEF/UN017649/UESLEI MARCELINO

Three forms of risk: Content, contact, conduct

Researchers now typically organize the wide range of risks encountered online into three categories – content, contact and conduct risks.[2]

Content risks: Where a child is exposed to unwelcome and inappropriate content. This can include sexual, pornographic and violent images; some forms of advertising; racist, discriminatory or hate-speech material; and websites advocating unhealthy or dangerous behaviours, such as self-harm, suicide and anorexia.

Contact risks: Where a child participates in risky communication, such as with an adult seeking inappropriate contact or soliciting a child for sexual purposes, or with individuals attempting to radicalize a child or persuade him or her to take part in unhealthy or dangerous behaviours.

Conduct risks: Where a child behaves in a way that contributes to risky content or contact. This may include children writing or creating hateful materials about other children, inciting racism or posting or distributing sexual images, including material they have produced themselves.

TYPOLOGY OF ICT-RELATED HARMS

	Content Child as recipient	Contact Child as participant in adult-initiated activity	Conduct Child as victim / actor
Aggression and violence	• Self-abuse and self-harm • Suicidal content • Discrimination • Exposure to extremist/violent/gory content	• Radicalization • Ideological persuasion • Hate speech	• Cyberbullying, stalking and harassment • Hostile and violent peer activity
Sexual abuse	• Unwanted/harmful exposure to pornographic content	• Sexual harassment • Sexual solicitation • Sexual grooming	• Child sexual abuse • Production and consumption of child abuse material • Child-produced indecent images
Commercial exploitation	• Embedded marketing • Online gambling	• Violation and misuse of personal data • Hacking • Fraud and theft • Sexual extortion	• Live streaming of child sexual abuse • Sexual exploitation of children • Trafficking for the purpose of sexual exploitation • Sexual exploitation of children in travel and tourism

Source: Burton, Patrick, Brian O'Neill and Monica Bulger, *A Global Review of Evidence of What Works in Preventing ICT-related Violence, Abuse and Exploitation of Children and in Promoting Digital Citizenship*, forthcoming.

While it is relatively easy to categorize various forms of risk in general, it is much harder to determine the risk relationship between, for instance, a particular online image or activity and an individual child. One reason for this is that attitudes towards what constitutes a risk vary greatly among cultures. For example, consensual sexual exploration among children using offline and online mediums, including texting or 'sexting', is acceptable in some cultures but not in others. Risks, therefore, are not always a function of the behaviour itself but are in some cases a reflection of how society perceives that behaviour.[3]

Equally, different children can have the same experience online and yet experience very different outcomes.[4] One 2009 pan-European survey found a range of responses among children to pornographic content seen online: Some children were not concerned about it, some thought it was funny and others wished they had never seen it[5] (a response that would normally be interpreted as indicating the child had suffered harm). When faced with these types of risks, most children in the study responded with strategies that were either positive (seeking help from others) or neutral (ignoring the risk). Others seemed less able to diminish the risk and ended up, in turn, perpetrating other 'conduct' risks themselves.

A final point: In and of itself, risk is not inherently bad. Developmental psychologists believe that some exposure to risk is essential for children to learn how to adapt and become resilient.[6] In the offline world, this idea is so familiar that it is usually taken for granted – think of when a child is first learning to swim or to ride a bicycle. But while tolerance of risk varies among societies, cultures, communities and individual families, most can agree that some risks are uncomfortably close to the line crossing into harm.

When risk becomes harm

Assessing the extent to which risks translate into actual harms is extremely difficult. The content-contact-conduct framework used to describe risks also provides a way of thinking about the actual harms that children may experience online, as the typology table shows.

But even if the number of children suffering severe harm is probably not that high, when harm does occur, according to one review of evidence in this area, its impact on the child can be very significant and justifies substantial resources and attention.[7] As numerous cases over the years have demonstrated, severe harm can manifest itself as much in mental distress as in real physical injuries, including self-harm and suicide. Major areas of concern in terms of harm include pro-eating disorder and pro-suicide

websites,[8] as well as cyberbullying and online child sexual abuse and exploitation.

Cyberbullying: "Nobody deserves this"

When Amanda Todd, a Canadian adolescent, was about 13, a man she met in a video chat room convinced her to expose her breasts on camera. He captured the image and used it to blackmail her, threatening to send the image to her friends and family. She ignored the threat and over the next two years was subject to bullying (both online and offline), harassment and physical assault. Despite her efforts to escape the torment – she moved both schools and cities – the attacks continued, both by the online offender and by her classmates. During this time, she struggled with depression, drug and alcohol abuse, isolation, loneliness and self-harm. Two years later, in October 2012, at 15, Amanda committed suicide.

The Cyberbullying Research Center defines cyberbullying as "willful and repeated harm inflicted through the use of computers, cell phones and other electronic devices." Whereas in previous generations, children being bullied could escape such abuse or harassment by going home or being alone, no such safe haven exists for children in a digital world. Carrying a mobile phone, laptop or other connected device means that texts, emails, chats and social media posts can arrive anytime, day or night. And online bullying carries on, spreading widely among peers and inflicting reputational harm whether the child is online or off.

The potential for bullies to hide behind a nameless profile, pose as someone other than themselves and – in a single click – instantly disseminate violent, hurtful or humiliating words or images is unprecedented. Moreover, once such

The potential for bullies to instantly disseminate violent, hurtful or humiliating words or images is unprecedented.

content is posted, deleting it is difficult, which increases the risk of victims being revictimized and makes it hard for them to recover.

Victims of cyberbullying are more likely to use alcohol and drugs, to not attend school, to experience in-person bullying, to receive poor grades and to experience lower self-esteem and more health problems than others. Survivors of such abuse express the severity of the impact, which sometimes leads to suicide or thoughts of suicide.[9]

Amanda's story, told above, illustrates both the potentially extreme impact of cyberbullying and the loss of control over content once it has appeared online *(see box: Self-generated sexually explicit material)*. Strong evidence shows that girls face much greater pressure to send sexually explicit images and suffer much harsher judgements when those images are shared beyond the intended recipient.[10]

Her experience also illustrates the fluidity between cyberbullying and traditional

bullying. A month before her suicide, using a series of 73 flashcards, Amanda told her story in a nine-minute video on YouTube. During one brutal in-person confrontation with classmates described on her cards, "In front of my new school (50) people… / A guy than *[sic]* yelled just punch her already / So she did… She threw me to the ground a *[sic]* punched me several times / Kids filmed it. I was all alone and left on the ground. / I felt like a joke in this world… I thought nobody deserves this:/"

Amanda's video went viral and by the time of this writing had received approximately 40 million views. Because of her story and those of other victims, in 2014, the Canadian government introduced legislation aimed at combating online harassment by making it illegal to distribute intimate images of a person without his or her consent. The bill has been criticized as a potential privacy violation because it allows police to access online data, phone records and digital tracking. In response to the criticisms, however, Carol Todd, Amanda's mother and founder of the Amanda Todd Legacy Society,

In Madagascar, 16-year-old Charmela's family can't afford to send her to school. She spends much of her time on the internet, where she has experienced online soliciting.
© UNICEF/ UN015588/PRINSLOO

Traffickers are able to recruit, advertise, organize and communicate primarily, or even exclusively, via mobile.

which participates in advocacy and outreach with a particular focus on adolescents' mental health issues, told the Commons Committee on Justice, "We should not have to choose between privacy and our safety."

Online child sexual abuse and exploitation

It has never been easier for child sex offenders to contact potential victims around the world, share images of their abuse and encourage each other to commit further crimes. "The scale of this crime is shocking," Jürgen Stock, secretary general of INTERPOL, has said, "made worse by the fact that these images can be shared online globally at the touch of a button and can exist forever. Each time an image or video clip is shared or viewed, the child is being re-victimized."

Advances in technology allow offenders to remain anonymous, cover their digital tracks, create false identities, pursue many victims at once and monitor their whereabouts. The increased use of mobile devices and greater access to broadband internet has made children more accessible than ever through unprotected social media profiles and online game forums. Offenders often begin grooming their victims on these platforms, where they gain a child's attention or trust, before moving the communication to video- and photo-sharing platforms, which can lead to content-driven or financially driven extortion or meeting offline.[11]

Old crimes, and new

A 12-year-old girl in the Philippines who was forced to live-stream sexual acts from her neighbour's house spoke about her experience: "When the foreigner says 'get naked,' then we undress…. The foreigners were from USA, Australia, UK, China. I would say, 'You want to buy a show?' And

the foreigner would say, 'Yes'." She would earn the equivalent of about US$3.00 for each 'show'. At one point, one of her online abusers travelled from the United States to meet her, but she was able to escape that encounter and was later rescued by the police in a raid. "My parents didn't know that I was doing the shows. I lied to them about it. But I regret that I did it." She is required to stay in a shelter until her neighbour is tried in court.[12]

The online world did not create crimes of child sexual abuse and exploitation, but it has changed them in two significant ways: It has facilitated existing 'common' forms and created wholly new forms.

These impacts are set out in a recent study by the United Nations Office on Drugs and Crime (UNODC),[13] which shows that new ICTs can increase access to victims and to child sexual abuse material, increase profits for criminal enterprises, reduce risk of identification and prosecution for perpetrators, provide social affirmation for offenders and increase levels of harm for victims. As a result, there is now greater opportunity for such 'common' forms of crime against children and greater potential for harm. As for the new forms of child abuse and exploitation described by UNODC, these include 'made-to-order' child sexual abuse material, self-generated content and the broadcasting of live sex abuse.

The UNODC study also examines the sexual exploitation of children – namely, trafficking in children for the purposes of sexual exploitation, and the sexual exploitation of children in travel and tourism. The study notes that ICTs have lowered the costs of trafficking operations. Traffickers are able to "recruit, advertise, organize and communicate primarily, or even exclusively, via mobile phone or devices such as tablets, effectively streamlining their activities and expanding their networks." This creates a new digital marketplace for modern-day slavery.[14] Offenders also have more control over their victims' movements. Not only can they require victims to call them at the beginning and end of each encounter, but they can also track their movements using GPS-enabled devices.[15]

A crime without borders

According to the Internet Watch Foundation (IWF), 57,335 uniform resource locators (URLs) contained child sexual abuse material in 2016. Of these, 60 per cent were hosted in Europe and 37 per cent in North America. Ninety-two per cent of all child sexual abuse URLs identified by the IWF are hosted in five countries: the Netherlands, the United States, Canada, France and the Russian Federation (listed by most to fewest URLs).[16]

Fifty-three per cent of the victims of such abuse were 10 years old or younger – a staggering figure, but also a drop from

69 per cent in 2015. However, the number of images of 11- to 15-year-old children increased: from 30 per cent in 2015 to 45 per cent in 2016. One reason for this shift is an increase in self-produced content shared online *(see box: Self-generated sexually explicit material)*.

In the 2016 *NetClean Report*, a survey of police officers in 26 countries showed that the material they handle in their investigations primarily depicts children from Europe and North America. One respondent to the survey explained that children are more likely to be victims if they live in "countries with high internet devices per person and reliable internet service" or in countries that have "poor or no laws prohibiting sex offenses against children and also have easy access to children."[17]

Europol's 2016 report points out that between 2012 and 2017, as many as

92% of all child sexual abuse URLs are hosted in 5 countries: the Netherlands, the United States, Canada, France and the Russian Federation.

Self-generated sexually explicit material

A new challenge in the identification of child sexual abuse material is the emergence of self-generated sexually explicit material.[19] This is often conflated with consensual 'sexting' but it can also include material produced non-consensually – for example, through online solicitation and grooming and sexual extortion.[20]

While this trend requires further research, a 2015 Internet Watch Foundation (IWF) report on youth-produced sexual content highlighted the extent to which control over the content is lost once it has appeared online: 89.9 per cent of the images and videos assessed as part of their study had been "harvested from the original upload location and

were being redistributed by third party websites."

While it is often assumed that material from self-generated sexual content is produced using mobile devices, 85.9 per cent of content depicting children 15 and under was created using a webcam.

A third key finding of this study was the high proportion of content depicting children 13 and under. IWF calls for "further research aimed at understanding the drivers for children to create and distribute such content" and the "need for awareness-raising campaigns aimed at younger age groups to highlight to younger children and their parents the risks which they are taking online."[21]

Children's attitudes to online risk can differ from those of adults: Where adults may consider meeting a stranger online as particularly dangerous, a child may view such encounters as an opportunity to make a new friend.
© UNICEF/UNI190722/D'AKI

"100 million children will be coming online for the first time … and that 80 per cent of those will be connecting via mobile devices. A significant proportion of these children will be connecting from African and South-East Asian countries." Without proper safeguards in place, more children will be vulnerable to online risks of harm in these emerging ICT-enabled countries and regions.

New challenges

One challenge of combating online sexual crimes against children is the constantly evolving nature of digital technology. Peer-to-peer networks (P2P) and, increasingly, the Dark web *(see graphic)* continue to facilitate the exchange of child sexual abuse material (CSAM), but there are also relatively new challenges, such as live-streaming of child sexual abuse and self-generated sexually explicit material *(see box Self-generated sexually explicit material)*, which are adding to the volume of CSAM.[18]

Digital currencies and the Dark web

Another factor contributing to the escalation in the live-streaming of child abuse is the growing use of cryptocurrencies, or anonymous payment systems and of end-to-end encrypted platforms for sharing media. These pose a real problem for law enforcement seeking to gather evidence of child abuse, as such content does not require downloading, and, even if downloaded, can be inaccessible or quickly wiped out by pre-installed software.[22] File sharing through P2P networks has transformed and expanded the distribution of CSAM,[23] whether on the Surface web or via the Deep web, the part of the internet not indexed by search engines and thus invisible to most users.

Within the Deep web is the 'Dark web', which contains intentionally concealed content. Special anonymity-granting web browsers are used to access it. One such

FIGURE 3.1 PARTS OF THE INTERNET

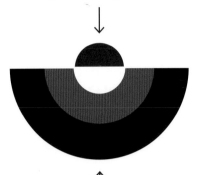

SURFACE WEB
Google, YouTube, Facebook, Snapchat, Instagram, etc.

DEEP WEB
Databases, records and documents (Medical, Academic, Legal, Financial), etc. Other content not indexed by standard search engines

DARK WEB
TOR, Peer-to-peer networks, Child sexual abuse material, Illegal content and activities, etc.

example is Tor (The Onion Router). As research by the Global Commission on Internet Governance (GCIG) points out, "The Dark Web poses a dilemma. Illegal markets, trolls and online child abuse rings proliferate due to the technology of Tor and other similar systems. However, the anonymity provided by such systems gives cover for people in repressive regimes that need the protection of technology in order to surf the Web, access censored content and otherwise exercise their genuine right to free expression."[24]

The GCIG paper concludes by recommending that "like every other aspect of human society, the Dark Web needs to be policed."[25] This means

Like every other aspect of human society, the Dark Web needs to be policed.

supporting local law enforcement's efforts to track down global criminals and bring them to justice – including by increasing resources for cybercrime and building capacity by training law enforcement officers to deal with cybercrime.

Which children are most vulnerable?

All children who go online face some level of risk, but not all face the same level of risk. Equally, some are more likely to suffer harm than others. Why? Not surprisingly, research increasingly indicates that children who are more vulnerable offline are more vulnerable online. Not only do children who report more offline risks report more online risks, they are also more likely to report harm resulting from those risks.[26] This link between online and offline vulnerability can deepen the challenges facing some of the world's most vulnerable and marginalized children.

Who are the most vulnerable children? Although there is a regrettable lack of research on some of the most marginalized communities and groups, existing evidence indicates that the children who are most vulnerable to online harms include girls, children from poor households, children in communities with a limited understanding of different forms of sexual abuse and exploitation of children, children who are out of school, children with disabilities, children who suffer depression or mental health problems and children from marginalized groups. Unguided digital access and a lack of awareness also put children at risk.[27]

Online and offline risks: "Two sides of the same coin"

The links between the online and offline contexts of cyberbullying are particularly striking. A large-scale study in the United Kingdom, involving responses from over 100,000 children, found that very few experienced cyberbullying without also being bullied offline.[28] "The main takeaway here is that it doesn't make sense to think of cyber-bullying as its own thing," a co-author of the study, Andrew Przybylski of the Oxford Internet Institute, told the BBC. "If you're a parent or you're running a school or designing an intervention, [online and offline bullying] are two sides of the same coin."[29]

The role of gender in cyberbullying and online harassment is also clear. According to the authors of an Australian study, harassment of women online, particularly those under 30, is in danger of becoming "an established norm."[30] Such harassment online is a clear continuation of offline sexism and misogyny. A 2015 report by the UN Broadband Commission for Digital Development titled *Cyber Violence Against Women and Girls: A world-wide wake-up call* notes, "Violence online and offline, or 'physical' VAWG [violence against women and girls] and 'cyber' VAWG, feed into each other."

Children's sexual identity also appears to be a factor. A 2013 study of 5,907 internet users in the United States aged 13–18 found that those who self-identified as lesbian, gay, bisexual or transgender were disproportionately at risk of online sexual harassment.[31] Similarly, a 2008 study of Swedish children found that bisexuality or homosexuality was a considerable factor in predicting online sexual solicitation.[32]

Another important factor is disability. Data collected as part of the Youth Internet Safety Survey, which covered ages 10–17, showed that children with special education needs were more likely to experience risk online.[33] Again, there were clear gender differences: Girls receiving special education services were three times more likely than boys to report online sexual solicitation.

Although specific evidence is lacking, there are reasons to be concerned about

Harassment of women online, particularly those under 30, is in danger of becoming "an established norm."

the possible online vulnerability of migrant children as well as children on the move or living in refugee camps.

Research in Italy indicates that migrant children tend to be at higher risk of bullying than native children.[34] In addition, there are particular risks for children on the move and those living in camps, with the United Nations High Commissioner for Refugees warning that some are at "heightened risk of violence and abuse." Given the documented links between offline and online violence, and how children on the move use digital technologies as a means of communication, entertainment and accessing information, the potential online risks facing these children deserve further investigation.

It is possible that children from minority groups are especially vulnerable to harm stemming from online violence and exploitation. The online space can be a refuge for children who seek companionship or information because they are 'different', a benefit of the internet that has been well documented.[35] That a space perceived as supportive can then be a place of harassment and bullying may exacerbate the trauma and harm attached to the incident.[36]

Vulnerability to online sexual abuse and exploitation

In the Philippines, where online child abuse was a leading form of cybercrime in 2014, an 8-year-old girl was forced to perform sexual acts three times a day in front of her neighbour's webcam for foreigners who would pay to watch. "I bought food [with the payment]. It was about 300 pesos" (US$6.00), she said. "My mother did not know anything about it." Following a police rescue operation, she is now required to stay in a shelter until the case against her neighbour is resolved. "I really miss my mother and my family." Reflecting on what she went through, she said, "I feel angry and I want to forget it."[37]

When it comes to online sexual abuse and exploitation, vulnerabilities can vary depending on the child's age. Younger children, for example, are particularly vulnerable to abuse by an adult or older peer within the family or in a setting or relationship where there is a position of trust.

By contrast, adolescents, are often exposed to a wider range of risks from abusers outside the family, including from offenders in the digital sphere. In El Salvador, a girl who was sexually exploited online at age 14 – not by a stranger but by her ex-boyfriend – explained that he asked for pictures of her "without a lot of clothes on or with no clothes at all," she said. "That made me more uncomfortable." After she broke up with him a few months later, he created a social media profile with her nude photos. "When I got the friend request ... I felt my world crumbling. He'd sent friend requests to all my friends, to my mother, to my sister." When the profile was made public, she went to the police. "They said it was my fault because I had sent the pictures." After the incident, she said, "I felt abused. I felt really hurt. He didn't get any punishment at all." She hopes that other children can learn from her experience: "I decided to tell my story to help other girls so this doesn't happen to them."[38]

Children's awareness of risks

In assessing vulnerabilities, it is also important to take account of children's own attitudes towards online risks – which often differ considerably from those of adults.

While adults might consider meeting a stranger online one of the most dangerous things that could happen to their children on the internet, children and teens may see this as an opportunity to meet new people – and even develop romantic relationships.[39] And while children value their privacy online *(see Special section: Protecting children's privacy online)*, they see risks

I decided to tell my story to help other girls so this doesn't happen to them.

What do adolescents think about … online risks and harms

When participants in the *State of the World's Children 2017* workshops* were asked about their concerns in the online world, they came up with a wide variety of responses. Some echoed adult concerns about content, contact and conduct risks *(see table: Typology of ICT-related harms)*, but others did not: For example, participants cited technological problems and parental intrusion in their online lives as things to be concerned about.

Nevertheless, their top concern was online privacy, especially the possibility of strangers accessing their personal information.
"I am careful to avoid privacy invasion." GIRL, 17, BRAZIL

"I take care of my privacy, I make sure not everyone can see what I share, my pictures and status." BOY, 15, GUATEMALA

"Social media has negative aspects because people can use my profile to create others, which is absolutely wrong." GIRL, 15, PORTUGAL

They understood that privacy breaches might lead to further issues, such as identity theft or exploitation of their images.
"I am concerned about leakage of personal information – because this means leakage of my money and personal information." BOY, 14, REPUBLIC OF KOREA

"I don't upload certain pics with which bad people can make dirty videos of us." GIRL, 16, BHUTAN

while a few also reported concerns that their parents or caregivers might view what they post online.
"I think, would my parents read my messages?" GIRL, 15, BURUNDI

They cited a wide range of strategies for protecting privacy, across a variety of platforms and devices.
"I am … careful not to disclose personal information, especially when chatting." GIRL, 16, DEMOCRATIC REPUBLIC OF THE CONGO

"I lock my Twitter account and make it a rule to not follow people I do not know in real life. I stop and think twice before uploading pictures of faces or locations." GIRL, 17, JAPAN

Another concern of participants was unpleasant or negative encounters online, or accessing inappropriate or suspicious websites.
"I try to be careful with the content of websites both for the issue of virus and [my information that] the website tries to transmit to the internet." GIRL, 16, BRAZIL

"The fact that sexual photos or obnoxious advertisements are being uploaded … leads me to avoid using Facebook." BOY, 14, REPUBLIC OF KOREA

Concerns over privacy and cyberbullying made some of them hesitate to use digital technology …
"I am personally most worried about attitudes such as cyberbullying, other ways of harassment and online discrimination, and every time I see, I try to stop." GIRL, 14, URUGUAY

"Cyberbullying. I am afraid of my friends commenting on my photo posted on Facebook." GIRL, 16, SOLOMON ISLANDS.

"I've been [cyberbullied by my friends] … they blame me because I have weird interest like anime and etc., and they keep mocking me until now." GIRL, 17, MALAYSIA

as did the possibility of encountering annoying or disturbing content – such as violence, persistent pop-ups and unsolicited advertising.
"Sometimes, when we use Google or social media on a laptop then there is like a pop-out of a porn website." GIRL, 16, MALAYSIA

They were particularly concerned about potential exposure to hacking, viruses and malware.

"I worry that one might publish bad things in my name if my account is hacked."
GIRL, 16, BURUNDI

"I am careful about the ads on the sites that can affect my PC. I worry about the viruses that can affect my PC." GIRL, 16, REPUBLIC OF MOLDOVA

Participants discussed their parents' concerns over adolescents' use of digital technology. Noting that these concerns sometimes differed from their own, participants said parents appeared to be primarily worried about the bad influence the internet might have on their children ...

"My parents worried that I learn bad things online like smoking, taking alcohol."
BOY, 17, MALAYSIA

"Parents are usually careful about people I don't know. Nowadays this type of caution makes sense because it is dangerous."
BOY, 16, BRAZIL

and that these online contacts might have serious consequences.

"I think that adults worry for our own good because it is also through the internet that many young people join terrorist groups."
BOY, 15, CENTRAL AFRICAN REPUBLIC

A few felt that parents and caregivers did not trust them to behave appropriately online.

"They are worried not so much about whether people are speaking ill of me as whether I am speaking ill of others." GIRL, 16, JAPAN

or worried about them viewing – intentionally or otherwise – inappropriate content, especially sexual content.

"We worry because our parents might think that we are using internet to see pornography." BOY, 13, TIMOR-LESTE

They also said that adults were worried about children being distracted from their schoolwork if they spent too much time on digital devices. Indeed, participants often shared those concerns.

"I am afraid of my school performance being worse." GIRL, 16, THAILAND

"My teacher was scared that I am not going to do homework that she gave me and then I am going to waste time online." BOY, 17, MALAYSIA

Despite occasional frustrations with the older generation, participants felt parents' concerns arose out of a genuine love for their children and a wish to keep them safe.

"They obviously worry about these things because they care and love us. They don't want us to get involved in some problems."
GIRL, 16, BHUTAN

"Because they want the best for us. Because they want a better future for us."
GIRL, 16, GUATEMALA

"Adults worry about those things because they see the child as a fragile person, easily fooled and who can get involved in bad stories and be kidnapped." BOY, 17, BURUNDI

IN SUMMARY

Adolescents have real concerns about the place of digital technology in their everyday lives. They are sensitive to the tensions created when their desire to engage online has to be weighed against their need to protect themselves, their responsibilities to themselves and others, and the responsibilities of adults to help them live and grow well in the digital age.

* Participants' responses have been shortened and edited for clarity where necessary.

to their privacy coming both from outside their sphere, such as from businesses and governments, and from within their own circle: overprotective parents, nosy parents and those who spy.[40]

One 2012 study of South African children aged 13–17 found that most were aware of the risks that could be encountered online, including how those risks translated from online to offline spaces. They also said they felt equipped to handle these risks and, importantly, that they were willing to take them in order to reap the benefits of going online, in particular, a sense of connectedness.[41]

There is variation, however, on how this sense of agency seems to play out across countries and among children of varying ages. In recent Global Kids Online studies in Argentina, the Philippines, Serbia and South Africa, the percentage of children aged 15–17 who knew how to activate and change their privacy settings ranged from 68 per cent to 98 per cent. Where younger children in the Philippines, Serbia and South Africa were surveyed, the rate was significantly lower, ranging from 5 per cent to 40 per cent.[42]

Preventing harm in the digital age

The wide range of risks that children can face online demands a great diversity of responses, some focusing on children's behaviour and others on technological solutions. What links all these responses, however, is the need for a broad vision: Protecting children online, regardless of the particular risk they're facing, requires holistic and coordinated responses that take account of the full circumstances of the child's life and the wide range of players – parents, teachers, governments, businesses and children themselves – who have a part to play in keeping them safe.

Understanding the full context of a child's life

Because children's offline and online vulnerabilities are so linked, the risks they face online need to be approached within the context of the child's total circumstances, including their offline risks. INSPIRE, a framework for preventing and responding to violence against children – developed by the World Health Organization in collaboration with UNICEF, the Global Partnership to End Violence Against Children and others, and promoted by the Special Representative of the United Nations Secretary-General on Violence against Children – identifies seven strategies for addressing violence, abuse and exploitation:

❯ **Implementation and enforcement of laws**
Laws banning violent punishment of children by parents, teachers or other caregivers; laws criminalizing all forms of sexual abuse and exploitation of children, including online; laws that prevent alcohol misuse; and laws limiting youth access to firearms and other weapons.

❯ **Norms and values**
Changing adherence to restrictive and harmful gender and social norms; community mobilization programmes; and bystander interventions.

❯ **Safe environments**
Reducing violence by addressing 'hotspots'; interrupting the spread of violence; and improving the built environment.

❯ **Parent and caregiver support**
Delivered through home visits, in groups in community settings and through comprehensive programmes.

❯ **Income and economic strengthening**
Through cash transfers; group saving and loans combined with gender equity training; and microfinance combined with gender norm training.

❯ Response and support services
Counselling and therapeutic approaches; screening combined with interventions; treatment programmes for juvenile offenders in the criminal justice system; and foster care interventions involving social welfare services.

❯ Education and life skills
Increase enrolment in preschool, primary and secondary schools; establish a safe and enabling school environment; improve children's knowledge about sexual abuse and how to protect themselves against it; life and social skills training; and adolescent intimate partner violence prevention programmes.

How do these strategies work in practice? As an example, cyberbullying can be prevented by changing norms and values so that they no longer enable such violence or condone it. Influencing what is considered acceptable and unacceptable can influence what peer bullies do.[43]

For example, the ConRed Cyberbullying Prevention Programme, which has been used primarily in Spain,[44] provides young people with a forum to discuss what is socially acceptable and desirable within their school environment. Students then promote empathy for the bullying victim and draw out the negative consequences of cyberbullying. Quasi-experimental evaluations of this programme find that

In El Salvador, the ex-boyfriend of this girl posted nude photos of her online after they split up. The images subsequently appeared on other websites.
© UNICEF/UN018651/ ZEHBRAUSKAS

Internet safety campaigns

Around the world, many national campaigns have been created to raise awareness of internet safety issues, to encourage responsible online behaviour and to promote policy change. In Argentina, for example, UNICEF and the provincial government of Buenos Aires designed the ongoing Digital Coexistence programme to promote children's rights online. Information guides were produced to show children how to use the internet safely and responsibly and to help parents support their children. UNICEF Argentina has also organized a campaign, using the hashtag #nodacompartir ('It's not cool to share'), with the Ministry of Justice and Human Rights to raise awareness among adolescents of the consequences of sharing offensive, insulting and discriminatory content online.

In Brazil, UNICEF's Surf Safe campaign promoted safe online behaviour among adolescents and addressed issues including cyberbullying and sexting, online friendships and privacy. The campaign, launched in 2015, reached almost 14.5 million people and generated more than a million social media views. UNICEF's implementing partner, Safernet, also maintains a helpline to assist children, adolescents and young people affected by online violence. The main topics addressed by the helpline in 2016 were cyberbullying,

with 312 cases; sexting, 301 cases; and problems with personal data, 273 cases.

In Albania, the #openyoureyes campaign was launched in December 2016 to increase awareness of internet safety issues and provide information to children, parents, teachers and service providers. The campaign, developed by UNICEF and supported with funding from the Government of the United Kingdom, used a combination of TV spots, billboards and posters to tell children that when they went online they would probably encounter risky content and behaviour, but they could handle those risks by supporting each other and talking to parents and teachers. Albania has also launched an online platform, <www.Isigurt.al>, for reporting of online abuse and offences.

In India, the #staysafeonline campaign has also aimed to raise awareness among boys and girls on how to safely navigate the online world and how to help each other to stay safe online. The campaign, which was designed in line with findings and recommendations from the UNICEF *Child Online Protection in India* report, launched in September 2016, has worked to disseminate three core messages among children: Be there for a friend in need, treat others with respect and advise others to be real friends.

it reduces cyberbullying (along with cyber-dependence) and improves students' perceptions of safety.[45]

Some programmes have focused on parents as gateways to child internet safety. The Cyber-Training for Parents Programme, part of the European Union's Lifelong Learning Programme, is a blended learning initiative that combines online training with traditional classroom teaching – parents go to online platforms to improve their own digital skills and at the same time are provided with key safety messages concerning how to prevent and identify cyberbullying.

Preventing online child sexual abuse and exploitation

Through global efforts such as the WePROTECT Global Alliance to End Child Sexual Exploitation Online, leading technology companies, international organizations and 77 countries have made an urgent commitment to end child sexual abuse and exploitation through a coordinated response.

UNICEF, as part of the WePROTECT initiative, has implemented a global programme to build the capacity of governments, civil society and the private sector to tackle online child sexual exploitation. Since 2013, more than 60,000 children, parents and teachers in 12 countries have been provided with information on how to mitigate online risks for children. More than 1,000 ICT industry representatives in 23 countries participated in consultations on their role and responsibilities in relation to online protection. And more than 1,000 law enforcement officers, prosecutors and judges in 14 countries improved their capacity to investigate and prosecute crimes of online child sexual exploitation.[46]

In nine countries, specialized units within law enforcement agencies and prosecutors' offices are enhancing national capacity to investigate and prosecute such crimes. For example, in Guatemala, the Cybercrime Investigation Unit and the National Prosecutor's Office have dismantled two networks that produced online child sexual abuse materials. In Jordan, a newly established police unit for online crimes against children received specialized training and visited schools to raise children's awareness of the risks of online exploitation and abuse, how to protect themselves and how to report these crimes. The unit has dealt with 21 cases since its opening in November 2016.

"It is important for children to be aware of how to use the internet safely," explains Captain Al-Refaie of the Cybercrime Unit in Jordan's Public Security Directorate. "Schools should provide them with the basic rules and awareness, as part of their education. Parents, too, play an essential role and should encourage an open dialogue with their children, but sometimes they lack knowledge of what is safe use. When children are not learning about safe use in schools or from their parents, we, as police, try to provide the necessary awareness."[47]

Among upcoming challenges, Europol points out that the increased use of digital currencies, anonymous payment systems and the development of new software encryptions help predators and traffickers conceal transactions for both online and offline child sexual abuse and exploitation. Facial recognition and geolocation software could also heighten risks for vulnerable children by allowing offenders to identify and locate potential victims[48] – but they can also help law enforcement identify and rescue victims.

Solutions using artificial intelligence

Over a decade of studies show that hundreds of searches for child abuse images occur every second, and hundreds of thousands of pieces of child sexual abuse material (CSAM) are shared through peer-to-peer (P2P) networks every year.[49] The sheer volume of material makes manual detection and identification close to impossible. Fortunately, some new tools using artificial intelligence may be helping meet this urgent challenge.

Digital forensic tools such as RoundUp and Child Protection System can monitor activity in P2P networks and offer geolocation and identification of points in the computer network that are involved in the sharing of CSAM.

Microsoft donated its PhotoDNA technology to the International Centre for Missing and Exploited Children. The technology, which was integrated into INTERPOL's International Child Sexual Exploitation (ICSE) database, creates a unique signature – a digital 'fingerprint' – from an image that allows for comparisons to find matching images, even if the image has been altered.[50]

The fingerprint is generated from the binary data of a photo or video and can be used to find the image anywhere online. This allows law enforcement agencies to maintain a database and detect modified versions of known CSAM. To date, use of the database has led to the identification of about 7,800 victims from

Schools should provide [children] with the basic rules and awareness, as part of their education.

R.AGE against predators

With more than 7 out of 10 people online in 2015,
Malaysia has seen rapid growth in internet connectivity.
But the pace of change in national laws and the social
understanding of internet-related crime has not always
been so quick. In 2016, the R.AGE group of young
journalists set out to draw attention to some of these
issues through a campaign backed by UNICEF, among
others. Their objective was clear: Catch on tape sexual
predators who use chat apps to groom children and show
how vulnerable children are to perpetrators exploiting
digital technology to sexually abuse children. At the time,
there was no comprehensive law against sexual grooming
in Malaysia.

In one secretly filmed sting, a 26-year-old reporter posed
as a 15-year-old girl to meet a man she had encountered
on a mobile chat app. He tried to convince her to come to
his hotel room, telling her, "You're not the only young girl I
know. There are many."

The R.AGE group's videos went viral, with over 3.7 million
views in just over six months, starting a public debate
and movement calling for stronger legislation. The facts
were undeniable: Grooming and online child sexual
abuse occurs in Malaysia and is perpetrated by Malaysian
nationals. "It shocked me to find out how prevalent this
issue was in Malaysia," wrote Samantha Chow,
a R.AGE reporter.

In support of legislative efforts undertaken by Dato' Seri
Azalina Othman Said, Malaysia's Minister of Law, the
journalists used social media and interactive mapping to
mobilize Members of Parliament one by one, under the
hashtag #MPsAgainstPredators. And it worked. In April
2017, Malaysia's Parliament passed the landmark Sexual
Offences Against Children Act. New offences are now
encompassed, including online grooming and exploitation
of children in pornography, to keep children safe online
and offline.

nearly 50 countries – an average of seven identifications per day – and the arrest of more than 3,800 offenders.[51]

To identify new or previously unknown CSAM being shared in P2P networks, researchers in Europe have developed a new software tool called 'iCOP'. It uses machine learning to triage thousands of files and go beyond matching files to known materials to looking for new file names. In addition to performing live forensic analysis outside of human capacities, the material detected by this software – new CSAM – is critical, as it can link to recent or even ongoing child abuse.[52]

Pointing the way forward

Any discussion of the risks and harms facing children in the digital age must not fail to consider two additional points: First, in a recent survey, most children who are online reported it as a real positive in their lives.[53] In seeking to protect children online, the focus should thus be less on restriction and more on open communication between children and caregivers and on developing children's digital awareness, resilience and capacity to manage risks – not only for the present but for the rest of their lives.

Second, there is a real tension between protecting children online and defending their rights to access information and make their voices heard. A recent UNICEF paper argued that "current public policy is increasingly driven by overemphasized, albeit real, risks faced by children online, with little consideration for potential negative impacts on children's rights to freedom of expression and access to information."[54] There is no easy resolution to this tension, which, in many countries, reflects deeper political issues of control over access to information and expression.

A shared responsibility

The task of keeping children safe online is not for any one sector or actor; collaboration and cooperation between caregivers, teachers, schools, governments, law enforcement, civil society and the private sector is essential.

In the area of sexual abuse and exploitation, for example, it is crucial to break the silence around sexual violence. To do this means to challenge attitudes, norms and behaviours that support child sexual abuse and exploitation through mobilization, education and raising awareness among children, families, teachers and communities – including religious communities, media, the travel and tourism sector and the ICT sector.

It is also imperative that law enforcement agencies receive adequate resources and frequent training to allow them to keep pace with the constant evolution of cybercrimes involving children, because it is difficult, if not impossible, for them to keep up with rapid technological change. To do so, they need the help of their governments and the private sector, among others. With the introduction of innovative tools, the tech industry and its researchers are playing a vital role in the detection, identification and removal of CSAM, as well as identifying victims and tracking down offenders.

The global and interconnected nature of the internet means that protecting children is not a challenge that any one country can meet on its own, which is why international efforts, such as those led by the WePROTECT Global Alliance Against Child Sexual Abuse Online, need to be supported. The urgency of this call only intensifies as more children around the world spend more time online. For the most disadvantaged – some of them connecting today for the very first time – the right, unified action could make the difference between a childhood blighted by abuse or exploitation and a gateway to expanded chances in life.

The tech industry plays a vital role in removing child sexual abuse material, identifying victims and tracking down offenders.

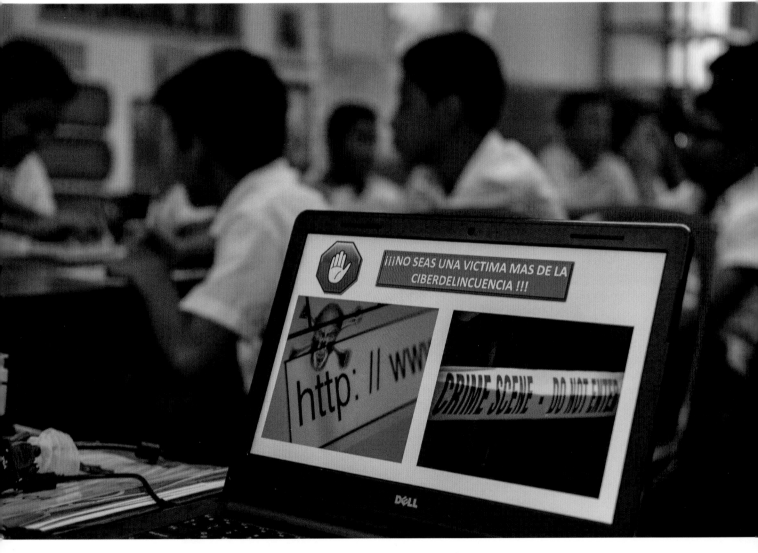

"Don't be a victim of cybercrime!!!" warns this screen during an internet safety class in El Salvador. © UNICEF/UN018678/ZEHBRAUSKAS

SPECIAL SECTION: Protecting children's privacy online

Every time a child posts a photo on social media, browses for products or searches for something online, he or she generates data. Those data, in turn, feed into an industry that processes the child's personal information, including identity, location, preferences and many other details.

Data processing from online and other activity affects everybody, and not always in negative ways *(see Special Section: How ICTs are supporting humanitarian action)*. However, there are significant concerns over how industrial-scale data processing, especially by business and the state, may affect the young. Children may have a very limited understanding of the risks such processing poses and may set low, or no, limits regarding all the bits of information they feed into the internet. Children also risk having their rights violated or abused[55] as 'big data' transform the internet into the Internet of Things and ultimately the Internet of Everything, where any and every bit of information can be seized upon as being useful to someone. Parents, too, often do not understand what data are collected from and about their children.[56]

Collecting personal data is now seen by companies as 'business critical'.[57] As *The Economist* recently commented, the most valuable resource for business today is not oil but data.[58] For businesses, children can be important targets as sources of data because they influence their friends' and families' consumer decisions.[59] Some may also be significant consumers themselves – both today and, crucially, in the future, when investment in securing their brand loyalty may really pay off.

'Behavioural' advertising, targeting online ads to specific behaviours, as well as other advertising techniques, can contribute

to the growing commercialization of childhood.[60] But beyond being targeted as consumers, children risk something even greater when businesses become interested in what they are doing online: Their whole private world may be opened up to the marketing machine, which will not only watch and record what a child is doing but also reconstruct and manipulate the online social environment in ways that impact the child's sense of self and security.

Children's privacy may also be targeted by the state. Governments can collect vast amounts of online personal data on children, a type of surveillance largely unimaginable in the pre-internet era.[61] Often neither lawful nor publicly acknowledged, mass surveillance now forms a key part of national security efforts in many countries. Not only does it undermine basic notions of privacy, it also threatens other basic human rights, such as freedom of expression, and opens the door to potential abuses of state power. As a recent UNICEF discussion paper noted, given the lack of information on how much data governments are collecting and how long they are holding the data for, the full implications of mass surveillance for children are unclear, but the potential outcomes are worrying: "If governments are able to link individual profiles with data intercepted by mass surveillance, as many believe feasible, this would allow authorities to build and maintain records of children's entire digital existence."[62]

The most valuable resource for business today is not oil but data.

"

'Sharenting', can harm a child's reputation, with potentially serious results.

A final potential source of abuse of children's data comes from their own parents. A 2010 survey found that 81 per cent of children under age 2 in 10 high-income countries (Australia, Canada, France, Germany, Italy, Japan, New Zealand, Spain, the United Kingdom and the United States) had a digital footprint, meaning that they had a profile or images of them posted online.[63]

Parents oversharing information about their children is nothing new. However, today's digital lifestyle can take it to a new level, turning parents into "potentially the distributors of information about their children to mass audiences."[64] Such 'sharenting', which is becoming more and more common,[65] can harm a child's reputation. It can create potentially serious results in an economy where individuals' online histories may increasingly outweigh their credit histories in the eyes of retailers, insurers and service providers.[66] Parents' lack of awareness can cause damage to a child's well-being when these digital assets depict a child without clothing, as they can be misused by child sex offenders. It can also harm child well-being in the longer term by interfering with children's ability to self-actualize, create their own identity[67] and find employment.[68]

Regulation of children's privacy

Despite the greatly expanding threats, national law does not always provide adequate protection of children's privacy rights. Similarly, international documents have had little to say on the topic. A rare exception came in early 2017, when the United Nations Human Rights Council passed a resolution that noted that violations of the right to privacy in the digital age could have "particular effects" on certain groups, among them children.[69]

Most regulatory approaches to protecting child privacy online have been based on principles of parental consent. Approaches

Simplifying the rules

Why do terms and conditions need to be so long? They probably don't. The pages of rules that many online service providers ask users to sign could in many cases be made more child-friendly and thus help build children's digital literacy. To show how this could be done, Jenny Afia, a privacy lawyer and member of a Children's Commissioner for England task force, examined a paragraph of text from one service provider that began, "You are responsible for any activity that occurs through your account and you agree you will not sell, transfer, license or assign your account, followers, username, or any account rights...." She rewrote the 112-word section as follows: "Don't use anybody else's account without their permission or try to find out their login details."[77]

vary among countries, but typically service providers are required, or in some cases advised, to obtain verified parental consent before offering services to, or collecting data from, children below a certain threshold age – for example, 13 in the United States,[70] 14 in Spain[71] and 18 in South Africa.[72]

This sort of approach is not without criticisms, including that it can impact children's freedom of expression, access to information and development of digital literacy.[73] Because in many cases children are not willing to share their online experiences with their parents, requiring parental consent for any data sharing on the part of the children would in effect reduce their autonomy and freedom online,[74] which runs counter to Convention on the Rights of the Child commitments that children be able to exercise agency based on their evolving capacities. Any regulatory approach would need to strike a balance between

protecting children online and respecting their independence as they grow up.

The need for parental consent may also contradict some recent evidence showing that children have some awareness of privacy threats and share some of the same concerns about identify theft and data mining as adults.[75] Research by Global Kids Online underscores how this plays out in the digital sphere, finding that the older children in its surveys typically know how to manage their privacy settings online, whereas younger children more often do not.[76]

There have been criticisms, too, of setting certain threshold ages for consent, such as age 16 in the European Union's General Data Protection Regulation (although member States can lower this to 13), which is set to take effect in 2018.[78] Arguably, this may encourage children to lie about their age to online service providers, a phenomenon that

some studies show is already widespread.[79] Critics argue it may also provide potential child groomers with a plausible defence that they assumed someone contacted through a social media site was at least 16 – the age of sexual consent in many countries.[80]

Some advocates point out that there are better ways than requiring parental consent to protect children's right to privacy while also safeguarding their other rights. These include education initiatives and changing default privacy settings.[81] But a greater burden of responsibility needs to be placed on online service providers to set clear limits to their collection, processing and retention of children's data. Policies should also include "transparency in methods of data collection and clear explanations of how resulting data will be used."[82] These explanations should also be adapted to children's information needs and understanding.

Regulatory approaches to protecting children's privacy online tend to be based on the principle of parental consent. Some argue this relieves online service providers of too much of the responsibility of safeguarding children's privacy and identity online.
© UNICEF/UN055396/ROMANA

A greater burden of responsibility needs to be placed on online service providers.

PERSPECTIVE

Are you tattooed ... yet?

Juan Enriquez

Most of you, dear readers, might initially think to answer that question with an emphatic "no." Tattoos are painful to acquire, pretty permanent and oft an embarrassment in later life. Most parents are adamant: Do Not Get a Tattoo. Period. If you must… then wait a long, long time, and be very careful what you choose. Seems like good advice. So why, then, do most parents allow their kids to get virtually tattooed? Let me explain…

When you use Facebook, Twitter, Instagram, Google, LinkedIn or a host of other services, you share parts of yourself. Pictures, activities, thoughts, quotes, tweets, friends, comments – all become breadcrumbs that, collectively, reflect you, your thoughts, interests, activities, talents, achievements, loves, break-ups and lives online. These images and words reflect what you think is important, what you care about. Just like tattoos. So in a sense, these are electronic tattoos, but more intimate and more descriptive than any ink on your skin.

Unless you chose to ink your face or hands, you can easily cover up most tattoos, say if you go to a job interview or choose not to show them on a date. The same is not true for electronic tattoos. Almost impossible to cover up. Removing a real tattoo is painful and messy, but possible. Removing an electronic tattoo is almost impossible. Go online and you can find out a whole lot about almost anyone. In a sense, we are all permanently tattooed. And it takes ever more work to remain even partially anonymous.

Legislating privacy on the extremes is far easier than legislating the everyday. Most privacy debates focus on actions like 'revenge porn', where an angry ex posts compromising pictures or videos of a former love. But that is nowhere near as common as the information we and our friends voluntarily share after an innocent party, site visit, job comment or family interaction. Because this data is so easy to access decades later, and because it is so widely disseminated, there are many who may eventually be amused, insulted, angered, surprised and entertained by the most innocent of electronic tattoos.

In a sense, we are all celebrities. According to an ex-mayor of London, "When you walk down the streets of London, you are a movie star. You are being filmed by more cameras than you can possibly imagine." Not surprising, given that there are by some estimates more than a million closed-circuit television cameras watching you. We now live under greater scrutiny than a major Hollywood figure or head of state might have lived under a few decades ago. But whereas it took a team of highly skilled investigative reporters or paparazzi to uncover the lives of the rich and famous of yore, today what we say, to whom, about what and how we looked can be easily scrutinized and shared.

As adults, today's children and adolescents will be subject to a scrutiny and historical record that we cannot begin to imagine. While most of us were, blessedly, able to forget, reimagine or reinvent part of our early lives, loves, jobs, thoughts, deeds, comments and mistakes, today's children will be in a very different spot. A single stupid comment can lead to decades of disdain and cyberbullying. A single stupid action can be reviewed by authorities, voters or employers decades later.

For better and worse, each of today's children has become an individual historical figure, subject to an ever more powerful and permanent panopticon. Even in utero, the details of each individual sometimes begin to become a public tattoo as parents share ultrasounds or even gene-sequence data. Before children hit their early teens and begin to share their own stories, there is already a broad tattoo out there that can define who they are perceived to be: Where do you live? Did your parents divorce? Who are they, anyway? What school did you go to? What did you look like? Played sports? All easy to find.

Hiding may not be a viable option. In a world of ever more prevalent and visible digital tattoos, coming across someone with no profile at all would really make one wonder. So as our kids face challenges we never faced, it is important that we have early conversations about one's public persona and profiles, about one's history and long-term reputation. In the same way as parents used to teach kids manners early, kids need to learn the rules and consequences

of being electronically tattooed. Turns out we are all tattooed, and we already all carry far more electronic ink on our bodies than the most colorfully decorated biker gangs…

Juan Enriquez is the managing director of Excel Venture Management, a fund that invests in entrepreneurial life science companies and big data platforms. He is a global speaker, futurist and best-selling author of books on politics, science and international affairs.

"We now live under greater scrutiny than a major Hollywood figure or head of state might have lived under a few decades ago," writes Juan Enriquez.
© UNICEF/UN036674/SHARMA

PERSPECTIVE

___

Look, Mum, no data!

Anab Jain

We are at a turning point in the development of toys and technology made for children and adolescents. In recent years, Apple's iPhone, iPod and iPad were named some of the most desirable toys of the year, marking the first time that technologies produced for adults, with significant online capabilities, were so widely touted as must-have toys for children. Infants play with tablets, smartphones and voice technologies before they can walk or talk. Childhood discovery is no longer constrained within a physical world children can touch and taste to understand. Their imagination can explore digital dimensions. Ways to learn and access information are endless.

Yet both producers and consumers face fresh challenges when toys are integrated into new technologies. The potential of toys and software accessible to children and adolescents reaches far beyond their marketed appeal. From environmental sensing, to passing data to the cloud, children's sensory and communicative capacities are extended, but so too are corporations' ability to influence children's thoughts, beliefs and decision-making.

In the 1980s, the deregulation of advertising aimed at children in the United States allowed marketers and companies to build huge franchises that demonstrably increased the emotional bonds children had to products. They did this through the development of cartoons, expensive advertising campaigns and blockbuster movies. Today there is precious little regulation holding back toy manufacturers and the technology industry. They continue to innovate and disrupt, faster than parents can understand, consumer groups can advise and governments can legislate.

From the smart toys that listen to children while they play, to the family use of Amazon Echo, and the abundance of other software and hardware in use around them, children are exploring an emergent frontier of life, play and learning driven by connected technology. New research has drawn attention to the nature of the invasion of children's privacy by toys that capture, record and share audio information during play. This raises serious questions about privacy and safety in the home and online. It also raises important issues about what companies can do with the information their products record during a child's play, how this can be used, how it should be protected and who is able to access it.

Children have always confided in their toys and teddy bears, but mainly in private, with the occasional overheard complaint or confession. Is it right to limit our children's privacy in this way, or should parents be given total access to their child's private moments to help aid their development? What are the incentives of the designers and producers?

The data gathered across our digital lives is often collected without privacy mandates, and it seems to be our responsibility to demand our data be encrypted. Reading the terms and conditions for every product is hardly something even the most diligent parent has time for. Consent becomes convoluted as our children's data is easily passed to third parties who can use it for marketing purposes or to train new systems and artificial intelligence.

The sheer mass of quantitative data we can gather on our children raises concerns about how parents use it. How are children going to be protected from well-meaning but increasingly invasive parental practices? Should children have agency in their technological experiences and, if so, how?

Ubiquitous technology in the home creates some challenges for children and their parents. Designers need to be aware of the ethical issues involved in developing new software and hardware that are accessible to minors, because these technologies have the opportunity to help shape and enhance young users' knowledge of the world and themselves.

But intentional design is crucial, because new technologies also expand opportunities for bullying, harassment and other more serious behaviour. Children and young people in their bedrooms can be exposed to crime, abuse and radicalisation. Software such as Snapchat has even been designed to limit the readability of shared content by making it unavailable after a user-determined time selection. WhatsApp, Signal and others offer encrypted communication channels. From a developmental perspective, how does the live streaming of our lives distort or develop who we are, and how do we nurture the best practices in our children?

With increasingly autonomous software and hardware, hidden discreetly within the technology that accompanies us wherever we go, we are ever more ignorant of how our devices actually work and the extent of what they are doing. Toy manufacturers and technology companies need to design their products and services with these things in mind. We need a better understanding of privacy, the fair use of data and the concerns of parents. As parents, we need to do a better job of holding these companies to account; we need to demand that our children be protected. We have more work to do in designing and building ethical, responsible and trustworthy technologies for children. We have more work to do understanding and using technology, and figuring out how to teach our children to steer themselves through the turbulence of our technological landscape.

Anab Jain is the director and co-founder of Superflux, a lab focused on emerging technologies for business, cultural and social purposes. She is also professor of industrial design at the University of Applied Arts Vienna. This essay was written in discussion with Jake Charles Rees, futures researcher at Superflux.

"Designers need to be aware of the ethical issues involved in developing new software and hardware that are accessible to minors, because these technologies have the opportunity to help shape and enhance young users' knowledge of the world and themselves," writes Anab Jain.
© UNICEF/UN040656/

04
Digital childhoods: Living online

ASHLEY TAN, 17, SINGAPORE

"It is pointless attempting to compare ourselves to unattainable standards that are reflected in social media posts, because many of these pictures are, in truth, just a warped version of reality."

Full articles by youth contributors featured in
The State of the World's Children 2017 can be found at:
<www.voicesofyouth.org/en/sections/content/pages/sowc-2017>

As children spend more and more time on digital devices, families, educators and children's advocates are growing more concerned – and more confused – by the lack of consensus among experts on the rewards and risks of connectivity. Many parents also struggle with conflicting messages that they should limit screen time, on the one hand, or get the latest device so their children can keep up, on the other.

As the debates continue, one thing is clear: Unlimited – and especially unsupervised – connectivity has the potential to cause harm, just as access to the wealth of information, entertainment and social opportunity has the potential to benefit children around the world. So the task is to find ways to provide children with the support and guidance they need to make the most of their online experiences.

Video games. Television. Comic books. Radio. A Google search on societal – and parental – worries about the impact of technology on children's well-being makes clear that such concerns are nothing new.

Radio was blamed for sleeplessness. Comic books for making children 'criminal and promiscuous'. Television for social isolation. And video games for offline aggression.[1]

As far back as the sixteenth century, some feared writing would increase forgetfulness, because people would no longer rely on memory for information. They also worried that books and the printing press would lead to what today we would call information overload.

Yet, compared with its innovative predecessors, the internet – and how children use it – raises concerns of a different magnitude. Connectivity and interactivity are harder to take away or turn off. Their use by children is harder to monitor. And while children access entertainment, information or social networks via a connected device, those devices gather information on them, too.

Questions about the impact of connectivity and interactivity abound among parents,

educators, policymakers and industry leaders. Is digital engagement a threat to children's well-being? Are they spending too much time at it? Is it making them depressed? Dependent? Obese? Who is most at risk? What can parents and caregivers do to allow children space to explore and develop independently while also providing enough oversight?

This chapter will examine these questions, summarize evidence on the impact of digital engagement on aspects of children's well-being (mental, social and physical) and present their perspectives on the subject.

As seen in previous chapters, whether and how much children benefit from digital experiences has much to do with their starting points in life. While those with strong social and familial relationships are likely to use the internet to bolster these relationships – leading to improved well-being – children experiencing loneliness, stress, depression or problems at home, for example, may find that the internet compounds some of these existing difficulties. Conversely, children who struggle with their social lives offline can sometimes develop friendships and receive social support online that they are not receiving elsewhere.[2]

How much children benefit from digital experiences has much to do with their starting points.

Questions of screen time for connected children, while still debated, are increasingly obsolete. This is because there is no clear agreement on when time spent on digital technology shifts from moderate to excessive; 'how much is too much' is highly individual, dependent on a child's age, individual characteristics and broader life context. And many children in high-connectivity contexts find it difficult to estimate how much time they spend with digital technology, because they are more or less using it *all of the time*.[3]

As these issues are debated and studied, some basic truths seem to be emerging. Rather than restricting children's digital media use, more attentive and supportive mediation by parents and educators holds the most promise for enabling children to draw maximum benefit and minimum risk from connectivity. More attention should be given to the content and activities of children's digital experiences – what they are doing online and why – rather than strictly to how much time they spend in front of screens. Finally, future research and policy should consider a child's full life context – age, gender, personality, life situation, social and cultural environment and other factors – to understand where to draw the line between healthy and harmful use.

A new generation gap

Parents, educators and those with an interest in children's health and well-being seem to be growing more concerned as children spend more time on digital devices. For every new article or study that says growing connectivity is harming children there is another that shoots down these claims with competing evidence.

Adults who think children spend too much time engaging with screens wonder whether children will miss out

on important areas of life – or the areas of life that were important to them as children: giggling with a friend after playing a practical joke, or climbing a tree, or being fascinated by an ant crawling across the ground.

Some parental concerns cut across cultural contexts. For example, a report from the Swedish Media Council described how parents in Sweden were at once quite positive about the benefits their children could reap by playing digital games and at the same time worried about how much time they spent doing it.[4] Likewise, in South Africa, parent focus groups acknowledged the benefits of the internet for their children even though they were also concerned about how much time their children spent online and the potential online risks their children faced.[5]

Sociologists and psychologists say that children today interact more with their phones than with each other, and speculate that they might miss out on important social experiences.[6] Others have noted the concern that children's social skills will be negatively affected or otherwise altered because their friendships and communications with peers are digitally mediated.[7]

Some experts say children still interact with one another as much as before and that the interactions are of similar quality. It is the venues for social interaction that have changed to digital.[8]

On the low- or no connectivity side of the digital divide, parents and caregivers may be concerned that their children are missing out on developing social fluencies, a digital identity or the skills and knowledge they will need to compete for jobs *(see Chapter 2)*.

Connected children point out that adults are the ones missing out, as one girl phrased it in an interview with *The*

More attention should be given to what children are doing online and why.

Washington Post, "on the whole world."[9] Other children complain that because their parents spend so much time online, they must compete with digital devices for their parents' attention.[10]

Despite these divergent views, children and their parents are finding ways to bridge the gap by regularly talking to each other about thoughtful, responsible digital behaviour *(see box: Parenting's new digital frontier)*.

Some say children now interact more with their phones than with each other; others argue that the only change is that the venues for children's social interactions are now increasingly digital. © UNICEF/UN036679/SHARMA

What do adolescents think about ... the impact of ICTs on families?

Adults often paint a picture of young people as being technologically connected but socially disconnected, and even participants in the *State of the World's Children 2017* workshops* admit this image has some truth.

"I think that the internet brought us closer to those who are far away and pulled us away from those who are close by. Within my family, there are times where we can all be in the same room without saying a single word because each of us is glued to the screen of our smartphone." GIRL, 16, DEMOCRATIC REPUBLIC OF THE CONGO

But, overall, they painted a much more positive picture of how digital technologies are changing family life. They were enthusiastic, for example, about how technology supported relationships with family members by allowing them to connect, communicate and share ...
"When we watch movies that make us laugh ... what makes us happy is to stay in harmony." GIRL, 10, PORTUGAL

"Playing games together on the desktop computer [with] my sister ... makes us feel happy." GIRL, 17, NIGERIA

"I sometimes show funny videos to my grandparents on YouTube." BOY, 17, PERU

and by giving families things to talk about.
"Each time we find something interesting on social media it brings up a conversation." GIRL, 16, TUNISIA

Digital technologies also allowed participants to stay in touch with relatives abroad ...
"My father is in Syria and I am in Jordan, I can communicate through social media and talk to him." GIRL, 16, JORDAN

"My sister made a video call from Spain and filled my family with joy." BOY, 16, PERU

enabled them to share moments in their lives ...
"My mom, she moved to Spain when I was a kid. I can share with her each moment that she or I live every day." GIRL, 17, PARAGUAY

"We use the phone to celebrate birthdays ... even just to say happy birthday through a call." GIRL, 14, TIMOR-LESTE

and created a sense of closeness that would not otherwise be possible.
"My brother lives abroad and the internet has helped us keep our close relationship. We talk all the time through Skype and I never felt that he left home." GIRL, 16, TUNISIA

"Now WhatsApp allows me to talk to my mother who is abroad without any problems. Before we had to buy credit but now with 100F [US$0.20] I can connect and chat with her and see her photos. Technology really makes our lives easier." GIRL, 14, SENEGAL

Digital technologies also helped during emergencies or when a family member needed support.
"My little sister was sick so I used my phone to call my mother and take her to the hospital." GIRL, 17, VANUATU

"A cousin who lives in South Africa had to have surgery, and afterwards she couldn't go out. So, with my sister and other cousins who live in different places around the world, we created a group, just to tell each other funny stories and distract her from her illness." GIRL, 14, DEMOCRATIC REPUBLIC OF THE CONGO

"My grandmother needs some medications that [are not available] in our country. So I used my PC to find them and order." BOY, 15, REPUBLIC OF MOLDOVA

But there were negatives: For example, many participants spoke of tensions with siblings over access to devices.
"Me and my siblings sometimes fight over my mother's computer to watch movies." GIRL, 17, VANUATU

In response, some tried to convince parents to help them buy their own devices …
"To save enough money to buy the device I want, I have to ask my parents for an increase in my allowance." BOY, 17, THAILAND

but often with little hope of success.
"I am trying to convince my father but I think that my father will not be convinced." BOY, 14, BANGLADESH

Some participants also spoke of arguments with parents or caregivers about how ICTs might be distracting them from their schoolwork or home responsibilities.
"I got on bad terms with my mom for spending too much time with digital devices and not spending enough time on school studies." GIRL, 13, REPUBLIC OF KOREA

"I have argued with my family because I didn't fulfil my responsibilities due to my distraction with the laptop." GIRL, 14, URUGUAY

Others experienced family frictions when they used digital technologies after bedtime or at the wrong time.
"I disturbed my father while on the mobile when it was prayer time." BOY, 16, JORDAN

But adolescents weren't the only ones distracted by glowing screens.
"When mum switches her computer on to work at home, she has no time to talk to us." GIRL, 18, BURUNDI

"When we all went dining outside, my mom got her feelings hurt because my dad and I only looked at our smartphones." GIRL, 14, REPUBLIC OF KOREA

There were other sources of tension: Sometimes parental monitoring of online activity led to misunderstandings …
"My family tends to spy on my private life through social media. In consequence, we fight over misunderstandings." GIRL, 16, TUNISIA

"Misunderstandings because porn sites appear as pop-ups and my parents think we search for them." GIRL, 16, GUATEMALA

and there were also intergenerational misunderstandings …
"My mother's use of emoji online does not reflect her feelings in reality. Therefore, I find it difficult to understand how my mother feels." GIRL, 17, JAPAN

as well as concerns over online safety …
"When my dad's account was hacked and everyone in my family was concerned." BOY, 16, PERU

that could even lead to arguments between parents or caregivers.
"I shared on Facebook something that my mom thought was inappropriate, and she and my dad had a strong argument about that." GIRL, 15, PARAGUAY

But it wasn't just adolescents' use of technology that created family tensions.
"I get upset when my mom posts a photo of mine without my permission." GIRL, 15, PARAGUAY

"[It's wrong] when parents neglect their children while concentrating on their devices." BOY, 16, FIJI

IN SUMMARY
Adolescents see the impact of digital technologies on family dynamics as both positive and negative. Interestingly, the views of participants on these issues were strikingly similar around the world, suggesting there may be opportunities for countries to collaborate in creating solutions to support families in making effective use of technologies.

* Participants' responses have been shortened and edited for clarity where necessary.

Parenting's new digital frontier

**JASMINA BYRNE AND
SONIA LIVINGSTONE**

*Jasmina Byrne is a Child
Protection Specialist who leads
UNICEF Office of Research –
Innocenti's work on children's
rights in the digital age as
well as research on family
and parenting support. Sonia
Livingstone OBE is Professor
of Social Psychology in the
Department of Media and
Communications at London
School of Economics and
Political Science.*

Parents are the first line of responsibility in protecting children and helping them learn and grow into productive adults – and their responsibilities to help their children realize the benefits of a digital world are no different. Yet many parents feel unprepared for this role. In a new and rapidly evolving realm, they must take on an age-old challenge: allowing independent exploration while providing parental oversight.[11]

In an environment where digital media is constantly becoming more personal and complex, parental anxiety around their children's internet use can be intense. Many parents and caregivers do not have the time, knowledge or resources to promote their children's digital opportunities or minimize their risks. Many also struggle with conflicting messages that they should "limit screen time" on the one hand, or "get the latest device" – so their children can "keep up" – on the other.

To whom do children turn when they encounter problems online? Generally, not to adults.[12] Studies consistently show that children tend to first turn to other children to talk about their online experiences. One study in South Africa showed that the number going to peers when they faced risks online was double the number reaching out to adults.[13] This was echoed in Global Kids Online research in Argentina, the Philippines and Serbia.[14] The reason is unsurprising: In places like Argentina, children believe their peers know more about technology, social media and the internet than adults do.[15]

On this new frontier of parenting, parents can feel disempowered and ignorant of what their children are doing online – and thus more likely to exaggerate concerns about internet predators and pornography. As a result, many parents are restrictive in managing their children's internet access.

In response, children often find ways to avoid adult oversight. These can include creating multiple profiles on social media so that they can 'friend' their parents in one and keep the others for their real use.[16] As a result, their parents may be even more in the dark – with the effect of making their children potentially more vulnerable to the very threats they fear.

At the same time, such restrictive parental mediation, one of the most common parenting styles vis-à-vis the internet, may limit the quality of children's online experience, preventing them from experiencing a range of appropriate, informative and entertaining content.[17]

While parents' concerns about children's online usage are fairly consistent, their ways of managing it are not. Parental mediation differs according to the age of the child: In one large-scale study in eight European countries, parents seemed to adapt their style from a more restrictive strategy with younger children to a more enabling strategy for older children. It also differs according to gender. A study involving children between the ages of 7 and 18 in Bahrain found that restrictions around use of digital media led girls to conceal activity online that would be considered 'unacceptable' by their parents.[18] A third variable concerns the parents: Research shows that poorer and less-educated parents prefer 'restrictive mediation',[19] and it is these same families that are struggling to update digital technology at home and acquire the skills to use it and guide their children's use.[20]

Whether parenting online or offline, one thing is clear: Key dimensions of parenting developed by the World Health Organization in 2007 still hold. Connection, behaviour control, respect for a child's individuality, modelling appropriate behaviour and provision and protection have a positive effect on adolescent well-being.

Being online and well-being: The evidence

Research is also struggling to keep up with the ever-evolving subject of children's well-being online. In preparation for this report, UNICEF's Office of Research performed a literature review to answer the question "How does the time children spend using digital technology impact their well-being?" While the evidence is mixed, recent research shows that children's use of digital tech has a mostly positive effect. The evidence summarized here looks at screen time and its impact on mental well-being, social relationships and physical activity, considers the debate over digital dependency and, finally, examines the effects digital experiences have on children's brains.

Assumptions about restricting screen time

While parents and caregivers may think they are protecting their children by restricting the time spent on digital technology, this may not be the case.

Common measures to restrict internet use – by governments, businesses, parents and others – usually take the form of parental controls, content blocking and internet filters. While well meaning, these are not always well designed to achieve their desired purpose and may even create unintended negative effects. For example, such restrictions can cut adolescents, especially, off from their social circles, from access to information and from the relaxation and learning that come from play. Tension around these restrictions can also damage trust between parents and children. And extreme restrictions can hold children back from developing the digital literacy skills needed to critically evaluate information and communicate safely, responsibly and effectively through digital technology – skills they will need for their future.

Without consensus on screen time, it is important for parents, policymakers, researchers and the media not to jump to conclusions about what is healthy or unhealthy digital use. Considering the full context of a child's life – together with an emphasis on content and experiences rather than screen time – may prove more useful for understanding the effects of digital connectivity on children's well-being.

A common assumption is that time spent online will detract from other activities thought to be more valuable, such as face-to-face socializing, reading books or exercising. This is sometimes referred to as the 'displacement theory' (discussed later in this chapter). While this assumption originally received support and served to inform policy statements, such as the former digital media guidelines of the American Academy of Pediatrics (AAP), more recent evidence suggests it might be simplistic or even inaccurate. One reason for this shift is the growing recognition that digital technologies offer many opportunities for children to pursue developmentally valuable activities, and these opportunities are both increasing and improving. For example, some video games positively influence cognitive, motivational, emotional and social development.[21] This recognition is reflected in the AAP's updated policy, which contains less-restrictive recommendations concerning both time and age limits.

Recent research suggests that youth seem quite resilient to screen consumption at higher levels – up to six hours daily – than is typically recommended by most policy statements.[22] That said, while it is a relief that children are not harmed by the sheer amount of time spent online, more research is needed to understand the benefits of spending up to a third of one's waking hours online. In addition, users – children and adults alike – should consider just who is benefiting the most, the user or the tech company *(see box: The role of (un)ethical design)*.

Parents, policymakers, researchers and the media should not jump to conclusions about what is healthy or unhealthy digital use.

PERSPECTIVE

Hey, Alexa, should I wear the pink or the sparkly dress today?

Rachel Botsman

I invited 'Alexa', also known as the Amazon Echo, into my home for an experiment with my daughter, Grace, 3. Pointing at the black cylindrical device, I explained it was a talking speaker, a bit like 'Siri' but different. "You can ask it anything you want," I said.

"Hello, Alexa," said Grace. "Will it rain today?" The turquoise rim around the speaker glowed into life. "Currently, it is 60 degrees," a female voice answered and assured her it wouldn't rain.

Over the next hour, Grace quickly figured she could ask Alexa to play her favourite music from the film *Sing*. She realized Alexa could tell jokes, do maths or give interesting facts. "Hey, Alexa, what do brown horses eat?" Her favourite interaction was realizing she could tell the assistant to stop with a simple command. "Alexa, shut up," Grace barked in a raised voice. Looking a little sheepish, she asked me if it was okay to be rude to *her*. Did she think it had feelings or even deserved respect?

By the next morning, Alexa was the first 'person' Grace said hello to as she bounded into the kitchen. My preschool daughter, who can't yet ride a bike, read a book or properly decipher good from bad, had also quickly mastered that she could buy things. "Alexa, buy the movie *Frozen*," she said. Of course, Grace had no idea that Amazon, the world's biggest retailer, was the corporate master behind the helpful assistant.

This simple experiment is a telling illustration of a profound technological shift. It's easy enough for adults to be coaxed into giving away their trust to a seemingly 'helpful' bot cleverly designed by marketing and technology experts. But when it comes to children, few checks and balances exist to deter them from giving away their trust very quickly.

Two days in of living with Alexa, something significant happened. "Alexa, what should I do today?" Grace asked nonchalantly. It

was shortly followed by a question about her fashion choice. "Alexa, what should I wear today?" I unplugged the thing.

In April 2017, Amazon launched the Echo Look device, which comes with a camera. In other words, Alexa doesn't just hear you, it sees you. The Style Check feature uses machine learning algorithms to judge our outfit choices, awarding them an overall rating from Alexa.

Confronting, isn't it? We're no longer trusting machines just to *do* something but to *decide* what to do and when to do it.

For generations, our trust in technology has resided in a confidence that the technology will do what it's expected to do – we trust a washing machine to clean our clothes or an ATM machine to dispense money. But what happens if I, say, step into an autonomous car? I'll need to trust the system itself to *decide* whether to go left or right, to swerve or stop. It's an often-cited example of how technology is enabling millions to take what I call a 'trust leap' – when we take a risk and do something new or in a fundamentally different way.

The artificial intelligence trust leap, and others like it, raises a new and pressing question: When an automated machine can have so much power over our children's lives, how do they set about trusting its intentions?

The next generation will grow up in an age of autonomous agents making decisions in their homes, schools, hospitals and even their love lives. The question for them won't be, "How will we trust robots?" but "Do we trust them too much?" In our rush to reject the old and embrace the new, children may end up placing too much trust, too easily, in the wrong places.

One of our key challenges is deciding where and when it is appropriate to make trust a matter of computer code. We need to be giving children the tools

to judge whether automated machines are trustworthy (or secure) enough to make decisions. Beyond security concerns, the bigger question is whether we can trust these bots to act ethically. Specifically, how do they 'learn' what's right and wrong?

It would be a shame to find ourselves in a world so automated that we depend solely on machines and algorithms to make decisions about whom to trust. That's a world devoid of the colour and movement born of human imperfection, and, if we take our hands off the wheel too much, possibly even dangerous. It's humans, with all our wonderful quirks and mutations, who make trust possible – not technology or mathematics.

If we want the upcoming generation to understand that, we need to design for a 'trust pause', an interval in which children stop and think before they automatically click, swipe, share or accept. To ask "Are you sure?" And we need to provide them with the knowledge and education that helps them decide: Is this person, information or thing worthy of my trust?

Rachel Botsman is an author, speaker, university lecturer and global expert on trust. Her work examines how technology is transforming human relationships. She is the author of Who Can You Trust? *(Penguin Portfolio, 2017) and co-author of* What's Mine Is Yours *(HarperCollins, 2010). She teaches the world's first MBA course on the collaborative economy, which she designed, at the University of Oxford's Saïd Business School.*

In our rush to reject the old and embrace the new, children may end up placing too much trust, too easily, in the wrong places," writes Rachel Botsman.
© UNICEF/UN040853/BICANSKI

The role of (un)ethical design

Never before has such a small number of tech designers had such a big impact on how a billion people around the world spend their time. In some places, people check their phones more than 150 times per day. Knowledge workers spend a third of their day in email. Some teenagers send 4,000 texts per month, or every six minutes awake.

Designers themselves say today's technologies are deliberately designed to exploit human weaknesses. They try to grab users' attention – and keep it for as long as possible – in order to tap into psychological biases and vulnerabilities. The aim is to play on the desire for social acceptance and exploit the fear of rejection. While the average user might disengage from the platform minutes or hours later than intended, coming away with little or no benefit, tech companies come away with financial gain from advertisers, plus their users' time, attention and personal data. Adolescents, already experiencing new and complex emotions, might not realize the potential impacts on their privacy or how they spend their time.

Until tech companies start thinking about ethical design, users – especially children and young people – will continue to face the consequences of technologies designed for social media firms' financial incentives and not users' real needs.

It is the collective responsibility of civil society, in particular the tech industry and governments, to advocate for children's best interests to be represented in debates on the design of technologies.

If not, technologies of tomorrow, such as artificial intelligence and the Internet of Things, might come at a cost to children's privacy and well-being. A first step is to learn from the organic food and green car movements. These started with educating consumers and creating new incentives for businesses that align with what's good for people.

This box is based on a Conversations with Thought Leaders Series event, 'Ethical Design for Digital Natives', held at UNICEF House on 31 January 2017 with Tristan Harris, former design ethicist and product philosopher at Google and co-founder of the Time Well Spent movement.

Social media bolsters existing friendships

Overall, research on the impact of social connections online has shifted over the past several decades. Early research, from the 1990s, tended to find internet use detrimental to social well-being.[23] One reason could be that, at the time, the bulk of people's social networks were yet to come online, so it was difficult to use the internet to maintain existing friendships, make new ones or renew old ones. More recent evidence portrays a mostly positive picture of how internet connection affects friendships and social capital[24] – and this is true for children as well as adults.

For example, adolescents' use of social networking sites has been found to provide greater feelings of connectedness to peers[25] – bolstering existing friendships[26] – and to contribute to less peer-related loneliness.[27] One reason for this, as studies from the past decade have shown, is that it is easier to talk about sensitive or personal topics online[28], in particular for boys.[29] However, among adolescents using social media to compensate for weak social cognitive skills, such use was found to increase feelings of loneliness.[30]

In terms of social networking and happiness, several studies have found a negative association between passive social media use (browsing friends' posts

> **"**
>
> *Today's technologies are deliberately designed to exploit human weaknesses.*

without interacting) and well-being,[31] which researchers hypothesize stems from increased feelings of envy[32] or from users' (undergraduates, in the case of this particular study) impression that other posters were happier than they were.[33]

Screen Time: Not too little, not too much

Despite concerns, mainly among parents and educators, regarding the effects of extensive screen time *(see section: The debate over digital dependency)*, a recent large-scale cross-sectional study of more than 120,000 15-year-olds in the United Kingdom found that the time children spent using digital tech had only a negligible impact. This study, which controlled for gender, ethnicity and economic factors, included watching TV and movies, playing video games, using computers and using smartphones. The activities differed somewhat in their respective impacts, but the authors conclude that, in general, no use at all was associated with lower mental well-being, while moderate use (between approximately two and five hours per day, depending on the activity) seemed to have a small positive effect on mental well-being.[34]

This 'Goldilocks effect'[35] – not too much, not too little, but just the right amount – seemed to be fine for children.

To give some perspective on the relative importance of screen time compared to other daily life activities, the negative effect of excessive gaming (defined in this study as more than seven hours per day) on mental well-being was less than a third of the positive effect of eating breakfast regularly or getting enough sleep.[36]

For very young children, findings from a large cohort study in 2010 of more than 13,000 5-year-old children in the United Kingdom found no evidence that longer duration of screen usage was associated with any other mental health

problems investigated for boys or girls, such as hyperactivity, peer problems or prosocial problems.[37]

However, the day and time digital technologies are used – for example, weekday versus weekend[38] – has been shown to matter. Intensive use on weekdays might have a stronger negative influence than use on weekends, indicating that for some children screen time might interfere with other structured activities during the week, such as homework.

Taken together, the impact of digital tech on child well-being seems to depend on the activity, how much time is spent and when time is spent. However, these effects – positive or negative – are generally weak and only contribute a very small part to explaining children's overall well-being.[39]

To improve children's mental well-being, it is important to take a holistic approach and focus on other factors known to have a stronger impact than screen time, such as family functioning, social dynamics at school and socio-economic conditions,[40] while also encouraging the moderate use of digital technology.

Limitations in the research

Still relatively new, the evidence is describing the impact of ever-evolving technologies on a young population that is diverse, also ever-evolving and using technologies in a variety of ways and from different starting points.

Another limitation is the research methodology used for most studies in this field *(see box: Research challenges)*. Studies have found associations between the use of digital technologies and reduced well-being.[41] However, it remains unclear if the use of digital technology is the cause or consequence of reduced well-being. For example, is spending too much time online making children feel lonely or are children

Focus on factors known to have a stronger impact than screen time, such as family functioning, social dynamics and socio-economic conditions.

Research challenges

Studies looking at mental, social or physical well-being have often been correlational (looking to identify relationships between two or more variables) or drawn from cross-sectional samples (where the data are taken at only one point in time). From these types of studies, it is difficult to determine what is cause and what is effect; it is also hard to estimate long-term consequences of the use of digital technology. To assess causality and long-term effects reliably will require longitudinal studies and other improvements in research methodology.

Another issue with current research is the tendency to focus on a limited number of background variables, when studies have shown that there are indeed major individual differences in how regular, excessive or problematic use of digital technology impacts children – based on their age, gender, personality, life situation, social and cultural environment, and other factors.[42] Thus, there is an inclination to either overestimate digital technology's effect on children or to assume that digital technology has an effect when that effect actually stems from another cause.[43]

The last caveat regarding the evidence is to look at how studies are counting and what they are covering. Studies that focus on time use alone, without describing or assessing the content or activity engaged in during that time, have limited value. Similarly, neurobiological studies (related to online behaviours) that focus on an unrepresentative portion of the developing population should not be applied to the majority of adolescents.

who already feel lonely spending more time online?

It is also important to note that much of the research has centred on children in high connectivity settings and may not be applicable to contexts of low connectivity.

Opportunity costs: Is time online replacing physical activity?

Any parent who has ever watched a child sit before a screen for hours inside on a beautiful day has considered the possibility that time online is cutting down on time engaged in physical activity. However, evidence on the impact of time spent using digital technology on physical activity[50] is decidedly mixed. Some studies show a link between online activity and reduced physical activity, while others show no associations between the two.[51]

Unfortunately, several key studies are based only on estimates of time use, with little disaggregation by digital device, activity or content, when these have been shown to matter.

But some large-scale studies are trying to find answers. One cross-national 2010 study drawing on survey data from over 200,000 adolescents aged 11–15 in Europe and North America found that spending two hours or more per day on screen-based activities resulted on average in half an hour less per week spent on leisure-type physical activity – but that the relationship differed according to age, gender and nationality.[52] And, the

Theories about friendships online

Three key hypotheses put forward and studied by researchers echo parents' concerns and perceptions about the impact of online behaviours on young people's relationships.

The displacement theory offers the idea that online interaction replaces face-to-face interaction, resulting in children and young people having lower social capital and fewer personal acquaintances.[44] As previously discussed, while this hypothesis initially received some support, new evidence suggests that it may be simplistic or even inaccurate today.

The 'rich-get-richer' theory asserts that those with strong social skills and networks offline will benefit more from online social opportunities than those who have weaker social connections to begin with.[45] An alternative to the 'rich-get-richer' hypothesis is the social compensation hypothesis, which suggests that online communication will benefit those who are socially anxious and even isolated, because it will be easier for them to develop friendships online than offline.

Lastly, the stimulation hypothesis holds that online communication stimulates communication with existing friends and is mostly positive.[46]

form of screen-based activity adolescents engaged in mattered, too: Regular computer use was associated with an increase in physical activity, while gaming and TV watching were associated with a decrease.

The study generally concluded that physical inactivity is unlikely to be a direct consequence of adolescents spending too much time on screen-based activities.

Some studies suggest that online activity and physical activity may be more independent of one another than they seem. Some hypothesize that children are not forgoing physical activity because they want to go online. Instead, they may be going online because they are already physically inactive, for a variety of reasons.[53] Or they may be less physically active, and also go online, as two separate outcomes to their circumstances.

Digital use is just one part of a complex picture of what children are doing, and why. Some children's circumstances make it difficult to engage in physical activity –

because their neighborhoods are unsafe to play in, because they don't live close to parks, playgrounds or sports facilities, or because their parents don't have the time, the interest or the resources to accompany and encourage them.

Finally, interventions targeting screen time alone are unlikely to significantly increase time spent on physical activity.[54] Instead of asking "How does screen time affect physical activity?," perhaps the right question is "Are children leading lives where they can get a healthy, balanced amount of activity for optimal growth and well-being?" Promoting physical activity and a healthy diet might prove a better strategy than merely reducing screen time.

The debate over digital dependency

Who hasn't seen or heard about an adolescent who can barely put

Promoting physical activity and a healthy diet might prove a better strategy than merely reducing screen time.

Although children seem resilient to relatively high levels of screen time, much more research is needed to understand the impact of spending up to a third of one's waking hours online. © UNICEF/ UN046200/KLJAJO

Who hasn't heard about an adolescent who can barely put down her smartphone?

down her smartphone, or a tween who loses control when his iPad privileges are taken away, or a young online gamer who seems to do little else?

There is no consensus on how to label the problem behaviour that many parents and educators are concerned about: children and adolescents who spend so much time with digital technology that it often seems as if they are actually as dependent on their screens as substance abusers are to their drugs of choice.

Some believe 'addiction' is a useful term to describe this problem behaviour – and the chilling possibility that it may be accurate drives headlines that in turn deepen parents' concerns. But the analogy is just an analogy.

In fact, there is very little evidence demonstrating that any significant number of children and adolescents are so dependent on their devices that they experience severe impairment in a major area of life – the definition of addiction – or are at risk of significant and snowballing health risks as a result.

As yet, researchers have not found robust evidence that any severe negative life outcomes from excessive use of digital technology are directly attributable to the use of technology alone.[55] Few studies have even explored in-depth which problems may occur as a consequence of excessive use of technology.[56] And there is little indication that such severe cases constitute a growing problem in society.

Still, the fears of parents are grounded in direct experience of their children's altered

How do new media change teens' social lives and identities?

MIZUKO ITO

Mizuko Ito is a cultural anthropologist, educational researcher, entrepreneur and advocate. She is director of the Connected Learning Lab at the University of California, Irvine, and a co-founder of Connected Camps, a non-profit organization offering online project-based, social STEM learning for kids in all walks of life.

Ever since the early days of the internet and mobile communications, researchers have debated whether these new technologies bring us together or push us apart. Adults have fretted that teens' real life communication skills are atrophying, and that social media encourages empty exchanges that ultimately make them lonely and isolated. We often jump to the question of whether these new media are good or bad, but it's important to first understand the role they play in young people's everyday social lives.

People of all ages take to mobile and social media because they offer a greater range of choice and flexibility for when and with whom we communicate. Misa Matsuda, who conducted some of the first studies of mobile communication in Japan, described the growth of 'selective sociality' in teen relationships.[47] When interviewing high school students, she noticed a new term, *chu-tomo* (a friend from middle school), that didn't exist before the advent of mobile phones. In the past, if students split up to go to high school, they would lose track of their friends from middle school. Now they can keep in touch with friends even if they aren't in the same school or community. The question is not whether we are more or less connected, but with whom we are connected. Matsuda also looked at how mobile media changed family communication. What she found was that text messaging increased parent-child communication for families who were close and connected, but for those who weren't, it had the opposite effect. In other words, we connect more with people we feel closest to.

In a study of teens in the United States during the first major wave of social media adoption in the early 2000s, we found different genres in how young people socialized online.[48] Most youth were engaged in casual social communication with peers they knew from school. A smaller number were going online to connect with specialized communities around gaming, popular culture and other interests. Often

the identities young people cultivated were quite different in these two kinds of settings. For example, one young man we spoke to projected his identity as a popular athlete with his school peer group on Myspace, but was also active in the online community for the game The Sims. He kept these identities and social networks quite separate.

The only constant today is greater choice and diversity in how new media play out in young people's lives. Young people can take to online communication to mobilize millions through a Facebook cause, or spend their time exchanging mindless gossip. It's futile to speculate whether these technologies are generically good or bad for all young people. It's more important to ask how we can best support the positives.

Given the broader range of experiences that new media open up for young people, we shoulder a greater responsibility in guiding them to making wise choices. It's not enough to say yes or no to specific devices or platforms or to clock screen time. We have to look at the substance and specifics of digital content and communities where young people are connecting, and actively engaging. I'm part of a community of researchers, educators and technology makers who have been advocating for 'connected learning', an approach to guiding young people to productive learning and relationships online.[49]

Our research has identified a persistent generation gap in how young people and adults view the value of new communications technologies. While young people see mobile phones and the internet as a lifeline to media, information and social connection, adults often view young people's engagement with these technologies as a waste of time. This generation gap represents a missed opportunity. New media can be a vehicle for parents, educators and young people to come together around shared interests and concerns rather than something that drives us apart.

When it comes to setting limits on screen time, the child's age, individual characteristics, culture and life context all need to be taken into account. © UNICEF/ UN017636/UESLEI MARCELINO

behaviour, and founded in legitimate concerns for their children's overall well-being. These concerns must be considered and addressed.

Many studies conducted over the past two decades suggest that problems might arise as children use digital technology to cope with difficult real-life situations as a form of self-medication. For example, if a child is feeling sad or stressed, he or she might go online to be distracted from the sadness or stress, facilitated by an application where immersion or distraction is afforded, such as an online game or a social networking site. The consequences can be both positive (he or she might feel better temporarily) and negative (the real cause may not be addressed). In the long run, this might make the coping behaviour a recurring habit, unless the underlying problem is

resolved. Researchers tend to agree that the underlying problems that can prompt life-impairing digital engagement need to be addressed to successfully overcome this problem behaviour, whereas a forced reduction in screen time would represent a surface intervention that is unlikely to serve its purpose.[57]

Quite possibly, labelling excessive screen use as an addiction may just be a proxy for expressing concerns about the impact disagreements about screen time are having on family dynamics. For the great majority of connected children, disagreements over screen time are likely a new iteration of generational tension between the old and the young. But wildly divergent views of how much screen time is too much can trigger serious family fights. In this respect, parents and caregivers face a difficult but important task in mediating their children's use – and their own use – of digital technology.

Such divergent views on digital technology can lead to arguments and fights at home, which are then used by some parents and researchers as evidence that the addiction to technology is real, while the actual cause of the arguments might be found in intergenerational disagreements around how children should spend their time.[58]

There are risks in employing addiction terminology to describe concerns regarding children's growing use of digital technology. Careless use of addiction terminology downplays the very real consequences of the behaviour for those who are seriously affected, while overstating the risk of harm for those who at times engage in somewhat excessive, but ultimately not harmful, use of digital technology. Applying clinical concepts to children's everyday behaviour does not help support them in developing healthy screen time habits.

And conflating the screen time debate with addiction can even be harmful. For example, in some countries, the idea of addiction to technology has been used to justify the incarceration of children in treatment camps despite a lack of evidence for the efficacy of such approaches.[59] Media reports from these camps suggest that disciplinary methods employed by staff involved physical punishment and electric shocks.[60]

According to one research team focused on the East Asian phenomenon of corrective boot camps: "Internet addiction, although descriptively meaningful, is diagnostically of questionable value because it is conceptually vague, possesses a degree of cultural loading and fails to distinguish between symptoms and primary conditions."[61]

This is your child's brain on digital

Right next to fears that digital technology could be addictive is the idea that it can, on a neurophysiological level, rewire a child's brain, interfere with the brain's own reward system or affect brain development in other ways.

Investigating the impact of digital tech on brain development and cognitive processes

Current research shows that children's experiences and environment during early childhood have an impact on the development of their brains. Whether a child receives adequate nutrition, is stimulated, loved and protected from adversity and stress all affect the formation of neural connections – with potentially lifelong impact. The first 1,000 days of life are a unique window of opportunity to support a child's optimal brain development – and also a period of special vulnerability.

But research also shows that experience and environment have an impact on adolescent brain development, too – that adolescence is period of consolidation and pruning of neural connections.

Key cognitive processes are developing in adolescence and into young adulthood: working memory, taking in and responding to social cues and the ability to choose what to pay attention to and what to ignore. Internet use seems to have an impact on all these areas, both positive and negative, and with many uncertainties and caveats.[62]

This has led some to wonder whether excessive use of digital technology might be among the experiences with a potential impact on brain development. Do common activities associated with children's online lives – use of social media and media

> **"**
>
> *Internet use seems to have an impact on cognitive areas, both positive and negative, and with many uncertainties and caveats.*

What do adolescents think about ... technology and health in the digital age?

For participants in *the State of the World's Children 2017* workshops,* the connections between digital technology and health and well-being – both their own and that of others – were complex. Reflecting their generally positive views of connectivity, they saw great hope in how digital technology could treat illness and support a healthy lifestyle. But they also had clear views on how it could affect their happiness and mental well-being, both for better and worse.

Participants believed digital technology was advancing medical knowledge and the availability of treatments ...
"Digital technology allows improving medical practices." GROUP RESPONSE, DEMOCRATIC REPUBLIC OF THE CONGO

and enabling people living with disabilities to participate more fully in everyday activities.
"Digital technology helps people in need: lenses, artificial limbs, special computers for people who can't speak or move." GROUP RESPONSE, REPUBLIC OF MOLDOVA

"New digital technologies for communication will help children with special needs to feel at ease with their classmates." GROUP RESPONSE, BELARUS

They also pointed to the role digital technology played in alerting them to the latest medical and/or health innovations ...
"[It] helps people to know about the latest evolution in the world." GROUP RESPONSE, DEMOCRATIC REPUBLIC OF THE CONGO

and helping them to access information on particular health issues.
"You can find ... information that describes your health condition, so it's really useful for our health and happiness." GROUP RESPONSE, REPUBLIC OF MOLDOVA

Participants felt that digital technology could support both their physical health ...
"Technology aids physical exercise by listening to music while working out." GROUP RESPONSE, NIGERIA

and their mental health, for example by promoting social connection and providing them with access to entertainment.
"It is good for our health, because watching funny videos distracts us. It also helps us de-stress a little." GROUP RESPONSE, PERU

On the negative side, participants argued that digital technology could exacerbate risks to health and well-being. They noted that overuse of digital technology could impair their hearing and vision ....
"The brightness of your phone or computer ... can also destroy your eyes." BOY, 17, KIRIBATI

and distract from other activities, such as exercise, thereby increasing the incidence of obesity.
"We do less sport. We walk less." GIRL, 17, NIGERIA

And they were sceptical about the idea that biometric devices could support positive physical health outcomes.
"App to track your health doesn't really work." GROUP RESPONSE, NIGERIA

They were also concerned about health misinformation.
"Some health ideas and tips online are wrong." GROUP RESPONSE, NIGERIA

In particular, participants highlighted the negative impacts of digital technology for their mental health and well-being. Prominent concerns centred on discriminatory or hurtful exchanges and content shared online, both of which could prompt powerful negative effects.
"I had an argument with a friend on Facebook. I experienced dreadful moments on Facebook. I saw miserable/regrettable posts. I received embarrassing comments." BOY, 14, SENEGAL

"When you publish something [online] and suddenly others attack you with no reason, without knowing you." GIRL, 14, URUGUAY

"I … posted a photo on Facebook and I received a comment that threw me into a panic." BOY, 14, SENEGAL

Interestingly, some children noted that they were affected – sometimes deeply – by the negative online experiences of their friends.
"One of my friends posted a photo and one of her enemies made a bad comment and that really affected me because she's one of my best friends." GIRL, 16, SENEGAL

Others were very aware that their own online engagements might impact others.
"We can destroy other people's happiness with what we publish." GROUP RESPONSE, DEMOCRATIC REPUBLIC OF THE CONGO

They also noted that engaging with digital technology could be frustrating, which could lead to increased anxiety or anger.
"It creates stress because it's very slow." GROUP RESPONSE, PERU

Some participants said that online platforms were not amenable to communicating feelings in ways that made them feel understood.
"We talk less often [because parents, siblings or I play games or spend time on social networking services]: My parents are not able to grasp my state, [such as mental health or problems at school]." BOY, 15, JAPAN

Children in some countries expressed concern about excessive use of digital technologies.
"Addiction to technology – a thing that spoils the relationship with relatives." BOY, 14, REPUBLIC OF MOLDOVA

"There have been so many devices around since childhood and it is so easy to get addicted." BOY, 15, JAPAN

Other participants suggested that digital technology could cause depression, anxiety and loss of contact with reality, noting, for example, that laptops, smartphones and computers can produce
"social isolation … by creating a virtual part-real world." BOY, 16, REPUBLIC OF MOLDOVA

"Digital technology also causes moral anxiety. If digital technology causes moral anxiety, how will it now aid health and happiness?" GROUP RESPONSE, NIGERIA

The displacement of other activities by digital technology meant, for some, that
"[people] forget the little things that [cause] happiness." GROUP RESPONSE, NIGERIA

IN SUMMARY
Despite their concerns about the potential negative impacts of digital technology on their health and happiness, the vast majority of participants stated either that technology's effects were positive or were a balance of positives and negatives.

* Participants' responses have been shortened and edited for clarity where necessary.

*Video games may
even have beneficial
effects on children's
visual faculty and
ability to learn.*

multitasking – affect how their brains function? If so, can we say how? Just as the possibility of addiction to digital technology has spawned fevered media stories, so too does the possibility of 'brain damage' send parents into frenzies of concern.

Fortunately, for the vast majority of children and adolescents, these fears are unfounded. Very few adolescents are excessive users of the internet or gamers whose total play time exceeds healthy bounds.[63] No evidence exists to suggest that moderate use of any digital technology has a negative impact on children's brains.

This is not to say that evidence of the impact of excessive use should be ignored. Studies measuring the relationship between online behaviours and brain development may focus on a very small percentage of adolescents, but the findings of some studies do demonstrate an impact in extreme cases. They also show that it is not necessarily how much time is spent online as the kinds of activities pursued while online.

An oft-expressed concern of parents is that excessive participation in violent video games can cause children to act violently offline, but there is no evidence that demonstrates such a connection. In fact, new studies show that video games may even have beneficial effects on children's visual faculty[64] and ability to learn.[65]

Effect of 'likes' on the brain

Adolescents spend considerable time engaging with the content their peers post online and reacting to it. In a digital world 'likes' are a coin of the adolescent realm, influencing preferences and behaviour – and possibly even registering in the brain.

When exposed to different types of photographs, accompanied by the number of 'likes' for each photograph, adolescents in one naturalistic experimental study

using MRIs showed greater activity in the areas of the brain associated with social understanding and reward processing.[66] The study also found that looking at pictures showing health-risking behaviours was linked to less activity in the parts of the brain affecting cognitive control and inhibition of actions.

However, despite these associations, there is not yet evidence on whether these variations in brain patterns have an actual impact or actually make adolescents *behave* in a certain way. Researchers do not know what the corresponding cognitive processes of the brain activity as seen on the MRI are and cannot predict whether the adolescents will indeed make certain behavioural choices when exposed to certain stimuli. Also, such 'peer pressure' may be the same offline – where it is much harder to measure with precision.

Benefits of media multitasking

Adolescents are known to multitask on their devices, flipping from watching a video to messaging their friends and back again, and then glancing to check social media status updates. Adults do it, too, of course – leading to a plethora of articles about whether the use of digital technology is causing attention-deficit/hyperactivity disorder (ADHD).

Studies show that adolescents and young adults who engage in more media multitasking need to employ more executive control and effort when working in distracting environments.[67] But researchers have not been able to determine whether the increased brain activity in those areas of the brain was the result of media multitasking, or whether engagement in media multitasking[68] is affected by brain activity. Similar research looked at how daily gaming affects memory and multitasking. The study measured how fluidly the young subjects between the ages of 13 and 24 switched attention while keeping track of multiple items at once while undergoing an MRI scan. The findings showed that, based on their brain activity, subjects who were more frequent gamers might be better at switching attention and keeping track of a lot of information than those who reported less daily gaming.[69]

Pointing the way forward

The temptation to draw overarching conclusions from limited research is understandable but not useful to evaluate and address risks and benefits of online activity among children and adolescents. There is a need for longitudinal, representative studies and much more child-centred research. In addition, in an age when some children feel like they use internet all the time, researchers face new challenges in measuring and controlling their studies of use or excessive use.

In terms of identifying thresholds for use – How much is normal? How much is too much? Is it interfering with sleep or meals or homework? – the answers will depend on the child's age, individual characteristics, culture and life context. At the same time, parents and caregivers must learn to pay greater attention to content and children's online experiences and less attention to time use alone. Responses to problematic or unhealthy digital behaviours should first consider the broader life factors, such as school environment and relationships with family and friends.

Another issue in making recommendations with regard to screen time is that adult perceptions of excessive use tend to drive the debate. Children use digital technology for specific reasons and it is important to take their opinions and explanations seriously.

Children are in many ways the pioneers and experts in this area. Some are creating apps and programmes on their own. To effectively adjust to this situation and build constructive dialogues around healthy and harmful use of digital technology in the family, school and society at large, we will need to rely more on children's voices and experiences.

Media outlets also play an important role in the public's understanding of the impact of digital media use on children's well-being. Media coverage can both reflect and influence societal fears, which emphasizes the importance of providing a nuanced picture. This is not easy to do, however, given that evidence in this area is inconclusive and conflicting. Too many news articles share evidence from studies that are methodologically weak or exaggerate or misrepresent the evidence provided. This can distract attention from more pressing issues for children, or lead to situations where research and policy seek to address problems too quickly via interventions that have not been properly evaluated. This is not necessarily the fault of the media outlets or journalists: It also signals that there may be problems in the way universities and research institutes communicate their findings. One way to tackle this issue is for researchers to play a more direct role in how their findings are presented to the world, so they can highlight limitations and prevent overstating or mischaracterizing findings.

Adapting to increased use of digital technology will demand some adjustments in how parents raise children, how researchers undertake studies and how decision-makers develop policies and recommendations. As discussed, some have called for reducing screen time, but the evidence to date does not justify such interventions given the lack of evidence for notable negative effects on children's lives or on the quality of their online experience. A better, shared understanding of how to use the internet – through mediation and positive and supportive parenting rather than restriction – holds the most promise for advancing children's digital opportunities while minimizing their risks.

"

Too many news articles share evidence from studies that are methodologically weak or exaggerate or misrepresent the evidence provided.

PERSPECTIVE

—

Empowering children to engage in the digital world

Niels B. Christiansen

At the LEGO Group, children are our role models. They are always exploring, creating and discovering. They are intuitive learners with a hands-on and minds-on approach to life. Play is critical to inspiring this innate approach to learning, and creative play experiences can empower children to learn and develop critical life skills.

I have seen how important play was for my own two children. It encouraged them to invent, problem-solve, collaborate and have fun. It is a powerful force and an essential element of every child's development. Research has consistently shown that play is not just enjoyable – it also fulfils a crucial role in learning and preparing children for challenges in childhood and throughout adulthood.

As more and more children around the world connect digitally, the importance of delivering playful experiences within safe online playgrounds has become a vital issue for the toy industry to address. For 85 years our company values of imagination, creativity, fun, learning, caring and quality have been instrumental in the LEGO Group's commitment to providing the best play experiences with LEGO® bricks. Those same values now guide our ambition to deliver inspiring and safe digital experiences.

Innovation in digital technology represents a tremendous opportunity for bringing playful and educational experiences to children around the world. However, it also presents fresh challenges for responsible brands that strive to deliver high levels of safety, while inspiring empowerment and creativity in children as they grow and develop.

Together with our partners and industry experts, we strive for our digital experiences to be as safe for children as our physical play materials. We were the first company in the toy industry to establish a global partnership with UNICEF, and we are committed to promoting and implementing the Children's Rights and Business Principles in our work. UNICEF and the International

Telecommunication Union's Guidelines for Industry on Child Online Protection have been incorporated into the development and implementation of the LEGO Group's Digital Child Safety policy. The policy affirms our respect and support for the rights of children, strengthens child protection governance across the company and underlines the LEGO Group's commitment to providing safe and enjoyable digital experiences, while empowering children to play, learn and share.

We've learned from millions of consumers around the world that parents understand that digital technology is now integral to their children's lives, and there is overwhelming support for trusted partners to provide social media channels designed for children's use.

Social media offers fantastic possibilities for children to connect with each other across the world and share creativity and play experiences. We believe children should have access to social networking and have developed LEGO® Life, a safe social platform just for children and 'tweens' that inspires them to build and share their stories and creations with thousands of other children around the world. It is designed to be a child's first digital social experience, taking users by the hand and introducing them to some of the core concepts of a social network.

Included in LEGO Life is our safety pledge, which provides support for parents to talk to their children about digital safety while establishing a shared commitment to ground rules for online social behaviour. We encourage parents to share digital experiences together with their children, take interest in their favourite apps, talk about digital protection and take the safety pledge (Be Safe, Be Cool, Respect Others and Have Fun) together with their children.

We believe that responsible brands, hand in hand with parents, have a significant role to play in ensuring that the evolution of technology contributes to children's

well-being and development. However, governments also have an important role to play – a role that is not simply about adding new rules and restrictions, but one that reflects on the broader legislative framework and seeks to ensure that this does not stifle children's creativity, nor tie the hands of responsible companies seeking to use technology to inspire and excite.

As we look to the future, therefore, it is important that we strike the right balance. A balance between protection and empowerment. A balance that gives children and parents the confidence necessary for fun and independent play but avoids the level of disruption that may drive children away from safe online spaces. A balance that respects children's right to privacy

and the importance of parental consent yet recognizes that digital play experiences can help children develop vital skills for the twenty-first century.

At the LEGO Group, we believe that the road to success is found through strong partnerships. By working together, industry, parents, policymakers and civil society can deliver safe, inspiring and empowering digital play experiences for children.

Niels B. Christiansen has been CEO of the LEGO Group since October 2017. Before joining the company, he was the CEO of Danfoss A/S and, earlier, executive vice president at GN Store Nord. Niels has a Master of Science in Engineering from the Technical University of Denmark and holds an MBA from INSEAD in France.

"Innovation in digital technology represents a tremendous opportunity for bringing playful and educational experiences to children around the world," writes Neils B. Christiansen.
© UNICEF/UN040222

05
Digital Priorities: Harness the good, limit the harm

**JENN LITTLE, 16
UNITED STATES**

"For me, it took exactly 20 clicks to reach out to an organization that provides students in the US with fundraising opportunities to help other kids go to school. ... To my peers in Generation Z: We must all remember that as children of the digital age we have immense power. Let's use it for good."

Full articles by youth contributors featured in
The State of the World's Children 2017 can be found at:
<www.voicesofyouth.org/en/sections/content/pages/sowc-2017>

It has been said that it's never a good idea to make predictions, especially about the future.☺

But there is no doubt that the futures of a rapidly growing number of children will be increasingly affected by digital technology.

Children already account for a substantial percentage of the global networked population, and their share will only increase in the future as internet penetration reaches ever further into regions with the most rapidly growing share of children and young people. Africa, for example, is expected by the middle of the century to become home to 40 per cent of all global under-fives, and 37 per cent of under-18s.[1]

More digital devices and online platforms, not fewer, will be available for children's use. ICTs will continue shaping children's lives, for better and for worse, just as emerging technologies like the Internet of Things and artificial intelligence help transform the digital landscape at a global scale.

As this report has shown, children will continue to experience these transformations in varied ways that also reflect how they experience 'the real world'. Not surprisingly, the most disadvantaged and marginalized are least likely to reap the benefits of the internet and connectivity and most likely to experience harm from the negative aspects of technology. Other critical factors – including gender, education status, traditional norms, language and location – all play a role in the impact digital technologies have in children's lives, for better and for worse.[2]

There are significant gaps in our understanding about those impacts, about the way children experience digital technology, and about the way they themselves regard the opportunities and risks of connectivity. There is an urgent need for more robust data collection, not only about whether children are or are not connected, but also why and how they

connect, and the conditions that facilitate or block their access. And more must be done to understand the opportunity costs for children living on both sides of digital divides – especially those lost by disadvantaged children with little or no access, but also offline opportunities potentially forgone by the most digitally connected children.

Especially in the absence of such information, policymakers face considerable challenges in keeping up with the rapid pace of technological change and its impact on children's lives. The internet as we know it was developed and has been regulated primarily with adult users in mind – and the assumption that users are adults continues to inform legislators, regulators and internet governance organizations.[3]

But today's children are digital natives and the internet is their second home. Policies and regulatory frameworks must catch up with this reality – especially when it comes to protecting children from the worst risks of connectivity, as those who use the internet to exploit and harm children make quick use of every loophole. But while less urgent, not less important is the need to develop policies and promote business practices that expand equitable access to online content.

The internet was developed primarily with adult users in mind.

To survive and thrive in the digital world, children need to develop a broad set of digital literacy skills.
© UNICEF/UN015600/PRINSLOO

There is no shortage of international instruments, guidelines, agreements and principles that deal with issues such as internet freedom, openness, net neutrality, accessibility and respect for human rights. What is needed are not more guidelines, per se, but agreed-upon principles and priority actions that recognize the responsibility we share to protect children from the perils of a digital world and to help all children benefit from the promise of connectivity.

This is not only in the best interests of children. In a digital world, it is also in the best interests of their societies, which can only benefit from children who are digitally literate, able to navigate among the myriad opportunities and risks of connectivity and chart a course to more productive futures.

Making the digital space better for children requires collaboration and cooperation among governments, United Nations agencies and other international children's organizations, civil society, the private sector, academia and the technical community, families and children themselves. Besides international guidelines and agreements, it requires child-focused national policy, coordinated response and sharing of best practice models.

The action points outlined here are by no means exhaustive, but together they reflect a core principle that should guide policymaking and practical action in the digital sphere: Respect and protect the child.

1. Provide all children with affordable access to high-quality online resources

Digital access is increasingly a determinant of equal opportunity for children, enabling them to benefit from access to information, knowledge, employment opportunities, community participation and social engagement. However, as discussed in Chapter 2, children face a range of barriers to accessing the internet and, if they do manage to get online, making the best use of online resources.

Chief among these, is the high cost of online access, but there are also physical barriers, including geography, poor infrastructure and lack of access to digital devices. Invisible barriers, such as gender and social norms, cultural practices and minority status, also play a role. Girls, for example, are particularly at risk of missing out on online access because of social concerns that the internet is a dangerous and inappropriate place for them. In addition, the lack of relevant content in children's own language greatly limits the usefulness of the internet for many, especially those speaking minority languages or living in remote regions.

There are issues, too, around the sort of devices that children use to access

the internet. Mobile devices have allowed some communities to leapfrog to connectivity, but these devices can provide only a 'second-best' experience, greatly limiting what children can do online in terms of extended writing and content creation. Similarly, some approaches to providing online access to underserved communities have relied on providing them with a 'walled garden' of online access – in other words, access to only a very limited number of websites.

There is real potential for all these digital divides to deepen existing socio-economic divisions. In response, it is essential to develop a full picture of how social and economic factors are shaping children's use of ICTs and the impact of ICTs on equity and opportunity.

❯ **Bring down the cost of connectivity.** Market strategies that foster innovation and competition among service providers can help lower the cost of connecting to the internet. Integrating fibre-optic cables into existing infrastructure construction for transportation, gas and electricity, telecoms and sewerage can also lower the cost of expanding connectivity. And providing tax and other incentives for the telecom industry to bring down the cost of connectivity for disadvantaged communities and families could make a significant difference.

❯ **Invest in public-access hotspots.** Public access points in schools, libraries, community centres, parks and shopping centres can dramatically increase access for unconnected children. In low-income neighbourhoods, mobile units, such as buses with Wi-Fi access, can similarly boost connectivity *(see 'Cuba's first online generation' and 'Mind the homework gap' boxes in Chapter 2).*

❯ **Promote the creation of content that is relevant to children and in their own languages.** Both the public and the private sectors should work to create

Digital access is increasingly a determinant of equal opportunity for children.

more locally developed and locally relevant content, especially in minority languages, and targeting remote areas with low population density.

❯ **Break cultural, social and gender barriers to equal online access.** Training programmes that provide girls with opportunities for safe internet use and enhance their digital skills can both build girls' confidence in using digital technology and help address family concerns *(see 'IT Girls: Bosnia and Herzegovina', Chapter 1).* Promoting community dialogue can help dispel myths around girls' use of technology and the internet. Assistive technologies and internet platforms can enable children living with disabilities to communicate more easily, support them in learning, and help them be more independent *(see iSign and Yuudee applications, Chapter 1).*

❯ **Provide children on the move with access to digital devices and connectivity.** Governments, aid agencies and the private sector should provide public internet access in refugee camps, immigration centres and other public spaces frequented by children on the move to help them stay in touch with families and friends *(see Chad box, Chapter 1).* Aid agencies should also consider working with the private sector more closely to include data services and digital devices as part of their overall aid packages.

2. Protect children from harm online

The digital age has amplified existing risks to children and created new ones. Child abuse, exploitation and trafficking online are still prevalent, not only on the Dark web but also on mainstream digital platforms and social media. In addition, children face a range of other online risks, including cyberbullying and exposure to unsuitable materials such as pornographic

or gambling sites. While most children navigate these latter risks successfully, for some the impact can be devastating and life-changing.

The international community has made some progress in formulating policies and approaches to eliminate the most egregious online risks, such as sexual exploitation, and there has been significant progress in law enforcement and support for victims. Initiatives such as the WePROTECT Global Alliance have created a framework that lays out what needs to be done at the levels of policy and governance, criminal justice, victim support, societal change, industry engagement and ethical and informed media reporting.

We need to build on these efforts – increasing coordination and knowledge sharing, scaling up approaches to help law enforcement stay ahead of online offenders, and working with the private sector to develop ethical standards that protect children.

❯ **Support law enforcement and child protection efforts.** The private sector, and particularly technology firms, have a vital role to play in sharing digital tools, knowledge and expertise with law enforcement agencies to protect children online *(see Chapter 3).*

❯ **Adopt and implement the WePROTECT Global Alliance strategic framework.** Designed to combat sexual exploitation online, the WePROTECT Global Alliance framework *(see above)* has already been adopted by 77 countries. The model sets out a coordinated response, with recommendations for action across a range of areas.

❯ **Tailor protections to reflect children's evolving capacities.** Strategies to promote children's safety online should take account of a child's age and maturity. Younger children are likely to need a great deal of support and guidance from parents, teachers and other trusted adults. But older children are likely to have greater agency and a desire to sometimes take risks. Within reason, such risk-taking is necessary for children to learn how to adapt and to develop resilience.

❯ **Support the people who can support children.** Evidence-based programmes and policies can guide us to develop strategies for parents and other caregivers to gain the skills they need to positively mediate – rather than simply restrict – children's use of ICTs. In addition, peer mentoring programmes can help children help each other more effectively, reflecting the reality that children often turn to their peers for support when they encounter online risks and harms.[4]

3. Safeguard children's privacy and identities online

In a world where every digital move can be recorded and content can reach vast audiences with a single click, children face new risks to their privacy, reputations and identities. Data generated through their use of social media, for example, can be used for inappropriate advertising and marketing, profiling and surveillance. In addition, toys connected to the internet can transmit the thoughts and feelings of even very young children to toy manufacturers and, potentially, other adults *(see 'Perspective' by Anab Jain in Special Section: Protecting children's privacy online)*.

Children often do not fully understand the risks associated with using digital media or the loss of control over content – how an embarrassing photograph or comment posted online has the potential to follow them into adulthood. More savvy children often have different views about privacy online than their parents, but they are concerned about violations committed by their peers through bullying, hate speech and harassment; by corporations and industry through the breach of their

privacy rights; by government prying and potentially interfering with their freedom of expression; and even by intrusive parents who use restrictive monitoring or spying techniques. Because children are key players in protecting their own privacy online, understanding their attitudes and opinions on these issues is important.

❯ **Put safeguards in place to protect children's privacy, personal information and reputation.** Governments, businesses, schools and many other institutions handle an increasing amount of data related to children that are either collected or stored online. All actors need to put in place safeguards to protect these data in accordance with international and ethical standards, such as consent, data anonymization, secure data storage and prohibition of unlawful disclosure of information.[5]

❯ **Set children's privacy settings at maximum by default.** Maximum privacy protection should be the basic setting for digital tools and platforms used by children, and privacy should be included in the design of all new technologies from the outset. In addition, social media and other platform companies should write their terms and conditions and privacy policies in clear language that children can understand and provide them with easy ways to report breaches of privacy or other concerns *(see 'Simplifying the Rules' in Special Section: Protecting children's privacy online)*.

❯ **Don't exploit children's personal data for commercial gain.** Businesses should not seek to monetize children's personal information, such as through targeted advertising. They should develop ethical protocols and implement heightened scrutiny and protection for the full range of data concerning children, including information on children's location and browsing habits and especially regarding their personal information.

❯ **Respect encryption for child-related and children's data.** Given children's potential vulnerabilities, additional layers of protection and privacy should be used to safeguard their data. Decisions to decrypt children's data to aid law enforcement agencies investigating online crimes, such as child sexual abuse and grooming, should be guided by the best interests of the child.

4. Teach digital literacy to keep children informed, engaged and safe online

Today's children are digital natives, but that doesn't mean they do not require guidance and support to make the most of connectivity. Similarly, they do not automatically understand their vulnerability to online risks or their own responsibility to be good digital citizens.

Digital literacy encompasses all these areas, implying a set of competencies that goes beyond digital and technical skills. It includes the ability to search, evaluate and manage information found online; interact, share and collaborate online; develop and create content; use safety and protection features, and solve problems and be creative.[6]

It also includes teaching children how to protect themselves from online dangers like cyberbullying, sextortion, loss of privacy and reputational risk. Seemingly innocuous activities, such as sharing photos, commenting on social media and filling in personal details on online forms, can have serious consequences, for example, if data fall into the wrong hands or if a private exchange between two children is spread more widely.

Investment in more sophisticated, complex digital skills is now becoming standard in schools in many higher-income countries, as well as in out-of-school initiatives that teach children coding and programming. As ICTs become more widespread in lower-income countries, similar investment will be needed to prepare children in less-wealthy countries both for life online and to equip them to work in the twenty-first century digital economy.

To improve digital literacy and make better use of ICTs in education ...

❯ **Teach digital literacy in schools.** With children going online at ever-younger ages, schools – and especially public schools – need to incorporate digital literacy programmes from the earliest years.

❯ **Provide children with access to proven online education opportunities.** The somewhat disappointing track record of ICTs in education underscores the need to pilot and test various models that really improve learning outcomes and can widen access to effective education opportunities.

❯ **Develop opportunities to learn ICT skills in non-formal education.** Disadvantaged children who have slipped outside, or were never part of, formal education systems frequently have the most to gain from online learning opportunities. Providing digital access in training centres, such as Women in Technology Uganda *(see Chapter 1)*, may be their only chance to engage with ICTs.

❯ **Support the development of teachers' digital skills and literacies.** Teachers need to be able to develop their own skills and knowledge to support their students' use of ICTs and to help them develop an understanding of safe internet use beyond the classroom.

❯ **Support the establishment of online libraries.** Online libraries, such as the Library for All, can open up a world of resources – including digital books and textbooks, videos and music – to children who would otherwise lack such access.

To teach children to keep themselves safe online and respect other users ...

❯ **Understand the risks of content creation and sharing.** Children need to be taught that everything they post online – from social media comments to videos – can no longer be considered private and potentially cannot be erased. Equally, children need to be made aware that self-generated content, such as sharing sexually explicit images, opens them up to the risk of extortion and their content may well end up being exchanged by strangers online.

❯ **Learn how to protect privacy and personal data online.** Children need to be taught how to control their privacy settings to protect their personal information – name, date of birth, address, friends, family, school and personal photographs – and understand the danger that if such data are made public it may lead to identity theft and data mining among other risks.

❯ **Strengthen the teaching of online tolerance and empathy.** Children need to be helped to understand the ways in which communicating online – with its lack of verbal and facial clues to meaning and its potential for anonymity – is different from traditional communication. Socio-emotional learning and the teaching of empathy can develop children's online resilience and help diminish online abuse and hateful language. Such themes need to be incorporated into curricula for digital literacy.

❯ **Be good digital role models for children.** It's not just children who

are fascinated by digital technologies. Parents and other adults need to offer children models of responsible and respectful use of ICTs.

5. Leverage the power of the private sector to advance ethical standards and practices that protect and benefit children online

The private sector has been a key driver of the digital revolution. As providers of internet access, producers and providers of content and other digital goods, and purveyors of online goods and services, businesses are now increasingly integrated into children's lives. As gatekeepers controlling the flow of information across the networks, they also have access to vast amounts of children's information and data. These roles provide businesses with considerable power and influence – and with these come heightened responsibilities.

Businesses have an indispensable role to play in protecting children, working with governments to take down child-abuse material or other inappropriate content, raising awareness of safe and responsible internet use, and protecting children's privacy. It is not enough to preach personal responsibility – the private sector must actively help children to guard their privacy, such as by changing default settings and providing regular advice to users.

The private sector must also lead in developing ethical technologies. For example, social media apps should aim to do more than simply keep children logged on for as long as possible *(see box, 'The role of (un)ethical design', Chapter 4)*. Instead, technology companies should set out to serve children's real needs, even if that means children spend less time online.

Everything children post online can no longer be considered private and potentially cannot be erased.

"

Internet policies fail to take sufficient account of children's distinctive needs and rights.

These issues will become ever more pressing as more powerful technologies like artificial intelligence and more immersive technologies like augmented and virtual reality become ever more integrated into children's lives.

These actions are not only the right thing to do; they are sound business decisions. There is a real risk of reputational harm for any business that is seen to be failing some of its most vulnerable customers – children.

❯ **Prevent networks and services from disseminating child-abuse material.**
Technology and internet companies should take steps to prevent their networks and services from being used by offenders to collect and distribute child sexual abuse images. Continuously monitoring the flow of goods, services, images and texts that pose the greatest threats to children and working with law enforcement and other stakeholders to find innovative solutions to online criminal activities can help keep children safer online and off. *(See, for example, 'Microsoft's Photo DNA' on page 87.)*

❯ **Promote non-discriminatory access.**
Companies can do more to provide children, particularly those in underserved areas, with access to the internet. They should also uphold shared principles, such as net neutrality, especially when these enable children to access a wide variety of sources and information.

❯ **Develop ethical standards for businesses and technologies.**
Businesses should work with policymakers and child rights advocates to develop minimum ethical standards for their services, and embrace the principle of 'safety by design', incorporating safety, privacy and security features into their products before they are made available to the public.

❯ **Offer parents the tools to create an age-appropriate online environment.**
Businesses should offer parents a fuller

range of easy-to-use tools – such as password protection, block/allow lists, age verification and filtering – that will allow them to create a safe online space for their children, especially younger children. Businesses should commit to constant monitoring and evaluation of these tools to make sure they really are contributing to child safety online without unfairly restricting children's legitimate freedoms.

6. Put children at the centre of digital policy

Despite estimates that children account for one third of internet users, current international and national internet policies fail to take sufficient account of children's distinctive needs and rights. Policies related to cybersecurity, artificial intelligence and machine learning, net neutrality and internet openness look first and foremost at the adult user. On the other hand, broader national policies that deal with children's rights and welfare, health and education have yet to universally embrace the power of digital technologies to help meet sectoral goals.[7]

To understand the power of the internet in helping to realize children's rights and to help create greater equality of opportunity, a determined effort is needed to collect data on barriers to access and on how and why children use ICTs. Children's needs must also be integrated in all ICT regulation and policy, the development of which should be informed by children's own views and outlooks.

❯ **Give children and young people a voice in the development of digital policies that affect their lives.** Policymakers should seek out children's distinctive experiences and needs by engaging institutions that uphold children's rights, including human

---

Internet governance

Who runs the internet? The simple answer is no one. Instead, a broad system of 'internet governance' is spread out across a range of entities, including international bodies, national governments, the private sector and civil society. Without central coordination, these entities have over time developed the principles, norms, rules, decision-making procedures and programmes that allow the internet to operate and expand its reach.

Initially, internet governance focused mainly on technical issues and infrastructure, but it gradually expanded to include issues such as cybersecurity, e-commerce, net neutrality, human rights and other issues.

More recently, there is growing interest in exploring how more coordinated internet governance can specifically support economic and social development. In 2015, the World Summit on the Information Society (WSIS+10) emphasized that access to ICTs has also become a development indicator and aspiration in and of itself. Even though none of the 17 Sustainable Development Goals focuses specifically on ICT, digital technology can contribute to the achievement of a number of child-focused goals, including ending poverty and hunger (SDGs 1 and 2), improving health and well-being (SDG 3), expanding educational opportunity (SDG 4), achieving gender equity (SDG 5) and tackling inequality (SDG 10).

Youth initiatives, such as Youth@IGF and NextGen@ICANN, focus on engaging young people in debates about the future of internet governance – though more can and should be done to incorporate children's experiences and perspectives now in shaping the debate around a safer and more inclusive internet.

---

rights commissioners, civil society organizations and children themselves. More broadly, government and civil society should encourage children to use digital platforms to improve their communities and societies.

❯ **Track disparities in, and barriers to, access.** To track the impact of internet access on equity and opportunity, it is vital to invest in the collection of data on children's connectivity *(see 'Information Poverty' in Chapter 2)*. Data should be disaggregated by wealth, geography, gender, age and other factors to spotlight disparities in access and opportunity and to target programmes and monitor progress. Evidence should be used to guide policymaking, monitor and evaluate the impact of government policies and strategies, and support the international sharing of best practices.

❯ **Integrate child- and gender-specific issues into national policies and strategies.** The legitimate needs and concerns of children should be integrated in all policies concerning ICTs and other emerging technologies, such as artificial intelligence. Policies should be guided by international standards and should seek to safeguard children's rights and guard against discrimination and the restriction of children's freedoms.

The testimonials and perspectives of children and young people in this report make it very clear that if given the chance – and provided with the skills – children will make the most of connectivity. Even with low access to ICTs, inadequate equipment, teachers who know less about digital technology than they do, and adults who are uncomfortable with the pace of change, millions of children around the world are already using the internet to learn, socialize and prepare themselves to take their place as adults in the workplace – and to make their mark upon the world.

They are eager for that chance – and they deserve it. It is up to all of us to see that every one of them gets it.

Endnotes

CHAPTER 1: DIGITAL OPPORTUNITIES: THE PROMISE OF CONNECTIVITY

1   Based on reporting by *The State of the World's Children* report team at Za'atari refugee camp in May 2017.

2   Réseau des journalistes amis de l'enfant (Journalists Network of Friends of the Child).

3   Gary Wolf, 'Steve Jobs: The next insanely great thing', *Wired*, 1 February 1996, pp. 102–163.

4   United Nations Educational, Scientific and Cultural Organization, *Leveraging Information and Communication Technologies to Achieve the Post-2015 Education Goal: Report of the International Conference on ICT and Post-2015 Education*, UNESCO, Paris, 2015, p. 22.

5   United Nations Children's Fund and Move, 'Igarité: Overview of face-to-face teaching with technological mediation in the state of Amazonas', UNICEF Brazil, 2017.

6   Pence, Audrey, 'Mobilizing Literacy: Cell phones help Afghan women learn to read', *Solutions*, vol. 6, no. 3, 2015, pp. 8–9.

7   United Nations Educational, Scientific and Cultural Organization, 'Study on International Collaboration on Open Educational Resources (OER)', Commissioned study prepared under a consultant contract for UNESCO, December 2016.

8   See Inoue, Keiko, et al., 'Out-of-School Youth in Sub-Saharan Africa: A policy perspective', World Bank, Washington, D.C., 2015; and Scott, Molly M., Simone Zhang and Heather Koball, 'Dropping Out and Clocking In: A portrait of teens who leave school early and work', Urban Institute, Washington, D.C., April 2015.

9   Njideka, Harry, 'Pioneering the Youth and Technology Movement in Africa and Beyond', *MIT Press Journals*, vol. 10, no. 1–2, 2015, p. 8.

10 Evaluation of UNDP/UNICEF/UN Women, IT Girls Project: Final report, Sarajevo, December 2016.

11 Toyama, Kentaro, 'Children's Education in a Digital Age', Background research paper for *The State of the World's Children 2017: Children in a Digital World*, University of Michigan, 2 February 2017.

12 Flores, Pablo, and Juan Pablo Hourcade, 'Under Development: One year of experiences with XO laptops in Uruguay', *Interactions*, vol. 16, no. 4, 2009, pp. 52–55.

13 Cristia, Julián P., et al., 'Technology and Child Development: Evidence from the One Laptop per Child Program', IZA Discussion Paper no. 6401, IZA, Bonn, March 2012, p. 4.

14 'Goodbye, One Laptop Per Child', *OLPC News*, 11 March 2014.

15 'The Learning Generation: Investing in education for a changing world', A Report on the International Commission for Financing Global Education Opportunity, New York, 2016, p. 59, fig. 13.

16 Toyama, 'Children's Education in a Digital Age'.

17 Banerjee, Abhijeet V., et al., 'Remedying Education: Evidence from two randomized experiments in India', *Quarterly Journal of Economics*, vol. 122, no. 3, 1 August 2007, pp. 1235–1264.

18 Muralidharan, Karthik, Abhijeet Singh and Alejandro J. Ganimian, *Disrupting Education? Experimental evidence on technology-aided instruction in India*,

NBER Working Paper no. 22923, National Bureau of Economic Research, Cambridge, Mass., 2016.

19 <www.avallainfoundation.org>

20 Avallain Foundation, 'The Avallain Foundation RCT-Based Impact Study: The impact of a-ACADEMY digital learning platform on children's performance in class 6 science in Kenya', 2017.

21 Focus group discussion conducted by *The State of the World's Children* report team with children in the Hanka Educational Centre, located in Mathare, Kenya.

22 Barrera-Osorio, Felipe, and Leigh L. Linden, 'The Use and Misuse of Computers in Education: Evidence from a randomized experiment in Colombia', Policy Research Working Paper no. 4836, World Bank, February 2009.

23 Fairlie, Robert W., and Jonathan Robinson, 'Experimental Evidence on the Effects of Home Computers on Academic Achievement among Schoolchildren', *American Economic Journal: Applied Economics*, vol. 5, no. 3, 2013, pp. 211–240.

24 Banerjee et al., 'Remedying Education'.

25 Toyama, 'Children's Education in a Digital Age'.

26 Organisation for Economic Co-operation and Development, 'Students, Computers and Learning: Making the connection', OECD Publishing, Paris 2015.

27 World Bank, *World Development Report 2018: Learning to realize education's promise*, World Bank, Washington, D.C., 2018, p. 145.

28   Toyama, *Children's Education in a Digital Age.*

29   Beland, Louis-Philippe, and Richard Murphy, 'Ill communication: Technology, distraction & student performance', *Labour Economics,* vol. 41, no. C, 2016, pp. 61–76. <www.sciencedirect.com/science/article/pii/S0927537116300136>

30   Duflo, Esther, Rema Hanna and Stephen P. Ryan, 'Incentives Work: Getting teachers to come to school', *American Economic Review,* vol. 102, no. 4, 2012, pp. 1241–1278.

31   Bannerjee et al., 'Remedying Education'; and Muralidharan et al., *Disrupting Education?*

32   Abdul Latif Jameel Poverty Action Lab, 'Remedial Education: Reorienting classroom instruction has improved learning opportunities for 47.7 million students in India, J-PAL.

33   Penuel, William R., 'Implementation and Effects of One-to-One Computing Initiatives: A research synthesis', *Journal of Research on Technology in Education,* vol. 38, no. 3, 2006, pp. 329–348 <www.tandfonline.com/doi/pdf/10.1080/15391523.2006.10782463>

34   Hagen, Erica, 'Mapping Change: Community information empowerment in Kibera (Innovations Case Narrative: Map Kibera)', *Innovations: Technology, Governance, Globalization,* vol. 6, no. 1, Winter 2011, MIT pp. 69–94.

35   Lazzeri, Thais, 'O menino tímido que abalou Brasília' (The shy boy who shook Brasília), *Epóca,* 17 July 2013; and Lima, Luciana, 'Em Brasília, jovem de 17 anos mobilizou mais de 10 mil pessoas' (In Brasilia, a 17-year-old young man mobilized 10,000 people), *Último Segundo',* 20 June 2013.

36   Kelly, Sanja, et al., 'Freedom on the Net 2016: Silencing the messenger – Communication apps under pressure', Freedom House, Washington, D.C., 2016, p. 19.

37   International Telecommunications Union, *Digital Opportunities: Innovative ICT solutions for youth employment,* ITU, Geneva, 2014; and World Bank, *World Development Report 2016: Digital dividends,* World Bank, Washington, D.C., 2016.

38   Raftree, Linda, 'Landscape Review: Mobiles for youth workforce development', JBS International, Rockland, Maryland, 2013, p. 25.

39   Ibid., p. 3.

40   <www.facebook.com/groups/oportunidadesp arainternacionalistas>

41   Raftree, 'Landscape Review', p. 2.

42   International Telecommunications Union, *Digital Opportunities,* ITU, Geneva, 2014, pp. 18–21.

43   Raftree, 'Landscape Review', p. 2.

44   World Bank, *World Development Report 2016,* p. xiii.

45   World Economic Forum, 'The Future of Jobs: Employment, skills and workforce strategy for the fourth industrial revolution', Global Challenge Insight Report, World Economic Forum, Geneva, January 2016, p. v.

46   Schwab, Klaus, 'The Fourth Industrial Revolution: What it means and how to respond', *Foreign Affairs,* December 2015.

47   Jütting, Johannes, and Christopher Garroway, 'The Rise of the Robots: Friend or foe for developing countries?', OECD Insights: Debate the issues, Organisation for Economic Co-operation and Development, 2 March 2016.

48   United Nations Educational, Scientific and Cultural Organization, *The Global Learning Crisis: Why every child deserves a quality education,* UNESCO, Paris, 2013, p. 2.

49   World Economic Forum, 'New Vision for Education: Unlocking the potential of technology', World Economic Forum, Geneva, 2015, p. 3.

50   Kautz, Tim, et al., 'Fostering and Measuring Skills: Improving cognitive and non-cognitive skills to promote lifetime success', Organisation for Economic Co-operation and Development, Paris, p. 54.

51   Morgenstern, Michael, 'Automation and Anxiety: Will smarter machines cause mass unemployment?', *The Economist,* 25 June 2016.

52   Ian Stewart, Debapratim De and Alex Cole, 'Technology and People: The great job-creating machine', Deloitte LLP, August 2015.

53   United Nations Children's Fund, *Uprooted: The growing crisis for refugee and migrant children,* UNICEF, New York, 2016, p. 1.

54   Maitland, Carleen, et al., 'Youth Mobile Phone and Internet Use: January 2015 – Za'atari Camp, Mafraq, Jordan', Penn State College of Information Sciences and Technology, October 2015, p. 3.

55   Raftree, Linda, Katie Appel and Anika Ganness, 'Modern Mobility: The role of ICTs in child and youth migration', Plan International, Washington, D.C., 2013, p. 17, 20–25.

56   Ibid., p. 3.

57   Vernon, Alan, Kamel Deriche and Samantha Eisenhauer, *Connecting Refugees: How internet and mobile connectivity can improve refugee well-being and transform humanitarian action,* UNHCR, Geneva, September 2016, pp. 12–13.

58   Ibid., p. 25.

59   United Nations Educational, Scientific and Cultural Organization, 'Debates on the implementation of the 2005 Convention on the Protection and Promotion of the Diversity of Cultural Expressions', UNESCO, Paris, 2015. p. 2.

60   Rice, Emma S., et al., 'Social Media and Digital Technology Use among Indigenous Young People in Australia: A literature review', *International Journal for Equity in Health,* vol. 15, no. 81, 2016.

61   Jenzen, Olu, and Irmi Karl, 'Make, Share, Care: Social media and LGBTQ youth engagement', *Ada: A Journal of Gender, New Media & Technology,* no. 5, 2014, p. 4.

62   The Gay, Lesbian & Straight Education Network, Center for Innovative Public Health Research and Crimes Against Children Research Center, 'Out Online: The experiences of lesbian, gay, bisexual and transgender youth on the internet', GLSEN, New York, 2013.

63   Child Helpline International, 'The Voices of Children and Young People. 2015 in Numbers: Child Helpline Global Highlights, CHI, Amsterdam, 2015, p. 1.

64   Child Helpline International, '2015 Annual Report', CHI, Amsterdam, p. 7.

65   United Nations Children's Fund, *The State of the World's Children 2013: Children with disabilities,* UNICEF, New York, 2013, p. 20.

66   Kaye, Stephen H., 'Disability and the Digital Divide', U.S. Department of Education, Washington, D.C., 2000; and Dobransky, Kerry, and Eszter Hargittai, 'The Disability Divide in Internet Access and Use', *Information Communication and Society,* vol. 9, no. 3, 2006, pp. 313–334.

67   Livingstone, Sonia, and Monica E. Bulger, 'A Global Agenda for Children's Rights in the Digital Age: Recommendations for developing UNICEF's research strategy', UNICEF Office of Research-Innocenti, Florence, September 2013.

68   Third, Amanda, 'Method Guide 6: Researching the benefits and opportunities for children online', Global Kids Online, London, November 2016, p. 21.

69   Byrne, Jasmina, et al., 'Global Kids Online Research Synthesis: 2015–2016', UNICEF Office of Research-Innocenti and London School of Economics and Political Science, Florence, November 2016, p. 11.

70   Based on an interview conducted by Brian Keeley and Céline Little (and translated by Samir Badran) with a family in the Za'atari Refugee Camp in Jordan on 14 May 2017.

71   United Nations Committee on the Rights of the Child, Report of the 2014 Day of General Discussion on Digital Media and Children's Rights, p. 9.

72   Jones, Lisa M., and Kimberly J. Mitchell, 'Defining and Measuring Youth Digital Citizenship', *News Media & Society,* vol. 18, no. 9, 2015, p. 2074.

73   Byrne et al., 'Global Kids Online Research Synthesis: 2015–2016', pp. 44–45.

74   United States Agency for International Development, 'Technical Brief: Use of technology in the Ebola response in West Africa', USAID, November 2014.

75   Ibid.

76   United Nations Global Pulse and GSMA, 'The State of Mobile Data for Social Good Report', UN Global Pulse and GSMA, 2017, p. 7.

77   Lopez Fernebrand, Tomas, 'How Travel Data Can Help Manage the Spread of the Zika Virus', UNICEF Stories of Innovation, 19 July 2016.

78   Fabian, Christopher, 'Can Big Data be Used as a Social Good in the Fight against Disease Epidemics?', UNICEF Stories of Innovation, 19 July 2016.

79   United Nations Children's Fund, *Education Uprooted: For every migrant, refugee and displaced child, education,* UNICEF, New York, September 2017.

80   Gaunt, Anna, 'UNHCR Cash Assistance: Improving refugee lives and supporting local economies – Post distribution monitoring for Syrian refugees', UNHCR, Jordan, 2016.

81   GSMA, 'Landscape Report: Mobile money, humanitarian cash transfers and displaced populations', GSMA, London, 2017, pp. 12–13.

82   United Nations Children's Fund, 'Cash Based Approaches in UNICEF's Humanitarian Action', UNICEF, May 2016, p. 2.

83   Global Innovation Exchange, 'Principles for Digital Payments in Humanitarian Response', 2016, p. 1.

84   Raymond, Nathaniel A., and Casey S. Harrity, 'Addressing the 'Doctrine Gap': Professionalising the use of information communication technologies in humanitarian action', Humanitarian Exchange, no. 66, Humanitarian Practice Network at the Overseas Development Institute, London, April 2016, p. 13.

85   Berman, Gabrielle, and Kerry Albright, 'Children and the Data Cycle: Rights and ethics in a big data world', Innocenti Working Paper 2017–05, UNICEF Office of Research-Innocenti, Florence, 2017, p. 10.

86   O'Brien, Stephen, 'This Is How We Build a Stronger, Data-Driven Humanitarian Sector', World Economic Forum, January 2017.

87   Raymond and Harrity, 'Addressing the 'Doctrine Gap', p. 13.

CHAPTER 2: DIGITAL DIVIDES: MISSED OPPORTUNITIES

1   ITU estimates for this report, 2017.

2   International Telecommunication Union, *ICT Facts and Figures 2016,* ITU, Geneva, p. 3; Facebook, *State of Connectivity 2015: A report on global internet access,* Facebook, Menlo Park, Calif., 2016, p. 36.

3   *Measuring the Information Society Report 2016,* ITU, Geneva, pp. 179–181, 190.

4   International Telecommunication Union, *ICT Facts and Figures 2016.*

5   Livingstone, Sonia, 'Method Guide 1: A framework for researching Global Kids Online – Understanding children's well-being and rights in the digital age', Global Kids Online, London, November 2016, p. 17.

6   Raftree, Linda, Katie Appel and Anika Ganness, 'Modern Mobility: The role of ICTs in child and youth migration', Plan International, Washington, D.C., 2013, p. 17, 20–25.

7   World Bank, *World Development Report 2016: Digital dividends,* World Bank, Washington, D.C., 2016, p. 14.

8   Organisation for Economic Co-operation and Development, 'Does Having Digital Skills Really

Pay Off?', Adult Skills in Focus No. 1, OECD Publishing, Paris, June 2015, p. 3.

9   Liu, CheWei, and Sunil Mithas, 'The Returns to Digital Skills: Evidence from India – 2005–2011', Research Paper submitted at the Thirty-Seventh International Conference on Information Systems, Dublin, 2016, p. 11.

10 Aissaoui, Najeh, and Lobna Ben Hassen, 'Skills-biased Technological Change, E-Skills and Wage Inequality: Evidence from Tunisia', *Journal of Economics Studies and Research,* vol. 2016, art. ID 492224, 2016, pp. 13–14.

11 Poushter, Jacob, 'Smartphone Ownership and Internet Usage Continues to Climb in Emerging Economies', Pew Research Center, 22 February 2016, p. 16.

12 Basu, Kaushik, 'Development in the digital age', *Let's Talk Development,* World Bank, Washington, D.C., 28 September 2015.

13 Kleine, Dorothea, David Hollow and Sammia Poveda, 'Children, ICT and Development: Capturing the potential, meeting the challenges', Innocenti Insight, Unicef Office of Research, Florence, 2013, p. 19.

14 International Telecommunication Union, *ICT Facts and Figures 2017,* ITU, Geneva, 2017, p. 1.

15 ITU estimates, 2017.

16 Eurostat, ITU and UNICEF, 2012–2016.

17 International Telecommunication Union, *Measuring the Information Society Report 2016,* p. 135.

18 Organisation for Economic Co-operation and Development, 'Students, Computers and Learning: Making the connection', OECD Publishing, Paris, 2015, p. 129.

19 International Telecommunication Union, *ICT Facts and Figures 2016.*

20 International Telecommunication Union and the United Nations Educational, Scientific and Cultural Organization, *The State of Broadband 2015: Broadband as a foundation for sustainable development,* ITU and UNESCO, Geneva, September 2015, p. 9.

21 GSM Association, 'Bridging the Gender Gap: Mobile access and usage in low- and middle-income countries', GSMA, London, 2015, pp. 6–9, 29.

22 Ibid., p. 6.

23 Horrigan, John B., 'The Numbers behind the Broadband 'Homework Gap', Pew Research Center, 20 April 2015.

24 Ibid.

25 McLaughlin, Clare, 'The Homework Gap: The "cruelest part of the digital divide"', *neaToday* (News and Features from the National Education Association), 20 April 2016.

26 Hispanic Heritage Foundation, myCollege Options and Family Online Safety Institute, 'Taking the Pulse of the High School Student Experience in America: Research Findings – 'Access to technology' Phase 1 of 6', 2015, p. 11.

27 Kang, Cecilia, 'Bridging a Digital Divide that Leaves Schoolchildren Behind', *The New York Times,* 22 February 2016.

28 Vick, Carl, 'internet for All', *Time,* 10 April 2017, pp. 34–35.

29 Kang 'Bridging a Digital Divide that Leaves Schoolchildren Behind'.

30 UNICEF India, *Child Online Protection in India,* UNICEF India, New Delhi, 2016, p. 46; and DNA India, 'Uttar Pradesh: Muslim village panchayat bans jeans, mobile phones for girls', D*aily News & Analysis (DNA),* 20 September 2015.

31 The study included a sample of 5,349 children from government, private and international schools. Information was also collected from school principals and IT teachers. Focus group discussions were also held with parents and heavy users.

32 UNICEF Sri Lanka, *Keeping Children in Sri Lanka Safe and Empowered Online: A study on Sri Lanka's digital landscape – potential risks to children and young people who are online,* UNICEF, Colombo, Sri Lanka, 2015.

33 Livingstone, Sonia, et al., 'Young Adolescents and Digital Media Uses, Risks and Opportunities in Low- and Middle-Income Countries: A Rapid Evidence review', Gender and Adolescence: Global Evidence (GAGE), London, 2017, p. 3.

34 Hargittai, Eszter, 'Second-Level Digital Divide: Differences in people's online skills', *First Monday,* vol. 7, no. 4, April 2002.

35 Van Deursen, Alexander J.A.M., and Jan A.G.M. van Dijk, 'The Digital Divide Shifts to Differences in Usage', *New Media & Society,* Vol. 16, no. 3, 2014, p. 520; Van DIJK, Jan A.G.M., 'The Evolution of the Digital Divide: The digital divide turns to inequality of skills and usage', *Digital Enlightenment Yearbook 2012,* IOS Press, Amsterdam, 2012, pp. 57–75; Pearce, Katy E., and Ronald E. Rice, 'Digital Divides from Access to Activities: Comparing mobile and personal internet users', *Journal of Communication,* vol. 63, no. 4, August 2013, pp. 721–744; and Hargittai, Eszter, and Amanda Hinnant, 'Differences in Young Adults' Use of the Internet', *Communication Research,* vol. 35, no. 5, 3 September 2008.

36 International Telecommunication Union, *Measuring the Information Society Report 2016,* pp. 199–201; Van Deursen and van Dijk, 'The Digital Divide Shifts to Differences in Usage'.

37 Van DIJK, Jan A.G.M., 'The Evolution of the Digital Divide'; and Andreasson, Kim, 'Redefining the Digital Divide: A Report from The Economist Intelligence Unit', The Economist Intelligence Unit Limited, London, 2013, pp. 8–9.

38 Sonck, N., et al, 'Digital Literacy and Safety Skills', *EU Kids Online,* London School of Economics and Political Science, London, July 2011, p. 2; Livingstone, Sonia, et al., 'EU Kids Online: Final report', London School of Economics and Political Science, London, 2011.

39 Organisation for Economic Co-operation and Development, 'Students, Computers and Learning' p. 137; and Van Deursen and van Dijk, 'The Digital Divide Shifts to Differences in Usage'.

40 Livingstone, Sonia, and Ellen Helsper, 'Gradations in Digital Inclusion: Children, young people and the digital divide', *New Media & Society,* vol. 9, no. 4, 2007, p. 6.

41   Napoli, Philip M., and Jonathan A. Obar, 'Mobile Leapfrogging and Digital Divide Policy: Assessing the limitations of mobile internet access', New America Foundation, Washington, D.C., April 2013, p. 9; Pearce and Rice, 'Digital Divides from Access to Activities', pp. 737–738; and Horrigan, John B., 'Smartphone and Broadband: Tech users see them as complements and very few would give up their home broadband subscription in favor of their smartphone', Discussion paper Prepared for the Silicon Flatirons/MIT Workshop 2015 on 'The internet & Television Expo', Cambridge, Mass., November 2014.

42   Caribou Digital, 'Digital Access in Africa', Farnham, Surrey, UK, p. 14.

43   Napoli, Philip M., and Jonathan A. Obar, 'Mobile Leapfrogging and Digital Divide Policy', p. 9.

44   Madden, Mary, et al., 'Teens and Technology 2013', Pew Research Center, Washington, D.C., 13 March 2013, p. 8.

45   Katz, Vikki, 'Opportunity for all? Digital equity in the lives of lower-income U.S. families', <http://digitalequityforlearning.org> Learning Research Network, 24 February 2017.

46   Byrne, Jasmina, et al., 'Global Kids Online Research Synthesis: 2015–2016', UNICEF Office of Research-Innocenti and London School of Economics and Political Science, Florence, 2016, pp. 36–37.

47   Malcolm, Jeremy, Corynne McSherry and Kit Walsh, 'Zero Rating: What it is and why you should care', Electronic Frontier Foundation, 18 February 2016.

48   International Telecommunication Union, Measuring the Information Society Report 2016, p. 101.

49   Surman, Mark, Corina Gardner and David Ascher, 'Local Content, Smartphones and Digital Inclusion', Innovations, vol. 9, 2014, p. 65.

50   International Telecommunication Union and the United Nations Educational, Scientific and Cultural Organization, The State of Broadband 2016: Broadband catalzying sustainable development, ITU and UNESCO, Geneva, p. 11; Pearce, Katy E., and Ronald E. Rice, 'The Language Divide: The persistence

of English proficiency as a gateway to the internet – The cases of Armenia, Azerbaijan, and Georgia', International Journal of Communication, vol. 8, 2014, pp. 2834–2859.

51   Facebook, State of Connectivity 2015, pp. 26–27; World Bank, World Development Report 2016, p. 104; and McKinsey & Company, 'Offline and Falling Behind: Barriers to internet adoption, technology, media, and telecom', McKinsey & Company, 2014.

52   Statista, The Statistics Portal, available at <www.statista.com/statistics/262946/share-of-the-most-common-languages-on-the-internet>; and Facebook, State of Connectivity 2015, pp. 26–27.

53   Facebook, State of Connectivity 2015, p. 27.

54   Ibid.

55   Johnson, Melvin, et al., 'Google's Multilingual Neural Machine Translation System: Enabling Zero-Shot translation', Transactions of the Association for Computational Linguistics, vol. 5, 2017, pp. 339–351.

56   Hargittai, Eszter, and Gina Walejko, 'The Participation Divide: Content creation and sharing in the digital age', Information, Communication and Society, vol. 11, no. 2, 2008, pp. 239–256 <https://soc334technologyandsociety.files.wordpress.com/2012/08/hargittaiwale jko2008.pdf>; and Graham, Mark, et al., 'Uneven Geographies of User-Generated Information: Patterns of increasing informational poverty', Annals of the Association of America Geographers, vol. 104, no. 4, 2014, pp. 746–764; and <http://geography.oii.ox.ac.uk/?page=the-geographically-uneven-coverage-of-wikipedia>.

57   Graham, Mark, et al., 'Uneven Geographies of User-Generated Information'.

58   Anderson, Monica, 'Wikipedia at 15: Millions of readers in scores of languages', Pew Research Center, Washington, D.C., 14 January 2016.

59   Graham, Mark, et al., 'Uneven Geographies of User-Generated Information'.

60   World Bank, World Development Report 2016: Digital dividends, p. 8.

61   Public Empiricus, 'From Snoring Camels to Product Diversification: A gendered analysis of internet participation in Ghana, Kenya, Nigeria and South Africa', 20 February 2017.

62   ETECSA Directorate of Institutional Communication, 2017.

63   Cuban Ministry of Commerce and Foreign Investment, 2017.

64   Organisation for Economic Co-operation and Development, 'Students, Computers and Learning', p. 16.

65   GSM Association, 'Accelerating affordable smartphone ownership in emerging Markets', GSM Association, London, July 2017, p. 9.

66   Caribou Digital, 'Digital Access in Africa', p. 13.

67   GSM Association, 'The Mobile Economy 2016', GSMA, London, 2016, pp. 2–4.

68   Kleine, Hollow and Poveda, 'Children, ICT and Development', p. 16; GSM Association, 'The Mobile Economy 2016', p. 4.

69   Data from UNICEF's Data and Analytics Section, Division of Research and Policy.

70   GSM Association, 'Connected Society: Consumer barriers to mobile internet adoption in Africa', GSMA, London, 2016, p. 6.

71   GSM Association, 'The Mobile Economy 2017', GSMA, London, 2016, p. 11.

72   Lall, Somik Vinay, et al., Africa's Cities: Opening Doors to the World, World Bank, Washington, D.C., 2017, p. 17.

73   United Nations Children's Fund, 'Generation 2030 Africa', UNICEF, New York, 2014, p. 9.

74   International Telecommunication Union, Measuring the Information Society Report 2016, p. 210.

75   ITU 2017 Data; Byrne, Jasmina, et al., 'Global Kids Online Research Synthesis: 2015–2016', p. 16.

76   Livingstone, Sonia, and Monica Bulger, 'A Global Agenda for Children's Rights in the Digital Age: Recommendations for developing UNICEF's research strategy', London School of Economics

and Political Science and UNICEF Office of Research-Innocenti, London and Florence, 2013, p. 4.

77 Lenhart, Amanda, 'Teens, Social Media & Technology Overview 2015', Pew Research Center, Washington, D. C., April 2015, p. 16.

78 Mascheroni, Giovanna, and Andrea Cuman, 'Net Children Go Mobile: Final Report (with country fact sheets) – Deliverables D6.4 and D5.2', Educatt, Milan, November 2014, pp. 5–6; Third, Amanda, et al., 'Children's Rights in the Digital Age: A Download from Children Around the world', Young and Well Cooperative Research Centre, Melbourne, 2014, p. 31.

79 Hajdinjak, Marko, et al., 'Online Experiences of Children in Bulgaria: Risks and safety – A National Representative survey', Bulgarian Safer Internet Centre, Applied Research and Communications Fund, Sofia, p. 4.

80 China Internet Network Information Center, 'Statistical Report on internet Development in China', CINIC, July 2016, p. 19.

81 Doneda, Danilo, and Carolina Rossini, 'ICT Kids online Brazil 2014: Survey on internet use by children in Brazil', Brazilian Internet Steering Committee, São Paulo, Brazil, 2015, p. 230.

82 GSM Association, 'Children's Use of Mobile Phones: An international comparison 2013', GSMA and NTT Docomo Inc.'s Mobile Society Research Institute, London and Tokyo, 2014, p. 9.

83 GSM Association, 'Children's Use of Mobile Phones: An international comparison 2015', GSMA and NTT Docomo Inc.'s Mobile Society Research Institute, London and Tokyo, 2016, pp. 6–7.

84 Mascheroni and Cuman, 'Net Children Go Mobile', p. 6; Hasebrink, Uwe, et al., 'Patterns of Risk and Safety Online: In-depth analysis from the EU Kids Online survey of 9- to 16-year-olds and their parents in 25 European countries', EU Kids Online, London, August 2011, p. 7.

85 GSM Association, 'Children's Use of Mobile Phones: An international comparison 2012', GSMA, and NTT Docomo Inc.'s Mobile Society Research Institute, London and Tokyo, 2013, p. 51; GSM Association, 'Children's Use of Mobile Phones: An international comparison 2013', pp. 44–45

<www.gsma.co m/publicpolicy/wp-content/uploads/2012/03/GSMA_ChildrensMobilePhones2013WEB.pdf>; and Mascheroni and Cuman, 'Net Children Go Mobile', p. 16.

86 Lenhart, Amada, et al., 'Teens, Technology and Friendships', Pew Research Center, Washington, D.C., August 2015, pp. 60–61.

87 Livingstone, Sonia, et al., 'Children's Online Risks and Opportunities: Comparative findings from EU Kids Online and Net Children Go Mobile', London School of Economics and Political Science, London, November 2014, p. 10.

88 Doneda and Rossini, 'ICT Kids online Brazil 2014', pp. 236–223.

89 Ravalli, María José, and Paoloni, Paola Carolina, 'Global Kids Online Argentina: Research study on the perceptions and habits of children and adolescents on the use of technologies, the internet and social media', Global Kids Online and United Nations Children's Fund, November 2016, p. 21.

90 Burton, Patrick, Lezanne Leoschut and Joanne Phyfer, 'South African Kids Online: A glimpse into children's internet use and online activities', Centre for Justice and Crime Prevention, Cape Town, South Africa, 2016, pp. 25–27.

91 Ravalli and Paoloni, 'Global Kids Online Argentina', p. 20; Burton, Leoschut and Phyfer, 'South African Kids Online' p. 23.

92 Global Kids Online database 2016.

93 Burton, Leoschut and Phyfer, 'South African Kids Online', p. 23.

94 The Global Kids Online research project <www.globalkidsonline.net> was developed as a collaborative initiative between the UNICEF Office of Research, the London School of Economics and Political Science, and the EU Kids Online network. The project has developed a global research toolkit that enables academics, governments, civil society and other actors to carry out reliable and standardized national research with children and their parents on the opportunities, risks and protective factors of children's internet use.

95 Livingstone, Sonia, and Brian O'Neill, 'Children's Rights Online: Challenges, dilemmas and emerging directions', in *Minding Minors Wandering the Web: Regulating online child safety,* edited by Simone van der Hof, et al., Asser Press, The Hague, 2014, pp. 20–38; and Third, Amanda, 'Method Guide 6: Researching the benefits and opportunities for children online', Global Kids Online, London, November 2016.

96 Ito, Mizuko, and Daisuke Okabe, 'Technosocial Situations: Emergent structures of mobile e-mail use', ch. 13 in *Personal, Portable, Pedestrian: Mobile phones in Japanese life,* edited by Matsuda Ito, Daisuke Okabe and Misa Matsuda, MIT Press, Cambridge, Mass., 2005. Based on interviews by UNICEF in March 2016.

CHAPTER 3: DIGITAL DANGERS: THE HARMS OF LIFE ONLINE

1 Based on interviews by UNICEF in March 2016.

2 Livingstone, Sonia, Giovanna Mascheroni and Elisabeth Staksrud, 'Developing a Framework for Researching Children's Online Risks and Opportunities in Europe', EU Kids Online, London, 2015.

3 Burton, Patrick, 'Risks and Harms for Children in the Digital Age', Background paper prepared for *The State of the World's Children 2017: Children in a Digital World,* United Nations Children's Fund, New York, 2017, p. 2.

4 Ibid., p. 1.

5 Staksrud, Elisabeth, and Sonia Livingstone, 'Children and Online Risk: Powerless victims or resourceful participants?' *Information, Communication & Society,* vol. 12, no. 3, 2009, pp. 364–387.

6   Coleman, John, and Ann Hagell, 'The Nature of Risk and Resilience in Adolescence', ch. 1 in *Adolescents, Risks and Resilience: Against the odds,* edited by John Coleman and Ann Hagell, John Wiley & Sons, Hoboken, N.J., 2007.

7   Vera Slavtcheva-Petkova, Victoria Jane Nash and Monica Bulger, 'Evidence on the Extent of Harms Experienced by Children as a Result of Online Risks: Implications for policy and research', *Information, Communication & Society,* vol. 18, no. 1, 2015, pp. 48–62.

8   Ibid.

9   Nixon, Charisse L., 'Current Perspectives: The impact of cyberbullying on adolescent health', *Adolescent Health, Medicine and Therapeutics,* vol. 5, August 2014, pp. 143–158; and Kowalski, Robin M., and Susan P. Limber, 'Psychological, Physical, and Academic Correlates of Cyberbullying and Traditional Bullying', *Journal of Adolescent Health,* vol. 53, no. 1, suppl., July 2013, pp. S13–S20.

10   Livingstone, Sonia, and Jessica Mason, 'Sexual Rights and Sexual Risks among Youth Online: A review of existing knowledge regarding children and young people's developing sexuality in relation to new media environments', report prepared for the European NGO Alliance for Child Safety Online (eNASCO), September 2015; and Boyd, Danah, Jenny Ryan and Alex Leavitt, 'Pro-Self-Harm and the Visibility of Youth-Generated Problematic Content', *I/S: A Journal of Law and Policy for the Information Society,* vol. 7, no. 1, 2011, p. 40.

11   European Police Office, 'Internet Organised Crime Threat Assessment (IOCTA) 2016', Europol, The Hague, pp. 24–27.

12   Based on interviews by UNICEF in March 2016.

13   United Nations Office on Drugs and Crime, 'Study on the Effects of New Information Technologies on the Abuse and Exploitation of Children', UNODC, Vienna, May 2015.

14   U.S. Department of State, 'Trafficking in Persons Report', U.S. Department of State, Washington, D.C., June 2013, p. 14.

15   'Study on the Effects of New Information Technologies'.

16   Internet Watch Foundation, 'Annual Report 2016', IWF, Cambridge, UK, 3 April 2017.

17   'The NetClean Report 2016: 10 important insights into child sexual abuse crime', NetClean, Gothenburg, Sweden, November 2016.

18   Ibid.

19   Ibid.

20   Europol's European Cybercrime Centre, 'Virtual Global Taskforce Child Sexual Exploitation Environmental Scan 2015', EC3-Europol, October 2015, p. 12.

21   Internet Watch Foundation and Microsoft, 'Emerging Patterns and Trends Report #1: Online-produced sexual content', Internet Watch Foundation, March 2015.

22   'IOCTA 2016', pp. 24–27.

23   Peersman, Claudia, et al., 'iCOP: Live forensics to reveal previously unknown criminal media on P2P networks', *Digital Investigation,* vol. 18, September 2016, pp. 50–64.

24   Jardine, Eric, 'The Dark Web Dilemma: Tor, anonymity and online policing', The Centre for International Governance Innovation and Chatham House, Ontario, Canada, and London, September 2015.

25   Ibid.

26   'Risks and Harms for Children in the Digital Age'.

27   Ibid.

28   Przybylski, Andrew K., and Lucy Bowes, 'Cyberbullying and Adolescent Well-Being in England: A population-based cross-sectional study', *The Lancet Child & Adolescent Health,* vol. 1, no. 1, September 2017, pp. 19–26.

29   Baraniuk, Chris, 'Cyber-Bullying Relatively Rare, Says Study', BBC News, 11 July 2017.

30   Hunt, Elle, 'Online Harassment of Women at Risk of Becoming "Established Norm", Study Finds', *The Guardian,* 7 March 2016.

31   Mitchell, Kimberly J., Michele L. Ybarra and Josephine D. Korchmaros, 'Sexual Harassment among Adolescents of Different Sexual Orientations and Gender Identifies', *Child Abuse and Neglect,* vol. 38, no. 1, 2014, pp. 43–71.

32   Suseg, Helle, et al., 'Seksuelle krenkelser via nettet – hvor stort er problemet?' (Sexual Harassment on the Internet – How great is the problem?), Report 16/2008, NOVA – Norwegian Social Research, Oslo, 2008.

33   Wells, Melissa, and Kimberly J. Mitchell, 'Patterns of Internet Use and Risk of Online Victimization for Youth with and without Disabilities', *The Journal of Special Education,* vol. 48, no. 3, 2014, pp. 204–213.

34   Caravita, Simona C. S., et al., 'Being Immigrant as a Risk Factor to Being Bullied: An Italian study on individual characteristics and group processes', *Child Abuse and Neglect,* vol. 18, no. 1, March 2016, pp. 59–87.

35   Livingstone and Mason, 'Sexual Rights and Sexual Risks among Youth Online'; and Boyd, Ryan and Leavitt, 'Pro-Self-Harm and the Visibility of Youth-Generated Problematic Content'.

36   Office of the United Nations Special Representative of the Secretary-General on Violence against Children, *Releasing Children's Potential and Minimizing Risks: ICTs, the internet, and violence against children,* Office of the United Nations Special Representative to the Secretary-General on Violence against Children, New York, October 2014, pp. 39–40.

37   Based on interviews by UNICEF in March 2016.

38   Based on interviews by UNICEF in April 2016.

39   Phyfer, Joanne, Patrick Burton and Lezanne Leoschut, 'South African Kids Online: Barriers, opportunities and risks – A glimpse into South African children's internet use and online activities', Centre for Justice and Crime Prevention, Cape Town, South Africa, 2016, pp. 25, 28; Mascheroni, Giovanna, and Andrea Cuman, 'Net Children Go Mobile: Final report (with country fact sheets) – Deliverables D6.4 & D5.2', Educatt, Milan, November 2014, <http://netchildrengomobile.eu/reports/>, accessed 1 November 2016.

40   Third, Amanda, et al., 'Children's Rights in the Digital Age: A download from children around the world', Young and Well Cooperative Research Centre, Melbourne, 2014, p. 47.

41   Samuels, Crystal, et al., 'Connected Dot Com: Young people's navigation of online risks – Social media, ICTs and online safety', Centre for Justice and Crime Prevention and UNICEF South Africa, Cape Town, 2013, pp. 5–6.

42   Byrne, Jasmina, et al., 'Global Kids Online Research Synthesis: 2015–2016', UNICEF Office of Research-Innocenti and The London School of Economics and Political Science, Florence, 2016, p. 50.

43   Menesini, Ersilia, and Christina Salmivalli, 'Bullying in Schools: The state of knowledge and effective interventions', *Psychology, Health & Medicine,* vol. 22, suppl. 1, January 2017, pp. 240–253.

44   Ortega-Ruiz, Rosario, Rosario Del Rey and José A. Casas, 'Knowing, Building and Living Together on Internet and Social Networks: The ConRed Cyberbullying Prevention Program', *International Journal of Conflict and Violence,* vol. 6, no. 2, 2012, pp. 302–312.

45   Ibid.

46   United Nations Children's Fund, 'UNICEF Global Programme to Build Capacity to Tackle Online Sexual Exploitation', Final Report to the Government of the United Kingdom of Great Britain and Northern Ireland, Reporting Period: 24 May 2015–30 March 2016, UNICEF Child Protection Section, Programme Division, New York.

47   Based on interviews by UNICEF in May 2017.

48   'IOCTA 2016', pp. 24–27.

49   Peersman, et al., 'iCOP: Live forensics to reveal previously unknown criminal media on P2P networks'.

50   Interpol, 'Annual Report 2015', Interpol, Lyon, France.

51   Interpol, 'Crimes against Children', Fact Sheet, Interpol.

52   Peersman et al., 'iCOP: Live forensics to reveal previously unknown criminal media on P2P networks'.

53   Byrne et al., 'Global Kids Online Research Synthesis: 2015–2016', p. 11.

54   United Nations Children's Fund, 'Freedom of Expression, Association, Access to Information and Participation', Discussion Paper Series: Children's Rights and Business in a Digital World, UNICEF Child Rights and Business Unit, June 2017, p. 4.

55   Olavsrud, Thor, '21 Data and Analytics Trends that Will Dominate in 2016', CIO, 18 January 2016.

56   Livingstone, Sonia, John Carr and Jasmina Byrne, 'One in Three: Internet governance and children's rights', Discussion paper 2016–01, UNICEF Office of Research-Innocenti, Florence, January 2016, p. 11.

57   As one example of this, see Cooper, Tim, and Ryan LaSalle, 'Guarding and Growing Personal Data Value', Accenture Consulting Co.

58   'Data Is Giving Rise to a New Economy', *The Economist,* 6 May 2017.

59   Doneda, Danilo, and Carolina Rossini, 'ICT Kids Online Brazil 2014: Survey on internet use by children in Brazil', Brazilian Internet Steering Committee, São Paulo, Brazil, 2015, p. 37.

60   Palfrey, John, Urs Gasser and Danah Boyd, 'Response to FCC Notice of Inquiry 09–94: Empowering parents and protecting children in an evolving media landscape', The Berkman Center for Internet & Society at Harvard University, Cambridge, Mass., 2010.

61   Brown, Duncan H., and Norma Pecora, 'Online Data Privacy as a Children's Media Right: Toward global policy principles', *Journal of Children and Media,* vol. 8, no. 2, 2014, p. 201.

62   United Nations Children's Fund, 'Privacy, Protection of Personal Information and Reputation Rights', Discussion Paper Series: Children's Rights and Business in a Digital World, UNICEF, March 2017.

63   'Digital Birth: Welcome to the online world', *Business Wire,* 6 October 2010.

64   LaFrance, Adrienne, 'The Perils of "Sharenting"', *The Atlantic,* 6 October 2016.

65   Steinberg, Stacey B., 'Sharenting: Children's privacy in the age of social media', University of Florida Levin College of Law Legal Studies Research Paper Series, vol. 66,839, 2016.

66   'Privacy, Protection of Personal Information and Reputation Rights'.

67   Steinberg, 'Sharenting: Children's Privacy in the Age of Social Media'.

68   Organisation for Economic Co-operation and Development, 'The Protection of Children Online: Risks faced by children online and policies to protect them', OECD Digital Economy Papers No. 179, OECD Publishing, Paris, 2011, p. 37.

69   United Nations, Human Rights Council Resolution, 'The Right to Privacy in the Digital Age', A/HRC/34/L.7/Rev.1, United Nations, New York, 2017, preamble and section 5.g.

70   U.S. Federal Trade Commission, 'Children's Online Privacy Protection Rule', § 312.5 Parental consent.

71   See Agencia Española de Protección de Datos (Spanish Data Protection Agency), 'Guidelines on Rights of Children and Duties of Parents', 2008.

72   2009 Protection of Personal Information Bill.

73   'Privacy, Protection of Personal Information and Reputation Rights', p. 9.

74   Shin, Wonsun, and Hyunjin Kang, 'Adolescent's Privacy Concerns and Information Disclosure Online: The role of parents and the internet', *Computers in Human Behavior,* vol. 54, January 2016, p. 114.

75   Jasmontaite, Lina, and Paul De Hert, 'The EU, Children under 13 years, and Parental Consent: A human rights analysis of a new, age-based bright-line for the protection of children on the internet', *International Data Privacy Law,* vol. 5, no. 1, 2015, pp. 28–29.

76   Byrne et al., 'Global Kids Online Research Synthesis: 2015–2016', p. 50.

77   Wang, Amy B., 'A Lawyer Rewrote Instagram's Terms of Use "In Plain English" So Kids Would Know Their Privacy Rights', *The Washington Post,* 8 January 2017.

78   Art. 8 (1), Regulation (EU) 2016/679 of the European Parliament and of the Council of the European Union of 27 April 2016 on the protection of

natural persons with regard to the processing of personal data and on the free movement of such data, and repealing Directive 95/46/EC (General Data Protection Regulation).

79 Coughlan, Sean, 'Safer Internet Day: Young ignore "social media age limit"', *BBC News, 9* February 2016.

80 Carr, John, 'The Point about 16: Implications of the GDPR for child grooming', The London School of Economics and Political Science Media Policy Project Blog, 1 December 2016.

81 Jasmontaite, and De Hert, 'The EU, Children under 13 years, and Parental Consent', p. 32.

82 Brown and Pecora, 'Online Data Privacy as a Children's Media Right', p. 205.

CHAPTER 4: DIGITAL LIVELIHOODS: LIVING ONLINE

1 Critcher, Chas, 'Making Waves: Panic discourses about the media and children or young people, past and present,' ch. 5 in *The International Handbook of Children, Media and Culture,* edited by Kirsten Drotner and Sonia Livingstone, Sage, London, 2008.

2 McKenna, Katelyn Y. A., Amie S. Green and Marci E. J. Gleason, 'Relationship Formation on the Internet: What's the big attraction?', *Journal of Social Issues,* vol. 58, no. 1, 2002, pp. 9–31. 6

3 Byrne, Jasmina, et al., 'Global Kids Online Research Synthesis: 2015–2016', UNICEF Office of Research-Innocenti and The London School of Economics and Political Science, Florence, November 2016, p. 28.

4 Statens Medieråd, 'Föräldrar & Medier: 2015', Statens Medieråd, Stockholm, 2015.

5 Burton, Patrick, Lezanne Leoschut and Joanne Phyfer, 'South African Kids Online: A glimpse into children's internet use and online activities', Centre for Justice and Crime Prevention, Cape Town, South Africa, 2016, p. 20.

6 Turkle, Sherry, *Alone Together: Why we expect more from technology and less from each other,* Basic Books, New York, 2011.

7 George, Madeleine J., and Candice L. Odgers, 'Seven Fears and the Science of How Mobile Technologies May Be Influencing Adolescents in the Digital Age', *Perspectives on Psychological Science,* vol. 10, no. 6, 2015, pp. 832–851.

8 Boyd, Danah, *It's Complicated: The social lives of networked teens,* Yale University Press, New Haven, Conn., 2014.

9 'Meet Generation Z' video, *The Washington Post,* 25 May 2016, available at <www.washingtonpost.com/video/entertainment/meet-gen eration-z/2016/05/ 25/290c2 c00-21db-11e6-b944-5 2f7b 1793dae_video.html>.

10 Henn, Steve, 'When Parents Are the Ones too Distracted by Devices', *All Things Considered,* National Public Radio, 16 April 2014.

11 Pew Research Center, *Parents, Teens and Digital Monitoring,* Pew Research Center, Washington, D.C., 2016.

12 Byrne et al., 'Global Kids Online Research Synthesis: 2015–2016'.

13 Burton, Leoschut and Phyfer, 'South African Kids Online', p. 41.

14 Byrne et al., 'Global Kids Online Research Synthesis: 2015–2016', p. 68.

15 Ravalli, María José, and Paoloni, Paola Carolina, 'Global Kids Online Argentina: Research study on the perceptions and habits of children and adolescents on the use of technologies, the internet and social media', Global Kids Online and United Nations Children's Fund, November 2016, p. 29.

16 Burton, Leoschut and Phyfer, 'South African Kids Online', p. 70.

17 Lupiáñez-Villanueva, Francisco, et al., 'Study on the Impact of Marketing through Social Media, Online Games and Mobile Applications on Children's Behaviour', Publications Office of the European Union, European Commission, Brussels, 2016.

18 Davidson, Julia, and Elena Martellozzo, 'Exploring Young People's Use of Social Networking Sites and Digital Media in the Internet Safety Context', *Information, Communication & Society,* vol. 16, no. 9, 2012, pp. 1456–1476.

19 Byrne, Jasmina, and Sonia Livingstone, 'Challenges of Parental Responsibility in a Global Perspective', Background paper prepared for *The State of the World's Children 2017: Children in a Digital World,* United Nations Children's Fund, New York, 2017.

20 Livingstone, Sonia, et al., *How Parents of Young Children Manage Digital Devices at Home: The role of income, education and parental style,* EU Kids Online, The London School of Economics and Political Science, London, 2015.

21 Granic, Isabela, Adam Lobel and Rutger C. M. E. Engels, 'The Benefits of Playing Video Games', *American Psychologist,* vol. 69, no. 1, 2014, pp. 66–78.

22 Ferguson, Christopher J., 'Everything in Moderation: Moderate use of screens unassociated with child behavior problems', article submitted to *Psychiatric Quarterly;* and Przybylski, Andrew, and Netta Weinstein, 'A Large-Scale Test of the Goldilocks Hypothesis: Quantifying the relations between digital-screen use and the mental well-being of adolescents', *Psychological Science,* vol. 28, no. 2, 2017, pp. 204–215.

23 Valkenburg, Patti M., and Jochen Peter, 'Social Consequences of the Internet for Adolescents: A decade of research', *Current Directions in Psychological Science,* vol. 18, no. 1, 2009, pp. 1–5.

24 McKenna, Katelyn Y. A., and John A. Bargh, 'Plan 9 from Cyberspace: The implications of the internet for personality and social psychology', *Personality and Social Psychology Review,* vol. 4, no. 1, 2000, pp. 57–75; and Peter, Jochen, Patti

M. Valkenburg, and Alexander P. Shouten, 'Developing a Model of Adolescent Friendship Formation on the Internet', *CyberPsychology & Behavior,* vol. 8, no. 5, October 2005, pp. 423–429.

25 Spies Shapiro, Laura A., and Gayla Margolin, 'Growing Up Wired: Social networking sites and adolescent psychosocial development', *Clinical Child and Family Psychology Review,* vol. 17, no. 1, 2014, pp. 1–18.

26 Kardefelt-Winther, Daniel, 'How Does the Time Children Spend Using Digital Technology Impact their Mental Well-Being, Social Relationships and Physical Activity? An evidence-focused literature review', Background paper written for *The State of the World's Children 2017: Children in a Digital World,* United Nations Children's Fund, New York, 2017.

27 Teppers, Eveline, et al., 'Loneliness and Facebook Motives in Adolescents: A longitudinal inquiry into directionality of effect', *Journal of Adolescence,* vol. 37, no. 5, July 2014, pp. 691–699.

28 Peter, Valkenburg and Shouten, 'Developing a Model of Adolescent Friendship Formation on the Internet'.

29 Valkenburg and Peter, 'Social Consequences of the Internet for Adolescents'.

30 Teppers et al., 'Loneliness and Facebook Motives in Adolescents'.

31 Chou, Hui-Tzu Grace, and Nicholas Edge, '"They Are Happier and Having Better Lives than I Am": The impact of using Facebook on perceptions of others' lives', *Cyberpsychology, Behavior, and Social Networking,* vol. 15, no.2, February 2012, pp. 117–121; and Verduyn, Philippe, et al., 'Passive Facebook Usage Undermines Affective Well-Being: Experimental and longitudinal evidence', *Journal of Experimental Psychology,* vol. 144, no. 2, 2015, pp. 480–488.

32 Verduyn et al., 'Passive Facebook Usage Undermines Affective Well-Being'.

33 Chou and Edge, '"They are Happier and Having Better Lives than I Am"'.

34 Przybylski and Weinstein, 'A Large-Scale Test of the Goldilocks Hypothesis', pp. 209–210.

35 Ibid.

36 Ibid.

37 Griffiths, Lucy. J. et al., 'Associations between Sport and Screen-Entertainment with Mental Health Problems in 5-Year-Old Children', *The International Journal of Behavioral Nutrition and Physical Activity,* vol. 7, no. 30, April 2010.

38 Przybylski and Weinstein, 'A Large-Scale Test of the Goldilocks Hypothesis'.

39 Kardefelt-Winther, 'How Does the Time Children Spend Using Digital Technology Impact Their Mental Well-Being, Social Relationships and Physical Activity?'.

40 Przybylski, Andrew K., 'Electronic Gaming and Psychosocial Adjustment', *Pediatrics, v*ol. 134, no. 3, September 2014, pp. e716–e722.

41 Caplan, Scott, Dmitri Williams and Nick Yee, 'Problematic Internet Use and Psychosocial Well-Being among MMO Players', *Computers in Human Behavior,* vol. 25, no. 6, 2009, pp. 1312–1319; and Lemmens, Jeroen S., Patti M. Valkenburg and Jochen Peter, 'Psychosocial Causes and Consequences of Pathological Gaming', *Computers in Human Behavior,* vol. 27, no. 1, 2011, pp. 144–152.

42 See Livingstone, Sonia, et al., Risks and Safety on the Internet: The perspective of European children – Full findings and policy implications from the EU Kids Online survey of 9–16–year–olds and their parents in 25 countries', EU Kids Online, The London School of Economics and Political Science, London, 2011; Livingstone, Sonia, 'A Framework for Researching Global Kids Online: Understanding children's well-being and rights in the Digital Age', Global Kids Online, London, November 2016; Kardefelt-Winther, Daniel, '*Excessive Internet Use: Fascination or compulsion?',* PhD thesis, The London School of Economics and Political Science, London, 2014; Byrne et al., 'Global Kids Online Research Synthesis: 2015–2016'; and Banaji, Shakauntala, '*Global Research on Children's Online Experiences: Addressing diversities and inequalities',* Global Kids Online, London, November 2016.

43 Kardefelt-Winther, 'How Does the Time Children Spend Using Digital Technology Impact Their Mental Well-Being, Social Relationships and Physical Activity?', p. 6.

44 Kraut, Robert, et al., 'Internet Paradox: A social technology that reduces social involvement and psychological well-being?', *American Psychologist,* vol. 53, no. 9, September 1998, pp. 1017–1031; Putnam, Robert D., *Bowling Alone: The collapse and revival of American community,* Simon and Schuster, New York, 2000; and Turkle, *Alone Together.*

45 Kraut, Robert, et al., 'Internet Paradox Revisited', *Journal of Social Issues,* vol. 58, no. 1, 2002, pp. 49–74.

46 Valkenburg, Patti. M., and Jochen Peter, 'Online Communication and Adolescent Well-Being: Testing the stimulation versus displacement hypothesis', *Journal of Computer-Mediated Communication,* vol. 12, no. 4, July 2007, pp. 1169–1182.

47 Matsuda, Misa, 'Mobile Communication and Selective Sociality', ch. 6 in *Personal, Portable, Pedestrian: Mobile phones in Japanese life,* edited by Mizuko Ito, Daisuke Okabe and Misa Matsuda, MIT Press, Cambridge, Mass., 2005.

48 Ito, Mizuko, et al., *Hanging Out, Messing Around, and Geeking Out: Kids living and learning with new media,* MIT Press, Cambridge, Mass., 2009.

49 Ito, Mizuko, et al., *Connected Learning: An agenda for research and design',* Digital Media and Learning Research Hub, Irvine, Calif., 2013.

50 World Health Organization, *Adolescent Obesity and Related Behaviours: Trends and inequalities in the WHO European Region – 2002–2014,* WHO Regional Office for Europe, Copenhagen, 2017, p. 44.

51 Laurson, Kelly R., et al., 'Concurrent Associations between Physical Activity, Screen Time, and Sleep Duration with Childhood Obesity', *ISRN Obesity,* vol. 2014, 2014.

52 Melkevik, Ole, et al., 'Is Spending Time in Screen-Based Sedentary Behaviors Associated with Less Physical Activity: A cross-national investigation', *International Journal of Behavioral*

Nutrition and Physical Activity, vol. 7, 2010.

53 Melkevik, 'Is Spending Time in Screen-Based Sedentary Behaviors Associated with Less Physical Activity'.

54 Iannotti, Ronald J., et al., 'Patterns of Adolescent Physical Activity, Screen-Based Media Use, and Positive and Negative Health Indicators in the U.S. and Canada', *Journal of Adolescent Health,* vol. 44, no. 5, May 2009, pp. 493–499.

55 Kardefelt-Winther, Daniel, et al., 'How Can We Conceptualize Behavioral Addiction without Pathologizing Common Behaviors?', *Addiction,* vol. 112, no. 10, October 2017, pp. 1–7.

56 Kardefelt-Winther, 'How Does the Time Children Spend Using Digital Technology Impact Their Mental Well-Being, Social Relationships and Physical Activity?'.

57 Griffiths, Mark D., et al., 'Working towards an International Consensus on Criteria for Assessing Internet Gaming Disorder: A critical commentary on Petry et al.', *Addiction,* vol. 111, no. 1, January 2016, pp. 167–175.

58 Bax, Trent, 'Internet Addiction in China: The battle for the hearts and minds of youth', *Deviant Behavior,* vol. 35, no. 9, 2014, pp. 687–702.

59 Aarseth, Espen, et al., 'Scholars' Open Debate Paper on the World Health Organization ICD-11 Gaming Disorder Proposal', *Journal of Behavioral Addictions,* vol. 6, no. 3, January 2017, pp. 1–4.

60 Russon, Mary-Ann, 'Abductions, Beatings and Death: The horrifying truth behind China's internet addiction boot camps', *International Business Times,* 23 September 2016; and Ives, Mike, 'Electroshock Therapy for Internet Addicts? China vows to end it', *New York Times,* 13 January 2017.

61 Kwee, Alex W., Eiko Komuro-Venovic and Janelle L. Kwee, 'Treatment Implications and Etiological and Diagnostic Considerations of Internet Addiction: Cautions with the boot camp approach', ResearchGate, 2014.

62 Mills, Kathryn L., 'Possible Effects of Internet Use on Cognitive Development in Adolescence', *Media and Communication,* vol. 4, no. 3, 2016, pp. 4–12.

63 Blinka, Lukas, et al., 'Excessive Internet Use in European Adolescents: What determines differences in severity?', *International Journal of Public Health,* vol. 60, no. 2, February 2015, pp. 249–256.

64 Granic, Lobel and Engels, 'The Benefits of Playing Video Games'.

65 Bejjanki, Vikranth R., et al., 'Action Video Game Play Facilitates the Development of Better Perceptual Templates', *Proceedings of the National Academy of Sciences of the United States of America,* vol. 111, no. 47, November 2014, pp. 16961–16966.

66 Sherman, Lauren E., et al., 'The Power of the Like in Adolescence: Effects of peer influence on neural and behavioral responses to social media', *Psychological Science,* vol. 27, no. 7, July 2016, pp. 1027–1035.

67 Moisala, Mona, et al., 'Media Multitasking is Associated with Distractibility and Increased Prefrontal Activity in Adolescents and Young Adults', *NeuroImage,* vol. 134, 2016, pp. 113–121.

68 Moisala, Mona, et al., 'Gaming Is Related to Enhanced Working Memory Performance and Task-Related Cortical Activity', *Brain Research,* vol. 1655, January 2017, pp. 204–215.

69 Ibid.

CHAPTER 5: DIGITAL PRIORITIES: HARNESS THE GOOD, LIMIT THE HARM

1 United Nations Children's Fund, *Generation 2030 Africa,* Child demographics in Africa, UNICEF, New York, August 2014, p. 5.

2 Byrne, Jasmina, et. al., 'Global Kids Online Research Synthesis: 2015–2016', UNICEF Office of Research-Innocenti and The London School of Economics and Political Science, Florence, p. 83.

3 Livingstone, Sonia, John Carr and Jasmina Byrne, 'One in Three: Internet governance and children's rights', Discussion Paper 2016–01, UNICEF Office of Research-Innocenti, Florence, 2016, p. 9.

4 GSM Association, 'Children's Use of Mobile Phones: An international

comparison 2012', GSM Association and NTT Docomo Inc.'s Mobile Society Research Institute, London and Tokyo, 2013, p. 50; and GSM Association, 'Children's Use of Mobile Phones: An international comparison 2013', GSM Association and NTT Docomo Inc.'s Mobile Society Research Institute, London and Tokyo, 2014, pp. 44–45.

5 Regulation (EU) 2016/679 of the European Parliament and of the Council of the European Union of 27 April 2016 on the protection of natural persons with regard to the processing of personal data and on the free movement of such data, and repealing Directive 95/46/EC (General Data Protection Regulation).

6 Vuorikari, Riina, et al., 'DigComp 2.0: The digital competence framework for citizens', JRC Science for Policy Report, European Union, Luxemburg, 2016.

7 Byrne, Jasmina, and Patrick Burton, 'Children as Internet Users: How can evidence better inform policy debate?', *Journal of Cyber Policy,* vol. 2, no. 1, 2017, pp. 39–52.

Methodologies for U-Report poll and adolescent workshops

U-Report poll

As part of *The State of the World's Children 2017* adolescent engagement strategy, a U-Report poll was organized in May and June 2017. U-Report sent four questions to U-Reporters worldwide. About 63,000 responses from 13-year-olds to 24-year-olds in 24 countries were analysed *(see below)*.

U-Report survey questions:

1. What do you dislike the most about the internet? Choose 1

a. I see violent stories, photos, videos
b. I see sexual content I don't want to see
c. There is bullying to me and my friend
d. People share embarrassing things
   about me
e. Scams
f. There is nothing I dislike

2. What are things you like the most about the internet?

a. Learn things (for school or health)
b. Read about politics and improving my
   community
c. Learn things important for my future
   (jobs, university)
d. Share things I like with people
e. Learn skills that I can't learn in school

3. How did you learn to use the Internet? From…

a. Parents/caregivers
b. Friends/siblings
c. Teachers at school
d. Clubs/organizations outside school
e. No one helped me

4. What would make the internet better for you?

a. Better internet coverage
b. Cheaper data plans
c. Easier access to mobile phones
   and computers
d. Higher speed connectivity
e. Other (open-ended)

Note: Questions and options were adapted in some cases to reflect local contexts.

Adolescent workshops

For *The State of the World's Children 2017*, adolescents' insights on their access to and use of digital technologies were collected using a process designed by the RErights. org team and UNICEF. RErights is a child-centred initiative led by Western Sydney University in partnership with Digitally Connected and UNICEF's Voices of Youth that enables adolescents (ages 10 to 19) to discuss and share their insights and experiences regarding the digital age.

RErights and UNICEF developed a distributed data-gathering methodology for use by UNICEF regional and country offices and national committees. The methodology was designed to facilitate four-hour face-to-face workshops with adolescents focusing on five to seven themes:

❯ Digital technology in their homes;

❯ Barriers to their digital technology use;

❯ Digital technology and learning;

❯ Digital technology and their futures;

❯ Using digital technology to create positive change;

❯ Concerns about digital technology (optional); and

❯ Digital technology and health (optional).

Workshops were held in 26 countries: Bangladesh, Belarus, Bhutan, Brazil, Burundi, Central African Republic, Democratic Republic of the Congo, Fiji, Guatemala, Japan, Jordan, Kiribati, Malaysia, Nigeria, Paraguay, Peru, Portugal, Republic of Korea Republic of Moldova, Senegal, Solomon Islands, Thailand, Timor-Leste, Tunisia, Uruguay and Vanuatu.

Key analytical issues

❯ Data were analysed by five categories: country, country income group, gender, age band and age.

❯ Only countries with a minimum of 100 respondents each were included in the 'country' category analysis, namely: Algeria, Bangladesh, Brazil, Burkina Faso, Burundi, Cameroon, Central African Republic, Chad, Chile, Côte d'Ivoire, El Salvador, Guatemala, Honduras, India, Indonesia, Liberia, Malaysia, Mexico, Mongolia, Pakistan, Peru, Philippines, Thailand and Ukraine.

❯ All invalid responses provided by respondents or submitted by country offices were discarded.

A total of 484 adolescents took part in 36 workshops (eight countries hosted more than one workshop). The average workshop size was 13 participants. Participating offices recruited a diverse sample of adolescents, and some also ran workshops with specific groups – for example, adolescent refugees in Jordan, homeless adolescents in Nigeria and LGBT adolescents in Brazil.

In advance of organizing the workshops, facilitators were briefed about workshop recruitment, content and administration.

The research received ethics approval from Western Sydney University's Human Research Ethics Committee (reference no. H11101).

Data collection and analysis

Data and analysis from the workshops are not statistically representative. Rather, the aim was to enable adolescents to use their own words to talk about their access to and use of digital technology and the meanings and aspirations they associate with their technology practices.

Apart from one short survey, the bulk of collected data was qualitative. Participants worked individually and in groups to complete surveys, short-answer questions, creative exercises (e.g., drawing), scenario-based exercises and small group discussions. Data gathered consisted of paper-based surveys, diagrams, drawings, written text and photographs. All data were digitized by participating offices and uploaded to secure digital repositories. The data were then collated by the RErights team using data analysis software. The research team worked in English, French and Spanish. All content received in other languages was translated into English by participating offices.

Thematic analysis was applied as the primary technique for understanding the data.

During data entry, individual researchers categorized relevant data blocks (e.g., phrases, quotes and sentences) according to the pre-existing themes and derived new themes in response to the data. The team then reviewed and discussed relevant data and individual analyses, checking and refining interpretations. Analyses were summarized and presented using quotes and images from participants; synopses, which included core insights and ideas derived from data; and charts and graphics depicting key concepts and general trends.

Where necessary, quotes from the workshops included in *The State of the World's Children 2017* have been edited and shortened for clarity.

A companion report, *Young and Online: Children's perspectives on life in the digital age*, containing more extensive results and analysis from the workshops will be published in late 2017 and will be available at <www.westernsydney.edu.au/__data/assets/pdf_file/0006/1334805/Young_and_Online_Report.pdf>

Statisical Tables

Overview

This reference guide presents the most recent key statistics on child survival, development and protection for the world's countries, areas and regions.

The statistical tables in this volume support UNICEF's focus on progress and results towards internationally agreed-upon goals and compacts relating to children's rights and development.

Efforts have been made to maximize the comparability of statistics across countries and time. Nevertheless, data used at the country level may differ in terms of the methods used to collect data or arrive at estimates, and in terms of the populations covered. Furthermore, data presented here are subject to evolving methodologies, revisions of time series data (e.g., immunization, maternal mortality ratios) and changing regional classifications. Also, data comparable from one year to the next are unavailable for some indicators. It is therefore not advisable to compare data from consecutive editions of *The State of the World's Children*.

The numbers presented in this reference guide are available online at <www.unicef. org/sowc2017> and via the UNICEF global statistical databases at <data.unicef.org>. Please refer to these websites for the latest tables and for any updates or corrigenda subsequent to printing.

General note on the data

Data presented in the following statistical tables are derived from the UNICEF global databases and are accompanied by definitions, sources and, where necessary, additional footnotes. The tables draw on inter-agency estimates and nationally representative household surveys such as Multiple Indicator Cluster Surveys (MICS) and Demographic and Health Surveys (DHS). In addition, data from administrative sources and other United Nations organizations have been used.

Data presented in this year's statistical tables generally reflect information available as of July 2017. More detailed information on methodology and data sources is available at <data.unicef.org>.

This volume includes the latest population estimates and projections from *World Population Prospects: The 2017 revision* and *World Urbanization Prospects: The 2014 revision* (United Nations Department of Economic and Social Affairs, Population Division). Data quality is likely to be adversely affected for countries that have recently suffered disasters, especially where basic country infrastructure has been fragmented or where major population movements have occurred.

Multiple Indicator Cluster Surveys (MICS): UNICEF assists countries in collecting and analyzing data in order to fill data gaps for monitoring the situation of children and women through its international household survey initiative, the Multiple Indicator Cluster Surveys (MICS). Since 1995, close to 300 surveys have been completed in more than 100 countries and areas.

MICS was a major source of data for monitoring progress on the Millennium Development Goals (MDG) indicators and will continue to be a major data source during the 2030 Sustainable Development Agenda to measure Sustainable Development Goal (SDG) indicators. More information is available at <mics.unicef.org>.

Child mortality estimates

Each year, in *The State of the World's Children*, UNICEF reports a series of mortality estimates for children – including the annual neonatal mortality rate, infant mortality rate, the under-five mortality rate (total, male and female) and the number of under-five deaths. These figures represent the best estimates available at the time of printing and are based on the work of the United Nations Inter-agency Group for Child Mortality Estimation (UN IGME), which includes UNICEF, the World Health Organization (WHO), the World Bank group and the United Nations Population Division.

UN IGME mortality estimates are updated annually through a detailed review of all newly available data points, which often results in adjustments to previously reported estimates. As a result, consecutive editions of *The State of the World's Children* should not be used for analysing mortality trends over time. Comparable global and regional under-five mortality estimates for the period 1990–2016 are presented on page 154. Country-specific mortality indicators for 1990 and 2016, based on the most recent UN IGME estimates, are presented in Table 1 and are available at <data.unicef.org/child-mortality/under-five> and <www.childmortality.org>.

Under-five mortality rate (per 1,000 live births)

UNICEF Region	1990	1995	2000	2005	2010	2015	2016
East Asia and the Pacific	57	49	40	30	22	17	16
Europe and Central Asia	31	28	22	16	13	10	10
Eastern Europe and Central Asia	47	45	36	27	20	15	14
Western Europe	11	8	6	5	5	4	4
Latin America and the Caribbean	55	44	33	26	25	18	18
Middle East and North Africa	66	53	43	34	28	25	24
North America	11	9	8	8	7	7	6
South Asia	129	112	94	77	63	50	48
Sub-Saharan Africa	181	173	155	127	101	81	78
Eastern and Southern Africa	164	156	138	108	82	64	61
West and Central Africa	199	191	173	145	119	98	95
Least developed countries	176	160	139	111	89	71	68
World	**93**	**87**	**78**	**64**	**52**	**42**	**41**

Under-five deaths (thousands)

UNICEF Region	1990	1995	2000	2005	2010	2015	2016
East Asia and the Pacific	2,329	1,706	1,221	899	692	537	510
Europe and Central Asia	388	307	223	169	139	112	107
Eastern Europe and Central Asia	331	266	192	143	117	93	88
Western Europe	58	41	30	26	23	20	19
Latin America and the Caribbean	652	513	387	293	270	194	187
Middle East and North Africa	558	427	330	277	255	242	237
North America	47	40	35	35	32	28	28
South Asia	4,730	4,149	3,523	2,904	2,313	1,794	1,713
Sub-Saharan Africa	3,893	4,152	4,149	3,767	3,312	2,923	2,860
Eastern and Southern Africa	1,851	1,945	1,893	1,632	1,352	1,134	1,104
West and Central Africa	2,042	2,207	2,256	2,135	1,959	1,789	1,756
Least developed countries	3,669	3,639	3,437	2,966	2,544	2,154	2,101
World	**12,598**	**11,293**	**9,868**	**8,344**	**7,014**	**5,831**	**5,642**

UNDER-FIVE MORTALITY RANKINGS

The following list ranks countries and areas in descending order of their estimated 2016 under-five mortality rate, a critical indicator of the well-being of children. Countries and areas are listed alphabetically in the tables on the following pages.

HIGHEST UNDER-FIVE MORTALITY RATE

Countries and areas	Under-5 mortality rate (2016) Value	Rank
Somalia	133	1
Chad	127	2
Central African Republic	124	3
Sierra Leone	114	4
Mali	111	5
Nigeria	104	6
Benin	98	7
Democratic Republic of the Congo	94	8
Lesotho	94	8
Côte d'Ivoire	92	10
Equatorial Guinea	91	11
Niger	91	11
South Sudan	91	11
Guinea	89	14
Guinea-Bissau	88	15
Burkina Faso	85	16
Angola	83	17
Mauritania	81	18
Cameroon	80	19
Pakistan	79	20
Togo	76	21
Comoros	73	22
Burundi	72	23
Mozambique	71	24
Afghanistan	70	25
Swaziland	70	25
Haiti	67	27
Liberia	67	27
Gambia	65	29
Sudan	65	29
Djibouti	64	31
Lao People's Democratic Republic	64	31
Zambia	63	33

Countries and areas	Under-5 mortality rate (2016) Value	Rank
Ghana	59	34
Ethiopia	58	35
United Republic of Tanzania	57	36
Zimbabwe	56	37
Malawi	55	38
Yemen	55	38
Congo	54	40
Kiribati	54	40
Papua New Guinea	54	40
Uganda	53	43
Myanmar	51	44
Turkmenistan	51	44
Timor-Leste	50	46
Kenya	49	47
Gabon	47	48
Senegal	47	48
Madagascar	46	50
Eritrea	45	51
Namibia	45	51
India	43	53
South Africa	43	53
Tajikistan	43	53
Botswana	41	56
Rwanda	39	57
Bolivia (Plurinational State of)	37	58
Marshall Islands	35	59
Nauru	35	59
Nepal	35	59
Bangladesh	34	62
Dominica	34	62
Sao Tome and Principe	34	62
Micronesia (Federated States of)	33	65

Countries and areas	Under-5 mortality rate (2016) Value	Rank
Bhutan	32	66
Guyana	32	66
Azerbaijan	31	68
Cambodia	31	68
Dominican Republic	31	68
Iraq	31	68
Guatemala	29	72
Vanuatu	28	73
Morocco	27	74
Philippines	27	74
Indonesia	26	76
Solomon Islands	26	76
Algeria	25	78
Tuvalu	25	78
Uzbekistan	24	80
Egypt	23	81
Fiji	22	82
Niue	22	82
Viet Nam	22	82
Cabo Verde	21	85
Ecuador	21	85
Kyrgyzstan	21	85
Democratic People's Republic of Korea	20	88
Nicaragua	20	88
Paraguay	20	88
Suriname	20	88
Honduras	19	92
State of Palestine	19	92
Trinidad and Tobago	19	92
Jordan	18	95
Mongolia	18	95
Syrian Arab Republic	18	95
Saint Vincent and the Grenadines	17	98

ABOUT 15,000 CHILDREN UNDER 5 YEARS OLD STILL DIE EVERY DAY.

LOWEST UNDER-5 MORTALITY RATE

Countries and areas	Under-5 mortality rate (2016)	
	Value	Rank
Samoa	17	98
Grenada	16	100
Palau	16	100
Panama	16	100
Republic of Moldova	16	100
Tonga	16	100
Venezuela (Bolivarian Republic of)	16	100
Belize	15	106
Brazil	15	106
Colombia	15	106
El Salvador	15	106
Iran (Islamic Republic of)	15	106
Jamaica	15	106
Mexico	15	106
Peru	15	106
Albania	14	114
Mauritius	14	114
Seychelles	14	114
Tunisia	14	114
Armenia	13	118
Libya	13	118
Saint Lucia	13	118
Saudi Arabia	13	118
Turkey	13	118
Barbados	12	123
Thailand	12	123
The former Yugoslav Republic of Macedonia	12	123
Argentina	11	126
Bahamas	11	126
Georgia	11	126
Kazakhstan	11	126
Oman	11	126
Brunei Darussalam	10	131

Countries and areas	Under-5 mortality rate (2016)	
	Value	Rank
China	10	131
Antigua and Barbuda	9	133
Costa Rica	9	133
Maldives	9	133
Qatar	9	133
Romania	9	133
Saint Kitts and Nevis	9	133
Sri Lanka	9	133
Ukraine	9	133
Uruguay	9	133
Bahrain	8	142
Bulgaria	8	142
Chile	8	142
Cook Islands	8	142
Kuwait	8	142
Lebanon	8	142
Malaysia	8	142
Russian Federation	8	142
United Arab Emirates	8	142
Malta	7	151
United States	7	151
Bosnia and Herzegovina	6	153
Cuba	6	153
Serbia	6	153
Slovakia	6	153
Canada	5	157
Croatia	5	157
Hungary	5	157
Latvia	5	157
Lithuania	5	157
New Zealand	5	157
Poland	5	157
Australia	4	164
Austria	4	164
Belarus	4	164

Countries and areas	Under-5 mortality rate (2016)	
	Value	Rank
Belgium	4	164
Denmark	4	164
France	4	164
Germany	4	164
Greece	4	164
Ireland	4	164
Israel	4	164
Montenegro	4	164
Netherlands	4	164
Portugal	4	164
Switzerland	4	164
United Kingdom	4	164
Andorra	3	179
Cyprus	3	179
Czechia	3	179
Estonia	3	179
Italy	3	179
Japan	3	179
Monaco	3	179
Norway	3	179
Republic of Korea	3	179
San Marino	3	179
Singapore	3	179
Spain	3	179
Sweden	3	179
Finland	2	192
Iceland	2	192
Luxembourg	2	192
Slovenia	2	192
Anguilla	-	-
British Virgin Islands	-	-
Holy See	-	-
Liechtenstein	-	-
Montserrat	-	-
Tokelau	-	-
Turks and Caicos Islands	-	-

Regional classification

Averages presented at the end of each of the 13 statistical tables are calculated using data from countries and areas as classified below.

East Asia and the Pacific

Australia; Brunei Darussalam; Cambodia; China; Cook Islands; Democratic People's Republic of Korea; Fiji; Indonesia; Japan; Kiribati; Lao People's Democratic Republic; Malaysia; Marshall Islands; Micronesia (Federated States of); Mongolia; Myanmar; Nauru; New Zealand; Niue; Palau; Papua New Guinea; Philippines; Republic of Korea; Samoa; Singapore; Solomon Islands; Thailand; Timor-Leste; Tokelau ; Tonga; Tuvalu; Vanuatu; Viet Nam

Europe and Central Asia

Eastern Europe and Central Asia; Western Europe

Eastern Europe and Central Asia

Albania; Armenia; Azerbaijan; Belarus; Bosnia and Herzegovina; Bulgaria; Croatia; Georgia; Kazakhstan; Kyrgyzstan; Montenegro; Republic of Moldova; Romania; Russian Federation; Serbia; Tajikistan; the former Yugoslav Republic of Macedonia; Turkey; Turkmenistan; Ukraine; Uzbekistan

Western Europe

 Andorra; Austria; Belgium; Cyprus; Czechia; Denmark; Estonia; Finland; France; Germany; Greece; Holy See; Hungary; Iceland; Ireland; Italy; Latvia; Liechtenstein; Lithuania; Luxembourg; Malta; Monaco; Netherlands; Norway; Poland; Portugal; San Marino; Slovakia; Slovenia; Spain; Sweden; Switzerland; United Kingdom

Latin America and the Caribbean

Anguilla; Antigua and Barbuda; Argentina; Bahamas; Barbados; Belize; Bolivia (Plurinational State of); Brazil; British Virgin Islands; Chile; Colombia; Costa Rica; Cuba; Dominica; Dominican Republic; Ecuador; El Salvador; Grenada; Guatemala; Guyana; Haiti; Honduras; Jamaica; Mexico; Montserrat; Nicaragua; Panama; Paraguay; Peru; Saint Kitts and Nevis; Saint Lucia; Saint Vincent and the Grenadines; Suriname; Trinidad and Tobago; Turks and Caicos Islands; Uruguay; Venezuela (Bolivarian Republic of)

Middle East and North Africa

Algeria; Bahrain; Egypt; Iran (Islamic Republic of); Iraq; Israel; Jordan; Kuwait; Lebanon; Libya; Morocco; Oman; Qatar; Saudi Arabia; State of Palestine; Syrian Arab Republic; Tunisia; United Arab Emirates; Yemen

North America

Canada; United States

South Asia

Afghanistan; Bangladesh; Bhutan; India; Maldives; Nepal; Pakistan; Sri Lanka

Sub-Saharan Africa

Eastern and Southern Africa; West and Central Africa

Eastern and Southern Africa

Angola; Botswana; Burundi; Comoros; Djibouti; Eritrea; Ethiopia; Kenya; Lesotho; Madagascar; Malawi; Mauritius; Mozambique; Namibia; Rwanda; Seychelles; Somalia; South Africa; South Sudan; Sudan; Swaziland; Uganda; United Republic of Tanzania; Zambia; Zimbabwe

West and Central Africa

Benin; Burkina Faso; Cabo Verde; Cameroon; Central African Republic; Chad; Congo; Côte d'Ivoire; Democratic Republic of the Congo; Equatorial Guinea; Gabon; Gambia; Ghana; Guinea; Guinea-Bissau; Liberia; Mali; Mauritania; Niger; Nigeria; Sao Tome and Principe; Senegal; Sierra Leone; Togo

Least developed countries/areas

[Classified as such by the United Nations High Representative for the Least Developed Countries, Landlocked Developing Countries and Small Island Developing States (UN-OHRLLS)].

Afghanistan; Angola; Bangladesh; Benin; Bhutan; Burkina Faso; Burundi; Cambodia; Central African Republic; Chad; Comoros; Democratic Republic of the Congo; Djibouti; Eritrea; Ethiopia; Gambia; Guinea; Guinea-Bissau; Haiti; Kiribati; Lao People's Democratic Republic; Lesotho; Liberia;

Madagascar; Malawi; Mali; Mauritania; Mozambique; Myanmar; Nepal; Niger; Rwanda; Sao Tome and Principe; Senegal; Sierra Leone; Solomon Islands; Somalia; South Sudan; Sudan; Timor-Leste; Togo; Tuvalu; Uganda; United Republic of Tanzania; Vanuatu; Yemen; Zambia

Notes on specific tables

TABLE 2. NUTRITION

Stunting, wasting and overweight: UNICEF, WHO and the World Bank have continued a process to harmonize anthropometric data used for computation and estimation of regional and global averages and trend analysis. As part of this process, regional and global averages for stunting, wasting and overweight prevalences are derived from a model described in M. de Onis et al., 'Methodology for Estimating Regional and Global Trends of Child Malnutrition' (International Journal of Epidemiology, vol. 33, 2004, pp. 1260–1270).

Vitamin A supplementation: Emphasizing the importance for children of receiving two annual doses of vitamin A (spaced 4–6 months apart), this report presents only full coverage of vitamin A supplementation. In the absence of a direct method to measure this indicator, full coverage is reported as the lower coverage estimate from semester 1 (Jan – June) and semester 2 (July – Dec), in a given year. The regional and global aggregates only contain the 82 countries indicated as priority countries for national level programmes. Hence the aggregates are published where at least 50 per cent of the population coverage for the priority countries in each region have been met. In other words, East Asia and Pacific estimates are presented despite there being no data for China, because China is not a priority country for a national level programme.

Low birthweight: The data have not been updated since October 2014 due to ongoing methodological work to revise the analysis method for estimates from household surveys where a large number of children are not weighed. New methods are currently being applied to generate estimates through an inter-agency process, and updates will be available in the next edition of *The State of the World's Children*.

Iodized salt: The definition of the indicator presented in this report has changed from the past when it was about households consuming adequately iodized salt. Now it is about salt with any iodine, as such, global and regional average prevalence estimates are not comparable to the averages published in previous editions of *The State of the World's Children*.

TABLE 3. HEALTH

Water, sanitation and hygiene: The drinking water, sanitation and hygiene estimates in this report come from the WHO/UNICEF Joint Monitoring Programme for Water Supply, Sanitation and Hygiene (JMP). Full details of the JMP methodology can be found at <www.washdata.org>. New estimates are released every 2 years which supersede all previous estimates and should not be compared.

Immunization: This report presents WHO and UNICEF estimates of national immunization coverage. Since 2000, the estimates are updated once annually in July, following a consultation process wherein countries are provided draft reports for review and comment. As the system incorporates new empirical data, each annual revision supersedes prior data releases, and coverage levels from earlier revisions are not comparable. A more detailed explanation of the process can be found at <data.unicef. org/child-health/immunization>.

Regional averages for the reported antigens are computed as follows:

- For BCG, regional averages include only those countries where BCG is included in the national routine immunization schedule.

- For DPT, polio, measles, HepB, Hib, PCV and rotavirus vaccines, regional averages include all countries, as these vaccines are universally recommended by WHO.

- For protection at birth (PAB) from tetanus, regional averages include only the countries where maternal and neonatal tetanus is endemic.

TABLE 4. HIV/AIDS
In 2017, the Joint United Nations Programme on HIV/AIDS (UNAIDS) released new global, regional and country-level HIV and AIDS estimates for 2016 that reflect the most up-to-date epidemiological estimates, as well as antiretroviral therapy (ART) for adults and children, and prevention of mother-to-child transmission (PMTCT) of HIV coverage data. The estimates are based on the most current available science and WHO programme guidelines, which have resulted in improvements in assumptions of the probability of HIV transmission from mother-to-child, fertility among women by age and HIV serostatus, net survival rates for HIV-infected children and more. Furthermore, this table includes the most recent and reliable data available from population-based surveys and programme service statistics. Based on the refined methodology, UNAIDS has retrospectively generated new estimates of HIV prevalence, the number of people living with HIV and those needing treatment, AIDS-related deaths, new HIV infections and the number of children whose parents have died due to all causes including AIDS for past years.

Only new estimates should be used for trend analysis as the global and regional figures published in *The State of the World's Children* are not comparable to estimates previously published. The new HIV and AIDS estimates included in this table are also available on <data.unicef.org> as well as <http://www.aidsinfoonline.org>. More information on HIV and AIDS estimates, methodology and updates can be found at <www.unaids.org>.

The indicators included in Table 4 have been revised from previous editions of *The State of the World's Children* in order to better reflect progress in current HIV/AIDS programmes and policy.

TABLE 7. WOMEN
Maternal mortality ratio (adjusted):
The table presents the 'adjusted' maternal mortality ratios for the year 2015, as published by the Maternal Mortality Estimation Inter-agency Group (MMEIG), composed of WHO, UNICEF, the United Nations Population Fund (UNFPA), The World Bank, and the United Nations Population Division, together with independent technical experts. To derive these estimates, the inter-agency group used a dual approach: making adjustments to correct misclassification and underreporting in existing estimates of maternal mortality from civil registration systems, and using a model to generate estimates for countries without reliable national-level estimates of maternal mortality. These 'adjusted' estimates should not be compared with previous inter-agency estimates. The full report – with complete country and regional estimates for the years 1990, 1995, 2000, 2005, 2010 and 2015, in addition to details on the methodology – can be found at <data.unicef.org/maternal-health/maternal-mortality.html>.

Demand for family planning satisfied with modern methods: This indicator has been added to replace contraceptive prevalence.

TABLE 8. CHILD PROTECTION
Birth Registration: Changes in the definition of birth registration were made from the second and third rounds of MICS (MICS2 and MICS3) to the fourth round (MICS4). In order to allow for comparability with later rounds, data from MICS2 and MICS3 on birth registration were recalculated according to the MICS4 indicator definition. Therefore, the recalculated data presented here may differ from estimates included in MICS2 and MICS3 national reports.

Child labour: The prevalence rates of child labour presented in the table vary widely across countries due to significant differences in survey methodology, questionnaire content, national definitions and thresholds used to establish child labour prevalence. Only a limited number of countries have produced child labour prevalence data based on international standards and classifications. Data from the fourth round of MICS (MICS4, 2009–2012) included in the table have been recalculated according to the indicator definition used in MICS3 surveys, to ensure cross-country comparability. In this definition, the activities of fetching water or collecting firewood are classified as household chores rather than as an economic activity. Under this approach, a child aged 5–14 would have to be engaged in fetching water or collecting firewood for at least 28 hours per week to be considered as a child labourer.

Female genital mutilation/cutting (FGM/C): Data on the prevalence of FGM/C among girls aged 0–14 were recalculated for technical reasons and may differ from that presented in original DHS and MICS country reports. For further details, refer to *Female Genital Mutilation/Cutting: A statistical overview and exploration of the dynamics of change*, UNICEF, New York, 2013. Regional estimates on the prevalence of FGM/C and attitudes towards the practice are based on available data from only practising countries with nationally representative data and therefore reflect the situation among those living in these affected countries within the region, and not the region as a whole, as there are some non-practising countries in each region as well.

Violent discipline: Estimates used in UNICEF publications and in MICS country reports prior to 2010 were calculated using household weights that did not take into account the last-stage selection of children for the administration of the child discipline module in MICS surveys. (A random selection of one child aged 2–14 is undertaken for the administration of the child discipline module.) In January 2010, it was decided that more accurate estimates are produced by using a household weight that takes the last-stage selection into

account. MICS3 data were recalculated using this approach.

TABLE 12. EARLY CHILDHOOD DEVELOPMENT

Father's support for learning: Data from the third and fourth rounds of MICS (MICS3 and MICS4) refer to father's engagement in one or more activities to promote learning and school readiness, while the definition was changed in the fifth round (MICS5) to reflect father's engagement in four or more activities. Therefore, estimates of father's support for learning from MICS3 and MICS4 are lower than those based on MICS5 results.

Children with inadequate supervision: This indicator was previously referred to as 'children left in inadequate care' but has been renamed to more accurately reflect the nature of the underlying construct.

TABLE 13. ECONOMIC INDICATORS

National monetary child poverty has been added in 2016 and 2017 to reflect Sustainable Development Goal 1, Target 1.2 that includes an explicit commitment to reduce poverty among children. This indicator measures "the percentage of children aged 0-17 years old living in households that have income or consumption level below the government defined national poverty threshold". Data come from official government sources such as Statistical Office tabulations, national household survey and poverty reports and from regional databases such as Eurostat. Note that the methodology used to calculate national poverty prevalence varies by country. For instance, some countries using income and others consumption, some applying an absolute poverty line and others a relative poverty threshold. Therefore, national child poverty rates should be used to monitor progress, but should not be used to compare or rank countries.

TABLE 1. BASIC INDICATORS

Countries and areas	Under-5 mortality rank	Under-5 mortality rate 1990	Under-5 mortality rate 2016	Under-5 mortality rate by sex 2016 male	Under-5 mortality rate by sex 2016 female	Infant mortality rate (under 1) 1990	Infant mortality rate (under 1) 2016	Neonatal mortality rate 2016	Total population (thousands) 2016	Annual number of births (thousands) 2016	Annual number of under-5 deaths (thousands) 2016	Life expectancy at birth (years) 2016	Total adult literacy rate (%) 2011–2016*	Primary school net enrolment ratio (%) 2011–2016*
Afghanistan	25	177	70	74	66	120	53	40	34,656	1,143	80	64	32	–
Albania	114	40	14	15	12	35	12	6	2,926	35	0	78	97	96
Algeria	78	49	25	27	24	41	22	16	40,606	949	24	76	75 x	97
Andorra	179	9	3	3	3	7	2	1	77	–	0	–	100	–
Angola	17	221	83	88	76	131	55	29	28,813	1,181	96	62	66	84
Anguilla	–	–	–	–	–	–	–	–	15	–	–	–	–	–
Antigua and Barbuda	133	26	9	9	8	25	5	4	101	2	0	76	99 x	87
Argentina	126	29	11	12	10	26	10	6	43,847	754	8	77	98	99
Armenia	118	50	13	15	12	42	12	7	2,925	40	1	75	100	96
Australia	164	9	4	4	3	8	3	2	24,126	311	1	83	–	97
Austria	164	10	4	4	3	8	3	2	8,712	83	0	82	–	–
Azerbaijan	68	95	31	34	28	75	27	18	9,725	176	5	72	100	94
Bahamas	126	24	11	11	10	20	9	6	391	6	0	76	–	98 x
Bahrain	142	23	8	8	7	20	7	3	1,425	21	0	77	95 x	96
Bangladesh	62	144	34	37	32	100	28	20	162,952	3,110	106	72	73	91 x
Barbados	123	18	12	13	11	16	11	8	285	3	0	76	–	91
Belarus	164	15	4	4	3	12	3	2	9,480	114	0	73	100 x	95
Belgium	164	10	4	4	4	8	3	2	11,358	129	1	81	–	99
Belize	106	39	15	16	13	32	13	10	367	8	0	70	–	96
Benin	7	178	98	102	93	107	63	31	10,872	397	38	61	33	96
Bhutan	66	128	32	36	29	90	27	18	798	15	0	70	57	86
Bolivia (Plurinational State of)	58	124	37	40	33	85	30	19	10,888	253	9	69	92	88
Bosnia and Herzegovina	153	18	6	7	5	16	5	5	3,517	33	0	77	97	–
Botswana	56	54	41	44	37	42	33	26	2,250	53	2	67	81 x	91
Brazil	106	64	15	16	14	53	14	8	207,653	2,966	45	76	92	93
British Virgin Islands	–	–	–	–	–	–	–	–	31	–	–	–	–	–
Brunei Darussalam	131	13	10	11	9	10	9	4	423	7	0	77	96	–
Bulgaria	142	18	8	8	7	15	7	4	7,131	67	1	75	98	93
Burkina Faso	16	199	85	89	80	99	53	26	18,646	716	60	60	35	69
Burundi	23	170	72	77	66	103	48	24	10,524	437	31	57	62	94
Cabo Verde	85	63	21	23	19	48	18	10	540	11	0	73	87	97
Cambodia	68	116	31	34	27	85	26	16	15,762	368	11	69	74 x	95
Cameroon	19	143	80	85	74	89	53	24	23,439	842	66	58	71 x	92
Canada	157	8	5	5	5	7	4	3	36,290	387	2	82	–	99
Central African Republic	3	174	124	130	117	114	89	42	4,595	166	20	52	37 x	71
Chad	2	211	127	133	121	111	75	35	14,453	615	77	53	22	79
Chile	142	19	8	9	8	16	7	5	17,910	239	2	80	96	94
China	131	54	10	11	9	42	9	5	1,403,500	17,035	168	76	95 x	–
Colombia	106	35	15	17	14	29	13	9	48,653	746	11	74	94	91
Comoros	22	126	73	78	68	88	55	33	796	26	2	64	49	79
Congo	40	91	54	58	49	59	39	21	5,126	176	9	65	79	91
Cook Islands	142	24	8	9	7	21	7	4	17	–	0	–	–	95
Costa Rica	133	17	9	10	8	14	8	6	4,857	70	1	80	97	96
Côte d'Ivoire	10	151	92	101	82	104	66	37	23,696	858	78	54	44	79
Croatia	157	13	5	5	4	11	4	3	4,213	39	0	78	99	89
Cuba	153	13	6	6	5	11	4	2	11,476	125	1	80	100	92
Cyprus	179	11	3	3	2	10	2	1	1,170	13	0	81	99	97
Czechia	179	12	3	4	3	10	3	2	10,611	109	0	79	–	–
Democratic People's Republic of Korea	88	43	20	22	18	33	15	11	25,369	350	7	72	–	94 x
Democratic Republic of the Congo	8	184	94	101	87	118	72	29	78,736	3,269	304	60	77	35 x
Denmark	164	9	4	5	4	7	4	3	5,712	59	0	81	–	98
Djibouti	31	118	64	70	58	91	54	33	942	22	1	62	–	53
Dominica	62	17	34	36	31	14	31	24	74	–	0	–	–	93 x
Dominican Republic	68	60	31	34	28	46	26	21	10,649	216	7	74	92	87
Ecuador	85	57	21	23	18	44	18	11	16,385	331	7	76	94	92
Egypt	81	86	23	24	22	63	19	13	95,689	2,541	57	71	75	98
El Salvador	106	60	15	17	13	46	13	8	6,345	118	2	74	88	91
Equatorial Guinea	11	191	91	97	84	129	66	32	1,221	41	4	58	88 x	56
Eritrea	51	151	45	49	39	93	33	18	4,955	160	7	65	65 x	39
Estonia	179	18	3	3	3	14	2	1	1,312	14	0	78	100	95
Ethiopia	35	203	58	64	53	121	41	28	102,403	3,230	187	65	39 x	86
Fiji	82	28	22	24	20	24	19	9	899	18	0	70	–	98
Finland	192	7	2	3	2	6	2	1	5,503	59	0	81	–	100

TABLE 1. BASIC INDICATORS

155

Countries and areas	Under-5 mortality rank	Under-5 mortality rate		Under-5 mortality rate by sex 2016		Infant mortality rate (under 1)		Neonatal mortality rate	Total population (thousands)	Annual number of births (thousands)	Annual number of under-5 deaths (thousands)	Life expectancy at birth (years)	Total adult literacy rate (%)	Primary school net enrolment ratio (%)
		1990	2016	male	female	1990	2016	2016	2016	2016	2016	2016	2011–2016*	2011–2016*
France	164	9	4	4	4	7	3	2	64,721	766	3	83	–	99
Gabon	48	92	47	52	43	60	34	22	1,980	58	3	66	82	–
Gambia	29	168	65	70	61	82	42	28	2,039	79	5	61	42	75
Georgia	126	47	11	12	9	40	10	7	3,925	55	1	73	100	99
Germany	164	9	4	4	4	7	3	2	81,915	711	3	81	–	99
Ghana	34	127	59	64	53	80	41	27	28,207	870	51	63	71 x	87
Greece	164	11	4	4	4	9	3	2	11,184	94	0	81	97	96
Grenada	100	22	16	17	15	18	14	8	107	2	0	74	–	96
Guatemala	72	82	29	31	26	60	24	14	16,582	417	12	73	81	85
Guinea	14	235	89	94	84	139	58	25	12,396	442	39	60	32	76
Guinea-Bissau	15	219	88	96	80	130	58	38	1,816	66	6	57	46	68 x
Guyana	66	60	32	37	28	46	27	20	773	16	1	67	86	81
Haiti	27	145	67	73	61	100	51	25	10,847	263	17	63	49 x	–
Holy See	–	–	–	–	–	–	–	–	1	–	–	–	–	–
Honduras	92	58	19	21	17	45	16	10	9,113	198	4	74	89	93
Hungary	157	17	5	6	5	15	4	3	9,753	88	0	76	–	91
Iceland	192	6	2	2	2	5	2	1	332	4	0	83	–	99
India	53	126	43	42	44	88	35	25	1,324,171	25,244	1,081	69	69	92
Indonesia	76	84	26	29	23	62	22	14	261,115	4,991	131	69	95	90
Iran (Islamic Republic of)	106	57	15	16	15	44	13	10	80,277	1,355	20	76	85	99
Iraq	68	54	31	34	28	42	26	18	37,203	1,212	38	70	44	92 x
Ireland	164	9	4	4	3	8	3	2	4,726	69	0	81	–	95
Israel	164	12	4	4	3	10	3	2	8,192	167	1	83	–	97
Italy	179	10	3	4	3	8	3	2	59,430	495	2	83	99	97
Jamaica	106	30	15	17	13	25	13	11	2,881	48	1	76	80 x	92 x
Japan	179	6	3	3	3	5	2	1	127,749	1,053	3	84	–	100
Jordan	95	37	18	19	17	30	15	11	9,456	243	4	74	98	89
Kazakhstan	126	52	11	13	10	44	10	6	17,988	385	4	70	100 x	87
Kenya	47	98	49	53	45	63	36	23	48,462	1,504	74	67	79	85
Kiribati	40	96	54	59	49	69	42	23	114	3	0	66	–	95
Kuwait	142	18	8	9	8	15	7	4	4,053	65	1	75	96	93
Kyrgyzstan	85	65	21	24	19	54	19	12	5,956	152	3	71	99 x	89
Lao People's Democratic Republic	31	162	64	70	58	111	49	29	6,758	163	10	67	58	93
Latvia	157	17	5	5	4	13	4	2	1,971	20	0	75	100	96
Lebanon	142	33	8	8	8	27	7	5	6,007	86	1	80	91 x	82
Lesotho	8	91	94	101	86	73	72	39	2,204	61	6	54	77	80
Liberia	27	258	67	72	62	172	51	23	4,614	157	10	63	43 x	38
Libya	118	42	13	14	12	36	11	7	6,293	127	2	72	–	–
Liechtenstein	–	–	–	–	–	–	–	–	38	–	–	–	–	94
Lithuania	157	15	5	6	5	12	4	3	2,908	31	0	75	100	98
Luxembourg	192	9	2	3	2	7	2	2	576	6	0	82	–	93
Madagascar	50	160	46	51	42	97	34	19	24,895	812	37	66	72	77 x
Malawi	38	232	55	60	50	137	39	23	18,092	653	36	63	62	97 x
Malaysia	142	17	8	9	8	14	7	4	31,187	524	4	75	93 x	98
Maldives	133	94	9	9	8	68	7	5	428	8	0	77	99	95
Mali	5	254	111	115	105	130	68	36	17,995	758	82	58	33	56
Malta	151	11	7	7	6	10	6	5	429	4	0	81	93	98
Marshall Islands	59	51	35	39	31	40	29	16	53	–	0	–	98	77
Mauritania	18	117	81	88	74	71	54	34	4,301	145	12	63	46 x	79
Mauritius	114	23	14	15	12	20	12	8	1,262	13	0	75	93	96
Mexico	106	46	15	16	13	37	13	8	127,540	2,330	34	77	94	95
Micronesia (Federated States of)	65	55	33	37	30	43	28	17	105	2	0	69	–	84
Monaco	179	8	3	4	3	6	3	2	38	–	0	–	–	–
Mongolia	95	109	18	21	14	77	15	10	3,027	73	1	69	98 x	97
Montenegro	164	17	4	4	4	15	4	2	629	7	0	77	98	93
Montserrat	–	–	–	–	–	–	–	–	5	–	–	–	–	92 x
Morocco	74	80	27	30	24	63	23	18	35,277	709	19	76	69	98
Mozambique	24	248	71	76	67	165	53	27	28,829	1,105	78	58	51 x	89
Myanmar	44	116	51	55	46	82	40	25	52,885	944	48	67	76	95
Namibia	51	71	45	49	41	48	32	18	2,480	72	3	64	88	90
Nauru	59	58	35	38	31	45	29	22	11	–	0	–	–	86
Nepal	59	141	35	37	32	98	28	21	28,983	573	20	70	60	97
Netherlands	164	8	4	4	3	7	3	3	16,987	179	1	82	–	98
New Zealand	157	11	5	6	5	9	5	3	4,661	62	0	82	–	99

TABLE 1. BASIC INDICATORS

Countries and areas	Under-5 mortality rank	Under-5 mortality rate		Under-5 mortality rate by sex 2016		Infant mortality rate (under 1)		Neonatal mortality rate	Total population (thousands)	Annual number of births (thousands)	Annual number of under-5 deaths (thousands)	Life expectancy at birth (years)	Total adult literacy rate (%)	Primary school net enrolment ratio (%)
		1990	2016	male	female	1990	2016	2016	2016	2016	2016	2016	2011–2016*	2011–2016*
Nicaragua	88	68	20	22	17	51	17	9	6,150	121	2	75	78 x	97 x
Niger	11	329	91	95	87	133	51	26	20,673	967	86	60	15	62
Nigeria	6	213	104	110	98	126	67	34	185,990	7,141	733	53	51 x	64 x
Niue	82	14	22	25	20	12	19	12	2	–	0	–	–	–
Norway	179	9	3	3	2	7	2	2	5,255	62	0	82	–	100
Oman	126	39	11	12	10	32	9	5	4,425	81	1	77	93	95
Pakistan	20	139	79	82	75	106	64	46	193,203	5,439	424	66	57	74
Palau	100	36	16	18	14	31	14	8	22	–	0	–	97	80
Panama	100	31	16	18	15	26	14	10	4,034	79	1	78	94 x	93
Papua New Guinea	40	88	54	59	50	64	42	24	8,085	221	12	66	57 x	86
Paraguay	88	47	20	22	18	37	17	11	6,725	140	3	73	95	89
Peru	106	80	15	17	14	57	12	9	31,774	615	9	75	94	94
Philippines	74	58	27	30	24	41	22	13	103,320	2,386	64	69	96	96
Poland	157	17	5	5	4	15	4	3	38,224	365	2	78	–	96
Portugal	164	15	4	4	3	12	3	2	10,372	83	0	81	94	98
Qatar	133	21	9	9	8	18	7	4	2,570	25	0	78	98	92
Republic of Korea	179	16	3	4	3	14	3	2	50,792	449	2	82	–	98
Republic of Moldova	100	33	16	18	14	27	14	12	4,060	43	1	72	99	87
Romania	133	31	9	10	8	25	8	4	19,778	192	2	75	99	87
Russian Federation	142	22	8	9	7	18	7	3	143,965	1,852	14	71	100 x	97
Rwanda	57	151	39	42	35	93	29	17	11,918	370	14	67	68	95
Saint Kitts and Nevis	133	32	9	10	8	26	8	6	55	–	0	–	–	78
Saint Lucia	118	21	13	15	12	18	12	9	178	2	0	75	–	93 x
Saint Vincent and the Grenadines	98	24	17	18	15	20	15	10	110	2	0	73	–	94
Samoa	98	31	17	19	16	26	15	9	195	5	0	75	99	96
San Marino	179	11	3	3	3	10	3	1	33	–	0	–	–	93
Sao Tome and Principe	62	105	34	37	30	67	26	15	200	7	0	67	90	95
Saudi Arabia	118	45	13	14	12	36	11	7	32,276	626	8	75	94	98
Senegal	48	140	47	51	43	72	34	21	15,412	542	25	67	43	71
Serbia	153	28	6	6	5	24	5	4	8,820	94	1	75	99	96
Seychelles	114	17	14	16	13	14	12	9	94	2	0	74	94 x	95
Sierra Leone	4	262	114	120	106	156	83	33	7,396	258	29	52	32	99
Singapore	179	8	3	3	3	6	2	1	5,622	50	0	83	97	–
Slovakia	153	15	6	6	5	13	5	3	5,444	57	0	77	–	–
Slovenia	192	10	2	3	2	9	2	1	2,078	21	0	81	–	98
Solomon Islands	76	38	26	28	23	31	22	10	599	17	0	71	77	71
Somalia	1	181	133	139	126	109	83	39	14,318	609	79	56	–	–
South Africa	53	57	43	48	39	45	34	12	56,015	1,176	51	63	94	83 x
South Sudan	11	256	91	96	85	152	59	38	12,231	431	38	57	27 x	31
Spain	179	9	3	4	3	7	3	2	46,348	415	1	83	98	99
Sri Lanka	133	21	9	10	9	18	8	5	20,798	323	3	75	91 x	99
State of Palestine	92	45	19	21	18	36	17	11	4,791	150	3	73	97	90
Sudan	29	131	65	70	60	82	45	29	39,579	1,290	83	64	54	54
Suriname	88	46	20	22	18	40	18	11	558	10	0	71	93	93
Swaziland	25	66	70	76	65	50	52	21	1,343	39	3	58	83 x	80
Sweden	179	7	3	3	3	6	2	2	9,838	119	0	82	–	99
Switzerland	164	8	4	4	4	7	4	3	8,402	86	0	83	–	93
Syrian Arab Republic	95	37	18	19	16	30	14	9	18,430	427	7	70	81 x	67
Tajikistan	53	107	43	48	38	84	37	20	8,735	251	11	71	99 x	98
Thailand	123	38	12	14	11	31	11	7	68,864	726	9	75	93	91
The former Yugoslav Republic of Macedonia	123	37	12	13	11	34	11	8	2,081	23	0	76	96 x	91
Timor-Leste	46	175	50	54	46	132	42	22	1,269	44	2	69	58 x	96
Togo	21	145	76	82	70	89	51	26	7,606	256	19	60	64	95
Tokelau	–	–	–	–	–	–	–	–	1	–	–	–	–	–
Tonga	100	22	16	15	18	19	14	7	107	3	0	73	99	88
Trinidad and Tobago	92	30	19	20	17	26	17	13	1,365	19	0	71	–	95 x
Tunisia	114	57	14	15	12	44	12	8	11,403	210	3	76	79	99
Turkey	118	74	13	13	12	56	11	7	79,512	1,294	16	76	96	94
Turkmenistan	44	86	51	60	42	70	43	22	5,663	144	7	68	–	–
Turks and Caicos Islands	–	–	–	–	–	–	–	–	35	–	–	–	–	–
Tuvalu	78	57	25	28	23	44	21	17	11	–	0	–	–	84
Uganda	43	175	53	58	48	104	38	21	41,488	1,715	90	60	70	94
Ukraine	133	19	9	10	8	17	8	5	44,439	479	4	72	100	96

TABLE 1. BASIC INDICATORS

157

Countries and areas	Under-5 mortality rank	Under-5 mortality rate		Under-5 mortality rate by sex 2016		Infant mortality rate (under 1)		Neonatal mortality rate	Total population (thousands)	Annual number of births (thousands)	Annual number of under-5 deaths (thousands)	Life expectancy at birth (years)	Total adult literacy rate (%)	Primary school net enrolment ratio (%)
		1990	2016	male	female	1990	2016	2016	2016	2016	2016	2016	2011–2016*	2011–2016*
United Arab Emirates	142	17	8	9	7	14	7	4	9,270	92	1	77	90 x	93
United Kingdom	164	9	4	5	4	8	4	3	65,789	805	3	82	–	100
United Republic of Tanzania	36	179	57	60	53	108	40	22	55,572	2,087	117	66	78	80
United States	151	11	7	7	6	9	6	4	322,180	4,003	26	79	–	94
Uruguay	133	23	9	10	8	21	8	5	3,444	49	0	77	99	94
Uzbekistan	80	72	24	27	21	59	21	14	31,447	663	16	71	100	95
Vanuatu	73	36	28	30	25	29	23	12	270	7	0	72	74 x	86
Venezuela (Bolivarian Republic of)	100	30	16	18	15	25	14	10	31,568	602	10	75	97	90
Viet Nam	82	51	22	25	18	37	17	12	94,569	1,582	34	76	94 x	98
Yemen	38	126	55	59	51	88	43	27	27,584	867	48	65	–	85
Zambia	33	182	63	68	58	110	44	23	16,591	620	39	62	83 x	87
Zimbabwe	37	75	56	62	51	50	40	23	16,150	535	30	61	89	86
SUMMARY														
East Asia and the Pacific	–	57	16	18	15	43	14	8	2,291,492	31,393	510	75	–	94 **
Europe and Central Asia	–	31	10	11	9	25	8	5	908,161	11,087	107	77	–	96
Eastern Europe and Central Asia	–	47	14	16	13	38	13	7	416,914	6,139	88	73	98	94
Western Europe	–	11	4	4	4	9	3	2	491,247	4,948	19	81	–	98
Latin America and the Caribbean	–	55	18	19	16	44	15	9	633,773	10,749	187	76	94	93
Middle East and North Africa	–	66	24	26	22	50	20	14	435,225	9,953	237	74	78	94
North America	–	11	6	7	6	9	6	4	358,469	4,389	28	80	–	94
South Asia	–	129	48	48	48	92	39	28	1,765,989	35,853	1,713	69	68	90
Sub-Saharan Africa	–	181	78	84	73	108	53	28	1,034,153	37,038	2,860	60	65	80
Eastern and Southern Africa	–	164	61	66	56	101	43	25	542,206	18,203	1,104	63	75	82
West and Central Africa	–	199	95	101	89	116	63	31	491,947	18,835	1,756	57	–	–
Least developed countries	–	176	68	73	63	109	48	26	979,388	31,163	2,101	64	63	81
World	–	**93**	**41**	**43**	**39**	**65**	**31**	**19**	**7,427,263**	**140,462**	**5,642**	**72**	**78**	**90 **

For a complete list of countries and areas in the regions, subregions and country categories, see page 150 or visit <data.unicef.org/regionalclassifications>.
It is not advisable to compare data from consecutive editions of *The State of the World's Children*.

DEFINITIONS OF THE INDICATORS

Under-5 mortality rate – Probability of dying between birth and exactly 5 years of age, expressed per 1,000 live births.

Infant mortality rate – Probability of dying between birth and exactly 1 year of age, expressed per 1,000 live births.

Neonatal mortality rate – Probability of dying during the first 28 days of life, expressed per 1,000 live births.

Life expectancy at birth – Number of years newborn children would live if subject to the mortality risks prevailing for the cross section of population at the time of their birth.

Total adult literacy rate – Percentage of population aged 15 years and over who can both read and write with understanding a short simple statement on his/her everyday life.

Primary school net enrolment ratio – Number of children enrolled in primary or secondary school who are of official primary school age, expressed as a percentage of the total number of children of official primary school age. Because of the inclusion of primary-school-aged children enrolled in secondary school, this indicator can also be referred to as a primary adjusted net enrolment ratio.

MAIN DATA SOURCES

Under-5, infant and neonatal mortality rates – United Nations Inter-agency Group for Child Mortality Estimation (UNICEF, World Health Organization, United Nations Population Division and the World Bank).

Total population and births – United Nations Population Division.

Under-five deaths – United Nations Inter-agency Group for Child Mortality Estimation (UNICEF, World Health Organization, United Nations Population Division and the World Bank).

Life expectancy at birth – United Nations Population Division.

Total adult literacy rate and primary school enrolment ratio – UNESCO Institute for Statistics (UIS).

NOTES

– Data not available.

x Data refer to years or periods other than those specified in the column heading. Such data are not included in the calculation of regional and global averages, with the exception of 2005–2006 data from India. Estimates from data years prior to 2000 are not displayed.

* Data refer to the most recent year available during the period specified in the column heading.

** Excludes China.

TABLE 2. NUTRITION

Countries and areas	Low birthweight (%)[u] 2011–2016*	Early initiation of breast-feeding (%)	Exclusive breast-feeding <6 months (%)	Introduction to solid, semi-solid or soft foods 6–8 months (%)	Minimum acceptable diet 6–23 months (%)	Breast-feeding at age 2 (%)	Stunting (%) moderate & severe[e]	Overweight (%) moderate & severe[e]	Wasting (%) moderate & severe[e]	Wasting (%) severe[e]	Vitamin A supplementation, full coverage[Δ] (%) 2015	Households consuming salt with iodine (%) 2011–2016*
				2011–2016*				2011–2016*				
Afghanistan	–	41	43	61	16	59	41	5	10	4	98 a	57 S
Albania	–	43 x	39 x	78 x	–	31 x	23 x	23 x	9 x	6 x	–	91 x,S
Algeria	6 x	36	26	28	–	27	12	12	4	1	–	81 S
Andorra	–	–	–	–	–	–	–	–	–	–	–	–
Angola	12 x	48	38	–	13	42	38	3	5	1	14 a	82 S
Anguilla	–	–	–	–	–	–	–	–	–	–	–	–
Antigua and Barbuda	6	–	–	–	–	–	–	–	–	–	–	–
Argentina	7	53	33	93	–	29	8 x	10 x	1 x	0 x	–	–
Armenia	8 x	41	45	90	24	22	9	14	4	2	–	99 S
Australia	6 x	–	–	–	–	–	2 x	8 x	0 x	0 x	–	–
Austria	7	–	–	–	–	–	–	–	–	–	–	–
Azerbaijan	10 x	20	12	77	22	16 x	18	13	3	1	96 a,w	94 y[b]
Bahamas	12	–	–	–	–	–	–	–	–	–	–	–
Bahrain	10	–	–	–	–	–	–	–	–	–	–	–
Bangladesh	22 x	51	55	65	23	87	36	1	14	3	99 a	69 y[a]
Barbados	12	40	20 p	–	–	–	8	12	7	2	–	37 S
Belarus	5	53	19	64	–	12	5 x	10 x	2 x	1 x	–	–
Belgium	7 x	–	–	–	–	–	–	–	–	–	–	–
Belize	11	68	33	79	–	35	15	7	2	1	–	85
Benin	15 x	47	41	73	14	46	34	2	5	1	95 a	69
Bhutan	10 x	78	51	87	–	61	34 x	8 x	6 x	2 x	– a	–
Bolivia (Plurinational State of)	6 x	78	64	83 x	–	40 x	18	9 x	2	1	– a	85 x,S
Bosnia and Herzegovina	5	42	19	71	–	12	9	17	2	2	–	–
Botswana	13 x	40 x	20 x	–	–	6 x	31 x	11 x	7 x	3 x	57 a	83 x,S
Brazil	9	43 x	39 x	94 x	–	26 x	7 x	7 x	2 x	0 x	–	98 x,S
British Virgin Islands	–	–	–	–	–	–	–	–	–	–	–	–
Brunei Darussalam	12	–	–	–	–	–	20 x	8 x	3 x	0 x	–	–
Bulgaria	9	–	–	–	–	–	9 x	14 x	3 x	1 x	–	92 y[a]
Burkina Faso	14 x	42	50	59	3	80	27	1	8	1	99 a	92 x,S
Burundi	13 x	74 x	83	70 x	10	81	56	1	5	1	71 a	87 x,S
Cabo Verde	6 x	73 x	60 x	–	–	13 x	–	–	–	–	–	–
Cambodia	11 x	63	65	82	30	37	32	2	10	2	63 a	68 S
Cameroon	11 x	31	28	83	17	19	32	7	5	1	99 a	86 S
Canada	6	–	–	–	–	–	–	10 x	–	–	–	–
Central African Republic	14 x	44 x	34 x	59 x	–	32 x	41	2	7	2 x	3 a	77 S
Chad	20 x	23	0	59	6	65	40	3	13	4	85 a	77 S
Chile	6	–	–	–	–	–	2	9	0	–	–	–
China	–	41 x	21	60 x	–	9 x	8	7 x	2	1 x	–	96 y[b]
Colombia	10	57 x	43 x	86 x	60 x	33 x	13 x	5 x	1 x	0 x	–	–
Comoros	25 x	34	12	81	6	57	32	11	11	4	12 a	82 S
Congo	13 x	25	33	84	6	11	21	6	8	3	99 a	90 S
Cook Islands	–	–	–	–	–	–	–	–	–	–	–	–
Costa Rica	7	60	33	86	–	28	6 x	8 x	1 x	–	–	–
Côte d'Ivoire	17 x	31	12	64	5	38	30	3	8	2	72 a	82 S
Croatia	5	–	–	–	–	–	–	–	–	–	–	–
Cuba	5	48	33	91	56	24	7 x	–	2 x	–	–	–
Cyprus	12 x	–	–	–	–	–	–	–	–	–	–	–
Czechia	8	–	–	–	–	–	3 x	4 x	5 x	1 x	–	–
Democratic People's Republic of Korea	6 x	28	69	66	–	22	28	0 x	4	1	99 a	–
Democratic Republic of the Congo	10 x	52	48	79	8	66	43	4	8	3	94 a	82 S
Denmark	5	–	–	–	–	–	–	–	–	–	–	–
Djibouti	10 x	55 x	1 x	35 x	–	18 x	34	8	22	9	72 a	4 x,S
Dominica	11	–	–	–	–	–	–	–	–	–	–	–
Dominican Republic	11 x	38	5	81	45	12	7	8	2	1	–	30 x,S
Ecuador	9	55	40 x	74	–	19	25	8	2	1	–	–
Egypt	13 x	27	40	77	23	20	22	16	10	5	– a	93 y[b]
El Salvador	9	42	47	90	67	57	14	6	2	0	–	–
Equatorial Guinea	13 x	21	7	76	11	5	26	10	3	2	– a	57 x,S
Eritrea	14 x	93 x	69 x	40 x	–	73 x	50 x	2 x	15 x	4 x	51 a	72 x,S
Estonia	5	–	–	–	–	–	–	–	–	–	–	–
Ethiopia	20 x	73	58	60	7	76	38	3	10	3	74 a	86 S
Fiji	10 x	57 x	40 x	–	–	–	8 x	5 x	6 x	2 x	–	–
Finland	4	–	–	–	–	–	–	–	–	–	–	–

TABLE 2. NUTRITION

Countries and areas	Low birthweight (%)[u] 2011–2016*	Early initiation of breast-feeding (%)	Exclusive breast-feeding <6 months (%)	Introduction to solid, semi-solid or soft foods 6–8 months (%)	Minimum acceptable diet 6–23 months (%)	Breast-feeding at age 2 (%)	Stunting (%) moderate & severe[e]	Overweight (%) moderate & severe[e]	Wasting (%) moderate & severe[e]	Wasting (%) severe[e]	Vitamin A supplementa-tion, full coverage[Δ] (%) 2015	Households consuming salt with iodine (%)
				2011–2016*					2011–2016*			2011–2016*
France	7	–	–	–	–	–	–	–	–	–	–	–
Gabon	14 x	32	6	82	5	4	18	8	3	1	– α	90 S
Gambia	10 x	52	47	47	8	42	25	3	11	4	27 α	69 S
Georgia	7	69	55 x	85 x	–	17 x	11 x	20 x	2 x	1 x	–	–
Germany	7	–	–	–	–	–	1 x	4 x	1 x	0 x	–	–
Ghana	11	56	52	73	13	50	19	3	5	1	28 α	57 S
Greece	10	–	–	–	–	–	–	–	–	–	–	–
Grenada	9	–	–	–	–	–	–	–	–	–	–	–
Guatemala	11 x	63	53	–	52	57	47	5	1	0	15 α	–
Guinea	12 x	17	21	43	4	66	31	4	10	4	69 α	61 S
Guinea-Bissau	11 x	34	53	71	8	51	28	2	6	1	87 α	26 S
Guyana	14 x	49	23	81	40	41	12	5	6	2	–	43 S
Haiti	23	47	40	87	14	31	22	4	5	1	21 α	16 S
Holy See	–	–	–	–	–	–	–	–	–	–	–	–
Honduras	10	64	31	70	54	43	23	5	1	0	– α	–
Hungary	9	–	–	–	–	–	–	–	–	–	–	–
Iceland	4	–	–	–	–	–	–	–	–	–	–	–
India	28 x	42	55	52	10	67	38	2 x	21	8	53 α	93 y[a]
Indonesia	9 x	49	42	91	37	55	36	12	14	7	82 α	92 y[b]
Iran (Islamic Republic of)	8	69	53	76	–	51	7	–	4	1	–	55 S
Iraq	13	43	20	36	–	23	23	12	7	4	–	55 S
Ireland	5	–	–	–	–	–	–	–	–	–	–	–
Israel	8	–	–	–	–	–	–	–	–	–	–	–
Italy	7 x	–	–	–	–	–	–	–	–	–	–	–
Jamaica	11	65	24	55	–	31	6	9	4	1 x	–	–
Japan	10	–	–	–	–	–	7 x	2 x	2 x	0 x	–	–
Jordan	13 x	19	23	92	33	13	8	5	2	1	–	88 x, y[b]
Kazakhstan	6	83	38	67	45	21	8	9	3	1	– α	94 S
Kenya	8 x	62	61	80	22	53	26	4	4	1	37 α	95 S
Kiribati	8	–	69 x	–	–	82 x	–	–	–	–	– α	–
Kuwait	8	–	–	–	–	–	5	6	3	1	–	–
Kyrgyzstan	6	83	41	85	36	23	13	7	3	1	– α	99 S
Lao People's Democratic Republic	15	39	40	52	–	40	44	2	6	2	88 α	80 S
Latvia	5	–	–	–	–	–	–	–	–	–	–	–
Lebanon	12 x	41 x	27 x	–	–	11 x	17 x	17 x	7 x	3 x	–	95 x,S
Lesotho	11 x	65	67	83	11	30	33	7	3	1	– α	85 S
Liberia	14 x	61	55	46	4	44	32	3	6	2	61 α	91 S
Libya	–	–	–	–	–	–	21 x	22 x	7 x	3 x	–	–
Liechtenstein	–	–	–	–	–	–	–	–	–	–	–	–
Lithuania	5	–	–	–	–	–	–	–	–	–	–	–
Luxembourg	7	–	–	–	–	–	–	–	–	–	–	–
Madagascar	16 x	66	42	90	–	83	49 x	6 x	15 x	6 x	97 α	68 x,S
Malawi	14 x	76	61	89	8	72	37	5	3	1	16 α	78 S
Malaysia	11	–	–	–	–	–	18	7	8	–	–	–
Maldives	11 x	64 x	48 x	91 x	–	68 x	20 x	7 x	10 x	3 x	79 α	–
Mali	18 x	53	33	42	3	53	30	2	14	3	88 α	81 x,S
Malta	7	–	–	–	–	–	–	–	–	–	–	–
Marshall Islands	18 x	73 x	31 x	–	–	53 x	–	–	–	–	– α	–
Mauritania	35	62	41	66	–	40	28	1	15	4	83 α	24 S
Mauritius	14 x	–	21 x	–	–	–	–	–	–	–	–	–
Mexico	9	51	31	82	53	24	12	5	1	0	– α	–
Micronesia (Federated States of)	11 x	–	–	–	–	–	–	–	–	–	– α	–
Monaco	6	–	–	–	–	–	–	–	–	–	–	–
Mongolia	5 x	71	47	95	35	53	11	11	1	0	38 α	80 S
Montenegro	5	14	17	95	66	9	9	22	3	1	–	–
Montserrat	–	–	–	–	–	–	–	–	–	–	–	–
Morocco	15 x	30	28	86 x	–	25	15	11	2	1	– α	–
Mozambique	17	69	41	95	11	52	43	8	6	2	99 α	43 S
Myanmar	9 x	67	51	75	16	64	29	1	7	1	88 α	81 S
Namibia	16 x	71	49	80	13	21	23	4	7	3	– α	74 S
Nauru	27 x	76 x	67 x	–	–	65 x	24 x	3 x	1 x	0 x	–	–
Nepal	18	55	66	84	32	89	36	1	10	2	79 α	94 S
Netherlands	6 x	–	–	–	–	–	–	–	–	–	–	–

TABLE 2. NUTRITION

Countries and areas	Low birthweight (%)[u] 2011–2016*	Early initiation of breast-feeding (%)	Exclusive breast-feeding <6 months (%)	Introduction to solid, semi-solid or soft foods 6–8 months (%)	Minimum acceptable diet 6–23 months (%)	Breast-feeding at age 2 (%)	Stunting (%) moderate & severe[e]	Overweight (%) moderate & severe[e]	Wasting (%) moderate & severe[e]	Wasting (%) severe[e]	Vitamin A supplementa-tion, full coverage[Δ] (%) 2015	Households consuming salt with iodine (%) 2011–2016*
				2011–2016*				2011–2016*				
New Zealand	6	–	–	–	–	–	–	–	–	–	–	–
Nicaragua	8	68	32	–	–	43	23 x	6 x	2 x	1 x	3 a	–
Niger	27 x	53	23	–	6	50	42	3	10	2	99 a	59 S
Nigeria	15	33	17	67	10	35	33	2	7	2	76 a	93 S
Niue	–	–	–	–	–	–	–	–	–	–	–	–
Norway	5 x	–	–	–	–	–	–	–	–	–	–	–
Oman	10	71	33	90	–	48	14	4	8	2	–	–
Pakistan	32 x	18	38	66	15	56	45	5	11	3	98 a	69 y[a]
Palau	7 x	–	–	–	–	–	–	–	–	–	–	–
Panama	8	47	22	61	–	34	19 x	–	1 x	0 x	–	–
Papua New Guinea	11 x	–	56 x	–	–	72 x	50	14	14	7	– a	–
Paraguay	6 x	47 x	24 x	–	–	14 x	11	12	3	0	–	93 y[b]
Peru	7	55	68	78	53	55 y	14	7	1	0	–	90 S
Philippines	21 x	50	34 x	90 x	–	41	33	4	7	2	72 a	52 y[b]
Poland	6	–	–	–	–	–	–	–	–	–	–	–
Portugal	9	–	–	–	–	–	–	–	–	–	–	–
Qatar	8 x	34	29	50	–	32	–	–	–	–	–	–
Republic of Korea	4 x	–	–	–	–	–	3	7	1	0	–	–
Republic of Moldova	6	61	36	62	–	12	6	5	2	1	–	58 S
Romania	8	12 x	16 x	–	–	–	13 x	8 x	4 x	1 x	–	–
Russian Federation	6	–	–	–	–	–	–	–	–	–	–	–
Rwanda	7 x	81	87	57	19	87	37	8	2	1	96 a	91 S
Saint Kitts and Nevis	10	–	–	–	–	–	–	–	–	–	–	–
Saint Lucia	10	50	–	–	–	–	3	6	4	1	–	75 S
Saint Vincent and the Grenadines	11	–	–	–	–	–	–	–	–	–	–	–
Samoa	10 x	88 x	51 x	–	–	74 x	5	5	4	1	–	96 S
San Marino	10	–	–	–	–	–	–	–	–	–	–	–
Sao Tome and Principe	10 x	38	74	74	22	24	17	2	4	1	42 a	91 S
Saudi Arabia	9	–	–	–	–	–	9 x	6 x	12 x	5 x	–	–
Senegal	19	31	33	63	10	48	17	1	7	1	29 a	57 S
Serbia	6	51	13	97	72	9	6	14	4	1	–	–
Seychelles	–	–	–	–	–	–	8	10	4	1	–	–
Sierra Leone	11 x	54	32	63	7	48	38	9	9	4	97 a	74 S
Singapore	10	–	–	–	–	–	4 x	3 x	4 x	1 x	–	–
Slovakia	8	–	–	–	–	–	–	–	–	–	–	–
Slovenia	6	–	–	–	–	–	–	–	–	–	–	–
Solomon Islands	13 x	75 x	74 x	–	–	67 x	32	4	8	3	–	–
Somalia	–	23 x	5 x	16 x	–	27 x	25 x	3 x	15 x	5 x	33 a	7 x,S
South Africa	–	61 x	32	–	23	13	27	13	3	1	– a	–
South Sudan	–	48 x	45 x	21 x	–	38 x	31 x	6 x	23 x	10 x	– a	60 x,S
Spain	8	–	–	–	–	–	–	–	–	–	–	–
Sri Lanka	17 x	80 x	76 x	–	–	84 x	17	2	15	3	74 a	–
State of Palestine	9 x	41	39	90	42	12	7	8	1	0	–	88 S
Sudan	–	69	55	51	15	49	38	3	16	5	72 a	34 S
Suriname	14 x	45 x	3 x	47 x	–	15 x	9 x	4 x	5 x	1 x	–	–
Swaziland	9 x	48	64	90	38	8	26	9	2	0	– a	90 S
Sweden	5	–	–	–	–	–	–	–	–	–	–	–
Switzerland	7	–	–	–	–	–	–	–	–	–	–	–
Syrian Arab Republic	10 x	46 x	43 x	–	–	25 x	28 x	18 x	12 x	6 x	–	–
Tajikistan	10 x	50	34	49	20	50	27	7	10	4	97 a	84 S
Thailand	11 x	40	23	85	56	16	11	8	5	1	–	85
The former Yugoslav Republic of Macedonia	6	21	23	41	–	13	5	12	2	0	–	–
Timor-Leste	12 x	93	62	97	18	39	50	2	11	2	61 a	76 x,S
Togo	11 x	61	58	67	12	61	28	2	7	2	6 a	77 S
Tokelau	–	–	–	–	–	–	–	–	–	–	–	–
Tonga	–	79	52	–	–	30	8	17	5	2	–	–
Trinidad and Tobago	12	41 x	13 x	83 x	–	22 x	5 x	5 x	5 x	1 x	–	53 x,S
Tunisia	7	40	9	27	–	19	10	14	3	2	–	–
Turkey	11 x	50	30	75	–	34	10	11	2	0	–	85 x,S
Turkmenistan	5	73	59	82	77	20	12	6	4	1	– a	100 S
Turks and Caicos Islands	–	–	–	–	–	–	–	–	–	–	–	–
Tuvalu	6 x	15 x	35 x	–	–	51 x	10 x	6 x	3 x	1 x	–	–
Uganda	12	53	66	67	14	43	29	4	4	1	– a	92 S

TABLE 2. NUTRITION

161

Countries and areas	Low birthweight (%)[U] 2011–2016*	Early initiation of breastfeeding (%)	Exclusive breastfeeding <6 months (%)	Introduction to solid, semi-solid or soft foods 6–8 months (%)	Minimum acceptable diet 6–23 months (%)	Breastfeeding at age 2 (%)	Stunting (%) moderate & severe[θ]	Overweight (%) moderate & severe[θ]	Wasting (%) moderate & severe[θ]	Wasting (%) severe[θ]	Vitamin A supplementation, full coverage[Δ] (%) 2015	Households consuming salt with iodine (%) 2011–2016*
	2011–2016*			2011–2016*					2011–2016*		2015	2011–2016*
Ukraine	5	66	20	43	–	22	4 x	27 x	0 x	4 x	–	36 S
United Arab Emirates	6 x	–	–	–	–	–	–	–	–	–	–	–
United Kingdom	7	–	–	–	–	–	–	–	–	–	–	–
United Republic of Tanzania	8 x	51	59	92	9	43	34	4	5	1	87 α	76 S
United States	8 x	–	24	–	–	–	2	6	1	0	–	–
Uruguay	8	77	–	–	–	–	11	7	1	0	–	–
Uzbekistan	5 x	67 x	26 x	47 x	–	38 x	20 x	13 x	5 x	2 x	98 α	82 x,S
Vanuatu	10 x	85	73	72	–	49	29	5	4	1	–	33 x,S
Venezuela (Bolivarian Republic of)	9	–	–	–	–	–	13 x	6 x	4 x	–	–	–
Viet Nam	5	27	24	91	59	22	25	5	6	1	97 α,w	61 S
Yemen	32 x	53	10	69	15	45	47	2	16	5	8 α	49 S
Zambia	11 x	66	73	82	11	42	40	6	6	3	– α	88 S
Zimbabwe	11	58	48	91	8	14	27	6	3	1	45 α	93 S
SUMMARY												
East Asia and Pacific	–	43	28	69	40 **	23	9	6	3	1	82	91
Europe and Central Asia	6	–	–	–	–	–	–	–	–	–	–	–
Eastern Europe and Central Asia	6	57	30	69	–	28 r	6 j	13 j	2 j	0 j	–	–
Western Europe	7	–	–	–	–	–	–	–	–	–	–	–
Latin America and Caribbean	9	54	38	82 N	51 N	32	11	7	1	0	–	–
Middle East and North Africa	–	40	32	63	–	29	15	11	7	3	–	–
North America	–	–	24	–	–	–	2	8	1	0	–	–
South Asia	–	39	52	56	12	68	36	4 k	16	5	66	88
Sub-Saharan Africa	–	51	42	71	11	50	34	4	8	2	72	80
Eastern and Southern Africa	–	63	55	75	13	53	34	4	7	2	65	78
West and Central Africa	–	40	29	68	9	47	34	4	9	3	78	81
Least developed countries	–	56	49	70	12	62	–	–	–	–	77	72
World	**–**	**45**	**40**	**66**	**17**	**45**	**23**	**6**	**8**	**3**	**70**	**86**

For a complete list of countries and areas in the regions, subregions and country categories, see page 150 or visit <data.unicef.org/regionalclassifications>.

It is not advisable to compare data from consecutive editions of *The State of the World's Children*.

DEFINITIONS OF THE INDICATORS

Low birthweight – Percentage of infants weighing less than 2,500 grams at birth.

Early initiation of breastfeeding – Percentage of infants who are put to the breast within one hour of birth.

Exclusive breastfeeding <6 months – Percentage of children aged 0–5 months who are fed exclusively with breast milk in the 24 hours prior to the survey.

Introduction of solid, semi-solid or soft foods (6–8 months) – Percentage of children aged 6–8 months who received solid, semi-solid or soft foods in the 24 hours prior to the survey.

Minimum Acceptable Diet (6–23 months) – Percentage of breastfed children 6–23 months of age who had at least the minimum dietary diversity and the minimum meal frequency during the previous day AND percentage of non-breastfed children 6–23 months of age who received at least 2 milk feedings and had at least the minimum dietary diversity not including milk feeds and the minimum meal frequency during the previous day.

Breastfeeding at age 2 – Percentage of children aged 20–23 months who received breast milk in the 24 hours prior to the survey.

MAIN DATA SOURCES

Low birthweight – Demographic and Health Surveys (DHS), Multiple Indicator Cluster Surveys (MICS), other national household surveys, data from routine reporting systems, UNICEF and WHO.

Infant and young child feeding – DHS, MICS, other national household surveys and UNICEF.

Stunting – Moderate and severe: Percentage of children aged 0–59 months who are below minus two standard deviations from median height-for-age of the WHO Child Growth Standards.

Overweight – Moderate and severe: Percentage of children aged 0–59 months who are above two standard deviations from median weight-for-height of the WHO Child Growth Standards (includes obesity).

Wasting – Moderate and severe: Percentage of children aged 0–59 months who are below minus two standard deviations from median weight-for-height of the WHO Child Growth Standards.

Wasting – severe: Percentage of children aged 0–59 months who are below minus three standard deviations from median weight-for-height of the WHO Child Growth Standards.

Vitamin A supplementation, full coverage – The estimated percentage of children aged 6–59 months reached with 2 doses of vitamin A supplements approximately 4–6 months apart in a given calendar year.

Households consuming salt with iodine – Percentage of households consuming salt with any iodine (>0 ppm).

Stunting, overweight, wasting and severe wasting – DHS, MICS, other national household surveys, WHO and UNICEF.

Vitamin A supplementation – UNICEF.

Iodized salt consumption – DHS, MICS, other national household surveys, school-based surveys and UNICEF.

NOTES

– Data not available.

x Data refer to years or periods other than those specified in the column heading. Such data are not included in the calculation of regional and global averages, with the exception of 2008 data from China for 'Early initiation of breastfeeding', 'Introduction to solids' and Breastfeeding at age 2'. Estimates from data years prior to 2000 are not displayed.

y Data differ from the standard definition or refer to only part of a country. If they fall within the noted reference period, such data are included in the calculation of regional and global averages. Surveys with a superscript footnote of "a" are mainly DHS surveys awaiting re-analysis to add the households that did not have salt to the estimate. Surveys with a superscript footnote "b" cannot be confirmed in whether the reported value includes households without salt or not.

p Based on small denominators (typically 25–49 unweighted cases). No data based on fewer than 25 unweighted cases are displayed.

θ Global and regional averages for stunting (moderate and severe), overweight (moderate and severe), wasting (moderate and severe) and wasting (severe) are estimated using statistical modelling data from the UNICEF-WHO-World Bank Group Joint Child Malnutrition Estimates, May 2017 Edition. For more information see <data.unicef.org/malnutrition>. Disaggregations for stunting (moderate and severe) as shown in tables 10 and 11, are population-weighted, which means using the most recent estimate for each country with data between 2011 and 2016; therefore disaggregations may not coincide with total estimates at the global and regional level presented in this table.

Δ Full coverage with vitamin A supplements is reported as the lower percentage of 2 annual coverage points (i.e., lower point between semester 1 (January–June) and semester 2 (July–December) of 2015). Data are only presented for VAS priority countries; thus aggregates are only based on and representative of these priority countries.

w Identifies countries with national vitamin A supplementation programmes targeted towards a reduced age range. Coverage figure is reported as targeted.

α Identifies countries which are designated 'priority'. Priority countries for national vitamin A supplementation programmes are identified as those having high under-five mortality rates (over 70 per 1,000 live births), and/or evidence of vitamin A deficiency among this age group, and/or a history of vitamin A supplementation programmes.

U The low birth weight database has not been updated since October 2014. Given that the data are out of date, aggregates for a number of regions and the global value have been suppressed. New methods are currently being applied to generate estimates through an inter-agency process and updates will be available in the next State of the World's Children Report.

j Estimates for Eastern Europe and Central Asia are based on a model fit for all of Europe and Central Asia. Data were not available for the Russian Federation and were mainly from countries in Eastern Europe and Central Asia.

k Due to consecutive low population coverage for the two most recent time periods of 2008–2012 and 2013–2016, overweight data for South Asia are not presented in SOWC; however, the estimates are available through the Joint Malnutrition Estimates which can be downloaded at <https://data.unicef.org/topic/nutrition/malnutrition/> but should be interpreted with caution.

S Re-analyzed by adjusting the denominator to include households without salt.

* Data refer to the most recent year available during the period specified in the column heading.

** Excludes China.

r Excludes the Russian Federation.

N Excludes Brazil.

TABLE 3. HEALTH

Countries and areas	Use of basic drinking water services (%) 2015			Use of basic sanitation services (%) 2015			Immunization coverage (%) 2016										Protection at birth (PAB) against tetanus^λ	Pneumonia Care seeking for children with symptoms of pneumonia (%)	Diarrhoea Treatment with oral rehydration salts (ORS) (%)	Malaria Care seeking for children with fever (%)	Children sleeping under ITNs (%)	Households with at least one ITN (%)
	total	urban	rural	total	urban	rural	BCG	DTP1β	DTP3β	polio3	MCV1	MCV2^	HepB3	Hib3	rota	PCV3			2011–2016*			
Afghanistan	63	89	53	39	56	33	74	73	65	60	62	39	65	65	0	65	65	62	46	63	5	26
Albania	91	93	90	98	98	97	99	99	98	98	96	98	98	98	0	98	92	70 x	54 x	71 x	–	–
Algeria	93	95	89	87	90	82	99	96	91	91	94	96	91	91	0	61	92	66	25	–	–	–
Andorra	100	100	100	100	100	100	–	99	98	98	97	90	94	98	0	92	–	–	–	–	–	–
Angola	41	63	23	39	62	21	58	79	64	66	49	26	64	64	53	58	78	49	43	51	22	31
Anguilla	98	98	–	97	97	–	–	–	–	–	–	–	–	–	–	–	–	–	–	–	–	–
Antigua and Barbuda	97	–	–	88	–	–	–	99	99	86	98	87	99	99	0	0	–	–	–	–	–	–
Argentina	100	100	100	95	95	94	92	97	92	87	90	88	92	92	75	82	–	94	18	–	–	–
Armenia	99	99	99	92	96	83	99	97	94	96	97	97	94	94	94	94	–	57 x	37	71	–	–
Australia	100	100	100	100	–	–	–	98	94	94	95	94	94	94	87	94	–	–	–	–	–	–
Austria	100	100	100	100	100	100	–	99	87	87	95	89	87	87	61	0	–	–	–	–	–	–
Azerbaijan	84	95	72	89	92	87	98	98	97	98	98	96	97	97	0	97	–	36 x	11	–	1 x	–
Bahamas	98	–	–	92	–	–	–	95	94	94	89	74	94	94	0	94	100	–	–	–	–	–
Bahrain	100	–	–	100	–	–	–	99	99	99	99	99	99	99	98	99	98	–	–	–	–	–
Bangladesh	97	98	97	47	54	43	99	99	97	97	94	93	97	97	0	97	97	42	77	55	–	–
Barbados	98	–	–	96	–	–	–	99	97	97	92	87	97	97	0	96	–	–	–	–	–	–
Belarus	98	98	99	94	94	95	98	99	98	98	98	98	96	11	0	0	–	93	45	–	–	–
Belgium	100	100	100	99	99	99	–	99	98	98	96	85	97	97	87	94	–	–	–	–	–	–
Belize	97	99	96	87	91	84	94	98	95	96	95	96	95	95	0	0	91	67	55	71	–	–
Benin	67	77	60	14	25	5	96	86	82	78	74	0	82	82	0	75	85	23	25	44	73	77
Bhutan	98	97	98	63	72	57	99	99	98	97	97	90	98	98	0	0	89	74 x	61 x	–	–	–
Bolivia (Plurinational State of)	93	99	79	53	64	27	99	99	99	99	99	0	99	99	99	97	87	62	22	–	–	–
Bosnia and Herzegovina	98	97	98	95	99	92	97	90	78	79	83	78	78	69	0	0	–	87	36	–	–	–
Botswana	79	95	58	60	75	39	98	98	95	96	97	74	95	95	95	95	92	14 x	43 x	75 x	31	53
Brazil	97	99	87	86	91	58	99	89	86	98	96	72	86	86	94	94	93	50 x	–	–	–	–
British Virgin Islands	100	–	–	97	–	–	–	–	–	–	–	–	–	–	–	–	–	–	–	–	–	–
Brunei Darussalam	100	100	99	96	96	97	99	99	99	99	98	97	99	99	0	0	95	–	–	–	–	–
Bulgaria	99	99	99	86	87	84	96	94	92	92	92	88	91	92	0	90	–	–	–	–	–	–
Burkina Faso	54	79	43	23	48	12	98	95	91	91	88	50	91	91	91	91	92	52	40	61	75	90
Burundi	56	88	52	50	46	51	93	97	94	94	93	72	94	94	96	94	85	63	36	69	40	46
Cabo Verde	86	93	74	65	73	51	96	96	96	95	92	95	96	96	0	0	92	–	–	–	–	–
Cambodia	75	96	70	49	88	39	97	92	90	87	81	58	90	90	0	87	93	69	35	61	4 x	5 x
Cameroon	65	84	43	39	56	19	70	92	85	83	78	0	85	85	80	84	85	28	16	33	55	71
Canada	99	–	–	99	–	–	–	96	91	91	90	86	55	91	0	79	–	–	–	–	–	–
Central African Republic	54	74	41	25	49	9	74	69	47	47	49	0	47	47	0	47	60	30 x	16 x	–	36 x	47 x
Chad	43	78	32	10	33	3	56	60	46	44	58	0	46	46	0	0	80	26	20	23	36	77
Chile	100	100	100	100	100	99	97	99	95	95	93	87	95	95	0	90	–	–	–	–	–	–
China	96	96	96	75	86	61	99	99	99	99	99	99	99	0	0	0	–	–	–	–	–	–
Colombia	97	100	86	84	88	72	88	93	91	91	93	87	91	91	90	89	90	64 x	54 x	54 x	–	3 x
Comoros	84	93	80	34	47	29	94	96	91	92	91	0	91	91	0	0	85	38	38	45	41	59
Congo	68	85	37	15	20	6	85	85	80	80	80	0	80	80	80	80	85	28	28	51	61	66
Cook Islands	100	–	–	98	–	–	99	99	99	99	90	90	99	99	0	0	–	–	–	–	–	–
Costa Rica	100	100	100	97	98	94	89	99	97	97	93	88	97	97	0	94	–	77	40	–	–	–
Côte d'Ivoire	73	89	54	30	45	13	95	98	85	80	77	0	85	85	0	83	90	38	17	43	37	67
Croatia	100	100	100	97	98	96	99	98	93	93	90	96	93	93	0	0	–	–	–	–	–	–
Cuba	95	97	90	91	92	88	99	99	99	99	99	99	99	99	0	0	–	93	61	93	–	–
Cyprus	100	100	100	99	100	99	–	98	97	97	90	88	97	96	0	81	–	–	–	–	–	–
Czechia	100	100	100	99	99	99	–	98	96	96	98	93	96	96	0	0	–	–	–	–	–	–
Democratic People's Republic of Korea	100	100	99	77	83	68	97	97	96	99	99	98	96	96	0	0	97	80 x	74 x	–	–	–
Democratic Republic of the Congo	42	70	21	20	23	18	80	80	79	74	77	0	79	79	0	77	85	42	39	55	56	70
Denmark	100	100	100	100	100	100	–	97	94	94	94	85	0	94	0	94	–	–	–	–	–	–
Djibouti	77	83	55	51	63	13	90	90	84	84	75	82	84	84	86	82	85	94	94	–	20 x	32
Dominica	97	–	–	78	–	–	98	99	99	99	96	92	99	99	0	0	–	–	–	–	–	–
Dominican Republic	94	97	86	83	85	74	99	98	87	82	85	0	80	73	75	30	90	73	48	65	–	–
Ecuador	93	100	80	86	89	80	84	94	83	79	86	76	84	84	80	84	88	–	46	–	–	–
Egypt	98	99	98	93	97	90	96	98	95	95	95	96	95	95	0	0	80	68	28	68	–	–
El Salvador	93	98	83	91	93	87	99	97	93	95	90	93	93	93	93	90	90	80	70	–	–	–
Equatorial Guinea	50	78	31	75	80	71	48	40	19	20	30	0	19	19	0	0	70	54	40	62	23	38
Eritrea	19	66	6	11	29	6	97	97	95	95	93	85	95	95	96	95	94	45 x	43 x	–	20 x	71 x
Estonia	100	100	99	100	100	100	95	94	93	93	93	92	93	93	85	0	–	–	–	–	–	–
Ethiopia	39	77	30	7	18	4	75	86	77	75	70	0	77	77	63	76	80	30	30	35	45	64
Fiji	94	98	89	96	96	95	99	99	99	99	94	94	99	99	99	99	94	–	–	–	–	–

TABLE 3. HEALTH

Countries and areas	Use of basic drinking water services (%) 2015 total	urban	rural	Use of basic sanitation services (%) 2015 total	urban	rural	BCG	DTP1β	DTP3β	polio3	MCV1	MCV2^	HepB3	Hib3	rota	PCV3	Protection at birth (PAB) against tetanus^	Care seeking for children with symptoms of pneumonia (%)	Treatment with oral rehydration salts (ORS) (%)	Care seeking for children with fever (%)	Children sleeping under ITNs (%)	House-holds with at least one ITN (%)
											Immunization coverage (%) 2016							Pneumonia 2011–2016*	Diarrhoea	Malaria		
Finland	100	100	100	99	99	99	–	99	92	92	94	85	0	92	84	87	–	–	–	–	–	–
France	100	100	100	99	99	99	–	99	97	97	90	79	88	96	0	91	–	–	–	–	–	–
Gabon	88	92	59	41	42	32	94	83	75	74	64	0	75	75	0	0	90	68	26	67	39	36
Gambia	80	88	68	42	46	35	98	99	95	95	97	79	95	95	95	95	92	68	59	65	47	69
Georgia	93	98	87	85	95	73	98	97	92	92	93	85	92	92	75	75	–	74 x	40 x	–	–	–
Germany	100	100	100	99	99	99	–	95	95	94	97	93	88	93	66	86	–	–	–	–	–	–
Ghana	78	88	66	14	19	9	94	94	93	95	89	75	93	93	94	93	88	56	49	77	47	68
Greece	100	100	100	99	99	98	–	99	99	99	97	83	96	99	20	96	–	–	–	–	–	–
Grenada	96	–	–	78	–	–	–	98	96	98	95	85	96	96	0	0	–	–	–	–	–	–
Guatemala	94	97	89	67	81	53	87	96	80	82	86	65	80	80	82	81	90	52	49	50	–	–
Guinea	67	88	55	22	34	15	72	65	57	42	54	0	57	57	0	0	80	37	34	37	26	47
Guinea-Bissau	69	85	54	21	35	8	94	95	87	87	81	0	87	87	61	80	80	34	35	51	81	90
Guyana	95	100	93	86	89	85	95	97	97	94	99	94	97	97	96	92	99	84	43	71	7	5
Haiti	64	81	40	31	37	22	72	78	58	56	53	26	58	58	48	0	88	38	53	40	12	19
Holy See	–	–	–	–	–	–	–	–	–	–	–	–	–	–	–	–	–	–	–	–	–	–
Honduras	92	99	84	80	84	75	99	99	97	97	88	0	97	97	97	97	94	64	60	62	–	–
Hungary	100	100	100	98	98	99	99	99	99	99	99	99	0	99	0	98	–	–	–	–	–	–
Iceland	100	100	100	99	99	100	–	96	91	91	91	95	0	91	0	90	–	–	–	–	–	–
India	88	93	85	44	65	34	89	91	88	86	88	76	88	80	4	0	87	73	51	71 x	–	–
Indonesia	90	97	81	68	77	57	81	95	79	80	76	56	79	79	0	0	85	75	39	74	3 x	3 x
Iran (Islamic Republic of)	95	97	89	88	92	79	99	99	99	99	99	98	99	99	0	0	95	76 x	61 x	–	–	–
Iraq	86	90	78	86	86	86	94	73	63	68	66	64	61	63	34	0	75	74	23	–	–	–
Ireland	99	99	99	92	91	95	18	98	95	95	92	0	95	95	0	91	–	–	–	–	–	–
Israel	100	100	100	100	100	100	–	94	94	94	97	97	95	94	81	93	–	–	–	–	–	–
Italy	100	100	100	99	99	99	–	97	93	93	85	83	93	93	0	89	–	–	–	–	–	–
Jamaica	93	97	88	85	84	87	96	99	99	99	95	85	98	99	0	0	80	82	64	–	–	–
Japan	99	–	–	100	–	–	84	99	99	99	96	93	0	99	0	99	–	–	–	–	–	–
Jordan	99	99	97	97	97	96	99	99	98	98	96	99	98	98	97	0	90	77	20	69	–	–
Kazakhstan	91	97	84	98	97	99	95	93	82	82	99	99	82	82	0	97	–	81	62	–	–	–
Kenya	58	83	50	30	35	28	99	96	89	88	75	32	89	89	74	78	85	66	54	72	56	59
Kiribati	64	90	44	40	49	32	79	82	81	82	80	79	81	81	79	79	90	81 x	62 x	27 x	–	–
Kuwait	100	–	–	100	–	–	99	99	99	99	93	96	99	99	0	99	95	–	–	–	–	–
Kyrgyzstan	87	97	82	97	93	99	97	97	96	97	97	98	96	96	0	0	–	60	33	56	–	–
Lao People's Democratic Republic	80	92	73	73	93	60	78	85	82	83	76	0	82	82	0	78	90	54	42	–	43	50
Latvia	99	99	98	93	97	84	96	99	98	98	93	89	98	98	83	82	–	–	–	–	–	–
Lebanon	92	–	–	95	–	–	–	84	81	75	79	75	81	81	0	0	–	74 x	44 x	–	–	–
Lesotho	72	87	66	44	46	43	98	98	93	90	90	82	93	93	0	93	85	63	53	61	–	–
Liberia	70	80	60	17	28	6	97	99	79	79	80	0	79	79	48	79	89	51	60	78	44	62
Libya	97	–	–	100	–	–	99	98	97	97	97	96	97	97	97	96	–	–	–	–	–	–
Liechtenstein	100	–	–	100	–	–											–	–	–	–	–	–
Lithuania	97	100	93	94	97	86	98	DTP1	97	DTP3	94	94	94	92	95	94	0	82	–	–	–	–
Luxembourg	100	100	100	98	97	99	–	99	99	99	99	86	94	99	89	95	–	–	–	–	–	–
Madagascar	51	82	34	10	16	6	70	84	77	75	58	0	77	77	78	76	78	41	15	46	73	80
Malawi	67	87	63	44	49	43	86	89	84	83	81	61	84	84	81	83	89	78	65	67	43	57
Malaysia	96	99	89	100	100	99	98	99	98	98	96	99	96	98	0	0	90	–	–	–	–	–
Maldives	98	96	100	96	93	98	99	99	99	99	99	99	99	99	0	0	99	22 x	57 x	84 x	–	–
Mali	74	91	63	31	46	22	92	86	68	67	75	0	68	68	60	70	85	23	22	49	79	93
Malta	100	100	100	100	100	100	–	97	97	97	93	86	97	97	0	0	–	–	–	–	–	–
Marshall Islands	78	79	68	99	95	66	94	87	71	69	75	49	73	58	38	51	–	34	38 x	63 x	–	–
Mauritania	70	86	45	45	48	17	85	87	73	67	70	0	73	73	73	73	80	34	19	35	18	67
Mauritius	100	100	100	93	94	93	98	97	96	96	92	92	72	96	92	10	95	–	–	–	–	–
Mexico	98	100	94	89	91	81	99	99	97	96	96	98	93	97	72	92	90	73	61	–	–	–
Micronesia (Federated States of)	88	97	86	–	–	–	85	95	69	68	70	74	76	61	46	63	–	–	–	–	–	–
Monaco	100	100	–	100	100	–	89	99	99	99	99	0	99	99	0	0	–	–	–	–	–	–
Mongolia	83	94	56	59	66	41	99	99	99	99	98	90	99	99	0	0	–	70	42	–	–	–
Montenegro	98	97	99	96	98	92	88	97	89	89	47	86	75	89	0	0	–	89 x	16 x	74	–	–
Montserrat	97	–	–	89	–	–	–	–	–	–	–	–	–	–	–	–	–	–	–	–	–	–
Morocco	83	96	64	83	89	75	99	99	99	99	99	99	99	99	99	98	90	70	22	–	–	–
Mozambique	47	79	32	24	47	12	95	90	80	80	91	51	80	80	76	80	83	50	55	56	36	51
Myanmar	68	82	60	65	76	59	88	94	90	89	91	86	90	90	0	14	87	58	62	65	19	27
Namibia	79	97	63	34	55	15	94	98	92	92	85	0	92	92	86	81	88	68	72	63	6	24
Nauru	100	100	–	66	66	–	99	98	91	91	98	96	91	91	0	0	–	69 x	23 x	51 x	–	–
Nepal	88	89	87	46	52	45	93	92	87	85	83	25	87	87	0	46	82	85	37	46	–	–

TABLE 3. HEALTH

Countries and areas	Use of basic drinking water services (%) 2015			Use of basic sanitation services (%) 2015			Immunization coverage (%)											Pneumonia	Diarrhoea	Malaria		
	total	urban	rural	total	urban	rural	BCG	DTP1β	DTP3β	polio3	MCV1	MCV2^	HepB3	Hib3	rota	PCV3	Protection at birth (PAB) against tetanus^	Care seeking for children with symptoms of pneumonia (%)	Treatment with oral rehydration salts (ORS) (%)	Care seeking for children with fever (%)	Children sleeping under ITNs (%)	Households with at least one ITN (%)
							2016											2011–2016*				
Netherlands	100	100	100	98	98	100	–	98	95	95	94	91	93	95	0	94	–	–	–	–	–	–
New Zealand	100	100	100	100	100	100	–	92	92	92	92	89	92	92	66	93	–	–	–	–	–	–
Nicaragua	82	97	61	76	86	63	98	99	98	99	99	0	98	98	98	98	85	58 x	65	–	–	–
Niger	46	89	36	13	44	6	77	87	67	67	74	37	67	67	61	64	85	59	41	51	20	61
Nigeria	67	82	54	33	39	27	64	64	49	49	51	0	49	49	0	26	63	35	34	66	44	69
Niue	98	–	–	97	–	–	99	99	99	99	99	99	99	99	0	99	–	–	–	–	–	–
Norway	100	100	100	98	98	98	–	99	96	96	96	91	0	96	0	94	–	–	–	–	–	–
Oman	91	95	78	99	99	99	99	99	99	99	99	99	99	99	0	99	98	56	59	–	–	–
Pakistan	89	92	87	58	74	48	85	79	72	72	61	53	72	72	0	72	80	64	38	65	0 x	1
Palau	100	100	97	100	100	100	–	99	98	98	96	95	98	98	98	98	–	–	–	–	–	–
Panama	95	99	87	77	86	59	99	96	73	72	90	92	73	73	92	83	–	82	52	–	–	–
Papua New Guinea	37	84	29	19	55	13	89	87	72	73	70	0	66	72	0	20	75	63 x	–	–	–	–
Paraguay	99	99	98	91	98	81	99	99	93	89	99	92	93	93	92	99	85	–	–	–	–	–
Peru	90	95	72	77	82	58	90	94	89	88	88	66	89	89	87	86	85	62	32	61	–	–
Philippines	91	96	86	75	79	72	76	87	86	72	80	66	86	86	0	36	90	64	49	50	–	–
Poland	98	99	96	98	98	98	94	99	98	92	96	94	96	98	0	0	–	–	–	–	–	–
Portugal	100	100	100	99	99	100	32	99	98	98	98	95	98	98	0	0	–	–	–	–	–	–
Qatar	100	–	–	100	–	–	97	99	98	98	99	92	98	98	99	97	–	–	–	–	–	–
Republic of Korea	100	–	–	100	–	–	97	98	98	98	99	97	98	98	0	98	–	–	–	–	–	–
Republic of Moldova	87	96	79	78	89	70	97	94	89	91	89	95	90	89	70	77	–	79	42	–	–	–
Romania	100	100	100	82	93	68	84	96	89	89	86	76	90	89	0	0	–	–	–	–	–	–
Russian Federation	96	99	90	89	93	76	96	97	97	97	98	97	97	0	0	35	–	–	–	–	–	–
Rwanda	57	77	49	62	57	64	99	99	98	99	95	90	98	98	98	98	90	54	28	57	68	81
Saint Kitts and Nevis	–	–	–	–	–	–	96	99	99	99	97	98	98	98	0	0	–	–	–	–	–	–
Saint Lucia	98	98	98	91	86	92	96	95	95	95	99	88	95	95	0	0	–	–	–	–	–	–
Saint Vincent and the Grenadines	95	–	–	87	–	–	99	99	98	97	99	99	98	99	0	0	–	–	–	–	–	–
Samoa	96	99	95	97	98	96	76	95	62	57	68	44	55	55	0	0	–	78	63	59	–	–
San Marino	100	–	–	100	–	–	–	78	66	66	62	36	66	65	0	12	–	–	–	–	–	–
Sao Tome and Principe	80	83	74	40	47	28	92	97	96	96	93	76	96	96	24	96	99	69	49	66	61	78
Saudi Arabia	100	–	–	100	–	–	98	98	98	97	98	96	98	98	95	98	–	–	–	–	–	–
Senegal	75	91	63	48	66	35	97	96	93	92	93	75	93	93	93	93	91	48	32	49	55	77
Serbia	91	88	95	95	98	91	98	97	92	93	82	90	91	92	0	0	–	90 x	36 x	–	–	–
Seychelles	96	–	–	100	–	–	99	98	96	96	97	99	97	96	0	0	100	–	–	–	–	–
Sierra Leone	58	75	47	15	24	8	92	97	84	84	83	50	84	84	95	84	90	72	85	72	49	64
Singapore	100	100	–	100	100	–	99	98	97	96	95	88	96	96	57	78	–	–	–	–	–	–
Slovakia	98	99	97	99	99	98	0	99	96	96	95	97	96	96	0	96	–	–	–	–	–	–
Slovenia	100	100	99	99	99	99	–	98	94	94	92	93	0	94	0	50	–	–	–	–	–	–
Solomon Islands	64	90	56	31	76	18	98	99	99	99	99	0	99	99	0	87	85	79	37	61	70	86
Somalia	40	70	20	16	28	8	37	52	42	47	46	0	42	42	0	0	67	13 x	13 x	–	11 x	12 x
South Africa	85	97	63	73	76	69	74	78	66	66	75	70	66	66	73	69	80	88	51	68	–	–
South Sudan	50	60	48	10	28	6	37	35	26	31	20	0	26	26	0	0	75	48 x	39 x	57	46	66
Spain	100	100	100	100	100	100	–	99	97	97	97	95	97	97	0	0	–	–	–	–	–	–
Sri Lanka	92	96	91	94	89	95	99	99	99	99	99	99	99	99	0	0	95	58 x	51 x	85 x	3 x	5 x
State of Palestine	88	86	94	95	95	99	99	99	99	99	99	99	99	99	0	99	–	77	32	–	–	–
Sudan	59	73	52	35	58	23	96	97	93	93	86	69	93	93	90	93	77	48	20	–	30 x	25 x
Suriname	95	98	88	79	88	61	–	92	91	91	90	44	91	91	0	0	93	76 x	42 x	–	43 x	61 x
Swaziland	68	95	60	58	58	58	97	92	90	90	89	89	90	90	95	90	90	60	84	63	2 x	10 x
Sweden	100	100	100	99	99	100	26	99	98	98	97	95	67	98	0	97	–	–	–	–	–	–
Switzerland	100	100	100	100	100	100	–	99	97	97	94	89	0	97	0	81	–	–	–	–	–	–
Syrian Arab Republic	97	99	94	93	96	89	66	61	42	48	62	52	50	42	0	0	91	77 x	50 x	–	–	–
Tajikistan	74	92	68	95	94	96	98	98	96	97	97	97	97	97	96	0	–	63	60	57	1 x	2 x
Thailand	98	99	97	95	94	96	99	99	99	99	99	99	99	0	0	0	95	80	73	76	–	–
The former Yugoslav Republic of Macedonia	97	96	98	91	97	83	99	97	95	95	82	93	94	94	0	0	–	93 x	62	–	–	–
Timor-Leste	70	91	60	44	73	30	85	95	85	83	78	22	85	85	0	0	81	71 x	71 x	73 x	41 x	41 x
Togo	63	90	45	14	28	5	79	93	89	89	87	0	89	89	90	89	83	49	19	58	43	65
Tokelau	100	–	100	93	–	93	–	–	–	–	–	–	–	–	–	–	–	–	–	–	–	–
Tonga	100	100	100	93	97	92	80	83	78	80	84	85	78	78	0	0	–	–	64	–	–	–
Trinidad and Tobago	97	–	–	92	–	–	–	97	97	84	86	65	97	97	0	91	–	74 x	–	–	–	–
Tunisia	94	100	83	93	98	83	95	99	98	98	96	97	98	98	0	0	96	60	65	–	–	–
Turkey	99	99	100	96	99	89	96	98	98	98	98	85	98	98	0	98	90	–	–	–	–	–
Turkmenistan	94	91	98	97	94	99	98	99	98	98	99	99	98	98	0	0	–	59	47	–	–	–
Turks and Caicos Islands	94	–	–	88	–	–	–	–	–	–	–	–	–	–	–	–	–	–	–	–	–	–
Tuvalu	99	100	99	91	92	91	98	99	94	94	96	92	94	94	0	0	–	–	44 x	79 x	–	–

UNICEF – THE STATE OF THE WORLD'S CHILDREN 2017

TABLE 3. HEALTH   165

Countries and areas	Use of basic drinking water services (%) 2015			Use of basic sanitation services (%) 2015			Immunization coverage (%)										Protection at birth (PAB) against tetanus^	Pneumonia — Care seeking for children with symptoms of pneumonia (%)	Diarrhoea — Treatment with oral rehydration salts (ORS) (%)	Malaria — Care seeking for children with fever (%)	Malaria — Children sleeping under ITNs (%)	Malaria — House-holds with at least one ITN (%)
	total	urban	rural	total	urban	rural	BCG	DTP1β	DTP3β	polio3	MCV1	MCV2^	HepB3	Hib3	rota	PCV3	2016	2011–2016*				
Uganda	39	73	32	19	28	17	93	89	78	82	82	0	78	78	0	78	87	80	47	81	62	78
Ukraine	98	97	100	96	97	93	75	42	19	56	42	31	26	47	0	0	–	92	59	–	–	–
United Arab Emirates	100	100	100	100	100	100	99	99	99	99	99	99	99	99	92	99	–	–	–	–	–	–
United Kingdom	100	100	100	99	99	99	–	98	94	94	92	89	0	94	90	92	–	–	–	–	–	–
United Republic of Tanzania	50	79	37	24	37	17	99	99	97	93	90	71	97	97	96	96	90	55	45	50	54	66
United States	99	100	97	100	100	100	–	97	95	94	92	0	93	93	73	93	–	–	–	–	–	–
Uruguay	99	100	94	96	96	95	98	97	95	95	95	92	95	95	0	94	–	91	–	–	–	–
Uzbekistan	–	99	–	100	100	100	99	99	99	99	99	99	99	99	99	99	–	68 x	28 x	–	–	–
Vanuatu	91	99	87	53	61	51	73	75	64	65	53	0	64	64	0	0	78	72	48	57	51	83
Venezuela (Bolivarian Republic of)	97	99	86	95	98	72	99	98	84	82	88	53	84	84	47	7	75	72 x	38 x	–	–	–
Viet Nam	91	92	91	78	91	72	95	96	96	95	99	95	96	96	0	0	94	81	51	–	9	10
Yemen	70	85	63	60	90	44	73	76	71	65	70	49	71	71	59	71	70	34	25	33	–	–
Zambia	61	86	44	31	49	19	99	99	91	87	93	58	91	91	90	90	85	70	64	75	41	68
Zimbabwe	67	94	54	39	54	31	95	94	90	90	95	63	90	90	91	90	80	51	41	50	9	48
SUMMARY																						
East Asia and Pacific	94	96	91	77	87	63	93	97	94	93	93	87	90	38	1	11	89 **	72 **	47 **	67 **	–	–
Europe and Central Asia	98	99	94	96	98	92	91	95	92	94	93	88	81	76	22	62	–	–	–	–	–	–
Eastern Europe and Central Asia	95	98	90	93	95	87	95	93	90	93	93	88	90	61	16	54	–	–	–	–	–	–
Western Europe	100	100	99	99	99	99	66	98	96	95	93	88	69	95	30	71	–	–	–	–	–	–
Latin America and Caribbean	96	99	86	86	90	68	95	94	90	92	92	73	89	89	77	81	89	72	48	–	–	–
Middle East and North Africa	93	96	87	89	94	81	94	91	88	88	89	87	88	88	29	32	84	65	27	–	–	–
North America	99	100	97	100	100	100	–	97	95	94	92	8	90	93	67	92	–	–	–	–	–	–
South Asia	88	93	86	46	65	37	89	89	86	84	84	72	86	80	3	22	86	69	51	61 ‡	–	5 ‡
Sub-Saharan Africa	58	82	43	28	42	20	80	83	74	73	72	24	74	74	45	65	80	47	38	57	48	66
Eastern and Southern Africa	53	82	40	30	48	21	84	88	80	80	76	36	80	80	66	76	82	56	42	56	48	62
West and Central Africa	62	82	46	27	37	19	76	77	67	65	67	11	67	67	25	54	77	39	34	57	48	70
Least developed countries	62	83	52	32	46	26	84	87	80	78	77	37	80	80	42	72	84	49	44	53	46	60
World	**89**	**95**	**80**	**68**	**83**	**50**	**88**	**91**	**86**	**85**	**85**	**64**	**84**	**70**	**25**	**42**	**84 ****	**62 ****	**44 ****	**59 ‡****	**–**	**–**

For a complete list of countries and areas in the regions, subregions and country categories, see page 150 or visit <data.unicef.org/regionalclassifications>.
It is not advisable to compare data from consecutive editions of *The State of the World's Children.*

DEFINITIONS OF THE INDICATORS

Population using basic drinking water services – Percentage of the population using an improved drinking water source, where collection time is not more than 30 minutes for a round trip including queuing (improved sources include: piped water; boreholes or tubewells; protected dug wells; protected springs; rainwater; and packaged or delivered water.

Population using basic sanitation services – Percentage of the population using an improved sanitation facility that is not shared with other households (improved facilities include: flush/pour flush to piped sewerage systems, septic tanks or pit latrines; ventilated improved pit latrines; composting toilets or pit latrines with slabs.

EPI – Expanded Programme on Immunization: The first diseases targeted by the EPI were diphtheria, pertussis (whooping cough) and tetanus (DPT); measles; poliomyelitis; and tuberculosis (TB). Additional vaccines have been added to the original six recommended in 1974 and include vaccines to protect against hepatitis B (HepB), and *Haemophilus influenzae* type b (Hib). Pneumococcal conjugate vaccine (PCV) and rotavirus vaccine, also recommended by the WHO, are increasingly being added to national schedules.

BCG – Percentage of live births who received bacille Calmette-Guérin (vaccine against tuberculosis).

DTP1 – Percentage of surviving infants who received the first dose of diphtheria, pertussis and tetanus vaccine.

DTP3 – Percentage of surviving infants who received three doses of diphtheria, pertussis and tetanus vaccine.

Polio3 – Percentage of surviving infants who received three doses of the polio vaccine.

MCV1 – Percentage of surviving infants who received the first dose of the measles-containing vaccine.

MCV2 – Percentage of children who received the second dose of measles-containing vaccine as per national schedule.

HepB3 – Percentage of surviving infants who received three doses of hepatitis B vaccine.

Hib3 – Percentage of surviving infants who received three doses of *Haemophilus influenzae* type b vaccine.

Rota – Percentage of surviving infants who received the last dose of rotavirus vaccine as recommended.

PCV3 – Percentage of surviving infants who received three doses of pneumococcal conjugate vaccine.

Protection at birth (PAB) – Percentage of newborns protected at birth against tetanus with Tetanus Toxoid.

Care-seeking for children with symptoms of pneumonia – Percentage of children under age 5 with symptoms of pneumonia (cough and fast or difficult breathing due to a problem in the chest) in the two weeks preceding the survey for whom advice or treatment was sought from a health facility or provider.

Diarrhoea treatment with oral rehydration salts (ORS) – Percentage of children under age 5 who had diarrhoea in the two weeks preceding the survey and who received oral rehydration salts (ORS packets or pre-packaged ORS fluids).

Care-seeking for children with fever – Percentage of children under five years of age with fever for whom advice or treatment was sought from a health facility or provider. Excludes drug vendor, stores, shops and traditional healer. In some countries, particularly non-malaria endemic countries, pharmacies have also been excluded from the calculation.

Children sleeping under ITNs – Percentage of children under age 5 who slept under an insecticide-treated mosquito net the night prior to the survey.

Households with at least one ITN – Percentage of households with at least one insecticide-treated mosquito net.

MAIN DATA SOURCES

Use of basic drinking water services and basic sanitation services – WHO/UNICEF Joint Monitoring Programme for Water Supply, Sanitation and Hygiene (JMP).

Immunization – WHO and UNICEF estimates of national immunization coverage, 2016 revision.

Care-seeking for children with symptoms of pneumonia – Demographic and Health Surveys (DHS), Multiple Indicator Cluster Surveys (MICS) and other national household surveys.

Diarrhoea treatment with oral rehydration salts (ORS) – DHS, MICS and other national household surveys.

Malaria prevention and treatment – DHS, MICS, Malaria Indicator Surveys (MIS) and other national household surveys.

NOTES

–   Data not available.

x   Data refer to years or periods other than those specified in the column heading. Such data are not included in the calculation of regional and global averages. Estimates from data years prior to 2000 are not displayed.

β   Coverage for DTP1 should be at least as high as DPT3. Discrepancies where DPT1 coverage is less than DPT3 reflect deficiencies in the data collection and reporting process. UNICEF and WHO are working with national and territorial systems to eliminate these discrepancies.

^   Generally, the second dose of measles containing vaccine (MCV2) is recommended for administration during the second year of life; however, in many countries, MCV2 is scheduled after the second year. For the calculation of regional aggregates, the coverage of the countries that did not report MCV2 data for 2016 is considered to be 0%, e.g. the regional coverage calculation for North America includes the United States with 0% MCV2 coverage in 2016.

λ   WHO and UNICEF employ a complex process employing adminitrative data, surveys (routine and supple-mental), serosurveys, and information on other vaccines to calculate the percentage of births that can be considered as protected against tetanus because pregnant women were given two doses or more of tetanus toxoid (TT) vaccine. The complete methodology can be found at <http://who.int/immunization/monitoring_surveillance/data/en/>.

*   Data refer to the most recent year available during the period specified in the column heading.

**   Excludes China.

‡   Excludes India.

TABLE 4. HIV/AIDS

Countries and areas	HIV incidence per 1,000 uninfected population 2016 — All ages	— children <5	— adolescents 15–19	People living with HIV 2016 — All ages	— children <15	— adolescents 10–19	New HIV infections 2016 — All ages	— children <5	— adolescents 15–19	AIDS-related deaths 2016 — All ages	— children <15	— adolescents 10–19	Pregnant women receiving ARVs for PMTCT (%) 2016*	People living with HIV receiving antiretroviral therapy (ART) (%) 2016* — All ages	— children <15	— adolescents 10–19	Condom use among adolescents with multiple partners (%) 2011–2016* — male	— female	Adolescents tested for HIV in the last 12 months and received results (%) 2011–2016* — male	— female
Afghanistan	0.03	0.01	0.02	7,500	<500	<500	<1,000	<100	<100	<500	<100	<100	5	7	17	16	–	–	<0.1	1
Albania	0.08	0.04	0.16	1,700	–	–	<500	–	<100	<100	–	–	–	30	–	–	–	–	0 x	0 x
Algeria	0.02	0.01	0.05	13,000	<500	<500	<1,000	<100	<200	<200	<100	<100	49	76	>95	77	–	–	–	1
Andorra	–	–	–	–	–	–	–	–	–	–	–	–	–	–	–	–	–	–	–	–
Angola	0.94	0.76	0.81	280,000	23,000	13,000	25,000	3,600	2,400	11,000	2,100	<500	44	22	14	–	39	31	4	16
Anguilla	–	–	–	–	–	–	–	–	–	–	–	–	–	–	–	–	–	–	–	–
Antigua and Barbuda	–	–	–	–	–	–	–	–	–	–	–	–	–	–	–	–	100 x	54 x	–	–
Argentina	0.13	0.02	0.28	120,000	1,200	3,700	5,500	<100	<1,000	2,400	<100	<100	91	64	>95	–	–	–	–	–
Armenia	0.09	<0.01	0.18	3,300	–	–	<500	–	<100	<200	–	–	–	36	–	–	–	–	0	1
Australia	0.05	<0.01	0.02	25,000	<100	<100	1,100	<100	<100	<500	<100	<100	>95	90	93	–	–	–	–	–
Austria	–	–	–	–	–	–	–	–	–	–	–	–	–	–	–	–	–	–	–	–
Azerbaijan	0.10	0.01	0.05	9,200	<200	<100	<1,000	<100	<100	<500	<100	<100	75	30	76	36	–	–	–	–
Bahamas	–	–	–	8,200	–	–	–	–	–	–	–	–	–	28	–	–	–	–	–	–
Bahrain	0.04	0.02	0.02	<500	–	–	<100	–	<100	<100	–	–	–	42	–	–	–	–	–	–
Bangladesh	0.01	<0.01	<0.01	12,000	<500	<500	1,500	<100	<100	1,000	<100	<100	17	16	39	23	–	–	–	–
Barbados	0.58	0.08	0.33	2,600	–	–	<200	–	<100	<100	–	–	–	46	–	–	–	–	–	10
Belarus	0.20	0.01	0.13	19,000	<100	<200	1,800	<100	<100	<200	<100	<100	92	45	>95	–	–	–	15	15
Belgium	–	–	–	–	–	–	–	–	–	–	–	–	–	–	–	–	–	–	–	–
Belize	0.75	0.46	1.48	4,300	<200	<500	<500	<100	<100	<200	<100	<100	35	32	64	–	–	–	–	14
Benin	0.34	0.25	0.58	67,000	6,300	5,100	3,600	<500	<1,000	2,400	<500	<200	>95	57	32	–	43	38	6	7
Bhutan	–	–	–	–	–	–	–	–	–	–	–	–	–	–	–	–	–	–	–	3 x
Bolivia (Plurinational State of)	0.10	0.01	0.21	19,000	<500	<1,000	1,100	<100	<500	<1,000	<100	<100	68	25	43	40	43 x	–	1 x	–
Bosnia and Herzegovina	–	–	–	–	–	–	–	–	–	–	–	–	–	–	–	–	–	–	<0.1	<0.1
Botswana	5.52	2.30	7.18	360,000	12,000	17,000	10,000	<1,000	1,400	3,900	<500	<500	>95	83	60	77	–	–	–	–
Brazil	0.24	0.04	0.48	830,000	11,000	30,000	48,000	<1,000	8,200	14,000	<1,000	<500	89	60	37	32	–	–	–	–
British Virgin Islands	–	–	–	–	–	–	–	–	–	–	–	–	–	–	–	–	–	–	–	–
Brunei Darussalam	–	–	–	–	–	–	–	–	–	–	–	–	–	–	–	–	–	–	–	–
Bulgaria	–	–	–	3,500	–	–	<500	–	–	<200	–	–	–	26	–	–	–	–	–	–
Burkina Faso	0.19	0.18	0.47	95,000	10,000	12,000	3,400	<1,000	<1,000	3,100	<500	<500	83	60	24	–	76 x,p	57 x,p	4 x	8 x
Burundi	0.20	0.20	0.15	84,000	12,000	8,100	2,200	<500	<200	2,900	<1,000	<500	84	61	25	–	–	–	8	13
Cabo Verde	–	–	–	2,800	<200	<200	<200	<100	–	<100	<100	<100	>95	57	65	40	–	–	–	–
Cambodia	0.04	0.05	0.08	71,000	4,200	3,300	<1,000	<100	<200	1,800	<100	<100	75	80	87	–	–	–	3	7
Cameroon	1.39	1.09	2.41	560,000	46,000	40,000	32,000	4,000	5,900	29,000	3,200	1,400	74	37	18	–	70	52	7	15
Canada	–	–	–	–	–	–	–	–	–	–	–	–	–	–	–	–	–	–	–	–
Central African Republic	1.80	0.80	1.51	130,000	9,200	8,700	8,700	<1,000	<1,000	7,300	<1,000	<500	81	24	18	25	50 x	28 x	7 x	15 x
Chad	0.34	0.38	0.38	110,000	11,000	7,600	4,800	<1,000	<1,000	2,800	<1,000	<500	63	39	14	–	–	54	2	5
Chile	0.28	0.08	0.59	61,000	<500	2,200	5,000	<100	<1,000	–	–	–	38	53	35	7	–	–	–	–
China	–	–	–	–	–	–	–	–	–	–	–	–	–	–	–	–	–	–	–	–
Colombia	0.12	0.01	0.22	120,000	<1,000	3,500	5,600	<100	<1,000	2,800	<100	<100	>95	–	–	–	–	45 x	–	8 x
Comoros	0.01	0.01	0.02	<200	–	–	<100	–	<100	<100	–	–	–	35	–	–	51 p	–	3	2
Congo	1.65	1.39	1.38	91,000	6,000	4,100	7,600	1,100	<1,000	3,800	<1,000	<200	16	23	25	–	56	46	4	8
Cook Islands	–	–	–	–	–	–	–	–	–	–	–	–	–	–	–	–	–	–	–	–
Costa Rica	0.19	0.02	0.36	13,000	<100	<500	<1,000	<100	<200	<500	<100	<100	65	49	80	–	–	59 p	–	9
Côte d'Ivoire	0.86	0.87	0.60	460,000	36,000	25,000	20,000	3,300	1,500	25,000	2,600	1,100	73	41	25	–	70	32	5	10
Croatia	0.02	<0.01	0.05	1,500	–	–	<100	–	<100	<100	–	–	–	70	–	–	–	–	–	–
Cuba	0.29	0.05	0.68	25,000	<200	1,100	3,300	<100	<500	<200	<100	<100	63	70	24	9	–	79 p	16	19
Cyprus	–	–	–	–	–	–	–	–	–	–	–	–	–	–	–	–	–	–	–	–
Czechia	0.04	<0.01	0.08	3,400	–	–	<500	–	<100	<100	–	–	–	52	–	–	–	–	–	–
Democratic People's Republic of Korea	–	–	–	–	–	–	–	–	–	–	–	–	–	–	–	–	–	–	–	–
Democratic Republic of the Congo	0.17	0.21	0.24	370,000	48,000	32,000	13,000	2,900	2,100	19,000	2,800	1,400	70	42	30	–	17	12	1	5
Denmark	–	–	–	–	–	–	–	–	–	–	–	–	–	–	–	–	–	–	–	–
Djibouti	0.58	0.68	0.40	8,600	<1,000	<1,000	<500	<100	<100	<1,000	<100	<100	35	26	9	10	–	–	–	–
Dominica	–	–	–	–	–	–	–	–	–	–	–	–	–	–	–	–	74 x	86 x	–	–
Dominican Republic	0.24	0.07	0.52	67,000	1,700	3,100	2,500	<100	<500	2,200	<100	<100	83	46	45	30	–	40	–	11
Ecuador	–	–	–	33,000	<500	1,400	1,900	<100	–	<1,000	<100	<100	>95	52	>95	–	–	–	–	–
Egypt	0.02	<0.01	0.04	11,000	<500	<1,000	1,600	<100	<500	<500	<100	<100	18	27	38	–	–	–	–	–
El Salvador	0.16	0.09	0.31	24,000	<500	<1,000	<1,000	<100	<200	<1,000	<100	<100	44	48	50	–	–	31 p	8	8
Equatorial Guinea	2.71	1.35	2.36	35,000	2,400	1,300	2,300	<200	<200	<1,000	<200	<100	90	43	16	–	31	17	7	27
Eritrea	0.15	0.22	0.11	15,000	1,500	1,300	<1,000	<200	<100	<1,000	<200	<100	37	59	34	–	–	–	–	–
Estonia	–	–	–	–	–	–	–	–	–	–	–	–	–	–	–	–	–	–	–	–
Ethiopia	0.33	0.26	0.23	710,000	62,000	67,000	30,000	3,800	2,700	20,000	2,900	2,500	69	59	35	–	57 p	–	9	12
Fiji	–	–	–	<1,000	–	–	<200	–	–	<100	–	–	–	32	–	–	–	–	–	–

TABLE 4. HIV/AIDS 167

Countries and areas	HIV incidence per 1,000 uninfected population 2016			People living with HIV 2016			New HIV infections 2016			AIDS-related deaths 2016			Pregnant women receiving ARVs for PMTCT (%) 2016*	People living with HIV receiving antiretroviral therapy (ART) (%) 2016*			Condom use among adolescents with multiple partners (%) 2011–2016*		Adolescents tested for HIV in the last 12 months and received results (%) 2011–2016*	
	All ages	children <5	adolescents 15–19	All ages	children <15	adolescents 10–19	All ages	children <5	adolescents 15–19	All ages	children <15	adolescents 10–19		All ages	children <15	adolescents 10–19	male	female	male	female
Finland	–	–	–	–	–	–	–	–	–	–	–	–	–	–	–	–	–	–	–	–
France	0.09	0.01	0.25	180,000	<500	2,800	6,000	<100	<1,000	<1,000	<100	<100	>95	78	>95					
Gabon	0.92	0.95	1.57	48,000	3,700	2,900	1,700	<500	<500	1,500	<500	<100	76	63	39	61	77	58	6	20
Gambia	0.65	0.47	0.23	20,000	1,600	<1,000	1,300	<200	<100	1,100	<200	<100	69	30	33	–	–	–	2	6
Georgia	0.28	0.06	0.15	12,000	<100	<100	1,100	<100	<100	<500	<100	<100	46	32	50	62	–	–	–	2 x
Germany	–	–	–	–	–	–	–	–	–	–	–	–	–	–	–	–	–	–	–	–
Ghana	0.78	0.79	0.83	290,000	32,000	23,000	20,000	3,000	2,200	15,000	2,500	1,100	56	34	15	–	–	22 p	1	5
Greece	–	–	–	–	–	–	–	–	–	–	–	–	–	–	–	–	–	–	–	–
Grenada	–	–	–	–	–	–	–	–	–	–	–	–	–	–	–	–	80 x	92 x	–	–
Guatemala	0.18	0.15	0.35	46,000	1,800	2,300	2,900	<500	<1,000	1,600	<200	<100	19	36	42	25	66	38	2	5
Guinea	0.67	0.68	1.08	120,000	10,000	8,700	8,300	1,300	1,400	5,800	<1,000	<500	43	35	18	–	46 p	30	1	3
Guinea-Bissau	0.72	0.72	0.56	36,000	4,200	2,100	1,300	<500	<200	2,000	<500	<200	85	33	15	–	60	41	2	5
Guyana	0.77	0.32	1.62	8,500	<500	<1,000	<1,000	<100	<200	<200	<100	<100	66	58	69	–	83 p	–	10	16
Haiti	0.77	0.50	0.59	150,000	7,200	6,200	7,900	<1,000	<1,000	4,600	<500	<200	71	55	49	53	58	42	4	9
Holy See	–	–	–	–	–	–	–	–	–	–	–	–	–	–	–	–	–	–	–	–
Honduras	0.11	0.05	0.21	21,000	<1,000	1,300	<1,000	<100	<200	<1,000	<100	<100	54	51	69	60	73	39	3	10
Hungary	–	–	–	–	–	–	–	–	–	–	–	–	–	–	–	–	–	–	–	–
Iceland	–	–	–	–	–	–	–	–	–	–	–	–	–	–	–	–	–	–	–	–
India	0.06	–	–	2,100,000	130,000	130,000	80,000	9,100	16,000	62,000	7,000	3,100	41	49	33	–	39 x	–	0 x	1 x
Indonesia	0.19	0.13	0.29	620,000	14,000	17,000	48,000	3,200	6,300	38,000	1,900	<500	14	13	21	–	–	–	–	–
Iran (Islamic Republic of)	0.06	0.01	0.03	66,000	1,000	<1,000	5,000	<100	<200	4,000	<100	<100	51	14	28	19	–	–	–	–
Iraq	–	–	–	–	–	–	–	–	–	–	–	–	–	–	–	–	–	–	–	0
Ireland	0.06	<0.01	0.03	6,200	<100	<100	<500	<100	<100	–	–	–	>95	77	>95	–	–	–	–	–
Israel	–	–	–	–	–	–	–	–	–	–	–	–	–	–	–	–	–	–	–	–
Italy	0.06	0.02	0.04	130,000	<1,000	<500	3,600	<100	<200	–	–	–	58	80	94	–	–	–	–	–
Jamaica	–	–	–	30,000	<500	1,300	1,700	<100	–	1,300	<100	<100	>95	35	>95	–	75	56 p	20	35
Japan	–	–	–	–	–	–	–	–	–	–	–	–	–	55	–	–	–	–	–	–
Jordan	<0.01	<0.01	0.01	<500	–	–	<100	–	<100	<100	–	–	–	55	–	–	–	–	–	–
Kazakhstan	0.16	0.03	0.08	26,000	<500	<500	2,900	<100	<100	<1,000	<100	<100	87	31	89	>95	94 p	–	–	11
Kenya	1.46	0.87	2.69	1,600,000	120,000	140,000	62,000	6,100	14,000	36,000	4,800	3,300	80	64	65	–	64	26	27	35
Kiribati	–	–	–	–	–	–	–	–	–	–	–	–	–	–	–	–	29 x	–	–	–
Kuwait	0.02	0.01	0.03	<500	–	–	<100	–	<100	<100	–	–	–	80	–	–	–	–	–	–
Kyrgyzstan	0.13	0.02	0.07	8,500	<200	<200	<1,000	<100	<100	<500	<100	<100	–	28	88	>95	–	–	–	11
Lao People's Democratic Republic	0.10	0.10	0.10	11,000	<1,000	<500	<1,000	<100	<100	<500	<100	<100	50	41	34	–	–	–	1	1
Latvia	0.23	0.02	0.63	6,600	<100	<200	<500	<100	<100	<500	<100	<100	>95	26	93	–	–	–	–	–
Lebanon	0.02	0.02	0.05	2,200	–	–	<200	–	<100	<100	–	–	–	51	–	–	–	–	–	–
Lesotho	12.68	7.57	13.73	330,000	–	–	21,000	–	2,900	9,900	–	–	66	53	–	–	22 p	27	4	13
Liberia	0.66	0.47	1.49	43,000	4,200	5,000	2,900	<500	<1,000	2,800	<500	<500	70	19	11	–	–	–	–	–
Libya	–	–	–	–	–	–	–	–	–	–	–	–	–	–	–	–	–	–	–	–
Liechtenstein	–	–	–	–	–	–	–	–	–	–	–	–	–	–	–	–	–	–	–	–
Lithuania	0.09	<0.01	0.05	2,900	–	–	<500	–	<100	<200	–	–	–	23	–	–	–	–	–	–
Luxembourg	0.18	0.03	0.40	–	–	–	<200	<100	<100	<100	<100	<100	56	–	–	–	–	–	–	–
Madagascar	0.18	0.09	0.37	31,000	1,900	3,200	4,300	<500	<1,000	1,600	<500	<100	3	5	2	52	5	6 p	1	2
Malawi	2.29	1.61	2.58	1,000,000	110,000	90,000	36,000	4,300	4,800	24,000	4,100	3,200	84	66	49	–	59	44	22	32
Malaysia	0.19	0.01	0.07	97,000	<500	<1,000	5,700	<100	<200	7,000	<100	<100	73	37	>95	71	–	–	–	–
Maldives	–	–	–	–	–	–	–	–	–	–	–	–	–	–	–	–	–	–	–	–
Mali	0.33	0.51	0.62	110,000	14,000	9,900	5,900	1,600	1,200	6,100	<1,000	<500	35	35	21	7	47	26	1	8
Malta	–	–	–	<500	–	–	<100	–	–	<100	–	–	–	75	–	–	–	–	–	–
Marshall Islands	–	–	–	–	–	–	–	–	–	–	–	–	–	–	–	–	–	–	–	–
Mauritania	–	–	–	11,000	<1,000	<1,000	<500	<100	–	<1,000	<100	<100	34	23	23	15	–	–	–	–
Mauritius	–	–	–	–	–	–	–	–	–	–	–	–	–	–	–	–	–	–	–	–
Mexico	0.10	0.02	0.19	220,000	2,500	7,200	12,000	<500	2,200	4,200	<200	<100	58	60	74	28	–	36 p	–	7
Micronesia (Federated States of)	–	–	–	–	–	–	–	–	–	–	–	–	–	–	–	–	–	–	–	–
Monaco	–	–	–	–	–	–	–	–	–	–	–	–	–	–	–	–	–	–	–	–
Mongolia	0.01	<0.01	0.02	<500	–	–	<100	–	<100	<100	–	–	–	33	–	–	78 p	–	–	–
Montenegro	0.11	0.05	0.30	<500	–	–	<100	–	<100	<100	–	–	–	60	–	–	64 p	–	<0.1	0
Montserrat	–	–	–	–	–	–	–	–	–	–	–	–	–	–	–	–	–	–	–	–
Morocco	0.03	0.01	0.06	22,000	<500	<1,000	<1,000	<100	<200	<1,000	<100	<100	62	48	>95	–	–	–	–	–
Mozambique	3.63	2.77	3.03	1,800,000	200,000	120,000	83,000	13,000	9,000	62,000	9,200	4,400	80	54	38	–	39	43 p	10	25
Myanmar	0.22	0.12	0.49	230,000	9,300	11,000	11,000	<1,000	2,300	7,800	<500	<200	87	55	78	–	–	61	2	1
Namibia	4.37	1.32	5.31	230,000	15,000	13,000	9,600	<500	1,300	4,300	<500	<500	>95	64	66	–	75	61	14	29
Nauru	–	–	–	–	–	–	–	–	–	–	–	–	–	–	–	–	–	–	–	–
Nepal	0.03	0.02	0.02	32,000	1,200	<1,000	<1,000	<100	<100	1,700	<100	<100	64	40	83	–	–	–	3	3

TABLE 4. HIV/AIDS

Countries and areas	HIV incidence per 1,000 uninfected population 2016			People living with HIV 2016			New HIV infections 2016			AIDS-related deaths 2016			Pregnant women receiving ARVs for PMTCT (%) 2016*	People living with HIV receiving antiretroviral therapy (ART) (%) 2016*			Condom use among adolescents with multiple partners (%) 2011–2016*		Adolescents tested for HIV in the last 12 months and received results (%) 2011–2016*	
	All ages	children <5	adolescents 15–19	All ages	children <15	adolescents 10–19	All ages	children <5	adolescents 15–19	All ages	children <15	adolescents 10–19		All ages	children <15	adolescents 10–19	male	female	male	female
Netherlands	0.03	<0.01	0.07	23,000	<100	<500	<500	<100	<100	<200	<100	<100	>95	80	>95	–	–	–	–	–
New Zealand	–	–	–	–	–	–	–	–	–	–	–	–	–	–	–	–	–	–	–	–
Nicaragua	0.06	0.01	0.13	8,900	<200	<500	<500	<100	<100	<500	<100	<100	>95	43	71	33	–	–	–	–
Niger	0.09	0.13	0.18	48,000	5,800	4,400	1,800	<1,000	<500	3,400	<500	<500	52	32	17	14	–	–	2	4
Nigeria	1.23	1.19	2.18	3,200,000	270,000	240,000	220,000	37,000	40,000	160,000	24,000	7,900	32	30	21	–	46 p	38	2	4
Niue	–	–	–	–	–	–	–	–	–	–	–	–	–	–	–	–	–	–	–	–
Norway	–	–	–	–	–	–	–	–	–	–	–	–	–	–	–	–	–	–	–	–
Oman	–	–	–	–	–	–	–	–	–	–	–	–	–	–	–	–	–	–	–	–
Pakistan	0.10	0.04	0.05	130,000	3,300	2,300	19,000	<1,000	<1,000	5,500	<500	<100	4	7	10	85	–	–	–	–
Palau	–	–	–	–	–	–	–	–	–	–	–	–	–	–	–	–	–	–	–	–
Panama	0.34	0.08	0.70	21,000	–	–	1,300	–	<500	<1,000	–	–	–	54	–	–	–	–	–	–
Papua New Guinea	0.37	0.42	0.27	46,000	3,400	2,000	2,800	<500	<500	1,100	<500	<100	33	52	37	–	–	–	–	–
Paraguay	0.20	0.05	0.38	19,000	<500	<1,000	1,300	<100	<500	<1,000	<100	<100	71	35	55	25	–	50 x	–	–
Peru	–	–	–	70,000	1,300	2,400	2,700	<100	–	2,200	<100	<100	85	60	73	15	–	20	–	–
Philippines	0.11	0.01	0.25	56,000	<500	5,200	10,000	<200	2,400	<1,000	<100	<100	12	32	10	3	–	–	–	<0.1
Poland	–	–	–	–	–	–	–	–	–	–	–	–	–	–	–	–	–	–	–	–
Portugal	–	–	–	–	–	–	–	–	–	–	–	–	–	–	–	–	–	–	–	–
Qatar	0.02	0.03	0.04	<100	–	–	<100	–	<100	<100	–	–	–	86	–	–	–	–	–	–
Republic of Korea	–	–	–	–	–	–	–	–	–	–	–	–	–	–	–	–	–	–	–	–
Republic of Moldova	0.38	0.06	0.19	15,000	<200	<200	1,600	<100	<100	<500	<100	<100	>95	29	83	55	–	–	6	10
Romania	0.04	<0.01	0.10	16,000	<100	<500	<1,000	<100	<200	<200	<100	<100	>95	68	>95	66	–	–	–	–
Russian Federation	–	–	–	–	–	–	–	–	–	–	–	–	–	–	–	–	–	–	–	–
Rwanda	0.70	0.50	0.85	220,000	16,000	16,000	7,500	<1,000	<1,000	3,300	<1,000	<500	82	80	55	–	–	–	22	27
Saint Kitts and Nevis	–	–	–	–	–	–	–	–	–	–	–	–	–	–	–	–	54 x	50 x	–	–
Saint Lucia	–	–	–	–	–	–	–	–	–	–	–	–	–	–	–	–	–	–	–	12
Saint Vincent and the Grenadines	–	–	–	–	–	–	–	–	–	–	–	–	–	–	–	–	–	–	–	–
Samoa	–	–	–	–	–	–	–	–	–	–	–	–	–	–	–	–	–	–	1 x	0 x
San Marino	–	–	–	–	–	–	–	–	–	–	–	–	–	–	–	–	–	–	–	–
Sao Tome and Principe	–	–	–	–	–	–	–	–	–	–	–	–	–	–	–	–	79	–	8	22
Saudi Arabia	0.02	0.01	0.01	8,200	<500	<200	<500	<100	<100	<500	<100	<100	39	60	48	>95	–	–	–	–
Senegal	0.08	0.16	0.12	41,000	4,800	2,900	1,100	<500	<200	1,900	<500	<200	55	52	26	31	–	–	6	10
Serbia	0.03	0.01	0.06	2,700	–	–	<500	–	<100	<100	–	–	–	62	–	–	63 x	–	1 x	1 x
Seychelles	–	–	–	–	–	–	–	–	–	–	–	–	–	–	–	–	–	–	–	–
Sierra Leone	–	–	–	67,000	4,400	5,000	5,300	<500	–	2,800	<500	<200	87	26	18	–	24	10	3	11
Singapore	–	–	–	–	–	–	–	–	–	–	–	–	–	–	–	–	–	–	–	–
Slovakia	0.02	<0.01	0.04	<1,000	–	–	<200	–	<100	<100	–	–	–	59	–	–	–	–	–	–
Slovenia	0.03	<0.01	0.06	<1,000	–	–	<100	–	<100	<100	–	–	–	–	–	–	–	–	–	–
Solomon Islands	–	–	–	–	–	–	–	–	–	–	–	–	–	–	–	–	54 x,p	15 x,p	–	–
Somalia	0.17	0.18	0.13	24,000	2,500	1,400	1,800	<500	<200	1,700	<500	<100	7	11	5	–	–	–	–	–
South Africa	5.58	2.19	10.51	7,100,000	320,000	370,000	270,000	12,000	50,000	110,000	9,300	6,200	>95	56	55	–	88	–	29	38
South Sudan	1.35	1.25	1.08	200,000	18,000	10,000	16,000	2,400	1,500	13,000	1,700	<500	29	10	5	–	–	6 x,p	–	4 x
Spain	0.09	<0.01	0.21	140,000	<100	1,200	3,900	<100	<500	–	–	–	>95	77	>95	–	–	–	–	–
Sri Lanka	0.03	<0.01	0.06	4,000	–	–	<1,000	–	<100	<200	–	–	–	27	–	–	–	–	–	–
State of Palestine	–	–	–	–	–	–	–	–	–	–	–	–	–	–	–	–	–	–	–	–
Sudan	0.13	0.10	0.26	56,000	3,000	3,800	5,000	<1,000	1,100	3,000	<500	<100	4	10	16	–	–	–	–	–
Suriname	0.62	0.17	1.35	4,900	<200	<500	<500	<100	<100	<200	<100	<100	89	48	81	36	–	86 x,p	–	11 x
Swaziland	9.37	4.50	11.91	220,000	15,000	15,000	8,800	<1,000	1,400	3,900	<1,000	<500	95	79	64	91	–	–	30	41
Sweden	0.06	<0.01	0.14	11,000	<100	<200	<1,000	<100	<100	<100	<100	<100	>95	83	>95	–	–	–	–	–
Switzerland	–	–	–	–	–	–	–	–	–	–	–	–	–	–	–	–	–	–	–	–
Syrian Arab Republic	–	–	–	–	–	–	–	–	–	–	–	–	–	–	–	–	–	–	–	–
Tajikistan	0.15	0.02	0.07	14,000	<500	<500	1,300	<100	<100	<1,000	<100	<100	85	30	88	90	–	–	–	1
Thailand	0.10	0.01	0.23	450,000	4,100	9,700	6,400	<100	<1,000	16,000	<100	<100	95	69	86	>95	–	–	4	6
The former Yugoslav Republic of Macedonia	0.02	<0.01	0.03	<500	–	–	<100	–	<100	<100	–	–	–	48	–	–	–	–	–	–
Timor-Leste	–	–	–	–	–	–	–	–	–	–	–	–	–	–	–	–	–	–	–	–
Togo	0.59	0.65	0.49	100,000	12,000	7,600	4,100	<1,000	<500	5,100	<1,000	<500	86	51	26	27	–	–	7	11
Tokelau	–	–	–	–	–	–	–	–	–	–	–	–	–	–	–	–	–	–	–	–
Tonga	–	–	–	–	–	–	–	–	–	–	–	–	–	–	–	–	–	–	2	0
Trinidad and Tobago	0.29	0.05	0.60	11,000	<100	<500	<500	<100	<100	<500	<100	<100	95	62	>95	–	–	–	–	–
Tunisia	0.03	0.01	0.06	2,900	–	–	<500	–	<100	<100	–	–	–	29	–	–	–	–	–	<0.1
Turkey	–	–	–	–	–	–	–	–	–	–	–	–	–	–	–	–	–	–	–	–
Turkmenistan	–	–	–	–	–	–	–	–	–	–	–	–	–	–	–	–	–	–	–	5
Turks and Caicos Islands	–	–	–	–	–	–	–	–	–	–	–	–	–	–	–	–	–	–	–	–
Tuvalu	–	–	–	–	–	–	–	–	–	–	–	–	–	–	–	–	–	–	–	–

TABLE 4. HIV/AIDS   169

Countries and areas	HIV incidence per 1,000 uninfected population 2016			People living with HIV 2016			New HIV infections 2016			AIDS-related deaths 2016			Pregnant women receiving ARVs for PMTCT (%) 2016*	People living with HIV receiving antiretroviral therapy (ART) (%) 2016*			Condom use among adolescents with multiple partners (%) 2011–2016*		Adolescents tested for HIV in the last 12 months and received results (%) 2011–2016*	
	All ages	children <5	adolescents 15–19	All ages	children <15	adolescents 10–19	All ages	children <5	adolescents 15–19	All ages	children <15	adolescents 10–19		All ages	children <15	adolescents 10–19	male	female	male	female
Uganda	1.50	0.69	2.55	1,400,000	130,000	120,000	52,000	4,600	10,000	28,000	5,800	3,800	>95	67	47	–	52	26	28	39
Ukraine	0.38	0.17	0.57	240,000	4,000	5,100	17,000	<500	1,200	8,500	<200	<100	84	37	64	–	90	–	10	7
United Arab Emirates	–	–	–	–	–	–	–	–	–	–	–	–	–	–	–	–	–	–	–	–
United Kingdom	–	–	–	–	–	–	–	–	–	–	–	–	–	–	–	–	–	–	–	–
United Republic of Tanzania	1.19	1.28	1.04	1,400,000	110,000	98,000	55,000	10,000	5,500	33,000	6,500	3,200	84	62	48	–	45	38	13	21
United States	–	–	–	–	–	–	–	–	–	–	–	–	–	–	–	–	–	–	–	–
Uruguay	–	–	–	12,000	<100	<500	<1,000	<100	–	<500	<100	<100	83	53	>95	–	–	67 p	–	7
Uzbekistan	–	–	–	–	–	–	–	–	–	–	–	–	–	–	–	–	–	–	–	–
Vanuatu	–	–	–	–	–	–	–	–	–	–	–	–	–	–	–	–	–	–	–	–
Venezuela (Bolivarian Republic of)	0.21	0.10	0.44	120,000	2,500	4,400	6,500	<500	1,200	2,500	<200	<100	48	–	–	–	–	–	–	–
Viet Nam	0.12	0.04	0.06	250,000	5,800	3,200	11,000	<500	<500	8,000	<200	<100	66	47	84	–	–	–	–	4
Yemen	0.04	0.02	0.08	9,900	<500	<1,000	1,100	<100	<500	<500	<100	<100	8	18	21	–	–	–	–	–
Zambia	4.08	3.28	6.46	1,200,000	94,000	95,000	59,000	8,900	11,000	21,000	5,700	2,300	83	65	52	–	38	33	19	33
Zimbabwe	3.03	1.36	3.50	1,300,000	–	–	40,000	–	5,800	30,000	–	–	93	75	–	–	71	–	19	30

SUMMARY

Countries and areas	HIV incidence per 1,000 uninfected population 2016			People living with HIV 2016			New HIV infections 2016			AIDS-related deaths 2016			Pregnant women receiving ARVs for PMTCT (%) 2016*	People living with HIV receiving antiretroviral therapy (ART) (%) 2016*			Condom use among adolescents with multiple partners (%) 2011–2016*		Adolescents tested for HIV in the last 12 months and received results (%) 2011–2016*	
	All ages	children <5	adolescents 15–19	All ages	children <15	adolescents 10–19	All ages	children <5	adolescents 15–19	All ages	children <15	adolescents 10–19		All ages	children <15	adolescents 10–19	male	female	male	female
East Asia and Pacific	0.07	0.03	0.11	2,800,000	48,000	60,000	160,000	5,100	15,000	100,000	3,000	<1,000	54	48	62	–	–	–	–	–
Europe & Central Asia	0.25	0.02	0.19	2,400,000	–	–	220,000	–	9,900	49,000	–	–		46	–	–	–	–	–	–
Eastern Europe & Central Asia	0.47	0.03	0.28	1,600,000	–	–	190,000	–	7,200	41,000	–	–		29	–	–	–	–	–	–
Western Europe	0.06	0.01	0.11	840,000	–	–	29,000	–	2,700	8,400	–	–		77	–	–	–	–	–	–
Latin America and Caribbean	0.19	0.05	0.36	2,100,000	34,000	77,000	120,000	2,600	19,000	45,000	2,000	<1,000	75	57	53	–	–	–	–	–
Middle East and North Africa	0.03	0.01	0.04	150,000	3,000	4,000	11,000	<500	1,100	6,300	<200	<100	37	33	62	–	–	–	–	–
North America	–	0.01	0.24	–	–	–	–	–	–	–	–	–		–	–	–	–	–	–	–
South Asia	0.06	0.02	0.03	2,300,000	140,000	130,000	100,000	10,000	18,000	71,000	7,600	3,100	38	46	33	–	–	–	–	–
Sub-Saharan Africa	1.23	0.87	1.83	25,700,000	1,900,000	1,700,000	1,200,000	140,000	190,000	730,000	100,000	50,000	78	54	42	–	49	32	10	15
Eastern and Southern Africa	1.68	1.01	2.34	19,600,000	1,400,000	1,300,000	800,000	79,000	130,000	420,000	59,000	34,000	88	60	51	–	54	–	16	24
West and Central Africa	0.78	0.74	1.25	6,100,000	540,000	450,000	360,000	60,000	62,000	300,000	43,000	16,000	49	34	21	–	43	32	3	6
Least developed countries	0.54	0.46	0.70	10,800,000	980,000	800,000	490,000	69,000	68,000	320,000	52,000	27,000	81	56	40	–	–	–	8	13
World	**0.26**	**0.29**	**0.55**	**36,700,000**	**2,100,000**	**2,100,000**	**1,800,000**	**160,000**	**260,000**	**1,000,000**	**120,000**	**55,000**	**76**	**53**	**43**	**–**	**–**	**–**	**–**	**–**

For a complete list of countries and areas in the regions, subregions and country categories, see page 150 or visit <data.unicef.org/regionalclassifications>.

It is not advisable to compare data from consecutive editions of *The State of the World's Children*.

DEFINITIONS OF THE INDICATORS

HIV incidence per 1,000 uninfected population – Estimated number of new HIV infections per 1,000 uninfected population, 2016. Data reported for children (aged <5), adolescents (aged 15–19) and all ages.

People living with HIV – Estimated number of people living with HIV, 2016. Data reported for children (aged 0–14), adolescents (aged 10–19) and all ages.

New HIV infections – Estimated number of new HIV infections, 2016. Data reported for children (aged <5), adolescents (aged 15–19) and all ages.

AIDS-related deaths – Estimated number of AIDS-related deaths, 2016. Data reported for children (aged 0–14), adolescents (aged 10–19) and all ages.

Pregnant women receiving ARVs for PMTCT – Per cent of the estimated number of pregnant women living with HIV receiving effective regimens (excludes single-dose nevirapine)

of antiretroviral medicines (ARVs) for preventing mother-to-child transmission (PMTCT) of HIV, 2016.

People living with HIV receiving ART – Per cent of the estimated number of people living with HIV receiving antiretroviral therapy (ART), 2016. Data reported for children (aged 0–14), adolescents (aged 10–19) and all ages.

Condom use among adolescents with multiple partners – Among adolescent males and females (aged 15–19) who reported having had more than one sexual partner in the last 12 months, the percentage who reported the use of a condom the last time they had sex with any partner, 2011–2016.

Adolescents tested for HIV in the last 12 months and received results – Percentage of adolescent boys and girls (aged 15–19) who were tested for HIV in the last 12 months and received the result of the most recent test, 2011–2016.

MAIN DATA SOURCES

HIV incidence per 1,000 uninfected population – UNAIDS 2017 estimates, July 2017.

People living with HIV – UNAIDS 2017 estimates, July 2017.

New HIV infections – UNAIDS 2017 estimates, July 2017.

AIDS-related deaths – UNAIDS 2017 estimates, July 2017.

Pregnant women receiving ARVs for PMTCT – UNAIDS 2017 estimates, July 2017.

People living with HIV receiving ART – UNAIDS 2017 estimates, July 2017.

Condom use among adolescents with multiple partners – UNICEF global databases based on Multiple Indicator Cluster Surveys (MICS), Demographic and Health Surveys (DHS), AIDS Indicator Surveys (AIS), and other national household surveys.

Adolescents tested for HIV in the last 12 months and received results – UNICEF global databases based on MICS, DHS, AIS, and other national household surveys.

NOTES

– Data not available.

x Data refer to years or periods other than those specified in the column heading. Such data are not included in the calculation of regional and global averages. Estimates from years prior to 2006 are not displayed.

p Based on small denominators (typically 25–49 unweighted cases). No data based on fewer than 25 unweighted cases are displayed.

* Data refer to the most recent year available during the period specified in the column heading.

TABLE 5. EDUCATION

Countries and areas	Youth (15–24 years) literacy rate (%) 2011–2016*		Number per 100 population 2016		Pre-primary school participation Gross enrolment ratio (%) 2011–2016*		Primary school participation Gross enrolment ratio (%) 2011–2016*		Net enrolment ratio (%) 2011–2016*		Net attendance ratio (%) 2011–2016*		Out-of-school rate of children of primary school age (%) 2011–2016*		Survival rate to last primary grade (%) 2011–2016*		Lower secondary school participation Net enrolment ratio (%) 2011–2016*		Net attendance ratio (%) 2011–2016*	
	male	female	mobile phones	internet users	male	female	male	female	male	female	male	female	male	female	male	female	male	female	male	female
Afghanistan	62	32	66	11	–	–	132	91	–	–	73	53	–	–	–	–	62	38	48	28
Albania	99	99	105	66	90	87	116	112	96	95	92	93	3	5	95	96	91	90	90 x	92 x
Algeria	96 x	92 x	117	43	79	79	120	113	–	–	98	97	–	–	93	95	–	–	82	85
Andorra	100	100	87	98	–	–	–	–	–	–	–	–	–	–	71	70	–	–	–	–
Angola	85	71	55	13	64	94	157	100	95	73	76	76	5	27	–	–	–	–	32	31
Anguilla	–	–	178 x	82	–	–	–	–	–	–	–	–	–	–	–	–	–	–	–	–
Antigua and Barbuda	–	–	194	73	97	95	100	94	88	86	–	–	9	10	–	–	78	82	–	–
Argentina	99	99	151	70	72	73	110	110	100	99	98	99	0	1	96	96	–	–	75	77
Armenia	100	100	115	62	52	53	98	98	96	96	100	99	3	4	100	99	–	–	97	98
Australia	–	–	110	88	127	123	102	102	97	97	–	–	3	3	–	–	–	–	–	–
Austria	–	–	166	84	103	104	104	102	–	–	–	–	–	–	99	100	–	–	–	–
Azerbaijan	100	100	106	78	24	24	107	106	95	93	69 y	67 y	5	7	100	95	85	82	–	–
Bahamas	–	–	92	80	–	–	–	–	–	–	–	–	–	–	–	–	–	–	–	–
Bahrain	99 x	98 x	217	98	56	55	101	102	96	97	86 x	87 x	2	2	99	97	90	88	–	–
Bangladesh	91	94	78	18	31	31	116	125	–	–	90	93	–	–	–	–	61	75	51	60
Barbados	–	–	115	80	83	86	93	94	90	92	100	99	9	8	–	–	80	87	89	89
Belarus	100 x	100 x	124	71	106	101	101	101	95	96	93	90	5	4	98	99	–	–	94	97
Belgium	–	–	111	87	117	116	104	104	99	99	–	–	1	1	92	95	85	87	–	–
Belize	–	–	64	45	49	50	116	110	97	95	96	97	0	1	96	94	70	73	–	–
Benin	64	41	80	12	24	24	134	124	100	88	77	72	0	12	59	56	49	41	40	34
Bhutan	90	84	89	42	25	27	97	103	85	87	96	95	12	10	78	79	57	67	52	54
Bolivia (Plurinational State of)	99	99	91	40	71	71	98	96	89	88	97 x	97 x	9	11	96	97	64	66	–	–
Bosnia and Herzegovina	100	100	89	69	–	–	–	–	–	–	97	95	–	–	96	98	–	–	94	96
Botswana	92 x	96 x	159	39	18	18	109	106	90	92	–	–	9	8	93	95	46	57	–	–
Brazil	98	99	119	60	93	92	117	114	92	93	97	97	6	5	–	–	76	80	–	–
British Virgin Islands	–	–	199 x	38 x	–	–	–	–	–	–	–	–	–	–	–	–	–	–	–	–
Brunei Darussalam	99	100	121	75	71	73	108	108	–	–	–	–	–	–	98	95	–	–	–	–
Bulgaria	98	98	127	60	84	82	98	97	94	93	–	–	5	5	96	96	81	78	–	–
Burkina Faso	57	44	84	14	4	4	90	86	71	67	54	50	29	32	62	71	27	26	19	17
Burundi	85	75	48	5	13	13	123	124	93	95	85	84	6	4	41	48	21	25	12	11
Cabo Verde	98	99	122	48	74	73	113	107	97	97	–	–	3	3	88	90	66	75	–	–
Cambodia	88 x	86 x	125	26	17	19	117	116	94	96	92	94	6	4	41	55	44	49	47	54
Cameroon	85 x	76 x	68	25	38	38	123	111	97	87	87	84	0	9	65	67	44	40	51	49
Canada	–	–	84	90	74	73	100	101	–	–	–	–	–	–	–	–	–	–	–	–
Central African Republic	49 x	27 x	25	4	6	6	107	80	79	62	78	68	21	38	47	45	16	9	17	13
Chad	41	22	44	5	1	1	115	88	89	69	53	47	11	31	54	46	–	–	16	11
Chile	99	99	127	66	88	86	103	100	94	94	91 y	92 y	6	6	99	100	75	82	–	–
China	100 x	100 x	97	53	83	84	104	104	–	–	97 y	97 y	–	–	–	–	–	–	–	–
Colombia	98	99	117	58	85	84	115	112	91	91	94	95	7	7	86	91	72	78	74	81
Comoros	74	70	58	8	20	21	107	99	81	78	84	84	17	20	65	78	38	42	45	52
Congo	86	77	113	8	14	14	107	115	88	95	96	97	11	3	–	–	–	–	65	61
Cook Islands	–	–	56 x	54	84	97	106	99	97	93	–	–	2	3	79	74	90	91	–	–
Costa Rica	99	99	159	66	53	52	110	109	97	96	96	96	3	4	93	95	74	76	71	73
Côte d'Ivoire	59	47	126	27	7	7	99	88	84	75	79	74	16	25	85	80	39	28	26	20
Croatia	100	100	104	73	64	61	98	98	89	89	–	–	3	0	99	99	91	92	–	–
Cuba	100	100	35	39	102	103	100	95	92	92	–	–	8	8	94	95	91	95	–	–
Cyprus	100	100	134	76	81	80	99	99	97	98	–	–	2	2	98	97	94	95	–	–
Czechia	–	–	115	76	107	104	100	100	–	–	–	–	–	–	99	100	–	–	–	–
Democratic People's Republic of Korea	100 x	100 x	14	0 x	51	51	–	–	–	–	99	99	–	–	–	–	57	57	–	–
Democratic Republic of the Congo	91	80	39	6	4	4	112	102	–	–	88	85	–	–	56	55	–	–	39	31
Denmark	–	–	123	97	96	96	102	101	98	98	–	–	1	1	100	100	89	94	–	–
Djibouti	–	–	38	13	5	5	69	62	61	54	71 y	68 y	39	46	80	71	44	37	–	–
Dominica	–	–	107	67	87	88	117	115	–	–	–	–	–	–	81	77	–	–	–	–
Dominican Republic	97	98	81	61	43	45	108	99	88	86	94	96	11	12	77	81	48	58	58	72
Ecuador	99	99	84	54	70	73	107	114	91	93	97 y	97 y	3	1	81	83	74	78	–	–
Egypt	94	90	114	39	31	30	104	104	98	98	97	97	1	1	–	–	83	88	84	86
El Salvador	97	98	141	29	71	73	111	107	91	92	95	96	8	7	76	80	67	72	69	73
Equatorial Guinea	98 x	97 x	66	24	58	58	80	78	55	56	61 x	60 x	43	43	72	72	22	24	–	–
Eritrea	91 x	83 x	7	1	13	13	53	46	41	37	83 y	79 y	59	63	72	74	20	19	63 y	55 y
Estonia	100	100	149	87	90	87	98	99	94	95	–	–	6	4	98	98	–	–	–	–
Ethiopia	63 x	47 x	51	15	31	30	107	97	89	82	64 y	67 y	11	17	37	39	35	33	21	26
Fiji	–	–	103	47	–	–	106	105	99	97	–	–	2	2	98	96	87	91	–	–

UNICEF – THE STATE OF THE WORLD'S CHILDREN 2017

TABLE 5. EDUCATION　　171

Countries and areas	Youth (15–24 years) literacy rate (%) 2011–2016* male	female	Number per 100 population 2016 mobile phones	internet users	Pre-primary school participation Gross enrolment ratio (%) 2011–2016* male	female	Primary school participation Gross enrolment ratio (%) 2011–2016* male	female	Net enrolment ratio (%) 2011–2016* male	female	Net attendance ratio (%) 2011–2016* male	female	Out-of-school rate of children of primary school age (%) 2011–2016* male	female	Survival rate to last primary grade (%) 2011–2016* male	female	Lower secondary school participation Net enrolment ratio (%) 2011–2016* male	female	Net attendance ratio (%) 2011–2016* male	female
Finland	–	–	134	88	79	79	102	101	99	100	–	–	1	0	100	100	96	97	–	–
France	–	–	103	86	109	109	106	105	99	99	–	–	1	0	–	–	–	–	–	–
Gabon	87	89	144	48	36	38	144	140	–	–	97	98	–	–	–	–	–	–	51	59
Gambia	66	56	140	19	37	39	90	94	71	78	65	66	28	20	73	77	35	41	32	32
Georgia	100	100	129	50	–	–	116	118	–	–	98	97	–	–	99	99	93	91	99 y	99 y
Germany	–	–	115	90	112	111	105	105	–	–	–	–	–	–	97	96	–	–	–	–
Ghana	88 x	83 x	139	35	117	119	107	110	87	88	70	70	13	11	85	82	50	50	33	35
Greece	99	99	113	69	49	49	98	97	97	96	–	–	3	4	92	92	95	94	–	–
Grenada	–	–	111	56	89	83	107	103	96	95	–	–	2	2	–	–	79	82	–	–
Guatemala	95	93	115	35	44	45	104	100	86	85	94	93	12	12	75	74	47	46	54	50
Guinea	57	37	85	10	15	15	99	84	81	70	63	58	16	28	67	65	35	24	32	26
Guinea-Bissau	71	50	70	4	–	–	–	–	–	–	62	62	–	–	–	–	–	–	10	9
Guyana	96	97	66	36	95	93	87	84	83	80	97	97	14	16	90	95	77	75	92	95
Haiti	74 x	70 x	61	12	–	–	–	–	–	–	83	84	–	–	–	–	–	–	19	26
Holy See	–	–																		
Honduras	95	97	91	30	45	47	111	110	92	94	95 y	92 y	7	6	74	82	43	50	48	57
Hungary	–	–	119	79	80	78	102	101	91	90	–	–	4	4	98	98	90	89	–	–
Iceland	–	–	118	98	97	97	100	99	100	99	–	–	0	1	97	99	96	98	–	–
India	90	82	87	30	13	12	103	115	92	93	85 x	82 x	3	2	82	81	64	69	–	–
Indonesia	100	100	149	25	57	59	107	104	90	89	99	99	9	10	–	–	74	79	85 y	89 y
Iran (Islamic Republic of)	98	98	100	53	51	50	106	112	–	–	96	97	–	–	98	97	90	92	–	–
Iraq	57	49	82	21	–	–	–	–	–	–	93	87	–	–	–	–	–	–	51	47
Ireland	–	–	104	82	95	99	101	102	94	95	–	–	2	0	–	–	–	–	–	–
Israel	–	–	132	80	111	111	104	105	97	98	–	–	3	2	100	98	–	–	–	–
Italy	100	100	140	61	100	97	101	101	98	97	–	–	1	1	99	99	–	–	–	–
Jamaica	–	–	116	45	96	103	–	–	–	–	97	99	–	–	93	96	68	78	92	92
Japan	–	–	130	92	–	–	101	101	100	100	–	–	0	0	100	100	–	–	–	–
Jordan	99	99	196	62	33	32	97	98	89	89	98	98	11	11	–	–	82	83	92	94
Kazakhstan	100 x	100 x	150	77	59	60	109	111	88	87	100	100	0	0	99	99	–	–	99	100
Kenya	87	86	81	26	77	76	109	109	83	87	84	87	16	12	–	–	–	–	38	46
Kiribati	–	–	51	14	–	–	103	106	–	–	83	87	–	–	–	–	68	88	–	–
Kuwait	99	99	147	78	82	80	102	103	93	93	–	–	2	1	95	96	81	88	–	–
Kyrgyzstan	100 x	100 x	131	35	28	28	108	107	90	88	99	99	2	3	96	97	88	87	98	98
Lao People's Democratic Republic	77	67	55	22	35	36	114	109	93	92	85	85	7	8	77	80	55	57	40	44
Latvia	100	100	131	80	89	88	100	99	96	96	–	–	3	3	95	95	–	–	–	–
Lebanon	99 x	99 x	96	76	80	75	97	88	85	79	98	98	14	19	87	94	67	67	–	–
Lesotho	80	94	107	27	33	35	107	104	79	82	90	94	21	18	57	74	22	39	20	37
Liberia	63 x	37 x	83	7	159	153	99	96	39	36	42	43	61	64	–	–	7	6	14	15
Libya	–	–	120	20	–	–	–	–	–	–	–	–	–	–	–	–	–	–	–	–
Liechtenstein	–	–	116	98	102	106	106	105	91	90	–	–	3	2	–	–	90	84	–	–
Lithuania	100	100	141	74	92	91	103	104	98	98	–	–	1	0	98	98	97	96	–	–
Luxembourg	–	–	148	97	94	93	97	97	93	93	–	–	4	4	82	84	83	87	–	–
Madagascar	78	75	42	5	17	19	149	149	–	–	68 y	71 y	–	–	41	44	28	31	22 x	25 x
Malawi	72	73	40	10	81	82	144	147	–	–	93	95	–	–	54	55	29	30	25	31
Malaysia	98 x	98 x	141	79	92	96	102	102	98	98	–	–	2	2	92	92	85	89	–	–
Maldives	99	99	223	59	101	102	97	–	94	96	94	95	6	4	80	84	70	67	64 x	78 x
Mali	61	39	120	11	4	4	79	72	59	52	55	51	36	43	64	59	33	28	34	26
Malta	98	99	125	77	109	113	102	105	97	100	–	–	3	0	95	98	96	96	–	–
Marshall Islands	98	99	29 x	30	40	41	93	93	75	79	–	–	24	19	–	–	58	64	–	–
Mauritania	66 x	48 x	87	18	9	12	100	105	77	81	58	62	22	18	65	63	22	21	21	20
Mauritius	98	99	144	53	103	105	102	104	95	97	–	–	5	3	96	96	82	86	–	–
Mexico	99	99	88	60	68	70	104	103	95	95	98	98	3	2	95	96	79	82	86	89
Micronesia (Federated States of)	–	–	22	33	34	32	95	96	83	85	–	–	17	15	–	–	49	56	–	–
Monaco	–	–	86	95	–	–	–	–	–	–	–	–	–	–	–	–	–	–	–	–
Mongolia	98 x	99 x	114	22	85	86	102	100	97	96	98	99	2	3	–	–	–	–	91	95
Montenegro	99	99	167	70	57	54	95	93	93	92	98	98	6	7	80	81	93	93	93	96
Montserrat	–	–			97 x	55 x	–	–	–	–	–	–	–	–	–	–	–	–	–	–
Morocco	95	88	121	58	63	51	118	112	99	98	91 x	88 x	1	1	91	87	62	63	–	–
Mozambique	80 x	57 x	66	18	–	–	110	101	91	87	71	72	9	13	34	32	17	19	15	17
Myanmar	85	84	89	25	23	24	101	98	–	–	93	92	–	–	–	–	53	52	67	71
Namibia	93	95	109	31	21	22	113	110	88	91	92	93	11	8	89	92	41	55	54	67
Nauru	–	–	97	54 x	85	96	110	100	88	84	97 y	98 y	11	16	–	–	66	71	–	–

TABLE 5. EDUCATION

Countries and areas	Youth (15–24 years) literacy rate (%) 2011–2016*		Number per 100 population 2016		Pre-primary school participation Gross enrolment ratio (%) 2011–2016*		Primary school participation										Lower secondary school participation			
							Gross enrolment ratio (%) 2011–2016*		Net enrolment ratio (%) 2011–2016*		Net attendance ratio (%) 2011–2016*		Out-of-school rate of children of primary school age (%) 2011–2016*		Survival rate to last primary grade (%) 2011–2016*		Net enrolment ratio (%) 2011–2016*		Net attendance ratio (%) 2011–2016*	
	male	female	mobile phones	internet users	male	female	male	female	male	female	male	female	male	female	male	female	male	female	male	female
Nepal	90	80	112	20	85	83	131	141	97	97	76	76	3	3	75	78	55	53	42	46
Netherlands	–	–	130	90	95	97	105	104	98	99	–	–	2	1	–	–	–	–	–	–
New Zealand	–	–	125	88	93	93	100	99	99	99	–	–	1	1	–	–	97	98	–	–
Nicaragua	85 x	89 x	122	25	–	–	–	–	–	–	71 x,y	70 x,y	–	–	–	–	–	–	–	–
Niger	35	15	49	4	7	8	78	67	67	57	55	46	32	42	63	66	23	16	21	17
Nigeria	76 x	58 x	82	26	–	–	94	93	–	–	70	66	–	–	–	–	–	–	50	49
Niue	–	–	38 x	80 x	113	125	147	120	–	–	100	100	–	–	–	–	–	–	–	–
Norway	–	–	110	97	97	98	101	100	100	100	–	–	0	0	99	100	99	99	–	–
Oman	99	99	159	70	55	56	107	111	95	94	97	98	2	2	98	99	81	86	–	–
Pakistan	80	66	71	16	77	67	100	85	79	68	67	60	21	32	64	64	58	48	36	34
Palau	98	99	91 x	–	71	77	100	112	74	87	–	–	26	13	–	–	33	38	–	–
Panama	98 x	97 x	172	54	48	49	104	101	94	93	97	97	6	7	85	87	71	74	78	86
Papua New Guinea	69 x	64 x	49	10	–	–	120	109	89	83	–	–	10	16	–	–	17	14	–	–
Paraguay	98	99	105	51	38	38	108	104	89	88	90 y	91 y	11	11	83	86	58	63	–	–
Peru	99	99	117	45	88	89	102	102	94	94	92 y	91 y	2	2	89	92	71	72	85	87
Philippines	97	99	109	56	–	–	117	117	94	98	88 x	89 x	5	1	–	–	58	70	–	–
Poland	–	–	146	73	79	79	100	101	96	96	–	–	3	3	98	98	93	94	–	–
Portugal	99	99	109	70	94	93	109	105	98	98	–	–	2	2	–	–	–	–	–	–
Qatar	98	100	147	94	58	60	102	104	92	93	96	97	4	3	99	96	76	83	–	–
Republic of Korea	–	–	123	93	94	94	99	99	98	98	–	–	1	1	99	100	98	98	–	–
Republic of Moldova	99	100	111	71	84	83	93	92	87	86	99	98	10	10	95	95	83	82	96	97
Romania	99	99	106	60	91	91	91	89	87	87	92 y	91 y	10	10	94	94	84	83	90 y	90 y
Russian Federation	100 x	100 x	163	76	88	86	100	101	96	97	–	–	3	2	99	100	97	98	–	–
Rwanda	81	83	70	20	18	18	132	133	94	96	93	96	6	4	41	48	19	24	25	34
Saint Kitts and Nevis	–	–	137	77	91	81	82	83	77	80	–	–	21	18	96	95	80	82	–	–
Saint Lucia	–	–	95	47	56	59	–	–	–	–	100	99	–	–	90	90	74	75	95	90
Saint Vincent and the Grenadines	–	–	103	56	93	93	106	103	94	94	–	–	1	1	–	–	88	89	–	–
Samoa	99	99	69	29	39	42	107	107	96	96	88 y	89 y	3	2	92	89	66	68	–	–
San Marino	–	–	114	50 x	106	108	94	93	93	92	–	–	7	7	95	98	91	94	–	–
Sao Tome and Principe	97	96	85	28	52	56	118	111	96	94	94	94	3	5	–	–	50	60	46	57
Saudi Arabia	99	99	158	74	17	18	108	111	97	98	–	–	3	2	–	–	76	70	–	–
Senegal	61	51	99	26	14	16	78	87	68	75	53	55	30	24	56	60	39	42	27	30
Serbia	100	100	121	67	59	58	101	101	96	96	99	99	1	1	100	97	97	97	97	96
Seychelles	99 x	99 x	161	57	88	93	101	104	94	96	–	–	5	4	–	–	–	–	–	–
Sierra Leone	65	51	98	12	10	11	127	128	99	99	74	78	1	1	48	48	31	29	36	36
Singapore	100	100	147	81	–	–	–	–	–	–	–	–	–	–	–	–	–	–	–	–
Slovakia	–	–	128	80	95	93	100	99	–	–	–	–	–	–	–	–	99	99	–	–
Slovenia	–	–	115	75	95	92	99	99	97	98	–	–	3	2	99	99	95	97	–	–
Solomon Islands	–	–	70	11	100	100	115	114	70	71	65	68	30	29	68	78	23	25	–	–
Somalia	–	–	58	2	–	–	–	–	–	–	24 x	19 x	–	–	–	–	–	–	–	–
South Africa	99	99	142	54	77	78	102	97	–	–	97	97	–	–	–	–	–	–	–	–
South Sudan	44 x	30 x	25 x	16 x	10	10	75	53	35	27	26	21	65	73	–	–	1	1	6	3
Spain	100	100	110	81	97	96	104	106	99	100	–	–	1	0	97	98	–	–	–	–
Sri Lanka	98 x	99 x	118	32	93	93	103	101	98	96	–	–	2	4	99	99	96	96	–	–
State of Palestine	99	99	77	61	53	52	94	94	90	91	99	99	8	7	94	99	83	87	92	97
Sudan	69 x	63 x	69	28	36	48	74	67	52	55	69	67	47	44	80	79	–	–	31	32
Suriname	98	97	146	45	90	97	124	121	93	94	95	96	6	5	85	98	50	61	46	61
Swaziland	92 x	95 x	76	29	25	26	118	108	80	79	97	98	20	20	72	77	20	31	33	48
Sweden	–	–	127	92	94	94	121	126	99	99	–	–	0	0	99	100	–	–	–	–
Switzerland	–	–	136	89	105	104	104	104	93	93	–	–	1	0	–	–	87	87	–	–
Syrian Arab Republic	95 x	90 x	54	32	6	6	81	79	67	66	97 x	96 x	28	30	93	93	53	52	–	–
Tajikistan	100 x	100 x	107	20	12	10	100	98	97	98	85	86	2	0	99	99	98	95	86	84
Thailand	98	98	173	48	74	64	106	99	94	87	95	95	6	13	–	–	79	79	83	86
The former Yugoslav Republic of Macedonia	–	98 x	101	72	36	36	94	93	91	91	98	98	9	9	97	96	78	76	86	85
Timor-Leste	80 x	79 x	125	25	18	20	137	136	94	97	71	73	5	1	81	84	39	48	30	34
Togo	90	78	75	11	17	18	125	118	94	88	90	87	4	10	55	53	–	–	45	40
Tokelau	–	–	0 x	1 x	175	160	121	–	–	–	–	–	–	–	–	–	–	–	–	–
Tonga	99	100	75	40	39	38	109	107	92	94	93 y	93 y	5	3	–	–	78	84	–	–
Trinidad and Tobago	–	–	161	73	–	–	–	–	–	–	98 x	98 x	–	–	–	–	–	–	–	–
Tunisia	97	96	126	51	44	44	116	113	–	–	98	98	–	–	93	95	80	85	76	85
Turkey	100	99	97	58	30	28	103	102	95	94	94	97	5	6	88	88	88	86	–	–
Turkmenistan	–	–	158	18	64	62	90	89	–	–	98	98	–	–	–	–	–	–	98	98

TABLE 5. EDUCATION

173

Countries and areas	Youth (15–24 years) literacy rate (%) 2011–2016*		Number per 100 population 2016		Pre-primary school participation Gross enrolment ratio (%) 2011–2016*		Primary school participation													Lower secondary school participation			
							Gross enrolment ratio (%) 2011–2016*		Net enrolment ratio (%) 2011–2016*		Net attendance ratio (%) 2011–2016*		Out-of-school rate of children of primary school age (%) 2011–2016*		Survival rate to last primary grade (%) 2011–2016*		Net enrolment ratio (%) 2011–2016*		Net attendance ratio (%) 2011–2016*			
	male	female	mobile phones	internet users	male	female	male	female	male	female	male	female	male	female	male	female	male	female	male	female
Turks and Caicos Islands	–	–	100 x	0	–	–	–	–	–	–	–	–	–	–	–	–	–	–	–	–
Tuvalu	–	–	76	46	96	93	103	104	84	85	97 x,y	99 x,y	5	2	–	–	73	77	–	–
Uganda	86	82	55	22	11	12	109	111	92	95	86	87	8	5	21	22	–	–	15	20
Ukraine	100	100	133	52	86	84	103	105	95	97	100	100	4	2	68	68	91	91	98	98
United Arab Emirates	94 x	97 x	204	91	83	84	117	116	94	93	–	–	4	4	91	93	76	83	–	–
United Kingdom	–	–	122	95	88	88	108	108	100	100	–	–	0	0	–	–	96	96	–	–
United Republic of Tanzania	87	85	74	13	31	32	80	83	79	81	78	83	21	19	62	71	–	–	25	31
United States	–	–	127	76	72	70	100	100	93	94	–	–	6	5	–	–	87	90	–	–
Uruguay	99	99	149	66	88	89	110	107	94	94	97	98	5	6	99	100	68	73	75	77
Uzbekistan	100	100	77	47	26	26	106	101	96	93	–	–	2	4	99	100	94	92	–	–
Vanuatu	–	–	71	24	103	100	121	119	85	87	76 y	78 y	14	12	–	–	42	48	–	–
Venezuela (Bolivarian Republic of)	98	99	87	60	75	76	101	99	90	90	91 x	93 x	8	8	90	90	69	74	–	–
Viet Nam	97 x	97 x	128	47	84	82	109	108	–	–	98	98	–	–	94	98	93	95	89	92
Yemen	–	–	67	25	1	1	106	89	92	78	80	72	8	22	72	67	47	34	43	34
Zambia	91 x	87 x	75	26	–	–	103	104	86	88	86	88	12	10	57	54	31	30	46	51
Zimbabwe	88	93	83	23	42	43	101	99	85	86	94	96	14	13	75	78	33	41	48	63
SUMMARY																				
East Asia and Pacific	99	97	109	52	77	77	106	105	93 **	93 **	97	97	6 **	6 **	–	–	71 **	76 **	81 **	84 **
Europe and Central Asia	–	–	125	74	76	75	103	103	96	96	–	–	3	2	95	95	93	92	–	–
Eastern Europe and Central Asia	100	99	129	64	60	59	102	102	95	94	94	95	4	4	93	93	93	92	–	–
Western Europe	–	–	122	83	97	97	105	104	98	98	–	–	1	1	97	98	–	–	–	–
Latin America and Caribbean	98	99	109	56	76	76	109	107	93	93	96	96	5	4	90	92	74	77	76	79
Middle East and North Africa	91	88	112	48	35	34	106	104	93	91	94	93	6	8	91	90	74	74	72	72
North America	–	–	123	78	72	70	100	100	93	94	–	–	6	–	–	–	87	–	–	–
South Asia	88	80	85	26	22	21	105	112	90	89	–	–	5	6	80	79	63	66	43	44
Sub-Saharan Africa	79	72	75	20	31	32	104	98	82	78	75	74	17	21	55	56	32	31	32	32
Eastern and Southern Africa	87	85	71	21	39	40	106	100	83	81	78	79	17	19	48	51	29	30	24	29
West and Central Africa	69	55	80	19	20	21	101	95	–	–	72	68	–	–	63	63	–	–	39	36
Least developed countries	80	73	68	16	23	24	108	101	82	78	76	75	17	22	52	54	41	41	33	35
World	**92**	**85**	**101**	**46**	**49**	**48**	**105**	**105**	**90 ****	**89 ****	**87**	**85**	**8 ****	**9 ****	**76**	**77**	**66 ****	**68 ****	**53 ****	**54 ****

For a complete list of countries and areas in the regions, subregions and country categories, see page 150 or visit <data.unicef.org/regionalclassifications>.
It is not advisable to compare data from consecutive editions of *The State of the World's Children*.

DEFINITIONS OF THE INDICATORS

Youth literacy rate – Number of literate persons aged 15–24 years, expressed as a percentage of the total population in that group.

Mobile phones – The number of active subscriptions to a public mobile telephone service, including the number of prepaid SIM cards active during the past three months.

Internet users – The estimated number of Internet users out of the total population. This includes those using the Internet from any device (including mobile phones) in the last 12 months.

Pre-primary school gross enrolment ratio – Number of children enrolled in pre-primary school, regardless of age, expressed as a percentage of the total number of children of official pre-primary school age.

Primary school gross enrolment ratio – Number of children enrolled in primary school, regardless of age, expressed as a percentage of the total number of children of official primary school age.

Primary school net enrolment ratio – Number of children enrolled in primary or secondary school who are of official primary school age, expressed as a percentage of the total number of children of official primary school age. Because of the inclusion of primary-school-aged children enrolled in secondary school, this indicator can also be referred to as a primary adjusted net enrolment ratio.

Primary school net attendance ratio – Number of children attending primary or secondary school who are of official primary school age, expressed as a percentage of the total number of children of official primary school age. Because of the inclusion of primary-school-aged children attending secondary school, this indicator can also be referred to as a primary adjusted net attendance ratio.

Rate of out-of-school children of primary school age – Number of children of official primary school age who are not enrolled in primary or secondary education, expressed as a percentage of the population of official primary school age.

Out-of-school children of primary school age – Children in the official primary school age range who are not enrolled in either primary or secondary schools. Children enrolled in pre-primary education are excluded and considered out of school.

Survival rate to last primary grade – Percentage of children entering the first grade of primary school who eventually reach the last grade of primary school.

Lower secondary school net enrolment ratio – Number of children enrolled in lower secondary school who are of official lower secondary school age, expressed as a percentage of the total number of children of official lower secondary school age. Lower secondary net enrolment ratio does not include lower-secondary-school-aged children enrolled in tertiary education owing to challenges in age reporting and recording at that level.

Lower secondary school net attendance ratio – Number of children attending lower secondary or tertiary school who are of official lower secondary school age, expressed as a percentage of the total number of children of official lower secondary school age. Because of the inclusion of lower-secondary-school-aged children attending tertiary school, this indicator can also be referred to as a lower secondary adjusted net attendance ratio.

All data refer to official International Standard Classifications of Education (ISCED) for the primary and lower secondary education levels and thus may not directly correspond to a country-specific school system.

MAIN DATA SOURCES

Youth literacy – UNESCO Institute for Statistics (UIS).

Mobile phone and Internet use – International Telecommunications Union, Geneva.

Pre-primary, primary and lower secondary enrolment and rate of out-of-school children – UIS. Estimates based on administrative data from national Education Management Information Systems (EMIS) with UN population estimates.

Primary and lower secondary school attendance – Demographic and Health Surveys (DHS), Multiple Indicator Cluster Surveys (MICS) and other national household surveys.

Survival rate to last primary grade – Administrative data: UIS; survey data: DHS, MICS and other national household surveys.

NOTES

– Data not available.

x Data refer to years or periods other than those specified in the column heading. Such data are not included in the calculation of regional and global averages, with the exception of 2005–2006 data from India. Estimates from data years prior to 2000 are not displayed.

y Data differ from the standard definition or refer to only part of a country. If they fall within the noted reference period, such data are included in the calculation of regional and global averages.

* Data refer to the most recent year available during the period specified in the column heading.

** Excludes China.

TABLE 6. DEMOGRAPHIC INDICATORS

Countries and areas	Population (thousands) 2016 total	under 18	under 5	Population annual growth rate (%) 1990–2016	2016–2030°	Crude death rate 1970	1990	2016	Crude birth rate 1970	1990	2016	Life expectancy 1970	1990	2016	Total fertility rate 2016	Urbanized population (%) 2016	Average annual growth rate of urban population (%) 1990–2016	2016–2030°
Afghanistan	34,656	17,744	5,233	4.0	2.1	28	16	7	52	49	33	37	50	64	4.6	27	5.5	3.6
Albania	2,926	659	177	-0.4	0.0	8	6	7	32	25	12	67	72	78	1.7	58	1.5	1.4
Algeria	40,606	13,495	4,699	1.7	1.3	17	6	5	47	32	23	50	67	76	2.8	71	3.0	1.7
Andorra	77	13	3	1.3	0.1	–	–	–	–	–	–	–	–	–	–	85	1.1	0.2
Angola	28,813	15,416	5,277	3.3	3.1	27	23	9	53	53	42	37	42	62	5.7	45	5.3	4.2
Anguilla	15	4	1	2.2	0.5	–	–	–	–	–	–	–	–	–	–	100	2.2	0.5
Antigua and Barbuda	101	30	8	1.6	0.9	7	7	6	31	19	16	66	71	76	2.1	23	0.0	0.3
Argentina	43,847	13,076	3,736	1.1	0.8	9	8	8	23	22	17	66	72	77	2.3	92	1.2	0.8
Armenia	2,925	685	202	-0.7	0.0	6	8	10	23	22	13	70	68	75	1.6	63	-0.9	0.1
Australia	24,126	5,433	1,551	1.3	1.1	9	7	7	20	15	13	71	77	83	1.8	90	1.5	1.2
Austria	8,712	1,489	412	0.5	0.2	13	11	10	16	11	10	70	76	82	1.5	66	0.5	0.6
Azerbaijan	9,725	2,653	891	1.1	0.7	9	9	7	32	29	18	63	65	72	2.1	55	1.2	1.2
Bahamas	391	97	28	1.6	0.8	6	5	6	26	24	14	66	71	76	1.8	83	1.8	1.1
Bahrain	1,425	334	107	4.1	2.5	7	3	2	38	29	15	63	72	77	2.0	89	4.0	1.3
Bangladesh	162,952	56,869	15,236	1.6	0.9	19	10	5	48	35	19	48	58	72	2.1	35	3.8	2.7
Barbados	285	66	17	0.3	0.1	10	10	11	22	16	12	66	71	76	1.8	31	0.3	0.7
Belarus	9,480	1,821	579	-0.3	-0.2	9	11	13	16	14	12	71	71	73	1.7	77	0.2	-0.2
Belgium	11,358	2,309	643	0.5	0.4	12	11	10	14	12	11	71	76	81	1.8	98	0.5	0.3
Belize	367	141	40	2.6	1.8	8	5	5	42	36	23	66	71	70	2.5	44	2.2	2.0
Benin	10,872	5,379	1,775	3.0	2.6	24	15	9	47	46	37	42	54	61	5.0	44	4.1	3.4
Bhutan	798	259	70	1.5	1.0	24	13	6	49	39	18	40	53	70	2.1	39	4.8	2.3
Bolivia (Plurinational State of)	10,888	4,150	1,189	1.8	1.4	20	13	7	42	35	23	46	55	69	2.9	69	2.8	1.9
Bosnia and Herzegovina	3,517	628	157	-0.9	-0.2	7	8	11	24	15	9	66	71	77	1.4	40	-0.6	0.6
Botswana	2,250	840	259	1.9	1.6	13	8	7	46	34	24	55	62	67	2.7	58	2.8	1.4
Brazil	207,653	56,235	14,919	1.3	0.6	10	7	6	35	25	14	59	65	76	1.7	86	1.8	0.8
British Virgin Islands	31	9	3	2.4	1.0	–	–	–	–	–	–	–	–	–	–	47	3.0	1.4
Brunei Darussalam	423	120	34	1.9	1.0	6	4	4	37	29	16	67	73	77	1.9	78	2.6	1.3
Bulgaria	7,131	1,183	324	-0.8	-0.7	9	12	15	16	12	9	71	71	75	1.6	74	-0.4	-0.5
Burkina Faso	18,646	9,724	3,221	2.9	2.7	25	17	9	47	47	39	39	49	60	5.4	31	5.9	4.7
Burundi	10,524	5,372	1,901	2.6	2.9	21	18	11	47	50	42	44	48	57	5.7	12	5.3	5.1
Cabo Verde	540	200	55	1.8	1.2	14	8	6	42	40	21	54	65	73	2.3	66	3.0	1.5
Cambodia	15,762	5,854	1,761	2.2	1.3	20	13	6	43	42	23	42	54	69	2.6	21	3.3	2.7
Cameroon	23,439	11,578	3,804	2.7	2.4	19	15	10	45	45	36	46	52	58	4.7	55	3.9	3.2
Canada	36,290	6,999	1,929	1.0	0.8	7	7	7	17	14	11	73	77	82	1.6	82	1.3	1.0
Central African Republic	4,595	2,326	730	1.7	2.1	23	17	14	43	41	36	42	49	52	4.9	40	2.3	2.8
Chad	14,453	7,854	2,666	3.4	2.8	23	19	13	47	51	43	41	47	53	5.9	23	3.6	4.0
Chile	17,910	4,462	1,184	1.2	0.7	10	6	6	30	22	13	62	74	80	1.8	90	1.5	0.8
China	1,403,500	295,112	85,866	0.7	0.2	11	7	7	36	22	12	59	69	76	1.6	57	3.7	1.6
Colombia	48,653	14,055	3,712	1.3	0.6	9	6	6	38	26	15	61	68	74	1.9	77	2.0	1.3
Comoros	796	369	119	2.5	2.1	19	12	7	46	43	33	46	57	64	4.3	28	2.6	2.8
Congo	5,126	2,489	824	2.9	2.5	14	12	7	43	38	35	53	56	65	4.7	66	3.4	3.0
Cook Islands	17	6	2	-0.2	0.2	–	–	–	–	–	–	–	–	–	–	75	1.7	0.7
Costa Rica	4,857	1,296	346	1.7	0.8	7	4	5	33	27	14	66	76	80	1.8	78	3.6	1.6
Côte d'Ivoire	23,696	11,689	3,861	2.5	2.4	21	14	12	52	43	37	44	52	54	4.9	55	3.5	3.1
Croatia	4,213	756	196	-0.5	-0.6	11	11	13	15	11	9	68	72	78	1.5	59	-0.1	0.2
Cuba	11,476	2,260	636	0.3	0.0	7	7	8	29	17	11	70	75	80	1.7	77	0.4	-0.1
Cyprus	1,170	241	66	1.6	0.7	7	7	7	19	19	11	73	77	81	1.3	67	1.6	0.8
Czechia	10,611	1,881	534	0.1	-0.1	12	12	11	16	12	10	70	72	79	1.5	73	0.1	0.3
Democratic People's Republic of Korea	25,369	6,452	1,726	0.9	0.4	10	6	9	37	21	14	60	70	72	1.9	61	1.0	0.8
Democratic Republic of the Congo	78,736	41,553	14,494	3.2	3.0	20	17	10	47	46	42	44	49	60	6.1	43	4.2	3.6
Denmark	5,712	1,157	285	0.4	0.4	10	12	9	15	12	10	73	75	81	1.7	88	0.5	0.6
Djibouti	942	356	102	1.8	1.3	15	11	8	45	40	23	49	57	62	2.8	77	1.8	1.3
Dominica	74	22	6	0.1	0.4	–	–	–	–	–	–	–	–	–	–	70	0.5	0.7
Dominican Republic	10,649	3,750	1,060	1.5	0.9	11	6	6	42	30	20	58	68	74	2.4	80	2.9	1.5
Ecuador	16,385	5,606	1,611	1.8	1.3	12	6	5	41	30	20	58	69	76	2.5	64	2.4	1.7
Egypt	95,689	36,997	12,876	2.0	1.6	16	8	6	42	34	26	52	65	71	3.3	43	1.6	1.8
El Salvador	6,345	2,153	577	0.7	0.5	13	8	7	43	31	19	55	64	74	2.1	67	1.9	1.0
Equatorial Guinea	1,221	521	182	4.0	3.0	26	18	10	42	42	34	40	48	58	4.7	40	3.6	3.0
Eritrea	4,955	2,397	744	1.8	2.2	21	16	7	47	42	32	43	50	65	4.1	23	4.3	4.4
Estonia	1,312	247	68	-0.7	-0.3	11	13	12	15	14	11	70	69	78	1.6	67	-1.0	-0.3
Ethiopia	102,403	49,500	15,177	2.9	2.2	21	18	7	48	48	32	43	47	65	4.2	20	4.6	4.3
Fiji	899	303	87	0.8	0.5	8	6	7	34	29	19	60	66	70	2.5	54	1.8	0.9
Finland	5,503	1,078	297	0.4	0.3	10	10	10	14	13	11	70	75	81	1.8	84	0.6	0.4
France	64,721	14,080	3,842	0.5	0.3	11	9	9	17	13	12	72	77	83	2.0	80	0.8	0.7
Gabon	1,980	822	274	2.8	1.9	20	11	8	37	37	30	47	61	66	3.8	87	3.4	2.2

TABLE 6. DEMOGRAPHIC INDICATORS 175

Countries and areas	Population (thousands) 2016			Population annual growth rate (%)		Crude death rate			Crude birth rate			Life expectancy			Total fertility rate 2016	Urbanized population (%) 2016	Average annual growth rate of urban population (%)	
	total	under 18	under 5	1990–2016	2016–2030	1970	1990	2016	1970	1990	2016	1970	1990	2016			1990–2016	2016–2030
Gambia	2,039	1,065	360	3.1	2.8	26	14	8	50	47	39	38	52	61	5.4	60	4.8	3.6
Georgia	3,925	875	271	-1.2	-0.3	9	9	13	20	17	13	67	70	73	2.0	54	-1.0	-0.1
Germany	81,915	13,103	3,557	0.1	0.0	12	12	11	14	10	9	71	75	81	1.5	76	0.2	0.0
Ghana	28,207	12,689	4,085	2.5	2.0	16	11	8	47	39	31	49	57	63	4.0	55	4.0	2.7
Greece	11,184	1,937	474	0.3	-0.3	10	9	11	18	11	8	71	77	81	1.3	78	0.7	0.2
Grenada	107	34	10	0.4	0.3	9	9	7	28	28	19	64	69	74	2.1	36	0.7	0.4
Guatemala	16,582	7,047	2,023	2.2	1.8	14	9	5	45	39	25	53	62	73	3.0	52	3.3	3.0
Guinea	12,396	6,082	1,983	2.8	2.5	27	17	9	45	47	36	37	50	60	4.9	38	4.0	3.5
Guinea-Bissau	1,816	872	291	2.2	2.3	22	17	11	43	46	37	42	49	57	4.6	50	4.5	3.2
Guyana	773	277	76	0.2	0.5	9	8	8	36	28	21	62	63	67	2.5	29	0.3	1.1
Haiti	10,847	4,296	1,233	1.6	1.0	18	13	9	39	37	24	47	55	63	2.9	60	4.4	2.2
Holy See	1	0	0	0.2	0.0	–	–	–	–	–	–	–	–	–	–	100	0.2	0.0
Honduras	9,113	3,541	951	2.3	1.4	15	7	5	48	39	22	53	67	74	2.5	55	3.4	2.5
Hungary	9,753	1,694	436	-0.2	-0.4	11	14	13	15	12	9	69	69	76	1.4	72	0.1	0.2
Iceland	332	80	22	1.0	0.7	7	7	6	21	17	13	74	78	83	1.9	94	1.3	0.9
India	1,324,171	448,314	119,998	1.6	1.0	17	11	7	39	32	19	48	58	69	2.3	33	2.5	2.2
Indonesia	261,115	85,965	24,822	1.4	0.9	13	8	7	40	26	19	55	63	69	2.4	54	3.6	1.9
Iran (Islamic Republic of)	80,277	22,149	6,823	1.4	0.7	16	7	5	42	33	17	51	64	76	1.7	74	2.4	1.4
Iraq	37,203	17,460	5,738	2.9	2.6	12	7	5	46	38	33	58	66	70	4.4	70	2.8	2.6
Ireland	4,726	1,197	344	1.1	0.7	11	9	6	22	14	14	71	75	81	2.0	64	1.6	1.3
Israel	8,192	2,672	841	2.3	1.4	7	6	5	26	22	20	72	77	83	3.0	92	2.3	1.4
Italy	59,430	9,761	2,482	0.2	-0.2	10	10	10	17	10	8	72	77	83	1.5	69	0.4	0.3
Jamaica	2,881	820	205	0.7	0.1	8	7	7	35	25	17	68	72	76	2.0	55	1.1	0.9
Japan	127,749	20,051	5,343	0.1	-0.4	7	7	11	19	10	8	72	79	84	1.5	94	0.9	-0.1
Jordan	9,456	3,959	1,227	3.8	1.2	10	5	4	51	35	26	60	70	74	3.4	84	3.8	1.5
Kazakhstan	17,988	5,566	1,997	0.3	0.9	9	9	9	26	23	21	63	67	70	2.6	53	0.0	1.0
Kenya	48,462	23,094	7,023	2.8	2.3	15	10	6	51	42	31	52	58	67	3.9	26	4.5	4.0
Kiribati	114	47	14	1.8	1.5	13	10	7	35	37	28	54	60	66	3.7	44	2.5	1.9
Kuwait	4,053	989	316	2.5	1.3	6	3	3	48	23	16	66	72	75	2.0	98	2.2	2.0
Kyrgyzstan	5,956	2,167	760	1.2	1.2	11	8	6	32	32	25	60	66	71	3.0	36	0.9	2.0
Lao People's Democratic Republic	6,758	2,674	766	1.8	1.2	18	14	7	43	43	24	46	54	67	2.7	40	5.6	3.3
Latvia	1,971	350	97	-1.2	-0.9	11	13	15	14	14	10	70	69	75	1.5	67	-1.2	-0.5
Lebanon	6,007	1,743	483	3.1	-0.8	8	7	5	32	25	15	66	70	80	1.7	88	2.6	0.3
Lesotho	2,204	932	286	1.2	1.2	17	10	13	43	35	28	49	59	54	3.1	28	3.8	2.6
Liberia	4,614	2,249	715	3.0	2.4	24	18	8	49	45	34	39	47	63	4.6	50	2.6	3.2
Libya	6,293	2,111	627	1.3	1.1	13	5	5	51	29	20	56	69	72	2.3	79	1.7	1.4
Liechtenstein	38	7	2	1.0	0.6	–	–	–	–	–	–	–	–	–	–	14	0.4	1.1
Lithuania	2,908	519	152	-0.9	-0.5	9	11	14	17	15	11	71	71	75	1.7	67	-0.9	-0.2
Luxembourg	576	115	32	1.6	1.1	12	10	7	13	12	11	70	75	82	1.6	90	1.8	1.2
Madagascar	24,895	11,988	3,769	2.9	2.6	21	15	6	48	44	33	45	51	66	4.2	36	4.6	4.2
Malawi	18,092	9,265	2,908	2.5	2.7	25	19	7	54	49	37	41	47	63	4.6	16	3.8	4.2
Malaysia	31,187	9,350	2,612	2.1	1.2	7	5	5	34	28	17	64	71	75	2.0	75	3.7	1.8
Maldives	428	117	39	2.5	1.3	21	9	3	50	41	18	44	61	77	2.1	47	4.3	2.6
Mali	17,995	9,806	3,332	2.9	2.9	32	20	10	50	49	43	32	46	58	6.1	41	5.0	4.7
Malta	429	75	21	0.6	0.2	9	8	9	16	15	10	71	76	81	1.5	96	0.8	0.2
Marshall Islands	53	19	5	0.4	0.3	–	–	–	–	–	–	–	–	–	–	73	0.9	0.9
Mauritania	4,301	1,996	655	2.9	2.5	16	11	8	46	41	34	49	58	63	4.7	60	4.2	2.9
Mauritius	1,262	295	68	0.7	0.1	7	6	8	29	21	11	63	69	75	1.4	40	0.3	0.3
Mexico	127,540	41,600	11,581	1.5	1.0	10	5	5	44	29	18	61	71	77	2.2	80	1.9	1.2
Micronesia (Federated States of)	105	43	12	0.3	0.8	9	7	6	41	34	24	62	66	69	3.1	22	-0.2	1.6
Monaco	38	7	2	1.0	0.5	–	–	–	–	–	–	–	–	–	–	100	1.0	0.9
Mongolia	3,027	1,017	368	1.3	1.2	15	10	6	44	32	24	55	60	69	2.8	73	2.1	1.7
Montenegro	629	139	36	0.1	0.0	7	7	10	22	16	11	70	75	77	1.7	64	1.2	0.2
Montserrat	5	2	0	-2.8	0.3	–	–	–	–	–	–	–	–	–	–	9	-4.0	1.0
Morocco	35,277	11,491	3,508	1.3	1.1	14	7	5	43	29	20	53	65	76	2.5	61	2.1	1.6
Mozambique	28,829	14,929	4,950	3.0	2.8	25	21	10	48	46	39	39	43	58	5.2	33	3.8	3.5
Myanmar	52,885	17,485	4,538	1.0	0.8	15	10	8	39	27	18	51	59	67	2.2	35	2.3	2.0
Namibia	2,480	1,076	344	2.2	1.9	15	9	7	43	38	29	52	62	64	3.4	48	4.2	3.1
Nauru	11	4	1	0.8	0.1	–	–	–	–	–	–	–	–	–	–	100	0.4	0.5
Nepal	28,983	11,190	2,756	1.7	1.0	23	13	6	43	39	20	41	54	70	2.1	19	4.7	2.9
Netherlands	16,987	3,425	894	0.5	0.3	8	9	9	18	13	11	74	77	82	1.7	91	1.6	0.5
New Zealand	4,661	1,109	304	1.2	0.8	8	8	7	22	17	13	71	75	82	2.0	86	1.3	0.9
Nicaragua	6,150	2,174	597	1.5	1.0	13	7	5	46	36	20	54	64	75	2.2	59	2.1	1.7
Niger	20,673	11,752	4,218	3.6	3.8	28	23	10	57	56	48	36	44	60	7.2	19	4.5	5.7
Nigeria	185,990	93,965	31,802	2.6	2.5	23	19	12	46	44	39	41	46	53	5.5	49	4.5	3.9

TABLE 6. DEMOGRAPHIC INDICATORS

Countries and areas	Population (thousands) 2016			Population annual growth rate (%)		Crude death rate			Crude birth rate			Life expectancy			Total fertility rate	Urbanized population (%)	Average annual growth rate of urban population (%)	
	total	under 18	under 5	1990–2016	2016–2030	1970	1990	2016	1970	1990	2016	1970	1990	2016	2016	2016	1990–2016	2016–2030
Niue	2	1	0	-1.4	0.2	–	–	–	–	–	–	–	–	–	–	43	-1.1	0.2
Norway	5,255	1,130	306	0.8	0.9	10	11	8	17	14	12	74	77	82	1.8	81	1.2	1.1
Oman	4,425	1,118	401	3.4	2.1	16	5	3	48	38	19	50	67	77	2.7	78	4.0	1.4
Pakistan	193,203	79,005	24,963	2.2	1.7	15	11	7	43	40	28	53	60	66	3.5	39	3.0	2.6
Palau	22	8	2	1.4	1.0	–	–	–	–	–	–	–	–	–	–	88	2.2	1.3
Panama	4,034	1,324	388	1.9	1.4	8	5	5	38	26	20	66	73	78	2.5	67	2.7	1.8
Papua New Guinea	8,085	3,449	1,033	2.4	1.9	16	9	7	41	35	28	49	59	66	3.7	13	1.9	2.8
Paraguay	6,725	2,404	672	1.8	1.1	7	6	6	37	34	21	65	68	73	2.5	60	2.8	1.9
Peru	31,774	10,454	3,033	1.4	1.1	14	7	6	42	30	19	53	66	75	2.4	79	1.9	1.4
Philippines	103,320	39,204	11,530	2.0	1.4	9	7	7	39	33	23	61	65	69	2.9	44	1.6	1.8
Poland	38,224	6,785	1,819	0.0	-0.3	8	10	10	17	15	9	70	71	78	1.3	61	0.0	0.1
Portugal	10,372	1,764	431	0.2	-0.3	11	10	11	21	11	8	67	74	81	1.2	64	1.4	0.6
Qatar	2,570	417	130	6.5	1.6	5	2	2	36	22	10	68	75	78	1.9	99	6.5	1.0
Republic of Korea	50,792	8,678	2,226	0.6	0.3	9	6	6	30	15	9	61	72	82	1.3	83	1.0	0.5
Republic of Moldova	4,060	768	218	-0.3	-0.4	10	10	11	20	19	10	65	68	72	1.2	45	-1.1	-0.2
Romania	19,778	3,667	944	-0.7	-0.5	10	11	13	21	14	10	68	70	75	1.5	55	-0.2	0.1
Russian Federation	143,965	28,642	9,561	-0.1	-0.2	9	12	13	15	14	13	69	68	71	1.8	74	-0.1	-0.2
Rwanda	11,918	5,593	1,740	1.9	2.1	20	32	6	50	47	31	44	34	67	3.9	30	8.7	4.7
Saint Kitts and Nevis	55	16	5	1.1	0.7	–	–	–	–	–	–	–	–	–	–	32	0.9	1.5
Saint Lucia	178	43	11	1.0	0.3	9	6	8	39	28	12	63	71	75	1.5	19	-0.6	1.1
Saint Vincent and the Grenadines	110	32	8	0.1	0.2	9	7	7	40	25	16	65	70	73	1.9	51	0.9	0.7
Samoa	195	85	23	0.7	0.6	11	7	5	41	33	25	55	65	75	4.0	19	0.3	0.5
San Marino	33	6	1	1.2	0.3	–	–	–	–	–	–	–	–	–	–	94	1.2	0.3
Sao Tome and Principe	200	100	31	2.2	2.1	13	10	7	41	40	34	56	62	67	4.5	66	3.8	2.6
Saudi Arabia	32,276	9,641	2,966	2.6	1.4	15	5	4	47	36	20	53	69	75	2.5	83	2.7	1.3
Senegal	15,412	7,616	2,544	2.7	2.6	25	11	6	50	43	36	39	57	67	4.8	44	3.2	3.5
Serbia	8,820	1,780	469	-0.3	-0.4	9	10	13	19	15	11	68	71	75	1.6	56	0.2	-0.2
Seychelles	94	24	8	1.1	0.3	9	7	8	35	23	16	66	71	74	2.3	54	1.5	0.9
Sierra Leone	7,396	3,638	1,141	2.1	2.0	30	26	13	49	47	35	35	37	52	4.5	40	2.5	2.7
Singapore	5,622	1,062	265	2.4	0.9	5	4	5	23	18	9	68	76	83	1.2	100	2.5	1.0
Slovakia	5,444	996	281	0.1	-0.1	9	10	10	18	15	10	70	71	77	1.4	53	-0.1	0.1
Slovenia	2,078	363	107	0.1	-0.1	10	10	10	17	11	10	69	73	81	1.6	50	0.1	0.3
Solomon Islands	599	275	83	2.5	1.8	13	11	5	45	40	29	54	57	71	3.9	23	4.5	3.4
Somalia	14,318	7,642	2,617	2.5	2.9	23	20	11	47	48	43	41	45	56	6.3	40	3.4	4.0
South Africa	56,015	19,428	5,705	1.5	1.0	12	8	10	38	29	21	56	62	63	2.5	65	2.3	1.2
South Sudan	12,231	5,944	1,925	2.9	2.5	28	21	11	51	47	36	36	44	57	4.9	19	4.4	3.8
Spain	46,348	8,135	2,065	0.6	0.0	9	8	9	20	10	9	72	77	83	1.4	80	1.0	0.4
Sri Lanka	20,798	6,020	1,602	0.7	0.2	8	6	7	31	21	15	64	70	75	2.0	18	0.8	1.4
State of Palestine	4,791	2,231	712	3.2	2.4	13	5	3	50	46	32	56	68	73	4.0	75	3.5	2.6
Sudan	39,579	18,971	5,940	2.6	2.3	15	12	7	47	42	33	52	56	64	4.5	34	3.4	3.1
Suriname	558	179	50	1.2	0.7	9	7	7	37	28	18	63	67	71	2.4	66	1.2	0.7
Swaziland	1,343	592	180	1.7	1.5	18	9	10	49	43	29	48	60	58	3.1	21	1.3	1.6
Sweden	9,838	2,006	584	0.5	0.6	10	11	9	14	14	12	74	78	82	1.9	86	0.6	0.8
Switzerland	8,402	1,499	434	0.9	0.7	9	9	8	16	12	10	73	78	83	1.5	74	0.9	1.1
Syrian Arab Republic	18,430	8,231	2,100	1.5	2.6	11	5	6	46	36	21	59	71	70	2.9	58	3.0	2.6
Tajikistan	8,735	3,581	1,183	1.9	1.8	12	10	5	42	41	29	60	63	71	3.4	27	1.3	2.7
Thailand	68,864	14,961	3,768	0.8	0.1	10	6	8	38	19	10	59	70	75	1.5	52	2.8	1.5
The former Yugoslav Republic of Macedonia	2,081	425	118	0.2	0.0	7	8	10	25	18	11	66	71	76	1.5	57	0.1	0.3
Timor-Leste	1,269	650	206	2.0	2.1	23	16	6	43	43	35	40	48	69	5.5	33	3.6	3.4
Togo	7,606	3,668	1,176	2.7	2.3	19	12	9	48	42	34	47	56	60	4.5	40	3.9	3.4
Tokelau	1	0	0	-0.9	0.8	–	–	–	–	–	–	–	–	–	–	0	0	0
Tonga	107	46	13	0.5	0.9	7	6	6	36	31	24	65	70	73	3.6	24	0.6	1.5
Trinidad and Tobago	1,365	335	95	0.4	0.0	7	8	10	27	21	14	65	68	71	1.8	8	0.3	-0.4
Tunisia	11,403	3,205	1,052	1.3	0.8	16	6	6	41	26	18	51	69	76	2.2	67	1.8	1.1
Turkey	79,512	24,162	6,775	1.5	0.8	15	8	6	40	26	16	52	64	76	2.1	74	2.2	1.3
Turkmenistan	5,663	2,021	709	1.7	1.3	12	9	7	38	35	25	58	63	68	2.9	50	1.9	1.7
Turks and Caicos Islands	35	10	3	4.3	1.2	–	–	–	–	–	–	–	–	–	–	93	5.1	1.3
Tuvalu	11	4	1	0.8	1.0	–	–	–	–	–	–	–	–	–	–	61	1.9	1.5
Uganda	41,488	22,807	7,699	3.3	3.1	17	18	9	49	50	42	49	46	60	5.6	16	4.8	5.1
Ukraine	44,439	7,948	2,334	-0.6	-0.5	9	13	15	15	13	11	71	70	72	1.5	70	-0.4	-0.4
United Arab Emirates	9,270	1,498	464	6.2	1.3	7	3	2	37	26	10	62	72	77	1.7	86	6.8	1.9
United Kingdom	65,789	13,785	4,000	0.5	0.5	12	11	9	15	14	12	72	76	82	1.9	83	0.7	0.7
United Republic of Tanzania	55,572	28,698	9,655	3.0	2.9	18	15	7	48	44	38	47	50	66	5.0	32	4.9	4.6
United States	322,180	73,928	19,607	0.9	0.7	10	9	8	16	16	13	71	75	79	1.9	82	1.3	0.9
Uruguay	3,444	884	240	0.4	0.3	10	10	9	21	18	14	69	73	77	2.0	95	0.7	0.4

TABLE 6. DEMOGRAPHIC INDICATORS

177

Countries and areas	Population (thousands) 2016			Population annual growth rate (%)		Crude death rate			Crude birth rate			Life expectancy			Total fertility rate	Urbanized population (%)	Average annual growth rate of urban population (%)	
	total	under 18	under 5	1990–2016	2016–2030ᵃ	1970	1990	2016	1970	1990	2016	1970	1990	2016	2016	2016	1990–2016	2016–2030ᵃ
Uzbekistan	31,447	10,386	3,184	1.7	1.1	10	8	6	37	35	21	62	66	71	2.3	36	1.1	1.7
Vanuatu	270	114	34	2.4	1.9	14	8	5	42	36	26	52	63	72	3.3	26	3.7	3.0
Venezuela (Bolivarian Republic of)	31,568	10,493	2,974	1.8	1.1	7	5	6	37	29	19	65	70	75	2.3	89	2.0	1.2
Viet Nam	94,569	25,780	7,761	1.3	0.8	12	6	6	36	29	17	60	71	76	2.0	34	3.2	2.2
Yemen	27,584	12,957	4,075	3.2	2.1	25	11	6	53	52	32	41	58	65	4.0	35	5.1	3.4
Zambia	16,591	8,647	2,820	2.8	2.9	17	18	8	50	45	38	49	45	62	5.0	41	2.9	4.3
Zimbabwe	16,150	7,726	2,539	1.8	2.1	13	10	8	47	37	33	55	58	61	3.8	32	1.9	2.3
SUMMARY																		
East Asia and Pacific	2,291,492	545,358	156,758	0.9	0.4	11	7	7	35	22	14	60	69	75	1.8	57	3.0	1.5
Europe and Central Asia	908,161	191,748	55,778	0.3	0.2	10	11	10	18	15	12	69	72	77	1.8	71	0.5	0.4
Eastern Europe and Central Asia	416,914	100,514	31,087	0.2	0.2	10	11	11	21	18	15	66	68	73	1.9	64	0.3	0.4
Western Europe	491,247	91,234	24,691	0.3	0.1	11	10	10	16	12	10	71	75	81	1.6	76	0.6	0.4
Latin America and Caribbean	633,773	193,378	53,227	1.4	0.8	10	7	6	37	27	17	60	68	76	2.1	80	1.9	1.1
Middle East and North Africa	435,225	152,698	49,143	2.1	1.5	15	7	5	44	34	23	53	66	74	2.8	63	2.6	1.8
North America	358,469	80,927	21,535	0.9	0.7	9	9	8	16	16	12	71	75	80	1.8	83	1.3	0.9
South Asia	1,765,989	619,518	169,895	1.7	1.0	17	11	7	40	33	20	48	58	69	2.5	33	2.7	2.3
Sub-Saharan Africa	1,034,153	511,533	167,977	2.7	2.5	21	16	9	47	44	36	45	50	60	4.8	37	4.0	3.6
Eastern and Southern Africa	542,206	261,901	83,757	2.6	2.4	19	16	8	47	43	34	47	51	63	4.4	31	3.7	3.5
West and Central Africa	491,947	249,631	84,220	2.8	2.6	23	17	11	47	45	39	42	49	57	5.4	45	4.2	3.7
Least developed countries	979,388	454,924	142,971	2.5	2.2	21	15	8	47	42	32	44	52	64	4.1	31	4.0	3.6
World	**7,427,263**	**2,295,160**	**674,314**	**1.3**	**1.0**	**13**	**9**	**8**	**33**	**26**	**19**	**59**	**65**	**72**	**2.4**	**54**	**2.2**	**1.6**

For a complete list of countries and areas in the regions, subregions and country categories, see page 150 or visit <data.unicef.org/regionalclassifications>.
It is not advisable to compare data from consecutive editions of *The State of the World's Children*.

DEFINITIONS OF THE INDICATORS

Crude death rate – Annual number of deaths per 1,000 population.

Crude birth rate – Annual number of births per 1,000 population.

Life expectancy – Number of years newborn children would live if subject to the mortality risks prevailing for the cross section of population at the time of their birth.

Total fertility rate – Number of children who would be born per woman if she lived to the end of her childbearing years and bore children at each age in accordance with prevailing age-specific fertility rates.

Urbanized population – Percentage of population living in urban areas as defined according to the national definition used in the most recent population census.

MAIN DATA SOURCES

Population – United Nations Population Division. Growth rates calculated by UNICEF based on data from United Nations Population Division.

Crude death and birth rates – United Nations Population Division.

Life expectancy – United Nations Population Division.

Total fertility rate – United Nations Population Division.

NOTES

– Data not available.

ᵃ Based on medium-fertility variant projections.

TABLE 7. WOMEN

Countries and areas	Life expectancy: females as a % of males 2016	Adult literacy rate: females as a % of males 2011–2016*	Enrolment ratios: females as a % of males Primary GER 2011–2016*	Enrolment ratios: females as a % of males Secondary GER 2011–2016*	Survival rate to the last grade of primary: females as a % of males 2011–2016*	Demand for family planning satisfied with modern methods (%) 2011–2016*	Antenatal care (%) At least one visit 2011–2016*	Antenatal care (%) At least four visits 2011–2016*	Delivery care (%) Skilled birth attendant 2013–2016*	Delivery care (%) Institutional delivery 2011–2016*	Delivery care (%) C-section 2011–2016*	Post-natal health check (%) For newborns 2011–2016*	Post-natal health check (%) For mothers 2011–2016*	Maternal mortality ratio Reported 2011–2016*	Maternal mortality ratio Adjusted 2015	Maternal mortality ratio Lifetime risk of maternal death (1 in:) 2015
Afghanistan	104	39	69	56	–	42	59	18	51	48	3	9	40	1,300	396	52
Albania	105	98	97	94	101	13 x	97 x	67 x	99 x	97 x	19 x	1 x	83 x	6	29	1,900
Algeria	103	82 x	94	104	102	77	93	67	97	97	16	–	–	–	140	240
Andorra	–	100	–	–	99	–	–	–	–	–	–	–	–	–	–	–
Angola	110	67	64	65	–	24	82	61	50	46	4	21	23	–	477	32
Anguilla	–	–	–	–	–	–	–	–	–	–	–	–	–	–	–	–
Antigua and Barbuda	107	101 x	94	102	–	–	100 x	100	100	–	–	–	–	0 x	–	–
Argentina	110	100	100	107	100	–	98	90	100	99	29	–	–	39	52	790
Armenia	109	100	100	101	99	40	100	96	100	99	18	98	97	17	25	2,300
Australia	105	–	100	95	–	–	98 x	92 x	–	99	31 x	–	–	–	6	8,700
Austria	106	–	99	95	101	–	–	–	99	99	24 x	–	–	–	4	18,200
Azerbaijan	109	100	98	–	95	22 x	92	66	100	93	20	3 x	83	14	25	1,600
Bahamas	108	–	–	–	–	–	98 x	85	98	–	–	–	–	37	80	660
Bahrain	103	95 x	101	100	97	–	100 x	100	100	98 x	–	–	–	17 x	15	3,000
Bangladesh	105	92	108	113	–	73	64	31	42	37	23	32	36	180	176	240
Barbados	107	–	101	103	–	70	93	88	99	100	21	98	97	52	27	2,100
Belarus	116	100 x	100	99	100	74	100	100	100	100	25	100	100	0	4	13,800
Belgium	106	–	100	114	102	–	–	–	–	–	18 x	–	–	–	7	8,000
Belize	108	–	95	102	98	66	97	93	97	96	34	96	96	45	28	1,300
Benin	105	49	92	70	95	25	83	59	77	87	5	80	78	350	405	51
Bhutan	101	73	107	107	101	85 x	98	85	86 x	74	12 x	30 x	41 x	86	148	310
Bolivia (Plurinational State of)	108	92	97	98	101	43 x	90	75	85 x	71	27	76 x	77 x	310 x	206	160
Bosnia and Herzegovina	107	96	–	–	101	22	87	84	100	100	14	–	–	0	11	6,800
Botswana	109	102 x	97	–	103	82 x	94 x	73 x	99 x	100	–	–	–	130	129	270
Brazil	110	101	97	105	–	90	97	91	99	99	56	–	–	55	44	1,200
British Virgin Islands	–	–	–	–	–	–	–	–	–	–	–	–	–	–	–	–
Brunei Darussalam	104	97	100	100	97	–	99 x	93	100	100 x	–	–	–	–	23	2,300
Bulgaria	110	99	99	97	100	–	–	–	100	94	36	–	–	6	11	6,200
Burkina Faso	102	59	96	92	114	44	93	47	80	82	4	33	74	330	371	48
Burundi	107	78	101	91	118	33	99	49	85	84	4 x	8 x	49	500 x	712	23
Cabo Verde	106	89	95	112	101	73 x	98	72 x	92	76 x	11 x	–	–	10	42	900
Cambodia	106	80 x	99	–	134	56	95	76	89	83	6	79	90	170	161	210
Cameroon	104	83 x	90	86	104	40	83	59	65	61	2	69	65	780	596	35
Canada	105	–	101	100	–	–	100 x	99 x	100 x	98	26 x	–	–	11	7	8,800
Central African Republic	107	48 x	74	51	96	29	68 x	38 x	40 x	53 x	5 x	–	–	540 x	882	27
Chad	105	45	77	46	85	18	55	31	20	22	1	5	16	860	856	18
Chile	107	100	97	101	101	–	–	–	100	100	50	14	22	2,600		
China	104	95 x	100	103	–	97 x	97	69	100	100	41	–	–	20	27	2,400
Colombia	110	100	97	107	106	84 x	97	90	99	99	46	7 x	1	54	64	800
Comoros	105	75	93	107	121	28	92	49	82 x	76	10	14	49	170	335	66
Congo	105	84	107	87	–	39	93	79	94	92	5	86	80	440	442	45
Cook Islands	–	–	94	108	94	–	100 x	–	100 x	100 x	–	–	–	0	–	–
Costa Rica	106	100	99	104	101	89	98	90	99	99	22	–	–	28	25	2,100
Côte d'Ivoire	106	73	89	72	95	31	91	44	59 x	57	3	34	70	610	645	32
Croatia	109	99	100	105	99	–	–	92	100	–	21	–	–	3	8	7,900
Cuba	105	100	95	105	100	88	99	98	99	100	40	98	99	42	39	1,800
Cyprus	106	99	100	99	99	–	99 x	–	–	97	–	–	–	–	7	9,400
Czechia	108	–	100	101	100	86 x	–	–	100	100	20 x	–	–	1	4	14,800
Democratic People's Republic of Korea	110	–	–	101	–	90	100 x	94 x	100 x	95 x	13 x	–	–	77 x	82	660
Democratic Republic of the Congo	105	75	91	62	99	16	88	48	80	80	5	8	44	850	693	24
Denmark	105	–	98	104	100	–	–	–	–	–	21 x	–	–	–	6	9,500
Djibouti	105	–	91	82	88	–	88	23	87 x	87	11	–	–	380	229	140
Dominica	–	–	98	99	95	–	100 x	–	100	–	–	–	–	110	–	–
Dominican Republic	109	101	91	110	105	84	98	93	98	98	58	95	95	110	92	400
Ecuador	107	98	106	104	102	81	84 x	58 x	96	93	46	–	–	46	64	580
Egypt	106	81	100	99	–	80	90	83	92	87	52	14	82	49	33	810
El Salvador	113	96	96	101	105	82	96	90	100	98	32	97	94	42	54	890
Equatorial Guinea	105	86 x	98	–	100	21	91	67	68 x	67	7	–	–	310	342	61
Eritrea	107	73 x	86	85	103	20 x	89 x	57 x	34 x	34 x	3 x	–	5 x	490 x	501	43
Estonia	113	100	100	99	101	–	–	97	100 x	99	–	–	–	7	9	6,300
Ethiopia	106	59 x	91	96	105	59	62	32	28	26	2	0	17	410	353	64
Fiji	109	–	99	111	98	–	100 x	94	100	99	–	–	–	59	30	1,200

TABLE 7. WOMEN 179

Countries and areas	Life expectancy: females as a % of males (2016)	Adult literacy rate: females as a % of males (2011–2016*)	Enrolment ratios: females as a % of males — Primary GER (2011–2016*)	Enrolment ratios: females as a % of males — Secondary GER (2011–2016*)	Survival rate to the last grade of primary: females as a % of males (2011–2016*)	Demand for family planning satisfied with modern methods (%) (2011–2016*)	Antenatal care (%) — At least one visit (2011–2016*)	Antenatal care (%) — At least four visits (2011–2016*)	Delivery care (%) — Skilled birth attendant (2013–2016*)	Delivery care (%) — Institutional delivery (2011–2016*)	Delivery care (%) — C-section (2011–2016*)	Post-natal health check (%) — For newborns (2011–2016*)	Post-natal health check (%) — For mothers (2011–2016*)	Maternal mortality ratio — Reported (2011–2016*)	Maternal mortality ratio — Adjusted (2015)	Lifetime risk of maternal death (1 in:) (2015)
Finland	107	–	100	109	100	–	100 x	–	–	100	16 x	–	–	–	3	21,700
France	108	–	99	101	–	96 x	100 x	99 x	–	98	21 x	–	–	–	8	6,100
Gabon	105	94	97	–	–	34	95	78	89 x	90	10	25	60	320	291	85
Gambia	104	65	105	–	106	24	86	78	57	63	2	6	76	430	706	24
Georgia	112	100	102	100	100	53 x	98 x	88	100	100	41	–	–	32	36	1,500
Germany	106	–	99	94	100	–	100 x	99	–	99	29 x	–	–	–	6	11,700
Ghana	103	83 x	102	97	97	41	91	87	71	73	13	23	81	450 x	319	74
Greece	107	98	99	94	100	–	100 x	–	99	–	–	–	–	–	3	23,700
Grenada	107	–	96	100	–	–	100 x	–	99	–	–	–	–	23	27	1,500
Guatemala	109	88	96	93	99	66	91	86	66	65	26	8	78	140	88	330
Guinea	102	50	85	66	97	16	85	57	45 x	40	2	25	37	720	679	29
Guinea–Bissau	106	50	–	–	–	38	92	65	45	44	4	55	48	900	549	38
Guyana	107	99	97	99	105	53	91	87	86	93	17	95	93	86 x	229	170
Haiti	107	84 x	–	–	–	45	90	67	49	36	6	19	32	380	359	90
Holy See	–	–	–	–	–	–	–	–	–	–	–	–	–	–	–	–
Honduras	107	100	99	119	110	76	97	89	83 x	83	19	81	85	73 x	129	300
Hungary	110	–	99	100	100	–	–	–	99 x	–	31 x	–	–	15	17	4,400
Iceland	104	–	99	104	102	–	–	–	–	–	17 x	–	–	–	3	14,600
India	105	75	112	101	99	72	74 x	51	81	79	17	24	62	170	174	220
Indonesia	106	96	97	100	–	79	95	84	93	80	12	48	80	360	126	320
Iran (Islamic Republic of)	103	89	105	99	99	69	97 x	94 x	96 x	95 x	46 x	–	–	25 x	25	2,000
Iraq	107	72	–	–	–	59	78	50	91 x	77	22	–	–	35	50	420
Ireland	105	–	101	103	–	–	100 x	–	100 x	100	25 x	–	–	–	8	6,100
Israel	104	–	101	101	98	–	–	–	–	–	–	–	–	–	5	6,200
Italy	106	99	99	98	100	–	99 x	68 x	–	100	40 x	–	–	–	4	19,700
Jamaica	107	116 x	–	107	103	83 x	98	86	99 x	99	21	–	–	80	89	520
Japan	108	–	100	100	100	–	–	–	–	100	–	–	–	–	5	13,400
Jordan	105	99	101	106	–	58	99	95	100 x	99	28	75	82	19 x	58	490
Kazakhstan	115	100 x	102	103	101	80	99	95	99	99	15	99	98	13	12	3,000
Kenya	108	88	99	–	–	75	94	58	62	61	9	36	53	360	510	42
Kiribati	110	–	103	–	–	36 x	88 x	71 x	98 x	66 x	10 x	–	–	33	90	300
Kuwait	103	98	101	116	101	–	100 x	–	99 x	99	–	–	–	2	4	10,300
Kyrgyzstan	112	99 x	99	102	100	62	98	95	98	98	7	99	98	36	76	390
Lao People's Democratic Republic	105	74	96	93	104	61	54	37	40 x	38	4	41	40	210	197	150
Latvia	114	100	99	99	100	–	92 x	–	100 x	98	–	–	–	24	18	3,500
Lebanon	105	93 x	91	99	108	–	96 x	–	98 x	100 x	–	–	–	–	15	3,700
Lesotho	109	125	97	136	129	76	95	74	78	77	10	18	62	1,000	487	61
Liberia	103	44 x	90	78	–	37	96	78	61	56	4	35	71	1,100	725	28
Libya	108	–	–	–	–	30 x	93 x	–	–	100	–	–	–	–	9	4,200
Liechtenstein	–	–	98	78	–	–	–	–	–	–	–	–	–	–	–	–
Lithuania	115	100	100	96	100	–	100 x	–	100 x	–	–	–	–	7	10	6,300
Luxembourg	106	–	100	102	103	–	–	97	100 x	100 x	29 x	–	–	–	10	6,500
Madagascar	105	91	100	98	105	50 x	82	51	44	38	2	13 x	46 x	480	353	60
Malawi	109	79	102	90	102	75	95	51	90	91	6	60	42	440	634	29
Malaysia	106	95 x	100	108	101	–	97	–	99	99	–	–	–	24	40	1,200
Maldives	103	100	–	–	106	43 x	99 x	85 x	96 x	95 x	32 x	1 x	70 x	110	68	600
Mali	102	49	91	81	94	48	48	38	44	65	2	63	58	460 x	587	27
Malta	104	103	102	107	104	–	100 x	–	–	100	–	–	–	–	9	8,300
Marshall Islands	–	100	100	110	–	81 x	81 x	77 x	90 x	85 x	9 x	–	–	110	–	–
Mauritania	105	62 x	105	93	98	30	85	63	64	69	5	58	57	630	602	36
Mauritius	110	96	102	105	99	41	–	–	100	98 x	–	–	–	22 x	53	1,300
Mexico	107	98	100	107	102	81	99	94	99	97	41	95	95	35	38	1,100
Micronesia (Federated States of)	103	–	100	–	–	–	80 x	–	100 x	87 x	11 x	–	–	160	100	310
Monaco	–	–	–	–	–	–	–	–	–	–	–	–	–	–	–	–
Mongolia	113	100 x	98	102	–	68	99	90	98	98	23	99	95	26	44	800
Montenegro	106	98	98	100	102	34	92	87	99	99	20	99	95	0 x	7	8,300
Montserrat	–	–	–	–	–	–	–	–	–	–	–	–	–	–	–	–
Morocco	103	74	95	85	96	75	77	55	74 x	73	16	–	1 x	110 x	121	320
Mozambique	108	54 x	92	92	94	28	91	51	54 x	55	4	–	5 x	410	489	40
Myanmar	107	90	97	103	–	75	81	59	60	37	17	36	71	230	178	260
Namibia	109	99	97	–	104	75	97	63	88	87	14	20	69	390	265	100
Nauru	–	–	92	102	–	43 x	95 x	40 x	97 x	99 x	8 x	–	–	0	–	–
Nepal	105	68	108	107	104	56	84	69	58	57	9	58	57	280 x	258	150

TABLE 7. WOMEN

Countries and areas	Life expectancy: females as a % of males 2016	Adult literacy rate: females as a % of males 2011–2016*	Enrolment ratios: females as a % of males — Primary GER 2011–2016*	Enrolment ratios: females as a % of males — Secondary GER 2011–2016*	Survival rate to the last grade of primary: females as a % of males 2011–2016*	Demand for family planning satisfied with modern methods (%) 2011–2016*	Antenatal care (%) — At least one visit 2011–2016*	Antenatal care (%) — At least four visits 2011–2016*	Delivery care (%) — Skilled birth attendant 2013–2016*	Delivery care (%) — Institutional delivery 2011–2016*	Delivery care (%) — C-section 2011–2016*	Post-natal health check (%)⁺ — For newborns 2011–2016*	Post-natal health check (%)⁺ — For mothers 2011–2016*	Maternal mortality ratio† — Reported 2011–2016*	Maternal mortality ratio† — Adjusted 2015	Lifetime risk of maternal death (1 in:) 2015
Netherlands	105	–	99	101	–	–	–	–	–	–	14 x	–	–	–	7	8,700
New Zealand	104	–	100	106	–	–	–	–	–	97	23 x	–	–	–	11	4,500
Nicaragua	108	100 x	–	–	–	90	95	88	88 x	71	30	–	3 x	51	150	270
Niger	103	38	86	71	104	35	83	38	40	59	1	13	37	520	553	23
Nigeria	103	68 x	98	93	–	33	61	51	35	36	2	14	40	550	814	22
Niue	–	–	82	110	–	–	100 x	–	100 x	–	–	–	–	0	–	–
Norway	105	–	100	97	100	–	–	–	–	99	16 x	–	–	–	5	11,500
Oman	106	89	103	107	101	19 x	99	94	99	99	19	98	95	18	17	1,900
Pakistan	103	64	85	79	99	47	73	37	55	48	14	43	60	280 x	178	140
Palau	–	100	111	99	–	–	90 x	81 x	100	100 x	–	–	–	0 x	–	–
Panama	108	99 x	97	107	102	76	93	88	94	91	28	93	92	81	94	420
Papua New Guinea	108	80 x	91	76	–	41 x	79	55 x	53 x	43	–	–	–	730 x	215	120
Paraguay	106	98	97	107	104	84 x	96	83	96 x	97	49	–	–	82	132	270
Peru	107	94	100	100	103	63	97	96	92	91	32	96	93	93 x	68	570
Philippines	110	101	100	110	–	52	95	84	73	61	9	53	72	220	114	280
Poland	111	–	100	96	100	–	–	–	100 x	100	21 x	–	–	2	3	22,100
Portugal	108	96	96	97	–	–	100 x	–	100 x	99	31 x	–	–	–	10	8,200
Qatar	103	100	101	126	97	69	91	85	100	99	20	–	–	11	13	3,500
Republic of Korea	108	–	99	99	100	–	–	97	–	100	32 x	–	–	–	11	7,200
Republic of Moldova	113	100	99	101	100	60	99	95	100	99	16	–	87 x	30	23	3,200
Romania	110	99	98	99	100	47 x	76	76 x	95	95	34	–	–	14	31	2,300
Russian Federation	117	100 x	101	98	101	72	–	–	100 x	99	13	–	–	11	25	2,300
Rwanda	107	89	101	109	118	66	99	44	91	91	13	19	43	210	290	85
Saint Kitts and Nevis	–	–	102	105	98	–	100 x	–	100	–	–	–	–	310	–	–
Saint Lucia	107	–	–	99	100	72	97	90	99 x	100	19	100	90	34	48	1,100
Saint Vincent and the Grenadines	106	–	98	97	–	–	100 x	100 x	99	–	–	–	–	45	45	1,100
Samoa	109	100	100	111	97	39	93	73	83	82	5	–	63	29 x	51	500
San Marino	–	–	99	103	103	–	–	–	–	–	–	–	–	–	–	–
Sao Tome and Principe	107	90	94	113	–	50	98	84	93	91	6	91	87	160 x	156	140
Saudi Arabia	104	95	103	76	–	–	97 x	–	98	–	–	–	–	14	12	3,100
Senegal	106	64	112	98	108	44	95	47	53	75	5	50	74	430	315	61
Serbia	108	99	100	101	97	25	98	94	98	98	29	–	–	12	17	3,900
Seychelles	113	101 x	103	107	–	–	–	–	99 x	–	–	–	–	57 x	–	–
Sierra Leone	102	60	101	86	101	38	97	76	60	54	3	39	73	1,200	1,360	17
Singapore	105	97	–	–	–	–	–	–	–	100	–	–	–	–	10	8,200
Slovakia	110	–	99	101	101	–	97 x	–	99 x	–	24 x	–	–	0	6	12,100
Slovenia	107	–	100	100	100	–	100 x	–	100 x	100	–	–	–	0	9	7,000
Solomon Islands	104	–	99	94	114	60 x	89	69	86	85	6	16	69	150 x	114	220
Somalia	106	–	–	–	–	–	26 x	6 x	9 x	9 x	–	–	–	1,000 x	732	22
South Africa	112	98	95	127	–	81 x	94	76	97	96	26	–	84	580	138	300
South Sudan	104	55 x	71	54	–	6 x	62	17 x	19 x	12 x	1 x	–	–	2,100 x	789	26
Spain	107	99	101	100	100	–	–	–	–	–	26 x	–	–	–	5	14,700
Sri Lanka	109	97 x	98	105	100	69 x	99 x	93 x	99 x	100	32	–	–	32	30	1,600
State of Palestine	105	97	100	110	105	65	99	96	100	99	20	94	91	–	45	490
Sudan	105	–	90	95	99	30	79	51	78	28	9	28	27	220 x	311	72
Suriname	109	96	98	127	115	73 x	91 x	67 x	90 x	92 x	19 x	–	–	130	155	270
Swaziland	112	98 x	92	99	107	81	99	76	88	88	12	90	88	590 x	389	76
Sweden	104	–	104	114	100	–	100 x	–	–	–	–	–	–	–	4	12,900
Switzerland	105	–	100	97	–	–	–	–	–	–	30 x	–	–	–	5	12,400
Syrian Arab Republic	120	84 x	97	100	101	53 x	88	64 x	96 x	78 x	26 x	–	–	65 x	68	440
Tajikistan	109	100 x	99	90	101	51	79	53	98	77	4	54	81	29	32	790
Thailand	111	96	94	94	–	89	98	91	99	99	33	–	–	12 x	20	3,600
The former Yugoslav Republic of Macedonia	105	96 x	99	97	99	22	99	94	100	100	25	–	–	4	8	8,500
Timor-Leste	105	83 x	99	107	103	38 x	84	55 x	29 x	21 x	2 x	2 x	24 x	570 x	215	82
Togo	103	66	95	–	96	32	73	57	45	73	7	35	71	400	368	58
Tokelau	–	–	–	93	–	–	–	–	–	–	–	–	–	–	–	–
Tonga	109	100	99	109	–	48	99	70	96 x	98	17	–	–	36 x	124	230
Trinidad and Tobago	110	–	–	–	–	55 x	96 x	100	100	97 x	–	–	–	84	63	860
Tunisia	106	84	97	105	103	73	98	85	74 x	99	27	98	92	–	62	710
Turkey	109	94	99	97	99	60	97	89	97	97	48	72	88	29 x	16	3,000
Turkmenistan	111	–	98	96	–	76	100	96	100	100	6	100	100	7 x	42	940
Turks and Caicos Islands	–	–	–	–	–	–	–	–	–	–	–	–	–	–	–	–

TABLE 7. WOMEN
181

Countries and areas	Life expectancy: females as a % of males (2016)	Adult literacy rate: females as a % of males (2011–2016*)	Enrolment ratios: females as a % of males — Primary GER (2011–2016*)	Secondary GER	Survival rate to the last grade of primary: females as a % of males (2011–2016*)	Demand for family planning satisfied with modern methods (%) (2011–2016*)	Antenatal care (%) — At least one visit (2011–2016*)	At least four visits	Delivery care (%) — Skilled birth attendant (2013–2016*)	Institutional delivery (2011–2016*)	C-section (2011–2016*)	Post-natal health check (%) — For newborns (2011–2016*)	For mothers	Maternal mortality ratio — Reported (2011–2016*)	Adjusted (2015)	Lifetime risk of maternal death (1 in:) (2015)
Tuvalu	–	–	101	128	–	41 x	97 x	67 x	93 x	93 x	7 x	–	–	0 x	–	–
Uganda	108	78	102	91	103	48	97	60	57 x	73	5	11	54	340	343	47
Ukraine	115	100	102	98	100	68	99	87	99 x	99	12	99	96	14	24	2,600
United Arab Emirates	103	102 x	99	–	103	–	100 x	–	100 x	100	–	–	–	0 x	6	7,900
United Kingdom	105	–	100	104	–	–	–	–	–	–	26 x	–	–	–	9	5,800
United Republic of Tanzania	106	88	103	91	115	53	91	51	64	63	6	42	34	560	398	45
United States	106	–	100	102	–	83 x	–	97	99	–	31 x	–	–	28	14	3,800
Uruguay	110	101	98	111	101	–	97	77	100	100	30	–	–	17	15	3,300
Uzbekistan	108	100	96	98	101	–	99	–	100	100	14	–	–	19	36	1,000
Vanuatu	106	–	98	106	–	51	76	52	89	89	12	–	–	86 x	78	360
Venezuela (Bolivarian Republic of)	112	100	97	108	100	–	98	84	100	99	52	–	–	69	95	420
Viet Nam	113	95 x	99	–	104	70	96	74	94	94	28	89	90	67	54	870
Yemen	105	–	84	69	93	47	60	25	45	30	5	11	20	150	385	60
Zambia	108	88 x	101	–	94	64	96	56	63	67	4	16	63	400	224	79
Zimbabwe	106	99	98	98	104	85	93	76	78	77	6	73	57	650	443	52

SUMMARY

East Asia and Pacific	106	–	99	102	–	89	96	74	95	90	31	56 **	79 **	–	59	930
Europe and Central Asia	109	–	100	99	100	75	–	–	–	98	22	–	–	–	16	3400
Eastern Europe and Central Asia	113	98	100	98	100	68	96	87	99	97	22	–	–	–	25	2000
Western Europe	107	–	100	100	100	82	–	–	–	99	–	–	–	–	7	9600
Latin America and Caribbean	109	99	98	105	102	83	97	90	96	94	43	–	–	–	68	670
Middle East and North Africa	105	84	98	95	99	71	84	66	86	80	30	–	–	–	81	400
North America	106	–	100	102	–	86	–	97	99	–	–	–	–	–	13	4100
South Asia	104	75	107	99	99	71	69 ‡	46	73	70	17	28	59	–	182	200
Sub–Saharan Africa	106	78	95	87	102	50	80	52	56	56	5	24	46	–	546	36
Eastern and Southern Africa	107	88	94	94	105	61	85	52	60	57	7	24	40	–	409	52
West and Central Africa	104	–	95	81	99	35	75	52	52	56	3	24	50	–	679	27
Least developed countries	105	77	94	89	103	58	79	46	56	54	7	25	42	–	436	52
World	**106**	**85**	**100**	**98**	**100**	**78**	**86 ‡**	**62**	**78**	**75**	**20**	**34 ****	**59 ****	**–**	**216**	**180**

For a complete list of countries and areas in the regions, subregions and country categories, see page 150 or visit <data.unicef.org/regionalclassifications>.
It is not advisable to compare data from consecutive editions of *The State of the World's Children*.

DEFINITIONS OF THE INDICATORS

Life expectancy – Number of years newborn children would live if subject to the mortality risks prevailing for the cross section of population at the time of their birth.

Adult literacy rate – Percentage of the population aged 15 years and over who can both read and write with understanding a short, simple statement on his/her everyday life.

Primary gross enrolment ratio (GER) – Total enrolment in primary school, regardless of age, expressed as a percentage of the official primary-school-aged population.

Secondary gross enrolment ratio (GER) – Total enrolment in secondary school, regardless of age, expressed as a percentage of the official secondary-school-aged population.

Survival rate to last grade of primary – Percentage of children entering the first grade of primary school who eventually reach the last grade (administrative data).

Demand for family planning satisfied with modern methods – Percentage of women of reproductive age (15–49 years) who have their need for family planning satisfied with modern methods.

Antenatal care – Percentage of women (aged 15–49) attended at least once during pregnancy by skilled health personnel (doctor, nurse or midwife) and the percentage attended by any provider at least four times.

Skilled birth attendant – Percentage of births attended by skilled health personnel (doctor, nurse or midwife).

Institutional delivery – Percentage of women (aged 15–49) who gave birth in a health facility.

C-section – Percentage of births delivered by Caesarean section. NB: C-section rates between 5 per cent and 15 per cent expected with adequate levels of emergency obstetric care.

Post-natal health check for newborn – Percentage of last live births in the last 2 years who received a health check within 2 days after delivery. NB: For MICS, health check refers to a health check while in facility or at home following delivery or a postnatal visit.

Post-natal health check for mother – Percentage of women age 15–49 years who received a health check within 2 days after delivery of their most recent live birth in the last 2 years. NB: For MICS, health check refers to a health check while in facility or at home following delivery or a postnatal visit.

Maternal mortality ratio – Number of deaths of women from pregnancy-related causes per 100,000 live births during the same time period. The 'reported' column shows country-reported figures that are not adjusted for under-reporting and misclassification. For the 'adjusted' column, see note below (†). Maternal mortality ratio values have been rounded according to the following scheme: Reported: <100, no rounding; 100–999, rounded to nearest 10; and >1,000, rounded to nearest 100. Adjusted: <1000, rounded to nearest 1; and ≥1,000, rounded to nearest 10.

Lifetime risk of maternal death – Lifetime risk of maternal death takes into account both the probability of becoming pregnant and the probability of dying as a result of that pregnancy, accumulated across a woman's reproductive years. Lifetime risk values have been rounded according to the following scheme: <1000, rounded to nearest 1; and ≥1,000, rounded to nearest 10.

MAIN DATA SOURCES

Life expectancy – United Nations Population Division.

Adult literacy – UNESCO Institute for Statistics (UIS).

Primary and secondary school enrolment – UIS.

Survival rate to last grade of primary – UIS.

Demand for family planning satisfied with modern methods – SDG Global Database based on Demographic and Health Surveys (DHS), Multiple Indicator Cluster Surveys (MICS), Reproductive Health Surveys, other national surveys, National Health Information Systems (HIS)

Antenatal care – DHS, MICS and other nationally representative sources.

Skilled birth attendant – Joint UNICEF/WHO SBA database, November 2017 update, based on DHS, MICS and other nationally representative sources.

Institutional delivery – DHS, MICS and other nationally representative sources.

C-section – DHS, MICS and other nationally representative sources.

Post-natal health check for newborn and mother – DHS and MICS.

Maternal mortality ratio (reported) – Nationally representative sources, including household surveys and vital registration.

Maternal mortality ratio (adjusted) – United Nations Maternal Mortality Estimation Inter-agency Group (WHO, UNICEF, UNFPA, The World Bank and the United Nations Population Division).

Lifetime risk of maternal death – United Nations Maternal Mortality Estimation Inter-agency Group (WHO, UNICEF, UNFPA, The World Bank and the United Nations Population Division).

NOTES

– Data not available.

x Data refer to years or periods other than those specified in the column heading. Such data are not included in the calculation of regional and global averages. Estimates from data years prior to 2000 are not displayed.

+ Data collection method for this indicator varies across surveys and may affect comparability of the coverage estimates. For detailed explanation see General Note on the Data, page 146.

† The maternal mortality data in the column headed 'reported' refer to data reported by national authorities. The data in the column headed 'adjusted' refer to the 2015 United Nations inter-agency maternal mortality estimates. Periodically, the United Nations Maternal Mortality Estimation Inter-agency Group (WHO, UNICEF, UNFPA The World Bank and the United Nations Population Division) produces internationally comparable sets of maternal mortality data that account for the well-documented problems of under-reporting and misclassification of maternal deaths, including also estimates for countries with no data. Please note that owing to an evolving methodology, these values are not comparable with previously reported maternal mortality ratio 'adjusted' values. Comparable time series on maternal mortality ratios for the years 1990, 1995, 2000, 2005 and 2015 are available at < http://data.unicef.org/maternal–health/maternal–mortality.html>.

* Data refer to the most recent year available during the period specified in the column heading.

** Excludes China.

‡ Excludes India.

TABLE 8. CHILD PROTECTION

Countries and areas	Child labour (%)+ 2010–2016*			Child marriage (%) 2010–2016*		Birth registration (%)++ 2010–2016*	Female genital mutilation/cutting (%)+ 2004–2016*			Justification of wife-beating (%) 2010–2016*		Violent discipline (%)+ 2010–2016*		
							prevalence		attitudes					
	total	male	female	married by 15	married by 18	total	women[a]	girls[b]	support for the practice[c]	male	female	total	male	female
Afghanistan	29	34	24	9	35	42	–	–	–	72 y	80 y	74 y	75 y	74 y
Albania	5 y	6 y	4 y	0 x	10 x	99 x	–	–	–	36 x	30 x	77 x,y	81 x,y	73 x,y
Algeria	5 y	6 y	5 y	0	3	100	–	–	–	–	59 y	86 y	88 y	85 y
Andorra	–	–	–	–	–	100 v	–	–	–	–	–	–	–	–
Angola	23	22	25	8	30	25	–	–	–	20	25	–	–	–
Anguilla	–	–	–	–	–	–	–	–	–	–	–	–	–	–
Antigua and Barbuda	–	–	–	–	–	–	–	–	–	–	–	–	–	–
Argentina	4 y	5 y	4 y	–	–	100 y	–	–	–	–	2	72 y	74 y	71 y
Armenia	9 y	11 y	6 y	0	5	99	–	–	–	23	10	69	71	67
Australia	–	–	–	–	–	100 v	–	–	–	–	–	–	–	–
Austria	–	–	–	–	–	100 v	–	–	–	–	–	–	–	–
Azerbaijan	7 x,y	8 x,y	5 x,y	2	11	94 x	–	–	–	–	28	77 x,y	80 x,y	74 x,y
Bahamas	–	–	–	–	–	–	–	–	–	–	–	–	–	–
Bahrain	5 x,y	6 x,y	3 x,y	–	–	–	–	–	–	–	–	–	–	–
Bangladesh	4 y	5 y	4 y	22	59	20	–	–	–	–	28 y	82	83	82
Barbados	2 y	3 y	1 y	1	11	99	–	–	–	–	3	75 y	78 y	72 y
Belarus	1 y	1 y	2 y	0	3	100 y	–	–	–	4	4	65 y	67 y	62 y
Belgium	–	–	–	–	–	100 v	–	–	–	–	–	–	–	–
Belize	3 y	5 y	1 y	3	26	96	–	–	–	5	5	65	67	63
Benin	53	54	51	7	26	85	9	0	3	17	36	91	92	90
Bhutan	3 y	3 y	3 y	6	26	100	–	–	–	–	68	–	–	–
Bolivia (Plurinational State of)	26 x,y	28 x,y	24 x,y	3 x	22 x	76 x,y	–	–	–	–	16 x	–	–	–
Bosnia and Herzegovina	5 x,y	7 x,y	4 x,y	0	4	100 x	–	–	–	6	5	55 y	60 y	50 y
Botswana	9 x,y	11 x,y	7 x,y	–	–	83 y	–	–	–	–	–	–	–	–
Brazil	7 y	9 y	5 y	11 x	36 x	96	–	–	–	–	–	–	–	–
British Virgin Islands	–	–	–	–	–	–	–	–	–	–	–	–	–	–
Brunei Darussalam	–	–	–	–	–	–	–	–	–	–	–	–	–	–
Bulgaria	–	–	–	–	–	100 y	–	–	–	–	–	–	–	–
Burkina Faso	39 y	42 y	36 y	10	52	77	76	13	9	34	44	83 x,y	84 x,y	82 x,y
Burundi	26 y	26 y	27 y	3	20	75	–	–	–	44	73	–	–	–
Cabo Verde	6 y	–	–	3 x	18 x	91	–	–	–	17 x,y	17 x,y	–	–	–
Cambodia	19 y	20 y	19 y	2	19	73	–	–	–	27 y	50 y	–	–	–
Cameroon	47	50	44	10	31	66	1	1 y	7	39	36	85	85	85
Canada	–	–	–	–	–	100 v	–	–	–	–	–	–	–	–
Central African Republic	29 y	27 y	30 y	29	68	61	24	1	11	75	80	92 y	92 y	92 y
Chad	52	51	52	30	67	12	38	10	29	51	74	71	72	71
Chile	7 y	–	–	–	–	99 y	–	–	–	–	–	–	–	–
China	–	–	–	–	–	–	–	–	–	–	–	–	–	–
Colombia	8 y	10 y	5 y	5	23	99	–	–	–	–	–	–	–	–
Comoros	22 y	20 y	24 y	10	32	87	–	–	–	17	39	–	–	–
Congo	23	–	–	6	33	96	–	–	–	40	54	83	–	–
Cook Islands	–	–	–	–	–	–	–	–	–	–	–	–	–	–
Costa Rica	4 y	4 y	5 y	7	21	100 y	–	–	–	–	4	46 y	52 y	39 y
Côte d'Ivoire	26 y	25 y	28 y	10	33	65	38	10	14	42	48	91 x,y	91 x,y	91 x,y
Croatia	–	–	–	–	–	–	–	–	–	–	–	–	–	–
Cuba	–	–	–	5	26	100	–	–	–	7 y	4 y	36	37	35
Cyprus	–	–	–	–	–	100 v	–	–	–	–	–	–	–	–
Czechia	–	–	–	–	–	100 v	–	–	–	–	–	–	–	–
Democratic People's Republic of Korea	–	–	–	–	–	100 x	–	–	–	–	–	–	–	–
Democratic Republic of the Congo	38	36	41	10	37	25	–	–	–	61	75	82	82	81
Denmark	–	–	–	–	–	100 v	–	–	–	–	–	–	–	–
Djibouti	8 x,y	8 x,y	8 x,y	2 x	5 x	92 x	93	49 y	37	–	–	72 x,y	73 x,y	71 x,y
Dominica	–	–	–	–	–	–	–	–	–	–	–	–	–	–
Dominican Republic	13	17	9	12	36	88	–	–	–	–	2	63	64	61
Ecuador	5 y	5 y	5 y	4 x	22 x	94	–	–	–	–	–	–	–	–
Egypt	7	8	6	2	17	99	87	14 y	54	–	36 y	93	93	93
El Salvador	9 y	13 y	5 y	6	26	99	–	–	–	–	8	52	55	50
Equatorial Guinea	28 x,y	28 x,y	28 x,y	9	30	54	–	–	–	52	53	–	–	–
Eritrea	–	–	–	13	41	–	83	33	12	45	51	–	–	–
Estonia	–	–	–	–	–	100 v	–	–	–	–	–	–	–	–
Ethiopia	27 y	31 y	24 y	14	40	3	65	16	18	28	63	–	–	–
Fiji	–	–	–	–	–	–	–	–	–	–	–	72 x,y	–	–
Finland	–	–	–	–	–	100 v	–	–	–	–	–	–	–	–

TABLE 8. CHILD PROTECTION

183

| Countries and areas | Child labour (%)+ 2010–2016* | | | Child marriage (%) 2010–2016* | | Birth registration (%)++ 2010–2016* | Female genital mutilation/cutting (%)+ 2004–2016* | | | Justification of wife-beating (%) 2010–2016* | | Violent discipline (%)+ 2010–2016* | | |
| | | | | | | | prevalence | | attitudes | | | | | |
	total	male	female	married by 15	married by 18	total	women[a]	girls[b]	support for the practice[c]	male	female	total	male	female
France	–	–	–	–	–	100 v	–	–	–	–	–	–	–	–
Gabon	13 y	15 y	12 y	6	22	90	–	–	–	40	50	–	–	–
Gambia	19 y	21 y	18 y	9	30	72	75	56	65	33	58	90 y	90 y	91 y
Georgia	4 y	6 y	2 y	1	14	100	–	–	–	–	7 x	67 x,y	70 x,y	63 x,y
Germany	–	–	–	–	–	100 v	–	–	–	–	–	–	–	–
Ghana	22 y	23 y	21 y	5	21	71	4	1	2	13	28	94 y	94 y	94 y
Greece	–	–	–	–	–	100 v	–	–	–	–	–	–	–	–
Grenada	–	–	–	–	–	–	–	–	–	–	–	–	–	–
Guatemala	26 y	35 y	16 y	6	30	96 y	–	–	–	7	11	–	–	–
Guinea	28 y	29 y	27 y	21	52	58	97	46	76	66	92	–	–	–
Guinea-Bissau	51	50	53	6	24	24	45	30	13	29	42	82	83	82
Guyana	18	20	17	4	30	89	–	–	–	10	10	70	74	65
Haiti	24 y	25 y	24 y	3	18	80	–	–	–	15	17	85 y	85 y	84 y
Holy See	–	–	–	–	–	–	–	–	–	–	–	–	–	–
Honduras	14 y	21 y	8 y	8	34	94	–	–	–	10	12	–	–	–
Hungary	–	–	–	–	–	100 v	–	–	–	–	–	–	–	–
Iceland	–	–	–	–	–	100 v	–	–	–	–	–	–	–	–
India	12 x,y	12 x,y	12 x,y	18 x	47 x	72	–	–	–	42 x	47 x	–	–	–
Indonesia	7 x,y	8 x,y	6 x,y	1	14	73 y	–	49 y	–	18 y	35	–	–	–
Iran (Islamic Republic of)	11 y	13 y	10 y	3	17	99 y	–	–	–	–	–	–	–	–
Iraq	5 y	5 y	4 y	5	24	99	8	3 y	5	–	51	79 y	81 y	77 y
Ireland	–	–	–	–	–	100 v	–	–	–	–	–	–	–	–
Israel	–	–	–	–	–	100 v	–	–	–	–	–	–	–	–
Italy	–	–	–	–	–	100 v	–	–	–	–	–	–	–	–
Jamaica	3 y	4 y	3 y	1	8	100	–	–	–	–	5	85 y	87 y	82 y
Japan	–	–	–	–	–	100 v	–	–	–	–	–	–	–	–
Jordan	2 y	3 y	0 y	0	8	99	–	–	–	–	70 y	90 y	91 y	89 y
Kazakhstan	2 x,y	2 x,y	2 x,y	0	7	100	–	–	–	–	14	53	55	50
Kenya	26 x,y	27 x,y	25 x,y	4	23	67	21	3	6	36	42	–	–	–
Kiribati	–	–	–	3 x	20 x	94 x	–	–	–	60 x	76 x	81 x,y	–	–
Kuwait	–	–	–	–	–	–	–	–	–	–	–	–	–	–
Kyrgyzstan	26	30	22	1	12	98	–	–	–	–	33	57	60	54
Lao People's Democratic Republic	10 y	9 y	11 y	9	35	75	–	–	–	49	58	76 y	77 y	74 y
Latvia	–	–	–	–	–	100 v	–	–	–	–	–	–	–	–
Lebanon	2 x,y	3 x,y	1 x,y	1 x	6 x	100 x	–	–	–	–	10 x,y	82 x,y	82 x,y	82 x,y
Lesotho	23 x,y	25 x,y	21 x,y	1	17	43	–	–	–	40	33	–	–	–
Liberia	21 x,y	21 x,y	21 x,y	9	36	25 y	50	–	39	24	43	90 x,y	90 x,y	90 x,y
Libya	–	–	–	–	–	–	–	–	–	–	–	–	–	–
Liechtenstein	–	–	–	–	–	100 v	–	–	–	–	–	–	–	–
Lithuania	–	–	–	–	–	100 v	–	–	–	–	–	–	–	–
Luxembourg	–	–	–	–	–	100 v	–	–	–	–	–	–	–	–
Madagascar	23 y	23 y	23 y	12	41	83	–	–	–	46 y	45	–	–	–
Malawi	39	42	37	9	42	67	–	–	–	13	16	72	73	72
Malaysia	–	–	–	–	–	–	–	–	–	–	–	71 y	74 y	67 y
Maldives	–	–	–	0 x	4 x	93 x	–	–	–	14 x,y	31 x,y	–	–	–
Mali	56	59	52	17	52	87	83	76	75	51	73	73	73	73
Malta	–	–	–	–	–	100 v	–	–	–	–	–	–	–	–
Marshall Islands	–	–	–	6 x	26 x	96 x	–	–	–	58 x	56 x	–	–	–
Mauritania	38	–	–	14	34	66	67	53	36	21 y	27 y	80	–	–
Mauritius	–	–	–	–	–	–	–	–	–	–	–	–	–	–
Mexico	12	16	9	4	26	95	–	–	–	–	5	63	63	63
Micronesia (Federated States of)	–	–	–	–	–	–	–	–	–	–	–	–	–	–
Monaco	–	–	–	–	–	100 v	–	–	–	–	–	–	–	–
Mongolia	17	19	15	0	5	99	–	–	–	9 y	10	49	52	46
Montenegro	13	15	10	1	5	99	–	–	–	5	3	69	73	66
Montserrat	–	–	–	–	–	–	–	–	–	–	–	–	–	–
Morocco	8 x,y	9 x,y	8 x,y	3 x	16 x	94 y	–	–	–	–	64 x	91 x,y	92 x,y	90 x,y
Mozambique	22 x,y	21 x,y	24 x,y	14	48	48	–	–	–	20	23	–	–	–
Myanmar	9 y	10 y	9 y	2	16	81	–	–	–	49	51	77 y	80 y	75 y
Namibia	–	–	–	2	7	87 y	–	–	–	22	28	–	–	–
Nauru	–	–	–	2 x	27 x	83 x	–	–	–	–	–	–	–	–
Nepal	37	37	38	10	37	58	–	–	–	–	43	82	83	81
Netherlands	–	–	–	–	–	100 v	–	–	–	–	–	–	–	–
New Zealand	–	–	–	–	–	100 v	–	–	–	–	–	–	–	–

TABLE 8. CHILD PROTECTION

Countries and areas	Child labour (%)[+] 2010–2016*			Child marriage (%) 2010–2016*		Birth registration (%)[++] 2010–2016*	Female genital mutilation/cutting (%)[+] 2004–2016*			Justification of wife-beating (%) 2010–2016*		Violent discipline (%)[+] 2010–2016*		
							prevalence		attitudes					
	total	male	female	married by 15	married by 18	total	women[a]	girls[b]	support for the practice[c]	male	female	total	male	female
Nicaragua	15 x,y	18 x,y	11 x,y	10 x	41 x	85	–	–	–	–	14 x,y	–	–	–
Niger	31 y	31 y	30 y	28	76	64	2	2 y	6	27	60	82 y	82 y	81 y
Nigeria	25 y	24 y	25 y	17	43	30 y	25	17	23	25	35	91 y	91 y	90 y
Niue	–	–	–	–	–	–	–	–	–	–	–	–	–	–
Norway	–	–	–	–	–	100 v	–	–	–	–	–	–	–	–
Oman	–	–	–	–	–	–	–	–	–	–	8	–	–	–
Pakistan	–	–	–	3	21	34	–	–	–	32 y	42 y	–	–	–
Palau	–	–	–	–	–	–	–	–	–	–	–	–	–	–
Panama	3 y	4 y	1 y	7	26	96	–	–	–	–	6	45	47	43
Papua New Guinea	–	–	–	2 x	21 x	–	–	–	–	–	–	–	–	–
Paraguay	28 y	32 y	24 y	2 x	18 x	85 y	–	–	–	–	–	–	–	–
Peru	22 y	24 y	19 y	3	22	98 y	–	–	–	–	–	–	–	–
Philippines	11 y	14 y	8 y	2	15	90	–	–	–	–	13	–	–	–
Poland	–	–	–	–	–	100 v	–	–	–	–	–	–	–	–
Portugal	3 x,y	4 x,y	3 x,y	–	–	100 v	–	–	–	–	–	–	–	–
Qatar	–	–	–	0	4	100 y	–	–	–	16	7	50 y	53 y	46 y
Republic of Korea	–	–	–	–	–	–	–	–	–	–	–	–	–	–
Republic of Moldova	16 x,y	20 x,y	12 x,y	0	12	100	–	–	–	13	11	76 y	77 y	74 y
Romania	1 x,y	1 x,y	1 x,y	–	–	–	–	–	–	–	–	–	–	–
Russian Federation	–	–	–	–	–	100 v	–	–	–	–	–	–	–	–
Rwanda	29 y	27 y	30 y	0	7	56	–	–	–	18	41	–	–	–
Saint Kitts and Nevis	–	–	–	–	–	–	–	–	–	–	–	–	–	–
Saint Lucia	4 y	5 y	3 y	1	8	92	–	–	–	–	7	68 y	71 y	64 y
Saint Vincent and the Grenadines	–	–	–	–	–	–	–	–	–	–	–	–	–	–
Samoa	–	–	–	1	11	59	–	–	–	30	37	–	–	–
San Marino	–	–	–	–	–	100 v	–	–	–	–	–	–	–	–
Sao Tome and Principe	26	25	28	8	35	95	–	–	–	14	19	80	80	79
Saudi Arabia	–	–	–	–	–	–	–	–	–	–	–	–	–	–
Senegal	23	29	17	9	31	68	24	15	19	25	57	–	–	–
Serbia	10	12	7	0	3	99	–	–	–	–	4	43	44	42
Seychelles	–	–	–	–	–	–	–	–	–	–	–	–	–	–
Sierra Leone	37 y	38 y	37 y	13	39	77	90	31 y	69	34	63	82 y	81 y	82 y
Singapore	–	–	–	–	–	–	–	–	–	–	–	–	–	–
Slovakia	–	–	–	–	–	100 v	–	–	–	–	–	–	–	–
Slovenia	–	–	–	–	–	100 v	–	–	–	–	–	–	–	–
Solomon Islands	48 y	47 y	49 y	6	21	88	–	–	–	57	77	86 y	86 y	85 y
Somalia	49 x,y	45 x,y	54 x,y	8 x	45 x	3 x	98	46 y	65	–	76 x,y	–	–	–
South Africa	–	–	–	1 x	6 x	85 y	–	–	–	–	–	–	–	–
South Sudan	–	–	–	9	52	35	–	–	–	–	79	–	–	–
Spain	–	–	–	–	–	100 v	–	–	–	–	–	–	–	–
Sri Lanka	1 y	1 y	1 y	2 x	12 x	97 x	–	–	–	–	53 x,y	–	–	–
State of Palestine	6 y	7 y	4 y	1	15	99	–	–	–	–	–	92	93	92
Sudan	25	28	22	12	34	67	87	32	41	–	34	64	65	63
Suriname	4 y	4 y	4 y	5	19	99	–	–	–	–	13	86 y	87 y	85 y
Swaziland	7 y	8 y	7 y	1	5	54	–	–	–	17	20	88	89	88
Sweden	–	–	–	–	–	100 v	–	–	–	–	–	–	–	–
Switzerland	–	–	–	–	–	100 v	–	–	–	–	–	–	–	–
Syrian Arab Republic	4 x,y	5 x,y	3 x,y	3 x	13 x	96 x	–	–	–	–	–	89 x,y	90 x,y	88 x,y
Tajikistan	10 x,y	9 x,y	11 x,y	0	12	88	–	–	–	–	60	78 x,y	80 x,y	75 x,y
Thailand	8 x,y	8 x,y	8 x,y	4	23	100 v	–	–	–	9	9	75	77	73
The former Yugoslav Republic of Macedonia	13 y	12 y	13 y	1	7	100	–	–	–	–	15	69 y	71 y	67 y
Timor-Leste	4 x,y	4 x,y	4 x,y	3	19	55	–	–	–	81	86	–	–	–
Togo	28	29	27	6	22	78	5	0	1	18	29	81	81	80
Tokelau	–	–	–	–	–	–	–	–	–	–	–	–	–	–
Tonga	–	–	–	0	6	93	–	–	–	21	29	–	–	–
Trinidad and Tobago	1 x,y	1 x,y	1 x,y	2 x	8 x	97 x	–	–	–	–	8 x	77 x,y	78 x,y	77 x,y
Tunisia	2 y	3 y	2 y	0	2	99	–	–	–	–	30	93 y	94 y	92 y
Turkey	6 y	8 y	4 y	1	15	99 y	–	–	–	–	13	–	–	–
Turkmenistan	0	1	0	0	6	100	–	–	–	–	26	37 y	39 y	34 y
Turks and Caicos Islands	–	–	–	–	–	–	–	–	–	–	–	–	–	–
Tuvalu	–	–	–	0 x	10 x	50 x	–	–	–	73 x	70 x	–	–	–
Uganda	16 y	17 y	16 y	10	40	30	1	1	9	44	58	–	–	–
Ukraine	2 y	3 y	2 y	0	9	100	–	–	–	9	3	61 y	68 y	55 y
United Arab Emirates	–	–	–	–	–	100 y	–	–	–	–	–	–	–	–

TABLE 8. CHILD PROTECTION — 185

Countries and areas	Child labour (%)+ 2010–2016*			Child marriage (%) 2010–2016*		Birth registration (%)++ 2010–2016*	Female genital mutilation/cutting (%)* 2004–2016*			Justification of wife-beating (%) 2010–2016*		Violent discipline (%)+ 2010–2016*		
							prevalence		attitudes					
	total	male	female	married by 15	married by 18	total	women[a]	girls[b]	support for the practice[c]	male	female	total	male	female
United Kingdom	–	–	–	–	–	100 v	–	–	–	–	–	–	–	–
United Republic of Tanzania	29 y	29 y	28 y	5	31	26	10	0	3	40	58	–	–	–
United States	–	–	–	–	–	100 v	–	–	–	–	–	–	–	–
Uruguay	8 x,y	8 x,y	8 x,y	1	25	100	–	–	–	–	2	55 y	58 y	51 y
Uzbekistan	–	–	–	0 x	7 x	100 x	–	–	–	61 x	70 x	–	–	–
Vanuatu	15 y	15 y	16 y	3	21	43 y	–	–	–	60	60	84 y	83 y	84 y
Venezuela (Bolivarian Republic of)	8 x,y	9 x,y	6 x,y	–	–	81 y	–	–	–	–	–	–	–	–
Viet Nam	16	17	16	1	11	96	–	–	–	–	28	68	72	65
Yemen	23 x,y	21 x,y	24 x,y	9	32	31	19	16 y	19	–	49	79 y	81 y	77 y
Zambia	41 x,y	42 x,y	40 x,y	6	31	11	–	–	–	32	47	–	–	–
Zimbabwe	–	–	–	4	32	44	–	–	–	33	39	63	63	62
SUMMARY														
East Asia and Pacific	–	–	–	2 **	15 **	84 **	–	–	–	–	29 **	–	–	–
Europe and Central Asia	–	–	–	–	–	99	–	–	–	–	–	–	–	–
Eastern Europe and Central Asia	–	–	–	1	11	99	–	–	–	–	14	–	–	–
Western Europe	–	–	–	–	–	100	–	–	–	–	–	–	–	–
Latin America and Caribbean	11	13	8	–	–	95	–	–	–	–	–	–	–	–
Middle East and North Africa	7	8	6	3	17	92	–	–	–	–	45	87	88	86
North America	–	–	–	–	–	100	–	–	–	–	–	–	–	–
South Asia	–	–	–	–	–	60	–	–	–	–	–	–	–	–
Sub-Saharan Africa	29	30	29	12	38	43	37	15	20	34	48	–	–	–
Eastern and Southern Africa	26	27	24	9	35	41	45	12	17	32	48	–	–	–
West and Central Africa	32	32	32	14	41	45	31	17	23	35	48	86	87	86
Least developed countries	26	26	24	12	40	40	–	–	–	39	49	79	79	78
World	**–**	**–**	**–**	**6 *****	**25 *****	**71 *****	**–**	**–**	**–**	**–**	**–**	**–**	**–**	**–**

For a complete list of countries and areas in the regions, subregions and country categories, see page 150 or visit <data.unicef.org/regionalclassifications>.
It is not advisable to compare data from consecutive editions of *The State of the World's Children*.

DEFINITIONS OF THE INDICATORS

Child labour – Percentage of children 5–17 years old involved in child labour at the moment of the survey. A child is considered to be involved in child labour under the following conditions: (a) children 5–11 years old who, during the reference week, did at least one hour of economic activity or at least 28 hours of household chores, (b) children 12–14 years old who, during the reference week, did at least 14 hours of economic activity or at least 28 hours of household chores, (c) children 15–17 years old who, during the reference week, did at least 43 hours of economic activity or household chores, and (d) children aged 5–17 years old in hazardous working conditions.

Child marriage – Percentage of women 20–24 years old who were first married or in union before they were 15 years old and percentage of women 20–24 years old who were first married or in union before they were 18 years old.

Birth registration – Percentage of children under age 5 who were registered at the moment of the survey. The numerator of this indicator includes children reported to have a birth certificate, regardless of whether or not it was seen by the interviewer, and those without a birth certificate whose mother or caregiver says the birth has been registered.

Female genital mutilation/cutting (FGM/C) – (a) Women: percentage of women 15–49 years old who have undergone FGM/C; (b) girls: percentage of girls 0–14 years old who have undergone FGM/C (as reported by their mothers); (c) support for the practice: percentage of women 15–49 years old who have heard about FGM/C and think the practice should continue.

Justification of wife-beating – Percentage of women and men 15–49 years old who consider a husband to be justified in hitting or beating his wife for at least one of the specified reasons, i.e., if his wife burns the food, argues with him, goes out without telling him, neglects the children or refuses sexual relations.

Violent discipline – Percentage of children 1–14 years old who experience any violent discipline (psychological aggression and/or physical punishment).

MAIN DATA SOURCES

Child labour –Demographic and Health Surveys (DHS), Multiple Indicator Cluster Surveys (MICS) and other national surveys.

Child marriage – DHS, MICS and other national surveys.

Birth registration – DHS, MICS, other national surveys, censuses and vital registration systems.

Female genital mutilation/cutting – DHS, MICS and other national surveys.

Justification of wife-beating – DHS, MICS and other national surveys.

Violent discipline – DHS, MICS and other national surveys.

Italicized data are from different sources than the data presented for the same indicators in other tables of the report.

NOTES

– Data not available.

v Estimates of 100% were assumed given that civil registration systems in these countries are complete and all vital events (including births) are registered. Source: United Nations, Department of Economic and Social Affairs, Statistics Division, *Population and Vital Statistics Report*, Series A Vol. LXV, New York, 2013.

x Data refer to years or periods other than those specified in the column heading. Such data are not included in the calculation of regional and global averages.

y Data differ from the standard definition or refer to only part of a country. If they fall within the noted reference period, such data are included in the calculation of regional and global averages.

+ A more detailed explanation of the methodology and the changes in calculating these estimates can be found in the General Note on the Data, page 146.

++ Changes in the definition of birth registration were made from the second and third rounds of MICS (MICS2 and MICS3) to the fourth round (MICS4). In order to allow for comparability with later rounds, data from MICS2 and MICS3 on birth registration were recalculated according to the MICS4 indicator definition. Therefore, the recalculated data presented here may differ from estimates included in MICS2 and MICS3 national reports.

* Data refer to the most recent year available during the period specified in the column heading.

** Excludes China.

TABLE 9. ADOLESCENTS

Countries and areas	Adolescent population Aged 10–19 (thousands) 2016	Proportion of total population (%) 2016	Adolescents currently married/in union (%) 2010–2016* male	female	Births by age 18 (%) 2011–2016*	Adolescent birth rate 2009–2014*	Justification of wife-beating among adolescents (%) 2010–2016* male	female	Use of mass media among adolescents (%) 2010–2016* male	female	Lower secondary school gross enrolment ratio 2011–2016*	Upper secondary school gross enrolment ratio 2011–2016*	Comprehensive knowledge of HIV among adolescents (%) 2011–2016* male	female
Afghanistan	8,587	25	3	17	20	90 x	71 y	78 y	70 y	52 y	67	43	4	1
Albania	446	15	1 x	8 x	3 x	18	37 x	24 x	97 x	99 x	101	89	21 x	36 x
Algeria	5,942	15	–	3	1	12	–	55 y	–	–	132	63	–	7
Andorra	–	–	–	–	–	5	–	–	–	–	–	–	–	–
Angola	6,486	23	2	18	38	191	24	25	84	77	36	21	29	31
Anguilla	–	–	–	–	–	46 x	–	–	–	–	–	–	–	–
Antigua and Barbuda	17	17	–	–	–	67 x	–	–	–	–	117	82	55 x	40 x
Argentina	7,020	16	–	–	12	70	–	2	–	–	128	85	–	36
Armenia	356	12	0	5	1	23	25	9	88	92	88	90	9	15
Australia	2,897	12	–	–	–	14	–	–	–	–	112	186	–	–
Austria	873	10	–	–	–	8	–	–	–	–	100	100	–	–
Azerbaijan	1,358	14	–	9	4	47	–	24	–	98	91	–	2 x	3 x
Bahamas	55	14	–	–	–	40 x	–	–	–	–	–	–	–	–
Bahrain	158	11	–	–	–	15	–	–	–	–	101	103	–	–
Bangladesh	32,575	20	–	44	36	83	–	29 y	–	54 y	83	48	–	12
Barbados	37	13	–	1	7	49 x	–	5	–	98	107	113	–	66
Belarus	904	10	1	7	3 x	22	3	3	–	–	102	119	53	51
Belgium	1,253	11	–	–	–	8	–	–	–	–	185	158	–	–
Belize	78	21	11	21	17	64	8	6	92	92	91	60	–	39
Benin	2,440	22	1	16	19	98	19	31	68	57	70	38	29	22
Bhutan	148	19	–	15	15 x	28	–	70	–	–	96	69	–	22 x,p
Bolivia (Plurinational State of)	2,216	20	4 x	13 x	20 x	89 x	–	17 x	100 x	97 x	96	81	24 x	20 x
Bosnia and Herzegovina	410	12	0	1	–	11	5	1	100	100	–	–	41	42
Botswana	431	19	–	–	–	39	–	–	–	–	91	–	–	–
Brazil	33,760	16	1	4	–	65	–	–	–	–	106	91	–	–
British Virgin Islands	–	–	–	–	–	27 x	–	–	–	–	111	80	–	–
Brunei Darussalam	70	16	–	–	–	17 x	–	–	–	–	105	93	–	–
Bulgaria	620	9	–	2 y	5	43	–	–	–	–	90	108	–	–
Burkina Faso	4,306	23	2	32	28 x	136 x	40	39	61	55	47	13	31 x	29 x
Burundi	2,243	21	1	9	11 x	65 x	56	74	83	69	54	25	50	46
Cabo Verde	114	21	2 x	8 x	22 x	92 x	24 x	23 x	88 x	88 x	115	73	–	–
Cambodia	3,052	19	3	16	7	57	26 y	46 y	77	74	63	–	42	33
Cameroon	5,206	22	1	20	28	128 x	45	37	80	64	68	43	30	26
Canada	3,968	11	–	–	–	13	–	–	–	–	100	119	–	–
Central African Republic	1,117	24	11	55	45 x	229	83	79	–	–	23	9	26 x	17 x
Chad	3,433	24	3	38	51	203	54	69	30	23	26	18	12	10
Chile	2,591	14	–	–	–	50	–	–	–	–	103	100	–	–
China	159,642	11	1	2	–	6	–	–	–	–	99	90	–	–
Colombia	8,139	17	–	13	20	85 x	–	–	–	–	106	82	–	21 x
Comoros	173	22	8	16	17	71	29	43	79	67	66	52	21	18
Congo	1,083	21	2	16	26	147	76 y	73 y	56	68	65	38	25 p	16
Cook Islands	–	–	–	–	–	56	–	–	–	–	96	73	–	–
Costa Rica	759	16	2	10	13	67	–	3	–	–	133	109	–	29
Côte d'Ivoire	5,409	23	1	21	31	125	51	51	73	62	55	28	21	15
Croatia	447	11	–	–	–	12	–	–	–	–	104	93	–	–
Cuba	1,336	12	7	16	6	50	5 y	4 y	–	–	101	100	48	59
Cyprus	143	12	–	–	–	4	–	–	–	–	100	100	–	–
Czechia	936	9	–	–	–	11	–	–	–	–	101	110	–	–
Democratic People's Republic of Korea	3,839	15	–	–	–	1 x	–	–	–	–	92	95	–	7 y
Democratic Republic of the Congo	17,401	22	1	21	27	135	69	75	49	38	56	37	20	17
Denmark	690	12	–	–	–	2	–	–	–	–	117	144	–	–
Djibouti	196	21	1	3	–	21	–	–	–	–	53	41	–	16 x
Dominica	–	–	–	–	–	47 x	–	–	–	–	115	81	39 x	49 x
Dominican Republic	2,007	19	–	28	21	90	–	3	–	98	86	74	39	–
Ecuador	3,005	18	–	16 x	–	100 x	–	–	–	–	116	96	–	–
Egypt	17,041	18	–	14	7	56	–	46 y	100	100	99	73	5	3
El Salvador	1,289	20	–	16	18	63	–	10	–	98	99	61	25	28
Equatorial Guinea	217	18	5	22	42	177 x	56	57	91	91	39	–	12	17
Eritrea	1,085	22	1	17	19 x	–	60	51	70	54	39	23	32 x	22 x
Estonia	122	9	–	–	–	16	–	–	–	–	112	118	–	–
Ethiopia	24,772	24	1	17	22	71	33	60	38	31	43	18	32	24
Fiji	157	17	–	–	–	28 x	–	–	–	–	103	76	–	–
Finland	594	11	–	–	–	7	–	–	–	–	102	194	–	–

TABLE 9. ADOLESCENTS 187

Countries and areas	Adolescent population Aged 10–19 (thousands) 2016	Proportion of total population (%) 2016	Adolescents currently married/ in union (%) 2010–2016* male	female	Births by age 18 (%) 2011–2016*	Adolescent birth rate 2009–2014*	Justification of wife-beating among adolescents (%) 2010–2016* male	female	Use of mass media among adolescents (%) 2010–2016* male	female	Lower secondary school gross enrolment ratio 2011–2016*	Upper secondary school gross enrolment ratio 2011–2016*	Comprehensive knowledge of HIV among adolescents (%) 2011–2016* male	female
France	7,723	12	–	–	–	9	–	–	–	–	108	115	–	–
Gabon	379	19	1	14	28	115	47	58	95	94	–	–	35	29
Gambia	467	23	0	24	19	88	42	58	82	70	64	–	27	22
Georgia	450	11	–	11	6 x	40	–	5 x	–	–	114	95	–	–
Germany	7,795	10	–	–	–	8	–	–	–	–	101	105	–	–
Ghana	6,009	21	1	6	17	65	20	35	81	67	89	39	25	18
Greece	1,108	10	–	–	–	9	–	–	–	–	101	111	–	–
Grenada	19	17	–	–	–	53 x	–	–	–	–	100	98	67 x	59 x
Guatemala	3,787	23	6	20	20	92	12	14	95	90	72	55	18	20
Guinea	2,786	22	1	33	40	154	63	89	55	53	44	31	29	20
Guinea-Bissau	395	22	0	11	28	137	37	40	96	89	–	–	19	20
Guyana	165	21	13	13	16	97 x	14	10	95	96	93	83	33	48
Haiti	2,285	21	2	12	13	65	22	24	85	80	–	–	25	32
Holy See	–	–	–	–	–	–	–	–	–	–	–	–	–	–
Honduras	1,990	22	5	23	22	99	18	15	98	94	74	66	33	29
Hungary	996	10	–	–	–	20	–	–	–	–	100	110	–	–
Iceland	43	13	–	–	–	7	–	–	–	–	97	133	–	–
India	250,086	19	5 x	30 x	22 x	39	47 x	45 x	88 x	72 x	88	64	35 x	19 x
Indonesia	46,188	18	–	9 y	7	47	48 y	45	88 y,p	91	95	76	4 p	9
Iran (Islamic Republic of)	10,928	14	–	16 x	5 x	35	–	–	–	–	99	85	–	–
Iraq	8,019	22	–	21	12	68 x	–	50	–	–	–	–	–	3
Ireland	583	12	–	–	–	9	–	–	–	–	111	154	–	–
Israel	1,296	16	–	–	–	10	–	–	–	–	104	101	–	–
Italy	5,592	9	–	–	–	6	–	–	–	–	106	101	–	–
Jamaica	520	18	–	3	15	72 x	–	8	–	–	86	76	34	39
Japan	11,650	9	–	–	–	4	–	–	–	–	102	101	–	–
Jordan	1,918	20	–	6	4	27	–	84 y	–	100 y	87	74	–	6
Kazakhstan	2,269	13	–	6	2	31 x	–	8	–	96	114	103	30	–
Kenya	11,065	23	1	12	23	101	37	45	84	75	97	–	58	52
Kiribati	23	20	5 x	16 x	9 x	49	65 x	77 x	58 x	57 x	105	–	46 x	41 x
Kuwait	450	11	–	–	–	8	–	–	–	–	99	85	–	–
Kyrgyzstan	991	17	–	14	4	42	–	22	–	100	97	81	18	–
Lao People's Democratic Republic	1,432	21	9	25	18	94	50	56	92	93	76	43	25	23
Latvia	181	9	–	–	–	15	–	–	–	–	116	123	–	–
Lebanon	1,061	18	–	3 x	–	18 x	–	22 x,y	–	–	68	55	–	–
Lesotho	495	22	1	18	14	94	49	48	60	66	63	40	30	35
Liberia	1,041	23	2	14	37	147	29	45	59	47	44	29	19	35
Libya	1,093	17	–	–	–	4 x	–	–	–	–	–	–	–	–
Liechtenstein	–	–	–	–	–	2	–	–	–	–	98	139	–	–
Lithuania	307	11	–	–	–	14	–	–	–	–	106	114	–	–
Luxembourg	65	11	–	–	–	6	–	–	–	–	114	94	–	–
Madagascar	5,740	23	7	28	36	147 x	44	47	62	59	50	22	24	21
Malawi	4,262	24	3	24	31	143	24	21	50	35	53	22	43	39
Malaysia	5,513	18	5	6	–	13	–	–	–	–	89	69	–	–
Maldives	59	14	–	5 x	1 x	14	–	41 x,y	–	100 x	97	–	–	22 x
Mali	4,135	23	2	40	37	178	54	68	83	75	52	29	27	21
Malta	44	10	–	–	–	16	–	–	–	–	102	90	–	–
Marshall Islands	–	–	5 x	21 x	21 x	85	71 x	47 x	86 x	85 x	81	67	35 x	27 x
Mauritania	917	21	1	28	22	71	–	36	55 x	44 x	37	21	10	–
Mauritius	189	15	–	–	–	31	–	–	–	–	111	84	–	–
Mexico	23,416	18	6	15	21	84	–	6	–	96	116	65	–	28
Micronesia (Federated States of)	25	24	–	–	–	33	–	–	–	–	81	–	–	–
Monaco	–	–	–	–	–	–	–	–	–	–	–	–	–	–
Mongolia	448	15	1	5	3	40	9	14	98	98	93	90	17	18
Montenegro	81	13	0	2	3	12	5	2	–	–	95	86	35	42
Montserrat	–	–	–	–	–	36	–	–	–	–	–	–	–	–
Morocco	5,982	17	1	11	8 x	32 x	–	64 x	–	90 x	97	55	–	–
Mozambique	6,649	23	8	37	40	166	20	24	73	57	39	21	28	28
Myanmar	10,042	19	5	13	5	17 x	57	53	75	76	59	34	14	13
Namibia	539	22	1	5	15	78	30	28	65 y	69	92	–	51	56
Nauru	–	–	9 x	18 x	22 x	106	–	–	89 x	86 x	77	94	8 x	8 x
Nepal	6,625	23	–	25	16	87 x	–	35	–	77	93	50	24	18
Netherlands	2,021	12	–	–	–	5	–	–	–	–	136	134	–	–

TABLE 9. ADOLESCENTS

Countries and areas	Adolescent population Aged 10–19 (thousands) 2016	Proportion of total population (%) 2016	Adolescents currently married/ in union (%) 2010–2016* male	female	Births by age 18 (%) 2011–2016*	Adolescent birth rate 2009–2014*	Justification of wife-beating among adolescents (%) 2010–2016* male	female	Use of mass media among adolescents (%) 2010–2016* male	female	Lower secondary school gross enrolment ratio 2011–2016*	Upper secondary school gross enrolment ratio	Comprehensive knowledge of HIV among adolescents (%) 2011–2016* male	female
New Zealand	616	13	–	–	–	22	–	–	–	–	103	134	–	–
Nicaragua	1,207	20	–	24 x	28 x	92	–	19 x,y	–	95 x	–	–	–	–
Niger	4,704	23	3	61	48	210	41	54	35	44	27	10	21	12
Nigeria	41,050	22	1	29	29	123	27	33	54	50	52	60	29	22
Niue	–	–	–	–	–	16	–	–	–	–	119	95	–	–
Norway	633	12	–	–	–	6	–	–	–	–	100	125	–	–
Oman	480	11	–	3	2	12	–	10	–	–	113	96	–	–
Pakistan	38,907	20	2	14	8	48	33 y,p	53 y	59 y,p	49 y	57	35	5 p	1
Palau	–	–	–	–	–	27	–	–	–	–	78	119	–	–
Panama	696	17	–	14	–	89	–	9	–	96	94	57	–	–
Papua New Guinea	1,728	21	3 x	15 x	14 x	65 x	–	–	–	–	73	22	–	–
Paraguay	1,342	20	–	11 x	–	63 x	–	–	–	–	84	69	–	–
Peru	5,606	18	–	11	16	68	–	–	–	90	100	90	–	21 x
Philippines	20,667	20	–	10	8	59	–	14	–	90	92	77	–	19 x
Poland	3,814	10	–	–	–	14	–	–	–	–	101	115	–	–
Portugal	1,080	10	–	–	–	12	–	–	–	–	119	119	–	–
Qatar	200	8	1	4	–	16	22	6 y	98	98	100	82	23	10
Republic of Korea	5,686	11	–	–	–	2	–	–	–	–	103	95	–	–
Republic of Moldova	444	11	1	10	4	25	14	13	96	96	87	85	26	35
Romania	2,132	11	–	–	–	36	–	–	–	–	93	92	–	–
Russian Federation	13,260	9	–	–	–	27	–	–	–	–	101	114	–	–
Rwanda	2,607	22	0	3	6	41 x	24	45	78	71	42	31	60	62
Saint Kitts and Nevis	–	–	–	–	–	75 x	–	–	–	–	93	86	55 x	54 x
Saint Lucia	29	16	–	4	–	50 x	–	15	–	99	87	82	–	58
Saint Vincent and the Grenadines	19	17	–	–	–	70	–	–	–	–	120	86	–	–
Samoa	43	22	1	8	6	39	28	34	99	97	102	78	5 x	2 x
San Marino	–	–	–	–	–	1	–	–	–	–	94	95	–	–
Sao Tome and Principe	46	23	1	15	27	110 x	19	24	97	97	110	61	42	41
Saudi Arabia	4,818	15	–	–	–	7 x	–	–	–	–	108	108	–	–
Senegal	3,380	22	0	21	18	80	36	57	69	76	59	36	28	26
Serbia	1,063	12	–	4	1	22	–	2	99	100	102	91	43 x	53 x
Seychelles	12	12	–	–	–	62	–	–	–	–	112	59	–	–
Sierra Leone	1,704	23	1	19	36	131	32	55	55	49	61	28	29	28
Singapore	665	12	–	–	–	3	–	–	–	–	–	–	–	–
Slovakia	553	10	–	–	–	21	–	–	–	–	98	86	–	–
Slovenia	186	9	–	–	–	5	–	–	–	–	100	118	–	–
Solomon Islands	134	22	2	11	15	62 x	60	78	37	28	78	29	26 x	29 x
Somalia	3,333	23	–	25 x	–	123 x	–	75 x,y	–	–	–	–	–	3 x
South Africa	10,319	18	2 x	4 x	15 x	54 x	–	–	–	–	97	88	–	–
South Sudan	2,767	23	–	40	28 x	158 x	–	72	–	–	18	5	–	8 x
Spain	4,386	9	–	–	–	9	–	–	–	–	124	136	–	–
Sri Lanka	3,284	16	–	9 x	4 x	24 x	–	54 x,y	–	88 x,y	99	99	–	–
State of Palestine	1,083	23	–	9	22	67	–	–	–	–	88	66	–	5
Sudan	9,060	23	–	21	22	102	–	36	–	–	54	35	10	–
Suriname	99	18	–	12	–	66 x	–	19	–	99	101	54	–	40 x
Swaziland	302	23	0	4	17	89	29	32	89	86	75	52	44	45
Sweden	1,025	10	–	–	–	3	–	–	–	–	115	164	–	–
Switzerland	833	10	–	–	–	3	–	–	–	–	106	98	–	–
Syrian Arab Republic	4,586	25	–	10 x	9 x	75 x	–	–	–	–	61	32	–	6 x
Tajikistan	1,710	20	–	13	2	47	–	47	–	89	98	68	9	–
Thailand	9,207	13	7	14	9	60	9	9	–	–	128	130	45	47
The former yugoslav Republic of Macedonia	253	12	–	4	2	19	–	14	–	–	83	76	–	23 x
Timor-Leste	314	25	0	8	9 x	54 x	72	81	61	62	87	65	15 x	11 x
Togo	1,665	22	1	13	15	77	19	26	67	63	68	36	28	23
Tokelau	–	–	–	–	–	30	–	–	–	–	206	–	–	–
Tonga	24	23	4	5	2	30	29	27	92	95	103	56	13	10
Trinidad and Tobago	177	13	–	6 x	–	36 x	–	10 x	–	–	–	–	–	49 x
Tunisia	1,618	14	–	1	1	7	–	27	–	98	103	78	–	15
Turkey	13,335	17	–	7	6	29	–	10	–	–	99	106	–	–
Turkmenistan	954	17	–	6	1	21 x	–	17	–	100	73	120	–	19
Turks and Caicos Islands	–	–	–	–	–	29 x	–	–	–	–	–	–	–	–
Tuvalu	–	–	2 x	8 x	3 x	42 x	83 x	69 x	89 x	95 x	99	56	57 x	31 x
Uganda	9,920	24	2	20	33	140	52	62	88	82	–	–	40	41

TABLE 9. ADOLESCENTS | 189

TABLE 9. ADOLESCENTS

Countries and areas	Adolescent population — Aged 10–19 (thousands) 2016	Proportion of total population (%) 2016	Adolescents currently married/ in union (%) 2010–2016* male	female	Births by age 18 (%) 2011–2016*	Adolescent birth rate 2009–2014*	Justification of wife-beating among adolescents (%) 2010–2016* male	female	Use of mass media among adolescents (%) 2010–2016* male	female	Lower secondary school gross enrolment ratio 2011–2016*	Upper secondary school gross enrolment ratio 2011–2016*	Comprehensive knowledge of HIV among adolescents (%) 2011–2016* male	female
Ukraine	4,059	9	0	7	4	27	2	2	97	96	102	93	37	43
United Arab Emirates	682	7	–	–	–	34	–	–	–	–	92	–	–	–
United Kingdom	7,309	11	–	–	–	21	–	–	–	–	113	138	–	–
United Republic of Tanzania	12,505	23	2	23	22	128 x	50	59	61	57	43	9	42	37
United States	42,010	13	–	–	–	27	–	–	–	–	102	93	–	–
Uruguay	508	15	–	7	–	60	–	3	–	–	110	81	–	36
Uzbekistan	5,360	17	–	5 x	2 x	26 x	63 x	63 x	–	–	97	95	–	27 x
Vanuatu	54	20	4	11	13	78	63	56	58	58	70	34	–	14 x
Venezuela (Bolivarian Republic of)	5,655	18	–	16	24	101	–	–	–	–	97	79	–	–
Viet Nam	13,605	14	–	10	5	36	–	28	–	97	97	–	–	51
Yemen	6,297	23	–	17	17	67	–	49	–	85	58	39	–	2 x
Zambia	3,956	24	1	17	31	145	41	49	75	69	63	–	42	39
Zimbabwe	3,557	22	1	20	22	120	49	54	57	53	68	37	41	41

SUMMARY

Countries and areas	Adolescent population — Aged 10–19 (thousands) 2016	Proportion of total population (%) 2016	Adolescents currently married/ in union (%) 2010–2016* male	female	Births by age 18 (%) 2011–2016*	Adolescent birth rate 2009–2014*	Justification of wife-beating among adolescents (%) 2010–2016* male	female	Use of mass media among adolescents (%) 2010–2016* male	female	Lower secondary school gross enrolment ratio 2011–2016*	Upper secondary school gross enrolment ratio 2011–2016*	Comprehensive knowledge of HIV among adolescents (%) 2011–2016* male	female
East Asia and Pacific	297,721	13	2	6	7 **	21	43 **	34 **	–	89 **	96	87	13 **	22 **
Europe and Central Asia	101,795	11	–	–	–	19	–	–	–	–	104	112	–	–
Eastern Europe and Central Asia	50,903	12	–	7	4	29	–	12	–	–	100	102	–	–
Western Europe	50,892	10	–	–	–	11	–	–	–	–	109	119	–	–
Latin America and Caribbean	109,829	17	3	11	19	74	–	–	–	–	107	81	–	–
Middle East and North Africa	73,653	17	–	13	8	41	–	49	–	–	96	70	–	–
North America	45,978	13	–	–	–	25	–	–	–	–	102	96	–	–
South Asia	340,270	19	–	–	20 ‡	44	–	–	–	–	83	59	8 ‡	6 ‡
Sub-Saharan Africa	232,069	22	2	23	28	122	39	49	61	54	53	37	31	27
Eastern and Southern Africa	122,663	23	2	20	26	113	38	49	64	56	52	31	36	35
West and Central Africa	109,406	22	1	27	29	130	41	48	58	52	54	42	26	20
Least developed countries	217,756	22	2	26	27	112	45	50	62	57	55	33	27	23
World	**1,201,315**	**16**	**–**	**16**	**18 ‡****	**50**	**–**	**35 ****	**–**	**–**	**86**	**70**	**–**	**21 ‡****

For a complete list of countries and areas in the regions, subregions and country categories, see page 150 or visit <data.unicef.org/regionalclassifications>.
It is not advisable to compare data from consecutive editions of *The State of the World's Children.*

DEFINITIONS OF THE INDICATORS

Adolescents currently married/ in union – Percentage of boys and girls aged 15–19 who are currently married or in union. This indicator is meant to provide a snapshot of the current marital status of boys and girls in this age group. However, it is worth noting that those not married at the time of the survey are still exposed to the risk of marrying before they exit adolescence.

Births by age 18 – Percentage of women aged 20–24 who gave birth before age 18. This standardized indicator from population-based surveys captures levels of fertility among adolescents up to the age of 18. Note that the data are based on the answers of women aged 20–24, whose risk of giving birth before the age of 18 is behind them.

Adolescent birth rate – Number of births per 1,000 adolescent girls aged 15–19.

Justification of wife-beating among adolescents – The percentage of boys and girls aged 15–19 who consider a husband to be justified in hitting or beating his wife for at least one of the specified reasons: if his wife burns the food, argues with him, goes out without telling him, neglects the children or refuses sexual relations.

Use of mass media among adolescents – The percentage of boys and girls aged 15–19 who make use of at least one of the following types of information media at least once a week: newspaper, magazine, television or radio.

Lower secondary school gross enrolment ratio – Number of children enrolled in lower secondary school, regardless of age, expressed as a percentage of the total number of children of official lower secondary school age.

Upper secondary school gross enrolment ratio – Number of children enrolled in upper secondary school, regardless of age, expressed as a percentage of the total number of children of official upper secondary school age.

Comprehensive knowledge of HIV among adolescents – Percentage of young men and women aged 15–19 who correctly identify the two major ways of preventing the sexual transmission of HIV (using condoms and limiting sex to one faithful, uninfected partner), who reject the two most common local misconceptions about HIV transmission and who know that a healthy-looking person can be HIV-positive.

MAIN DATA SOURCES

Adolescent population – United Nations Population Division.

Adolescents currently married/ in union – Demographic and Health Surveys (DHS), Multiple Indicator Cluster Surveys (MICS), other national surveys and censuses.

Births by age 18 – DHS, MICS and other national surveys.

Adolescent birth rate – United Nations Population Division.

Justification of wife-beating among adolescents – DHS, MICS and other national surveys.

Use of mass media among adolescents – DHS, MICS and other national surveys.

Gross enrolment ratio – UNESCO Institute for Statistics (UIS).

Comprehensive knowledge of HIV among adolescents – AIDS Indicator Surveys (AIS), DHS, MICS and other national household surveys.

NOTES

– Data not available

p Based on small denominators (typically 25–49 unweighted cases).

x Data refer to years or periods other than those specified in the column heading. Such data are not included in the calculation of regional and global averages. Data from years prior to 2000 are not displayed.

y Data differ from the standard definition or refer to only part of a country. If they fall within the noted reference period, such data are included in the calculation of regional and global averages.

* Data refer to the most recent year available during the period specified in the column heading.

** Excludes China.

‡ Excludes India.

Italicized data are from different sources than the data presented for the same indicators in other tables of the report.

TABLE 10. DISPARITIES BY RESIDENCE

Countries and areas	Birth registration (%)++ 2010–2016*			Skilled birth attendant (%) 2011–2016*			Stunting prevalence in children under 5 (moderate & severe)⁸ 2011–2016*			Oral rehydration salts (ORS) treatment for children with diarrhoea (%) 2011–2016*			Primary school net attendance ratio 2011–2016*			Comprehensive knowledge of HIV/AIDS (%) Females 15–24 2011–2016*			Use of basic sanitation services (%) 2015		
	urban	rural	ratio of urban to rural	urban	rural	ratio of urban to rural	urban	rural	ratio of rural to urban	urban	rural	ratio of urban to rural	urban	rural	ratio of urban to rural	urban	rural	ratio of urban to rural	urban	rural	ratio of urban to rural
Afghanistan	64	36	1.8	79	42	1.9	–	–	–	44	47	0.9	80	59	1.4	2	1	2.1	56	33	1.7
Albania	99 x	98 x	1.0 x	100 x	99 x	1.0 x	23 x	23 x	1.0 x	–	–	–	93	92	1.0	51 x	26 x	2.0 x	98	97	1.0
Algeria	100	100	1.0	98	95	1.0	11	12	1.1	25	26	1.0	98	97	1.0	11	7	1.7	90	82	1.1
Andorra	–	–	–	–	–	–	–	–	–	–	–	–	–	–	–	–	–	–	100	100	1.0
Angola	33	14	2.4	68	21	3.2	32	46	1.4	49	32	1.5	84	61	1.4	42	9	4.4	62	21	2.9
Anguilla	–	–	–	–	–	–	–	–	–	–	–	–	–	–	–	–	–	–	97	–	–
Antigua and Barbuda	–	–	–	–	–	–	–	–	–	–	–	–	–	–	–	–	–	–	–	–	–
Argentina	–	–	–	–	–	–	–	–	–	–	–	–	–	–	–	–	–	–	95	94	1.0
Armenia	99	98	1.0	100	100	1.0	6	13	2.2	–	–	–	100	99	1.0	25	14	1.7	96	83	1.2
Australia	–	–	–	–	–	–	–	–	–	–	–	–	–	–	–	–	–	–	–	–	–
Austria	–	–	–	–	–	–	–	–	–	–	–	–	–	–	–	–	–	–	100	100	1.0
Azerbaijan	96 x	92 x	1.0 x	99	95	1.0	15	21	1.4	11	11	1.0	68 y	67 y	1.0 y	7 x	2 x	3.3 x	92	87	1.1
Bahamas	–	–	–	–	–	–	–	–	–	–	–	–	–	–	–	–	–	–	–	–	–
Bahrain	–	–	–	–	–	–	–	–	–	–	–	–	–	–	–	–	–	–	–	–	–
Bangladesh	23	19	1.2	61	36	1.7	31	38	1.2	83	75	1.1	91	92	1.0	14	8	1.8	54	43	1.2
Barbados	98	100	1.0	98	100	1.0	8	7	0.9	–	–	–	100	99	1.0	67	69	1.0	–	–	–
Belarus	–	–	–	100	100	1.0	3 x	8 x	2.6 x	–	–	–	91	93	1.0	56	57	1.0	94	95	1.0
Belgium	–	–	–	–	–	–	–	–	–	–	–	–	–	–	–	–	–	–	99	99	1.0
Belize	97	95	1.0	98	96	1.0	11	18	1.7	54	56	1.0	99	94	1.0	55	33	1.7	91	84	1.1
Benin	88	82	1.1	83	73	1.2	29	38	1.3	26	25	1.1	83	69	1.2	25	18	1.3	25	5	4.6
Bhutan	100	100	1.0	96	67	1.4	28 x	36 x	1.3 x	64 x	60 x	1.1 x	98	94	1.0	32 x	15 x	2.1 x	72	57	1.3
Bolivia (Plurinational State of)	79 x,y	72 x,y	1.1 x,y	94	68	1.4	14	25	1.8	23	20	1.2	98 x	96 x	1.0 x	32 x	9 x	3.5 x	64	27	2.4
Bosnia and Herzegovina	99 x	100 x	1.0 x	100	100	1.0	11	8	0.7	–	–	–	95	97	1.0	50	47	1.1	99	92	1.1
Botswana	78 x	67 x	1.2 x	99 x	90 x	1.1 x	–	–	–	–	–	–	–	–	–	–	–	–	75	39	1.9
Brazil	–	–	–	98 x	94 x	1.0 x	7 x	8 x	1.1 x	–	–	–	–	–	–	–	–	–	91	58	1.6
British Virgin Islands	–	–	–	–	–	–	–	–	–	–	–	–	–	–	–	–	–	–	–	–	–
Brunei Darussalam	–	–	–	–	–	–	–	–	–	–	–	–	–	–	–	–	–	–	96	97	1.0
Bulgaria	–	–	–	–	–	–	–	–	–	–	–	–	–	–	–	–	–	–	87	84	1.0
Burkina Faso	93	74	1.3	95	77	1.2	21 x	37 x	1.8 x	46	38	1.2	83	45	1.8	46 x	24 x	1.9 x	48	12	4.0
Burundi	87	74	1.2	96	84	1.1	28	59	2.1	30	36	0.8	91	84	1.1	61	51	1.2	46	51	0.9
Cabo Verde	–	–	–	91 x	64 x	1.4 x	–	–	–	–	–	–	–	–	–	–	–	–	73	51	1.4
Cambodia	84	72	1.2	98	88	1.1	24	34	1.4	30	36	0.8	97	92	1.1	55	33	1.7	88	39	2.3
Cameroon	84	53	1.6	88	49	1.8	23	38	1.7	24	12	2.1	94	79	1.2	37	18	2.1	56	19	2.9
Canada	–	–	–	–	–	–	–	–	–	–	–	–	–	–	–	–	–	–	–	–	–
Central African Republic	78	52	1.5	74 x	22 x	3.4 x	38	42	1.1	23 x	12 x	2.0 x	86	66	1.3	19 x	16 x	1.2 x	49	9	5.4
Chad	36	6	5.6	54	12	4.6	32	42	1.3	28	18	1.5	72	45	1.6	25	6	4.0	33	3	11.3
Chile	–	–	–	100 x	99 x	1.0 x	–	–	–	–	–	–	–	–	–	–	–	–	100	99	1.0
China	–	–	–	100	100	1.0	4	11	2.6	–	–	–	97 y	96 y	1.0 y	–	–	–	86	61	1.4
Colombia	99	98	1.0	99	88	1.1	11 x	17 x	1.5 x	57	49	1.2 x	94	94	1.0	26 x	17 x	1.5 x	88	72	1.2
Comoros	90	87	1.0	92	79	1.2	26	35	1.4	40	37	1.1	90	82	1.1	24	17	1.4	47	29	1.6
Congo	95	85	1.1	98	84	1.2	20	30	1.5	31	22	1.4	–	–	–	16	10	1.5	20	6	3.6
Cook Islands	–	–	–	–	–	–	–	–	–	–	–	–	–	–	–	–	–	–	–	–	–
Costa Rica	100	99	1.0	99	97	1.0	–	–	–	43	35	1.2	97	95	1.0	37	27	1.4	98	94	1.0
Côte d'Ivoire	85	54	1.6	84	45	1.9	22	34	1.6	22	14	1.5	85	71	1.2	22	8	2.7	45	13	3.5
Croatia	–	–	–	–	–	–	–	–	–	–	–	–	–	–	–	–	–	–	98	96	1.0
Cuba	100	100	1.0	99	100	1.0	–	–	–	62	59	1.0	–	–	–	61	63	1.0	92	88	1.0
Cyprus	–	–	–	–	–	–	–	–	–	–	–	–	–	–	–	–	–	–	100	99	1.0
Czechia	–	–	–	–	–	–	–	–	–	–	–	–	–	–	–	–	–	–	99	99	1.0
Democratic People's Republic of Korea	100 x	100 x	1.0 x	100 x	100 x	1.0 x	23 x	45 x	1.9 x	75 x	73 x	1.0 x	100	99	1.0	11 x	4 x	2.8 x	83	68	1.2
Democratic Republic of the Congo	30	22	1.3	94	74	1.3	33	47	1.4	44	37	1.2	93	84	1.1	24	15	1.6	23	18	1.3
Denmark	–	–	–	–	–	–	–	–	–	–	–	–	–	–	–	–	–	–	100	100	1.0
Djibouti	92 x	84 x	1.1 x	98	55	1.8	30	42	1.4	–	–	–	–	–	–	18 x	9 x	2.0 x	63	13	4.8
Dominica	–	–	–	–	–	–	–	–	–	–	–	–	–	–	–	–	–	–	–	–	–
Dominican Republic	90	82	1.1	98	97	1.0	7	6	0.9	50	42	1.2	–	–	–	49	38	1.3	85	74	1.2
Ecuador	95	91	1.0	98 x	99 x	1.0 x	–	–	–	52	35	1.5	97 y	97 y	1.0 y	–	–	–	89	80	1.1
Egypt	100	99	1.0	97	89	1.1	23	21	0.9	26	29	0.9	97	97	1.0	5	4	1.5	97	90	1.1
El Salvador	98	99	1.0	99	96	1.0	11	17	1.5	72	68	1.1	97	95	1.0	37	22	1.7	93	87	1.1
Equatorial Guinea	60	47	1.3	86	53	1.6	20	32	1.6	55	27	2.0	–	–	–	27	9	2.9	80	71	1.1
Eritrea	–	–	–	74 x	17 x	4.4 x	38 x	56 x	1.4 x	51 x	41 x	1.2 x	91 y	77 y	1.2 y	32 x	20 x	1.7 x	29	6	4.7
Estonia	–	–	–	–	–	–	–	–	–	–	–	–	–	–	–	–	–	–	100	100	1.0
Ethiopia	12	2	7.2	80	21	3.8	25	40	1.6	41	28	1.4	80 y	63 y	1.3 y	38	19	2.0	18	4	4.3
Fiji	–	–	–	–	–	–	–	–	–	–	–	–	–	–	–	–	–	–	96	95	1.0
Finland	–	–	–	–	–	–	–	–	–	–	–	–	–	–	–	–	–	–	99	99	1.0

TABLE 10. DISPARITIES BY RESIDENCE 191

Countries and areas	Birth registration (%)++ 2010–2016*			Skilled birth attendant (%) 2011–2016*			Stunting prevalence in children under 5 (moderate & severe)θ (%) 2011–2016*			Oral rehydration salts (ORS) treatment for children with diarrhoea (%) 2011–2016*			Primary school net attendance ratio 2011–2016*			Comprehensive knowledge of HIV/AIDS (%) Females 15–24 2011–2016*			Use of basic sanitation services (%) 2015		
	urban	rural	ratio of urban to rural	urban	rural	ratio of urban to rural	urban	rural	ratio of rural to urban	urban	rural	ratio of urban to rural	urban	rural	ratio of urban to rural	urban	rural	ratio of urban to rural	urban	rural	ratio of urban to rural
France	–	–	–	–	–	–	–	–	–	–	–	–	–	–	–	–	–	–	99	99	1.0
Gabon	89	91	1.0	93	69	1.3	15	30	2.0	27	21	1.3	98	98	1.0	32	15	2.2	42	32	1.3
Gambia	72	72	1.0	75	41	1.9	19	29	1.5	62	57	1.1	74 y	58 y	1.3 y	32	18	1.8	46	35	1.3
Georgia	100	100	1.0	99 x	98 x	1.0 x	10 x	12 x	1.2 x	44 x	36 x	1.2 x	98	97	1.0	–	–	–	95	73	1.3
Germany	–	–	–	–	–	–	–	–	–	–	–	–	–	–	–	–	–	–	99	99	1.0
Ghana	79	63	1.3	87	57	1.5	15	22	1.5	48	49	1.0	75	66	1.1	23	17	1.4	19	9	2.1
Greece	–	–	–	–	–	–	–	–	–	–	–	–	–	–	–	–	–	–	99	98	1.0
Grenada	–	–	–	–	–	–	–	–	–	–	–	–	–	–	–	–	–	–	–	–	–
Guatemala	97 y	96 y	1.0 y	84	55	1.5	35	53	1.5	51	48	1.1	96	92	1.0	30	16	1.9	81	53	1.5
Guinea	83	49	1.7	84	32	2.7	18	36	2.0	46	30	1.5	82	49	1.7	32	16	2.0	34	15	2.3
Guinea-Bissau	34	18	2.0	72	29	2.5	21	32	1.5	42	30	1.4	74	53	1.4	26	18	1.4	35	8	4.1
Guyana	91	88	1.0	99	82	1.2	10	13	1.3	–	–	–	96	97	1.0	64	47	1.4	89	85	1.0
Haiti	85	77	1.1	59	25	2.4	16	25	1.6	56	51	1.1	90	81	1.1	41	29	1.4	37	22	1.7
Holy See	–	–	–	–	–	–	–	–	–	–	–	–	–	–	–	–	–	–	–	–	–
Honduras	95	93	1.0	94	73	1.3	15	29	2.0	59	61	1.0	92	92	1.0	42	23	1.9	84	75	1.1
Hungary	–	–	–	–	–	–	–	–	–	–	–	–	–	–	–	–	–	–	98	99	1.0
Iceland	–	–	–	–	–	–	–	–	–	–	–	–	–	–	–	–	–	–	99	100	1.0
India	83	67	1.2	90	78	1.2	31	41	1.3	59	48	1.2	88 x	82 x	1.1 x	33 x	14 x	2.4 x	65	34	1.9
Indonesia	79 y	65 y	1.2 y	97	88	1.1	32	41	1.3	41	37	1.1	100	99	1.0	14	9	1.6	77	57	1.4
Iran (Islamic Republic of)	99 y	98 y	1.0 y	98 x	93 x	1.1 x	5	9	1.7	64 x	58 x	1.1 x	97	95	1.0	–	–	–	92	79	1.2
Iraq	99	99	1.0	94	85	1.1	22	24	1.1	25	19	1.3	94	84	1.1	4	1	3.7	86	86	1.0
Ireland	–	–	–	–	–	–	–	–	–	–	–	–	–	–	–	–	–	–	91	95	1.0
Israel	–	–	–	–	–	–	–	–	–	–	–	–	–	–	–	–	–	–	100	100	1.0
Italy	–	–	–	–	–	–	–	–	–	–	–	–	–	–	–	–	–	–	99	99	1.0
Jamaica	100	99	1.0	100	98	1.0	–	3	–	–	–	–	98	98	1.0	–	–	–	84	87	1.0
Japan	–	–	–	–	–	–	–	–	–	–	–	–	–	–	–	–	–	–	–	–	–
Jordan	99	100	1.0	100	100	1.0	8	9	1.2	20	23	0.9	98	98	1.0	8	11	0.7	97	96	1.0
Kazakhstan	100	100	1.0	99	99	1.0	7	9	1.2	–	–	–	99	100	1.0	31	21	1.5	97	99	1.0
Kenya	79	61	1.3	82	50	1.6	20	29	1.5	58	52	1.1	89	84	1.1	63	52	1.2	35	28	1.3
Kiribati	95 x	93 x	1.0 x	84 x	77 x	1.1 x	–	–	–	–	–	–	–	–	–	45 x	43 x	1.1 x	49	32	1.5
Kuwait	–	–	–	–	–	–	–	–	–	–	–	–	–	–	–	–	–	–	–	–	–
Kyrgyzstan	99	97	1.0	99	98	1.0	12	13	1.1	34	33	1.0	99	100	1.0	18	21	0.9	93	99	0.9
Lao People's Democratic Republic	88	71	1.2	79	29	2.7	27	49	1.8	65	40	1.6	95	83	1.1	39	18	2.2	93	60	1.6
Latvia	–	–	–	–	–	–	–	–	–	–	–	–	–	–	–	–	–	–	97	84	1.2
Lebanon	–	–	–	–	–	–	–	–	–	–	–	–	–	–	–	–	–	–	–	–	–
Lesotho	54	40	1.3	90	73	1.2	27	35	1.3	53	54	1.0	94	91	1.0	44	35	1.3	46	43	1.1
Liberia	29 y	20 y	1.5 y	73	50	1.5	31	34	1.1	57	63	0.9	52	31	1.7	40	27	1.5	28	6	4.7
Libya	–	–	–	–	–	–	–	–	–	–	–	–	–	–	–	–	–	–	–	–	–
Liechtenstein	–	–	–	–	–	–	–	–	–	–	–	–	–	–	–	–	–	–	–	–	–
Lithuania	–	–	–	–	–	–	–	–	–	–	–	–	–	–	–	–	–	–	97	86	1.1
Luxembourg	–	–	–	–	–	–	–	–	–	–	–	–	–	–	–	–	–	–	97	99	1.0
Madagascar	97	81	1.2	78	39	2.0	43 x	50 x	1.2 x	16	14	1.1	86 y	66 y	1.3 y	44	18	2.5	16	6	2.6
Malawi	75	66	1.1	95	89	1.1	25	39	1.6	60	66	0.9	97	93	1.0	47	40	1.2	49	43	1.1
Malaysia	–	–	–	–	–	–	–	–	–	–	–	–	–	–	–	–	–	–	100	99	1.0
Maldives	93 x	92 x	1.0 x	99 x	93 x	1.1 x	16 x	22 x	1.3 x	–	–	–	94	94	1.0	43 x	32 x	1.4 x	93	98	0.9
Mali	97	85	1.1	73 x	14 x	5.2 x	17	34	2.0	29 x	20 x	1.5 x	83	46	1.8	32	16	2	46	22	2.1
Malta	–	–	–	–	–	–	–	–	–	–	–	–	–	–	–	–	–	–	100	100	1.0
Marshall Islands	96 x	96 x	1.0 x	97 x	68 x	1.4 x	–	–	–	39 x	37 x	1.1 x	–	–	–	33 x	12 x	2.7 x	95	66	1.4
Mauritania	75	49	1.5	88	49	1.8	25	33	1.3	26	14	2.0	–	–	–	9	4	2.7	63	17	3.7
Mauritius	–	–	–	–	–	–	–	–	–	–	–	–	–	–	–	–	–	–	94	93	1.0
Mexico	96	94	1.0	99	94	1.1	10	19	1.9	61	63	1.0	98	98	1.0	33	25	1.3	91	81	1.1
Micronesia (Federated States of)	–	–	–	–	–	–	–	–	–	–	–	–	–	–	–	–	–	–	–	–	–
Monaco	–	–	–	–	–	–	–	–	–	–	–	–	–	–	–	–	–	–	100	–	–
Mongolia	99	99	1.0	99	98	1.0	8	15	1.7	46	38	1.2	99	98	1.0	36 x	21 x	1.7 x	66	41	1.6
Montenegro	99	100	1.0	99	100	1.0	10	9	1.0	–	–	–	97	99	1.0	47	49	1.0	98	92	1.1
Montserrat	–	–	–	–	–	–	–	–	–	–	–	–	–	–	–	–	–	–	–	–	–
Morocco	97 y	91 y	1.1 y	92	55	1.7	9	21	2.4	23	21	1.1	96 x	83 x	1.2 x	–	–	–	89	75	1.2
Mozambique	51	47	1.1	80	44	1.8	36	46	1.3	65	50	1.3	83	67	1.2	39	25	1.6	47	12	3.8
Myanmar	94	78	1.2	88	52	1.7	20	32	1.6	67	61	1.1	96	92	1.1	28	11	2.5	76	59	1.3
Namibia	89 y	86 y	1.0 y	95	82	1.2	16	27	1.7	75	69	1.1	95	91	1.0	67	55	1.2	55	15	3.6
Nauru	–	–	–	–	–	–	–	–	–	–	–	–	–	–	–	–	–	–	66	–	–
Nepal	57	58	1.0	68	47	1.4	32	40	1.3	36	38	0.9	80	76	1.1	25	14	1.7	52	45	1.2
Netherlands	–	–	–	–	–	–	–	–	–	–	–	–	–	–	–	–	–	–	98	100	1.0

TABLE 10. DISPARITIES BY RESIDENCE

Countries and areas	Birth registration (%)++ 2010–2016*			Skilled birth attendant (%) 2011–2016*			Stunting prevalence in children under 5 (moderate & severe)ᵉ (%) 2011–2016*			Oral rehydration salts (ORS) treatment for children with diarrhoea (%) 2011–2016*			Primary school net attendance ratio 2011–2016*			Comprehensive knowledge of HIV/AIDS (%) Females 15–24 2011–2016*			Use of basic sanitation services (%) 2015		
	urban	rural	ratio of urban to rural	urban	rural	ratio of urban to rural	urban	rural	ratio of rural to urban	urban	rural	ratio of urban to rural	urban	rural	ratio of urban to rural	urban	rural	ratio of urban to rural	urban	rural	ratio of urban to rural
New Zealand	–	–	–	–	–	–	–	–	–	–	–	–	–	–	–	–	–	–	100	100	1.0
Nicaragua	–	–	–	97	79	1.2	15 x	30 x	2.0 x	74	57	1.3	76 x,y	64 x,y	1.2 x,y	–	–	–	86	63	1.4
Niger	92	60	1.5	83	32	2.6	34	45	1.3	47	44	1.1	83	45	1.9	31	9	3.3	44	6	7.4
Nigeria	50 y	19 y	2.7 y	62	21	3.0	26	43	1.7	45	28	1.6	87	57	1.5	30	20	1.4	39	27	1.4
Niue	–	–	–	–	–	–	–	–	–	–	–	–	100	100	1.0	–	–	–	–	–	–
Norway	–	–	–	–	–	–	–	–	–	–	–	–	–	–	–	–	–	–	98	98	1.0
Oman	–	–	–	99	98	1.0	14	15	1.1	58	62	0.9	98	97	1.0	–	–	–	99	99	1.0
Pakistan	59	23	2.6	71	44	1.6	37	48	1.3	42	37	1.1	75	59	1.3	–	–	–	74	48	1.5
Palau	–	–	–	–	–	–	–	–	–	–	–	–	–	–	–	–	–	–	100	100	1.0
Panama	98	93	1.1	100	78	1.3	–	–	–	61	44	1.4	97	97	1.0	–	–	–	86	59	1.4
Papua New Guinea	–	–	–	88 x	48 x	1.9 x	36 x	51 x	1.4 x	–	–	–	–	–	–	–	–	–	55	13	4.2
Paraguay	87 y	80 y	1.1 y	94 x	79 x	1.2 x	12	10	0.8	–	–	–	92 y	90 y	1.0 y	–	–	–	98	81	1.2
Peru	98 y	96 y	1.0 y	98	75	1.3	9	28	3.0	37	22	1.7	92 y	92 y	1.0 y	27 x	8 x	3.3 x	82	58	1.4
Philippines	–	–	–	83	64	1.3	28	38	1.3	54	45	1.2	90 x	87 x	1.0 x	23 x	17 x	1.4 x	79	72	1.1
Poland	–	–	–	–	–	–	–	–	–	–	–	–	–	–	–	–	–	–	98	98	1.0
Portugal	–	–	–	–	–	–	–	–	–	–	–	–	–	–	–	–	–	–	99	100	1.0
Qatar	–	–	–	–	–	–	–	–	–	–	–	–	–	–	–	–	–	–	–	–	–
Republic of Korea	–	–	–	–	–	–	–	–	–	–	–	–	–	–	–	–	–	–	–	–	–
Republic of Moldova	100	100	1.0	100	99	1.0	4	8	2.2	–	–	–	98	99	1.0	41	32	1.3	89	70	1.3
Romania	–	–	–	94	96	1.0	14 x	13 x	0.9 x	–	–	–	–	–	–	–	–	–	93	68	1.4
Russian Federation	–	–	–	–	–	–	–	–	–	–	–	–	–	–	–	–	–	–	93	76	1.2
Rwanda	55	56	1.0	97	89	1.1	27	40	1.5	33	27	1.3	96	94	1.0	74	62	1.2	57	64	0.9
Saint Kitts and Nevis	–	–	–	–	–	–	–	–	–	–	–	–	–	–	–	–	–	–	–	–	–
Saint Lucia	91	92	1.0	–	–	–	4	2	0.6	–	–	–	99	100	1.0	57	63	0.9	86	92	0.9
Saint Vincent and the Grenadines	–	–	–	–	–	–	–	–	–	–	–	–	–	–	–	–	–	–	–	–	–
Samoa	68	57	1.2	97	79	1.2	4	5	1.1	–	–	–	89 y	88 y	1.0 y	5 x	2 x	2.4 x	98	96	1.0
San Marino	–	–	–	–	–	–	–	–	–	–	–	–	–	–	–	–	–	–	–	–	–
Sao Tome and Principe	96	93	1.0	95	88	1.1	16	19	1.2	46	57	0.8	94	94	1.0	43	40	1.1	47	28	1.7
Saudi Arabia	–	–	–	–	–	–	–	–	–	–	–	–	–	–	–	–	–	–	–	–	–
Senegal	87	58	1.5	70	44	1.6	14	24	1.7	32	31	1.0	72	43	1.7	–	–	–	66	35	1.9
Serbia	100	99	1.0	98	99	1.0	7	5	0.8	50 x	22 x	2.3 x	100	98	1.0	63 x	41 x	1.5 x	98	91	1.1
Seychelles	–	–	–	–	–	–	–	–	–	–	–	–	–	–	–	–	–	–	–	–	–
Sierra Leone	80	76	1.1	79	53	1.5	30	40	1.4	86	85	1.0	88	71	1.2	38	22	1.7	24	8	2.8
Singapore	–	–	–	–	–	–	–	–	–	–	–	–	–	–	–	–	–	–	100	–	–
Slovakia	–	–	–	–	–	–	–	–	–	–	–	–	–	–	–	–	–	–	99	98	1.0
Slovenia	–	–	–	–	–	–	–	–	–	–	–	–	–	–	–	–	–	–	99	99	1.0
Solomon Islands	89	88	1.0	96	84	1.1	27	32	1.2	45	35	1.3	–	–	–	34 x	28 x	1.2 x	76	18	4.1
Somalia	6 x	2 x	3.7 x	21 x	3 x	7.4 x	32 x	48 x	1.5 x	25 x	9 x	3.0 x	39 x	11 x	3.4 x	7 x	2 x	4.1 x	28	8	3.5
South Africa	–	–	–	98	95	1.0	26 y	29 y	1.1 y	53	49	1.1	–	–	–	–	–	–	76	69	1.1
South Sudan	45	32	1.4	31 x	15 x	2.0 x	29 x	32 x	1.1 x	44 x	37 x	1.2 x	40	19	2.1	16 x	7 x	2.3 x	28	6	4.3
Spain	–	–	–	–	–	–	–	–	–	–	–	–	–	–	–	–	–	–	100	100	1.0
Sri Lanka	97 x	98 x	1.0 x	99 x	99 x	1.0 x	–	–	–	–	–	–	–	–	–	–	–	–	89	95	0.9
State of Palestine	99	100	1.0	100	100	1.0	8	8	1.0	30	34	0.9	99	99	1.0	8 x	6 x	1.3 x	95	99	1.0
Sudan	89	59	1.5	93	72	1.3	27	43	1.6	25	18	1.4	86	61	1.4	12	7	1.9	58	23	2.5
Suriname	100	98	1.0	93 x	84 x	1.1 x	7 x	12 x	1.8 x	33 x	55 x	0.6 x	97	94	1.0	45 x	33 x	1.4 x	88	61	1.4
Swaziland	64	51	1.3	93	86	1.1	19	27	1.4	64	90	0.7	98	98	1.0	56	47	1.2	58	58	1.0
Sweden	–	–	–	–	–	–	–	–	–	–	–	–	–	–	–	–	–	–	99	100	1.0
Switzerland	–	–	–	–	–	–	–	–	–	–	–	–	–	–	–	–	–	–	100	100	1.0
Syrian Arab Republic	97 x	95 x	1.0 x	99 x	93 x	1.1 x	28 x	28 x	1.0 x	56 x	44 x	1.3 x	98 x	96 x	1.0 x	7 x	7 x	1.0 x	96	89	1.1
Tajikistan	88	89	1.0	93	86	1.1	22	28	1.3	58	61	0.9	87	85	1.0	11	8	1.4	94	96	1.0
Thailand	99 y	100 y	1.0 y	99	100	1.0	10	11	1.1	68	75	0.9	95	95	1.0	55	56	1.0	94	96	1.0
The former Yugoslav Republic of Macedonia	100	100	1.0	94	88	1.1	4	6	1.4	19 x	30 x	0.6 x	98	98	1.0	33 x	18 x	1.8 x	97	83	1.2
Timor-Leste	50	57	0.9	59 x	20 x	2.9 x	39	55	1.4	65 x	74 x	0.9 x	80	70	1.1	14 x	12 x	1.2 x	73	30	2.4
Togo	95	69	1.4	82	24	3.4	16	33	2.1	18	19	0.9	96	85	1.1	28	19	1.5	28	5	6.2
Tokelau	–	–	–	–	–	–	–	–	–	–	–	–	–	–	–	–	–	–	–	93	0.0
Tonga	92	94	1.0	94	96	1.0	9	8	0.9	–	–	–	92 y	93 y	1.0 y	11	13	0.8	97	92	1.0
Trinidad and Tobago	–	–	–	–	–	–	–	–	–	–	–	–	–	–	–	–	–	–	–	–	–
Tunisia	100	98	1.0	77	67	1.1	8	14	1.7	69	59	1.2	99	97	1.0	22	13	1.7	98	83	1.2
Turkey	99 y	98 y	1.0 y	99	92	1.1	8	14	1.8	–	–	–	95	96	1.0	–	–	–	99	89	1.1
Turkmenistan	100	100	1.0	100	100	1.0	12	11	0.9	–	–	–	98	98	1.0	7 x	4 x	2.0 x	94	99	1.0
Turks and Caicos Islands	–	–	–	–	–	–	–	–	–	–	–	–	–	–	–	–	–	–	–	–	–
Tuvalu	60 x	38 x	1.6 x	93 x	93 x	1.0 x	10 x	11 x	1.1 x	–	–	–	98 x,y	99 x,y	1.0 x,y	38 x	41 x	0.9 x	92	91	1.0
Uganda	38	29	1.3	89	52	1.7	24	30	1.3	53	45	1.2	91	86	1.1	55	42	1.3	28	17	1.6

TABLE 10. DISPARITIES BY RESIDENCE   193

Countries and areas	Birth registration (%) 2010–2016* urban	rural	ratio of urban to rural	Skilled birth attendant (%) 2011–2016* urban	rural	ratio of urban to rural	Stunting prevalence in children under 5 (moderate & severe)θ (%) 2011–2016* urban	rural	ratio of rural to urban	Oral rehydration salts (ORS) treatment for children with diarrhoea (%) 2011–2016* urban	rural	ratio of urban to rural	Primary school net attendance ratio 2011–2016* urban	rural	ratio of urban to rural	Comprehensive knowledge of HIV/AIDS (%) Females 15–24 2011–2016* urban	rural	ratio of urban to rural	Use of basic sanitation services (%) 2015 urban	rural	ratio of urban to rural
Ukraine	100	100	1.0	99	99	1.0	–	–	–	–	–	–	100	100	1.0	52	45	1.1	97	93	1.1
United Arab Emirates	–	–	–	–	–	–	–	–	–	–	–	–	–	–	–	–	–	–	100	100	1.0
United Kingdom	–	–	–	–	–	–	–	–	–	–	–	–	–	–	–	–	–	–	99	99	1.0
United Republic of Tanzania	51	18	2.9	87	55	1.6	25	38	1.5	46	44	1.0	91	77	1.2	52	36	1.5	37	17	2.2
United States	–	–	–	–	–	–	–	–	–	–	–	–	–	–	–	–	–	–	100	100	1.0
Uruguay	100	100	1.0	*98*	*98*	*1.0*	–	–	–	–	–	–	97	97	1.0	34	–	–	96	95	1.0
Uzbekistan	100 x	100 x	1.0 x	100	100	1.0	18 x	19 x	1.1 x	*34 x*	*31 x*	*1.1 x*	–	–	–	33 x	30 x	1.1 x	100	100	1.0
Vanuatu	61 y	37 y	1.7 y	96	87	1.1	19	32	1.6	38	52	0.7	77 y	77 y	1.0 y	23 x	13 x	1.8 x	61	51	1.2
Venezuela (Bolivarian Republic of)	–	–	–	–	–	–	–	–	–	–	–	–	–	–	–	–	–	–	98	72	1.4
Viet Nam	97	96	1.0	99	92	1.1	*12*	*27*	*2.3*	58	49	1.2	98	97	1.0	54	47	1.1	91	72	1.3
Yemen	48	24	2.0	73	34	2.1	34	51	1.5	24	26	0.9	85	73	1.2	4 x	1 x	6.7 x	90	44	2.1
Zambia	20	7	3.0	88	51	1.7	36	42	1.2	68	62	1.1	92	84	1.1	50	34	1.5	49	19	2.6
Zimbabwe	67	34	1.9	93	71	1.3	22	29	1.3	46	38	1.2	98	94	1.0	56	41	1.4	54	31	1.7
SUMMARY																					
East Asia and Pacific	85 **	77 **	1.1 **	98	91	1.1	13	21	1.7	49 **	46 **	1.1 **	98	96	1.0	29 **	23 **	1.3 **	87	63	1.4
Europe and Central Asia	–	–	–	–	–	–	–	–	–	–	–	–	–	–	–	–	–	–	98	92	1.1
Eastern Europe and Central Asia	99	97	1.0	99	96	1.0	10 r	14 r	1.4 r	–	–	–	96	96	1.0	–	–	–	95	87	1.1
Western Europe	–	–	–	–	–	–	–	–	–	–	–	–	–	–	–	–	–	–	99	99	1.0
Latin America and Caribbean	96	93	1.0	–	–	–	13 N	23 N	1.8 N	–	–	–	95	93	1.0	–	–	–	90	68	1.3
Middle East and North Africa	96	87	1.1	93	76	1.2	17	21	1.2	27	27	1.0	96	91	1.0	–	–	–	94	81	1.2
North America	–	–	–	–	–	–	–	–	–	–	–	–	–	–	–	–	–	–	100	100	1.0
South Asia	73	56	1.3	84	68	1.2	32	42	1.3	57	49	1.2	86	79	1.1	13 ‡	7 ‡	1.8 ‡	65	37	1.8
Sub-Saharan Africa	57	35	1.6	80	46	1.7	26	39	1.5	43	36	1.2	86	68	1.3	37	23	1.6	42	20	2.1
Eastern and Southern Africa	52	33	1.6	86	50	1.7	26	38	1.5	47	39	1.2	87	73	1.2	45	30	1.5	48	21	2.2
West and Central Africa	60	38	1.6	76	41	1.8	26	40	1.5	41	32	1.3	86	61	1.4	28	17	1.7	37	19	2.0
Least developed countries	52	36	1.5	81	48	1.7	28	40	1.4	49	42	1.2	87	72	1.2	31	18	1.7	46	26	1.8
World	**82 **	**59 **	**1.4 **	**89**	**67**	**1.3**	**23**	**32**	**1.4**	**48 **	**42 **	**1.1 **	**92**	**81**	**1.1**	**30 ‡**	**20 ‡**	**1.5 ‡**	**83**	**50**	**1.7**

For a complete list of countries and areas in the regions, subregions and country categories, see page 150 or visit <data.unicef.org/regionalclassifications>.
It is not advisable to compare data from consecutive editions of The State of the World's Children.

DEFINITIONS OF THE INDICATORS

Birth registration – Percentage of children under age 5 who were registered at the moment of the survey. The numerator of this indicator includes children reported to have a birth certificate, regardless of whether or not it was seen by the interviewer, and those without a birth certificate whose mother or caregiver says the birth has been registered.

Skilled birth attendant – Percentage of births attended by skilled health personnel (doctor, nurse or midwife).

Stunting prevalence in children under 5–Percentage of children aged 0–59 months who are below minus two standard deviations from median height-for-age of the WHO Child Growth Standards.

Stunting – Moderate and severe: Percentage of children aged 0–59 months who are below minus two standard deviations from median height-for-age of the WHO Child Growth Standards.

Diarrhoea treatment with oral rehydration salts (ORS) – Percentage of children under age 5 who had diarrhoea in the two weeks preceding the survey and who received oral rehydration salts (ORS packets or pre-packaged ORS fluids).

Primary school net attendance ratio – Number of children attending primary or secondary school who are of official primary school age, expressed as a percentage of the total number of children of official primary school age. Because of the inclusion of primary-school-aged children attending secondary school, this indicator can also be referred to as a primary adjusted net attendance ratio.

Comprehensive knowledge of HIV – Percentage of young women (aged 15–24) who correctly identify the two major ways of preventing the sexual transmission of HIV (using condoms and limiting sex to one faithful, uninfected partner), who reject the two most common local misconceptions about HIV transmission and who know that a healthy-looking person can be HIV-positive.

Use of basic sanitation services – Percentage of the population using an improved sanitation facility that is not shared with other households (improved facilities include: flush/pour flush to piped sewerage systems, septic tanks or pit latrines; ventilated improved pit latrines; composting toilets or pit latrines with slabs.

MAIN DATA SOURCES

Birth registration – Demographic and Health Surveys (DHS), Multiple Indicator Cluster Surveys (MICS), other national surveys, censuses and vital registration systems.

Skilled birth attendant – DHS, MICS and other nationally representative sources.

Stunting prevalence in children under 5 – DHS, MICS, other national household surveys, WHO and UNICEF.

Diarrhoea treatment with oral rehydration salts (ORS) – DHS, MICS and other national household surveys.

Primary school attendance ratio – DHS, MICS and other national household surveys.

Comprehensive knowledge of HIV – AIDS Indicator Surveys (AIS), DHS, MICS, and other national household surveys; DHS STATcompiler, www.statcompiler.com.

Use of basic sanitation services – WHO/UNICEF Joint Monitoring Programme for Water Supply, Sanitation and Hygiene (JMP).

NOTES

– Data not available.

p Based on small denominators (typically 25–49 unweighted cases). No data based on fewer than 25 unweighted cases are displayed.

x Data refer to years or periods other than those specified in the column heading. Such data are not included in the calculation of regional and global averages, with the exception of 2005–2006 data on primary attendance from India. Estimates from data years prior to 2000 are not displayed.

y Data differ from the standard definition or refer to only part of a country. If they fall within the noted reference period, such data are included in the calculation of regional and global averages.

++ Changes in the definition of birth registration were made from the second and third rounds of MICS (MICS2 and MICS3) to the fourth round (MICS4). In order to allow for comparability with later rounds, data from MICS2 and MICS3 on birth registration were recalculated according to the MICS4 indicator definition. Therefore, the recalculated data presented here may differ from estimates included in MICS2 and MICS3 national reports.

θ Global and regional averages for stunting (moderate and severe) are estimated using statistical modelling data from the UNICEF-WHO-World Bank Group Joint Child Manutrition Estimates, May 2017 Edition. For more information see <data.unicef.org/malnutrition>. Disaggregations for stunting (moderate and severe) are population-weighted, which means using the most recent estimate for each country with data between 2011 and 2016; therefore disaggregations may not coincide with total estimates at the global and regional level.

* Data refer to the most recent year available during the period specified in the column heading.

** Excludes China.

‡ Excludes India.

r Excludes the Russian Federation.

N Excludes Brazil.

Italicized data are from different sources than the data presented for the same indicators in other tables of the report.

TABLE 11. DISPARITIES BY HOUSEHOLD WEALTH

Countries and areas	Birth registration (%)++ 2010–2016* poorest 20%	richest 20%	ratio of richest to poorest	Skilled birth attendant (%) 2011–2016* poorest 20%	richest 20%	ratio of richest to poorest	Stunting prevalence in children under 5 (moderate & severe)θ (%) 2011–2016* poorest 20%	richest 20%	ratio of poorest to richest	Oral rehydration salts (ORS) treatment for children with diarrhoea (%) 2011–2016* poorest 20%	richest 20%	ratio of richest to poorest	Primary school net attendance ratio 2011–2016* poorest 20%	richest 20%	ratio of richest to poorest	Comprehensive knowledge of HIV/AIDS (%) Females 15–24 2011–2016* poorest 20%	richest 20%	ratio of richest to poorest	Comprehensive knowledge of HIV/AIDS (%) Males 15–24 2011–2016* poorest 20%	richest 20%	ratio of richest to poorest
Afghanistan	30	70	2.3	24	85	3.6	49	31	1.6	45	42	0.9	59	83	1.4	0	5	23.0	–	–	–
Albania	98 x	99 x	1.0 x	98 x	100 x	1.0 x	27 x	13 x	2.1 x	–	–	–	91	94	1.0	20	60 x	3.0 x	10 x	38 x	3.8 x
Algeria	99	100	1.0	95	99	1.0	3	11	0.2	21	31	1.5	96	98	1.0	4	17	3.8	–	–	–
Andorra	–	–	–	–	–	–	–	–	–	–	–	–	–	–	–	–	–	–	–	–	–
Angola	10	55	5.7	17	90	5.2	47	7	6.8	29	57	1.9	56	95	1.7	8	58	7.3	10	46	4.8
Anguilla	–	–	–	–	–	–	–	–	–	–	–	–	–	–	–	–	–	–	–	–	–
Antigua and Barbuda	–	–	–	–	–	–	–	–	–	–	–	–	–	–	–	–	–	–	–	–	–
Argentina	99 y	100 y	1.0 y	–	–	–	–	–	–	26	6	0.2	98	99	1.0	–	54	–	–	–	–
Armenia	98	99	1.0	100	100	1.0	12	6	2.0	–	–	–	99	100	1.0	13	30	2.3	4	23	5.5
Australia	–	–	–	–	–	–	–	–	–	–	–	–	–	–	–	–	–	–	–	–	–
Austria	–	–	–	–	–	–	–	–	–	–	–	–	–	–	–	–	–	–	–	–	–
Azerbaijan	92 x	97 x	1.1 x	90	100	1.1	28	16	1.8	3 x	36 x	13.3 x	67 y	70 y	1.0 y	1 x	12 x	10.3 x	2 x	14 x	6.3 x
Bahamas	–	–	–	–	–	–	–	–	–	–	–	–	–	–	–	–	–	–	–	–	–
Bahrain	–	–	–	–	–	–	–	–	–	–	–	–	–	–	–	–	–	–	–	–	–
Bangladesh	15	28	1.8	18	74	4.2	50	21	2.4	72	81	1.1	88	93	1.1	2	18	8.9	–	–	–
Barbados	98	99	1.0	–	–	–	8	3	2.4	–	–	–	99	100	1.0	57	66	1.2	–	–	–
Belarus	–	–	–	100	100	1.0	11 x	2 x	5.3 x	–	–	–	93	93	1.0	55	55	1.0	42	43	1.0
Belgium	–	–	–	–	–	–	–	–	–	–	–	–	–	–	–	–	–	–	–	–	–
Belize	94	99	1.1	93	99	1.1	26	5	4.8	–	–	–	93	99	1.1	20	53	2.7	–	–	–
Benin	69	96	1.4	61	91	1.5	46	18	2.6	20	31	1.6	54	92	1.7	15	29	2.0	26	42	1.6
Bhutan	100	100	1.0	34 x	95 x	2.8 x	41 x	21 x	1.9 x	60 x	56 x	0.9 x	–	–	–	7 x	32 x	4.4 x	–	–	–
Bolivia (Plurinational State of)	68 x,y	90 x,y	1.3 x,y	57	99	1.7	32	9	3.5	18	27	1.5	95 x	99 x	1.0 x	5 x	40 x	8.4 x	11 x	45 x	4.3 x
Bosnia and Herzegovina	100 x	99 x	1.0 x	100	100	1.0	10	10	1.0	–	–	–	93	94	1.0	37	44	1.2	38	45	1.2
Botswana	–	–	–	–	–	–	38 x	20 x	1.9 x	–	–	–	–	–	–	–	–	–	–	–	–
Brazil	–	–	–	–	–	–	7 x	3 x	2.1 x	–	–	–	–	–	–	–	–	–	–	–	–
British Virgin Islands	–	–	–	–	–	–	–	–	–	–	–	–	–	–	–	–	–	–	–	–	–
Brunei Darussalam	–	–	–	–	–	–	–	–	–	–	–	–	–	–	–	–	–	–	–	–	–
Bulgaria	–	–	–	–	–	–	–	–	–	–	–	–	–	–	–	–	–	–	–	–	–
Burkina Faso	62	95	1.5	68	95	1.4	42 x	19 x	2.3 x	38	47	1.2	31	85	2.8	8 x	37 x	4.4 x	–	–	–
Burundi	64	87	1.4	77	96	1.2				34	38	1.1									
Cabo Verde	–	–	–	–	–	–	–	–	–	–	–	–	–	–	–	–	–	–	–	–	–
Cambodia	59	87	1.5	75	98	1.3	42	19	2.3	40	27	0.7	86	98	1.1	27	55	2.1	28	63	2.2
Cameroon	38	92	2.4	21	98	4.7	42	15	2.9	9	37	4.3	65	99	1.5	12 x	50 x	4.0 x	–	–	–
Canada	–	–	–	–	–	–	–	–	–	–	–	–	–	–	–	–	–	–	–	–	–
Central African Republic	46	85	1.8	18 x	79 x	4.3 x	45	30	1.5	11 x	28 x	2.5 x	57	90	1.6	12 x	21 x	1.7 x	19 x	29 x	1.5 x
Chad	6	39	6.5	11	58	5.3	41	32	1.3	14	30	2.2	44	76	1.7	6 x	18 x	2.9 x	–	–	–
Chile	–	–	–	–	–	–	–	–	–	–	–	–	–	–	–	–	–	–	–	–	–
China	–	–	–	–	–	–	–	–	–	–	–	–	–	–	–	–	–	–	–	–	–
Colombia	96	98	1.0	86	99	1.2	19 x	7 x	2.9 x	47 x	61 x	1.3 x	93	96	1.0	15 x	32 x	2.2 x	–	–	–
Comoros	85	93	1.1	66	93	1.4	38	22	1.7	39	36	0.9	72	95	1.3	–	–	–	–	–	–
Congo	80	99	1.2	78	99	1.3	35	9	3.7	22	37	1.7	–	–	–	5 x	12 x	2.4 x	12 x	27 x	2.3 x
Cook Islands	–	–	–	–	–	–	–	–	–	–	–	–	–	–	–	–	–	–	–	–	–
Costa Rica	99	100	1.0	97	99	1.0	–	–	–	–	–	–	94	98	1.0	20	54	2.7	–	–	–
Côte d'Ivoire	44	90	2.0	35	91	2.6	38	16	2.5	6	24	3.7	62	94	1.5	–	–	–	–	–	–
Croatia	–	–	–	–	–	–	–	–	–	–	–	–	–	–	–	–	–	–	–	–	–
Cuba	–	–	–	–	–	–	–	–	–	–	–	–	–	–	–	–	–	–	–	–	–
Cyprus	–	–	–	–	–	–	–	–	–	–	–	–	–	–	–	–	–	–	–	–	–
Czechia	–	–	–	–	–	–	–	–	–	–	–	–	–	–	–	–	–	–	–	–	–
Democratic People's Republic of Korea	–	–	–	–	–	–	–	–	–	–	–	–	–	–	–	–	–	–	–	–	–
Democratic Republic of the Congo	16	38	2.4	66	98	1.5	50	23	2.2	31	42	1.4	79	94	1.2	8 x	24 x	2.8 x	–	–	–
Denmark	–	–	–	–	–	–	–	–	–	–	–	–	–	–	–	–	–	–	–	–	–
Djibouti	–	–	–	–	–	–	–	–	–	–	–	–	–	–	–	–	–	–	–	–	–
Dominica	–	–	–	–	–	–	–	–	–	–	–	–	–	–	–	–	–	–	–	–	–
Dominican Republic	73	98	1.4	96	99	1.0	11	4	2.9	43	57	1.3	91	98	1.1	34	55	1.6	–	–	–
Ecuador	90	96	1.1	99 x	98 x	1.0 x	37	14	2.6	41	64	1.6	97 y	98 y	1.0 y	–	–	–	–	–	–
Egypt	99	100	1.0	82	99	1.2	24	23	1.0	27	23	0.9	95	98	1.0	6	14	2.1	2	10	5.8
El Salvador	98	99	1.0	94	99	1.1	24	5	4.5	71	68	1.0	92	99	1.1	17	46	2.8	17	46	2.8
Equatorial Guinea	60	60	1.0	48	88	1.8	28	19	1.5	–	–	–	–	–	–	–	–	–	–	–	–
Eritrea	–	–	–	9 x	90 x	10.5 x	57 x	27 x	2.1 x	42 x	50 x	1.2 x	71 y	96 y	1.3 y	9 x	37 x	4.3 x	21 x	43 x	2.0 x
Estonia	–	–	–	–	–	–	–	–	–	–	–	–	–	–	–	–	–	–	–	–	–
Ethiopia	1	10	11.9	13	67	5.1	40	27	1.6	32	37	1.2	49 y	82 y	1.7 y	–	–	–	–	–	–
Fiji	–	–	–	–	–	–	–	–	–	–	–	–	–	–	–	–	–	–	–	–	–
Finland	–	–	–	–	–	–	–	–	–	–	–	–	–	–	–	–	–	–	–	–	–

TABLE 11. DISPARITIES BY HOUSEHOLD WEALTH   195

Countries and areas	Birth registration (%)++ 2010–2016* poorest 20%	richest 20%	ratio of richest to poorest	Skilled birth attendant (%) 2011–2016* poorest 20%	richest 20%	ratio of richest to poorest	Stunting prevalence in children under 5 (moderate & severe)θ (%) 2011–2016* poorest 20%	richest 20%	ratio of poorest to richest	Oral rehydration salts (ORS) treatment for children with diarrhoea (%) 2011–2016* poorest 20%	richest 20%	ratio of richest to poorest	Primary school net attendance ratio 2011–2016* poorest 20%	richest 20%	ratio of richest to poorest	Comprehensive knowledge of HIV/AIDS (%) Females 15–24 2011–2016* poorest 20%	richest 20%	ratio of richest to poorest	Comprehensive knowledge of HIV/ AIDS (%) Males 15–24 2011–2016* poorest 20%	richest 20%	ratio of richest to poorest
France	–	–	–	–	–	–	–	–	–	–	–	–	–	–	–	–	–	–	–	–	–
Gabon	92	86	0.9	74	95	1.3	30	6	5.2	24	19	0.8	96	98	1.0	–	–	–	–	–	–
Gambia	69	75	1.1	46	82	1.8	30	15	1.9	56	58	1.0	60 y	80 y	1.3 y	20 x	48 x	2.4 x	–	–	–
Georgia	99	100	1.0	95 x	99 x	1.0 x	–	–	–	–	–	–	–	–	–	–	–	–	–	–	–
Germany	–	–	–	–	–	–	–	–	–	–	–	–	–	–	–	–	–	–	–	–	–
Ghana	58	88	1.5	42	94	2.2	25	9	2.9	47	50	1.1	63	84	1.3	18	53	2.9	19	49	2.6
Greece	–	–	–	–	–	–	–	–	–	–	–	–	–	–	–	–	–	–	–	–	–
Grenada	–	–	–	–	–	–	–	–	–	–	–	–	–	–	–	–	–	–	–	–	–
Guatemala	–	–	–	37	96	2.6	66	17	3.8	49	55	1.1	89	98	1.1	7	41	6.0	7	36	5.4
Guinea	38	89	2.4	19	92	4.9	34	15	2.2	25	49	1.9	38	87	2.3	–	–	–	–	–	–
Guinea-Bissau	13	43	3.3	26	83	3.2	31	15	2.1	26	30	1.2	56	76	1.4	21	27	1.3	13	32	2.5
Guyana	84	95	1.1	70	96	1.4	21	7	2.9	–	–	–	96	97	1.0	40	62	1.5	28	56	2.0
Haiti	71	92	1.3	10	78	8.1	31	7	4.7	52	62	1.2	73	96	1.3	18 x	41 x	2.2 x	28 x	52 x	1.9 x
Holy See	–	–	–	–	–	–	–	–	–	–	–	–	–	–	–	–	–	–	–	–	–
Honduras	92	95	1.0	58	98	1.7	42	8	5.3	63	52	0.8	–	–	–	13 x	44 x	3.4	–	–	–
Hungary	–	–	–	–	–	–	–	–	–	–	–	–	–	–	–	–	–	–	–	–	–
Iceland	–	–	–	–	–	–	–	–	–	–	–	–	–	–	–	–	–	–	–	–	–
India	57	86	1.5	64	95	1.5	51	22	1.9	33	45	1.4	70 x	96 x	1.4 x	4 x	45 x	11.7 x	15 x	55 x	3.8 x
Indonesia	41	88	2.2	63	98	1.6	48	29	1.7	39	34	0.9	99	100	1.0	3 x	23 x	7.5 x	2 x	27 x	12.2 x
Iran (Islamic Republic of)	–	–	–	–	–	–	21	1	17.3	–	–	–	–	–	–	–	–	–	–	–	–
Iraq	98	100	1.0	82	96	1.2	25	22	1.1	19	22	1.1	79	98	1.2	1	8	7.2	–	–	–
Ireland	–	–	–	–	–	–	–	–	–	–	–	–	–	–	–	–	–	–	–	–	–
Israel	–	–	–	–	–	–	–	–	–	–	–	–	–	–	–	–	–	–	–	–	–
Italy	–	–	–	–	–	–	–	–	–	–	–	–	–	–	–	–	–	–	–	–	–
Jamaica	99	100	1.0	97	100	1.0	4	8	0.5	–	–	–	98	99	1.0	–	–	–	–	–	–
Japan	–	–	–	–	–	–	–	–	–	–	–	–	–	–	–	–	–	–	–	–	–
Jordan	98	100	1.0	99	100	1.0	14	2	7.7	22	21	1.0	97	99	1.0	–	–	–	–	–	–
Kazakhstan	99	100	1.0	100	100	1.0	10	6	1.7	–	–	–	100	99	1.0	15	33	2.2	–	–	–
Kenya	52	89	1.7	31	93	3.0	36	14	2.6	52	55	1.0	69	94	1.4	29 x	61 x	2.1 x	42 x	68 x	1.6 x
Kiribati	93 x	94 x	1.0 x	76 x	93 x	1.2 x	–	–	–	–	–	–	–	–	–	42 x	49 x	1.2 x	38 x	51 x	1.3 x
Kuwait	–	–	–	–	–	–	–	–	–	–	–	–	–	–	–	–	–	–	–	–	–
Kyrgyzstan	96	99	1.0	97	99	1.0	18	11	1.7	–	–	–	99	100	1.0	22	18	0.8	–	–	–
Lao People's Democratic Republic	66	93	1.4	11	90	8.5	61	20	3.1	35	69	2.0	71	97	1.4	6	41	6.5	12	43	3.6
Latvia	–	–	–	–	–	–	–	–	–	–	–	–	–	–	–	–	–	–	–	–	–
Lebanon	–	–	–	–	–	–	–	–	–	–	–	–	–	–	–	–	–	–	–	–	–
Lesotho	34	63	1.8	60	94	1.6	46	13	3.4	–	–	–	88	95	1.1	26	48	1.8	19	36	1.9
Liberia	16 y	31 y	1.9 y	43	89	2.1	35	20	1.8	57	44	0.8	25	65	2.6	14 x	29 x	2.1 x	17 x	37 x	2.2 x
Libya	–	–	–	–	–	–	–	–	–	–	–	–	–	–	–	–	–	–	–	–	–
Liechtenstein	–	–	–	–	–	–	–	–	–	–	–	–	–	–	–	–	–	–	–	–	–
Lithuania	–	–	–	–	–	–	–	–	–	–	–	–	–	–	–	–	–	–	–	–	–
Luxembourg	–	–	–	–	–	–	–	–	–	–	–	–	–	–	–	–	–	–	–	–	–
Madagascar	72	94	1.3	27	73	2.7	48 x	44 x	1.1 x	11	17	1.6	54 y	82 y	1.5 y	10	40	4.1	13	41	3.2
Malawi	65	74	1.1	87	95	1.1	46	24	1.9	63	61	1.0	89	98	1.1	34	48	1.4	32	53	1.7
Malaysia	–	–	–	–	–	–	–	–	–	–	–	–	–	–	–	–	–	–	–	–	–
Maldives	92 x	94 x	1.0 x	89 x	99 x	1.1 x	22 x	16 x	1.4 x	–	–	–	94	94	1.0	23 x	48 x	2.0 x	–	–	–
Mali	69	98	1.4	6 x	81 x	12.6 x	41	15	3.0	18 x	25 x	1.4 x	27	86	3.2	12	33	2.7	17	53	3.2
Malta	–	–	–	–	–	–	–	–	–	–	–	–	–	–	–	–	–	–	–	–	–
Marshall Islands	92 x	98 x	1.1 x	68 x	99 x	1.5 x	–	–	–	–	–	–	–	–	–	12 x	39 x	3.3 x	37 x	58 x	1.6 x
Mauritania	33	84	2.6	27	96	3.6	39	18	2.2	9	33	3.8	–	–	–	2	12	7.9	–	–	–
Mauritius	–	–	–	–	–	–	–	–	–	–	–	–	–	–	–	–	–	–	–	–	–
Mexico	83	99	1.2	92	100	1.1	23	5	4.7	–	–	–	96	99	1.0	21	39	1.9	–	–	–
Micronesia (Federated States of)	–	–	–	–	–	–	–	–	–	–	–	–	–	–	–	–	–	–	–	–	–
Monaco	–	–	–	–	–	–	–	–	–	–	–	–	–	–	–	–	–	–	–	–	–
Mongolia	99	100	1.0	97	99	1.0	19	6	3.3	35	43	1.3	96	99	1.0	17 x	42 x	2.5 x	12 x	48 x,p	4.1 x,p
Montenegro	99	99	1.0	99	100	1.0	5	9	0.5	–	–	–	95	100	1.0	39	51	1.3	33	47 p	1.4
Montserrat	–	–	–	–	–	–	–	–	–	–	–	–	–	–	–	–	–	–	–	–	–
Morocco	–	–	–	38	96	2.5	28	7	4.2	14	23	1.7	77 x	97 x	1.3 x	–	–	–	–	–	–
Mozambique	42	60	1.4	32	90	2.8	51	24	2.1	41	70	1.7	58	93	1.6	19	44	2.3	20	44	2.2
Myanmar	69	97	1.4	36	97	2.7	38	16	2.4	–	–	–	84	97	1.2	–	–	–	–	–	–
Namibia	83 y	93 y	1.1 y	73	98	1.4	31	9	3.6	64	70	1.1	88	97	1.1	61 x	69 x	1.1 x	55 x	67 x	1.2 x
Nauru	71 x	88 x	1.2 x	97 x	98 x	1.0 x	52 x	18 x	2.9 x	–	–	–	–	–	–	13 x,p	10 x,p	0.8 x,p	–	25 x,p	–
Nepal	55	58	1.1	34	89	2.6	49	17	3.0	–	–	–	81	82	1.0	26	54	2.1	–	–	–
Netherlands	–	–	–	–	–	–	–	–	–	–	–	–	–	–	–	–	–	–	–	–	–

TABLE 11. DISPARITIES BY HOUSEHOLD WEALTH

Countries and areas	Birth registration (%)[++] 2010–2016*			Skilled birth attendant (%) 2011–2016*			Stunting prevalence in children under 5 (moderate & severe)[θ] (%) 2011–2016*			Oral rehydration salts (ORS) treatment for children with diarrhoea (%) 2011–2016*			Primary school net attendance ratio 2011–2016*			Comprehensive knowledge of HIV/AIDS (%) Females 15–24 2011–2016*			Comprehensive knowledge of HIV/AIDS (%) Males 15–24 2011–2016*		
	poorest 20%	richest 20%	ratio of richest to poorest	poorest 20%	richest 20%	ratio of richest to poorest	poorest 20%	richest 20%	ratio of poorest to richest	poorest 20%	richest 20%	ratio of richest to poorest	poorest 20%	richest 20%	ratio of richest to poorest	poorest 20%	richest 20%	ratio of richest to poorest	poorest 20%	richest 20%	ratio of richest to poorest
New Zealand	–	–	–	–	–	–	–	–	–	–	–	–	–	–	–	–	–	–	–	–	–
Nicaragua	–	–	–	42 x	99 x	2.4 x	35	6 x	6.0 x	53 x	64 x	1.2 x	–	–	–	–	–	–	–	–	–
Niger	50	89	1.8	12	71	6.0	47	35	1.4	34	49	1.4	35	81	2.3	6	30	5.0	6	42	7.2
Nigeria	7 y	65 y	9.7 y	5	81	15.6	54	18	3.0	20	53	2.6	28	95	3.3	15	33	2.2	23	43	1.9
Niue	–	–	–	–	–	–	–	–	–	–	–	–	100	100	1.0	–	–	–	–	–	–
Norway	–	–	–	–	–	–	–	–	–	–	–	–	–	–	–	–	–	–	–	–	–
Oman	–	–	–	–	–	–	–	–	–	–	–	–	–	–	–	–	–	–	–	–	–
Pakistan	5	71	14.3	30 x	85	2.9	62	23	2.7	34	48	1.4	39	87	2.2	–	–	–	–	–	–
Palau	–	–	–	–	–	–	–	–	–	–	–	–	–	–	–	–	–	–	–	–	–
Panama	90	97	1.1	72	100	1.4	–	–	–	–	–	–	96	97	1.0	–	–	–	–	–	–
Papua New Guinea	–	–	–	–	–	–	–	–	–	–	–	–	–	–	–	–	–	–	–	–	–
Paraguay	67 y	89 y	1.3 y	–	–	–	28	13	2.2	–	–	–	–	–	–	–	–	–	–	–	–
Peru	95 y	99 y	1.0 y	71	100	1.4	32	3	11.3	23	44	1.9	92 y	92 y	1.0 y	–	–	–	–	–	–
Philippines	–	–	–	42	96	2.3	49	15	3.3	–	–	–	79 x	92 x	1.2 x	14 x	26 x	1.8 x	–	–	–
Poland	–	–	–	–	–	–	–	–	–	–	–	–	–	–	–	–	–	–	–	–	–
Portugal	–	–	–	–	–	–	–	–	–	–	–	–	–	–	–	–	–	–	–	–	–
Qatar	–	–	–	–	–	–	–	–	–	–	–	–	–	–	–	–	–	–	–	–	–
Republic of Korea	–	–	–	–	–	–	–	–	–	–	–	–	–	–	–	–	–	–	–	–	–
Republic of Moldova	99	100	1.0	98	99	1.0	11	3	4.2	–	–	–	98	99	1.0	14	47	3.3	13	40	3.1
Romania	–	–	–	–	–	–	–	–	–	–	–	–	–	–	–	–	–	–	–	–	–
Russian Federation	–	–	–	–	–	–	–	–	–	–	–	–	–	–	–	–	–	–	–	–	–
Rwanda	43	64	1.5	84	97	1.2	49	21	2.3	22	37	1.7	88	97	1.1	–	–	–	–	–	–
Saint Kitts and Nevis	–	–	–	–	–	–	–	–	–	–	–	–	–	–	–	–	–	–	–	–	–
Saint Lucia	–	–	–	–	–	–	–	–	–	–	–	–	98	100	1.0	–	–	–	–	–	–
Saint Vincent and the Grenadines	–	–	–	–	–	–	–	–	–	–	–	–	–	–	–	–	–	–	–	–	–
Samoa	47	77	1.6	72	94	1.3	6	3	2.3	–	–	–	85 y	91 y	1.1 y	3 x	3 x	1.0 x	3 x	9 x	2.7 x
San Marino	–	–	–	–	–	–	–	–	–	–	–	–	–	–	–	–	–	–	–	–	–
Sao Tome and Principe	88	100	1.1	85	98	1.1	26	7	3.8	–	–	–	92	96	1.1	39	51	1.3	38	56	1.5
Saudi Arabia	–	–	–	–	–	–	–	–	–	–	–	–	–	–	–	–	–	–	–	–	–
Senegal	44	93	2.1	29	81	2.8	28	10	2.8	28	23	0.8	43	78	1.8	–	–	–	–	–	–
Serbia	97	100	1.0	98	95	1.0	14	4	3.3	–	–	–	97	100	1.0	28 x	69 x	2.4 x	28 x	66 x	2.4 x
Seychelles	–	–	–	–	–	–	–	–	–	–	–	–	–	–	–	–	–	–	–	–	–
Sierra Leone	77	80	1.0	51	84	1.6	43	28	1.5	87	88	1.0	62	92	1.5	14 x	36 x	2.6 x	–	–	–
Singapore	–	–	–	–	–	–	–	–	–	–	–	–	–	–	–	–	–	–	–	–	–
Slovakia	–	–	–	–	–	–	–	–	–	–	–	–	–	–	–	–	–	–	–	–	–
Slovenia	–	–	–	–	–	–	–	–	–	–	–	–	–	–	–	–	–	–	–	–	–
Solomon Islands	87	88	1.0	72	96	1.3	36.2	25	–	37	39	1.0	–	–	–	17 x	37 x	2.1 x	35 x	50 x	1.5 x
Somalia	1 x	7 x	6.6 x	1 x	27 x	27.1 x	52 x	25 x	2.0 x	7 x	31 x	4.8 x	4 x	50 x	13.2 x	1 x	8 x	13.5 x	–	–	–
South Africa	–	–	–	93	99	1.1	36	13	2.9	–	–	–	–	–	–	–	–	–	–	–	–
South Sudan	21	57	2.7	8 x	41 x	5.1 x	31 x	27 x	1.2 x	27 x	52 x	1.9 x	10	50	5.1	3 x	18 x	6.1 x	–	–	–
Spain	–	–	–	–	–	–	–	–	–	–	–	–	–	–	–	–	–	–	–	–	–
Sri Lanka	97 x	98 x	1.0 x	97 x	99 x	1.0 x	19	10	2.0	–	–	–	–	–	–	–	–	–	–	–	–
State of Palestine	100	99	1.0	100	99	1.0	8	7	1.1	23	31	1.3	99	99	1.0	5 x	10 x	2.1 x	–	–	–
Sudan	37	98	2.6	48	99	2.1	44	21	2.1	16	21	1.3	48	94	1.9	2	19	8.7	–	–	–
Suriname	98	100	1.0	83 x	94 x	1.1 x	13 x	6 x	2.4 x	–	–	–	92	97	1.1	26 x	52 x	2.0 x	–	–	–
Swaziland	39	78	2.0	76	95	1.2	30	9	3.3	–	–	–	97	98	1.0	38	54	1.4	40	69	1.7
Sweden	–	–	–	–	–	–	–	–	–	–	–	–	–	–	–	–	–	–	–	–	–
Switzerland	–	–	–	–	–	–	–	–	–	–	–	–	–	–	–	–	–	–	–	–	–
Syrian Arab Republic	93 x	99 x	1.1 x	75 x	99 x	1.3 x	35 x	25 x	1.4 x	46 x	59 x	1.3 x	92 x	99 x	1.1 x	4 x	10 x	2.9 x	–	–	–
Tajikistan	86	90	1.0	74 x	96	1.3	32	21	1.5	53	62	1.2	85	88	1.0	–	–	–	–	–	–
Thailand	100 y	100 y	1.0 y	98	100	1.0	13	12	1.1	78	81	1.0	92	97	1.1	42	53	1.3	37	53	1.4
The former Yugoslav Republic of Macedonia	99	100	1.0	78 x	97 x	1.2 x	7	2	3.6	–	–	–	96	99	1.0	9 x	45 x	5.0 x	–	–	–
Timor-Leste	50	56	1.1	10 x	69 x	6.9 x	59	39	1.5	70 x	71 x	1.0 x	60	84	1.4	9 x	16 x	1.8 x	11 x	35 x	3.0 x
Togo	67	97	1.5	11	87	8.1	33	11	3.2	28	25	0.9	80	97	1.2	18 x	42 x	2.3 x	20 x	55 x	2.7 x
Tokelau	–	–	–	–	–	–	–	–	–	–	–	–	–	–	–	–	–	–	–	–	–
Tonga	92	96	1.1	93	97	1.0	7	10	0.7	–	–	–	94 y	94 y	1.0 y	11	16	1.4	13	14	1.1
Trinidad and Tobago	96 x	99 x	1.0 x	98 x	99 x	1.0 x	–	–	–	–	–	–	95	98	1.0	48 x	62 x	1.3 x	–	–	–
Tunisia	98	100	1.0	63	89	1.4	16	8	2.0	–	–	–	96	99	1.0	10 p	29	2.8	–	–	–
Turkey	98 y	99 y	1.0 y	91	100	1.1	18	4	4.3	–	–	–	92	96	1.0	–	–	–	–	–	–
Turkmenistan	100	99	1.0	100	100	1.0	16	11	1.4	–	–	–	98	98	1.0	17 p	32	1.9	–	–	–
Turks and Caicos Islands	–	–	–	–	–	–	–	–	–	–	–	–	–	–	–	–	–	–	–	–	–
Tuvalu	39 x	71 x	1.8 x	95 x	90 x	1.0 x	8 x	13 x	0.6 x	–	–	–	99 x,y	100 x,y	1.0 x,y	34 x,p	39 x	1.2 x	–	67 x,p	–
Uganda	27	44	1.6	43	88	2.0	32	17	1.9	48	53	1.1	79	92	1.2	20 x,p	47 x	2.3 x	28 x	47 x	1.6 x

TABLE 11. DISPARITIES BY HOUSEHOLD WEALTH   197

Countries and areas	Birth registration (%)++ 2010–2016*			Skilled birth attendant (%) 2011–2016*			Stunting prevalence in children under 5 (moderate & severe)θ (%) 2011–2016*			Oral rehydration salts (ORS) treatment for children with diarrhoea (%) 2011–2016*			Primary school net attendance ratio 2011–2016*			Comprehensive knowledge of HIV/AIDS (%) Females 15–24 2011–2016*			Comprehensive knowledge of HIV/AIDS (%) Males 15–24 2011–2016*		
	poorest 20%	richest 20%	ratio of richest to poorest	poorest 20%	richest 20%	ratio of richest to poorest	poorest 20%	richest 20%	ratio of poorest to richest	poorest 20%	richest 20%	ratio of richest to poorest	poorest 20%	richest 20%	ratio of richest to poorest	poorest 20%	richest 20%	ratio of richest to poorest	poorest 20%	richest 20%	ratio of richest to poorest
Ukraine	100	99	1.0	99	100	1.0	–	–	–	–	–	–	100	100	1.0	41 p	53	1.3	40	54	1.3
United Arab Emirates	–	–	–	–	–	–	–	–	–	–	–	–	–	–	–	–	–	–	–	–	–
United Kingdom	–	–	–	–	–	–	–	–	–	–	–	–	–	–	–	–	–	–	–	–	–
United Republic of Tanzania	8	65	8.5	42	95	2.3	40	19	2.1	40	45	1.1	63	95	1.5	39 x,p	55 x	1.4 x	34 x	56 x	1.7 x
United States	–	–	–	–	–	–	–	–	–	–	–	–	–	–	–	–	–	–	–	–	–
Uruguay	–	–	–	–	–	–	–	–	–	–	–	–	97	98	1.0	–	–	–	–	–	–
Uzbekistan	100 x	100 x	1.0 x	99 x	100 x	1.0 x	21 x	15 x	1.4 x	27 x	19 x	0.7 x	–	–	–	25 x	33 x	1.3 x	–	–	–
Vanuatu	33 y	59 y	1.8 y	77	95	1.2	40	16	2.4	–	–	–	75 y	80 y	1.1 y	9 x	23 x	2.7 x	–	–	–
Venezuela (Bolivarian Republic of)	–	–	–	99	93	0.9	–	–	–	–	–	–	86	99	1.2	–	–	–	–	–	–
Viet Nam	91	98	1.1	73	100	1.4	41	6	6.7	–	–	–	94	98	1.0	30	65	2.2	–	–	–
Yemen	17	56	3.3	19	81	4.2	59	26	2.3	27	21	0.8	56	90	1.6	0 x	4 x	– x	–	–	–
Zambia	5	29	6.0	45	94	2.1	47	28	1.7	59	68	1.1	75	97	1.3	24 x	48 x	2.0 x	24 x	51 x	2.1 x
Zimbabwe	24	79	3.3	62	96	1.6	33	17	2.0	30	44	1.5	91	100	1.1	47	65	1.4	43	67	1.6
SUMMARY																					
East Asia and Pacific	59 **	92 **	1.6 **	60 **	98 **	1.6 **	44 **	20 **	2.2 **	–	–	–	95 **	99 **	1.0 **	–	–	–	–	–	–
Europe and Central Asia	–	–	–	–	–	–	–	–	–	–	–	–	–	–	–	–	–	–	–	–	–
Eastern Europe and Central Asia	98	98	1.0	93	99	1.1	18 r	8 r	2.4 r	–	–	–	94	96	1.0	–	–	–	–	–	–
Western Europe	–	–	–	–	–	–	–	–	–	–	–	–	–	–	–	–	–	–	–	–	–
Latin America and Caribbean	88	98	1.1	80	98	1.2	30 N	7 N	4.3 N	–	–	–	94	97	1.0	–	–	–	–	–	–
Middle East and North Africa	88	94	1.1	72	96	1.3	24	15	1.6	23	24	1.0	86	97	1.1	–	–	–	–	–	–
North America	–	–	–	–	–	–	–	–	–	–	–	–	–	–	–	–	–	–	–	–	–
South Asia	45	78	1.7	53	91	1.7	52	22	2.0	37	49	1.3	67	94	1.4	5 ‡	21 ‡	4.1 ‡	–	–	–
Sub-Saharan Africa	27	63	2.3	34	87	2.6	44	19	2.3	31	45	1.5	54	91	1.7	–	–	–	–	–	–
Eastern and Southern Africa	27	55	2.1	40	87	2.2	42	19	2.2	37	46	1.2	63	90	1.4	–	–	–	–	–	–
West and Central Africa	28	70	2.5	28	86	3.1	46	19	2.4	25	45	1.8	46	91	2.0	14	34	2.4	–	–	–
Least developed countries	30	56	1.9	36	85	2.4	45	21	2.1	39	47	1.2	64	89	1.4	–	–	–	–	–	–
World	**56 ****	**82 ****	**1.5 ****	**51 ****	**91 ****	**1.8 ****	**44**	**19**	**2.2**	**34 ****	**45 ****	**1.3 ****	**70 ****	**94 ****	**1.3 ****	–	–	–	–	–	–

For a complete list of countries and areas in the regions, subregions and country categories, see page 150 or visit <data.unicef.org/regionalclassifications>.

It is not advisable to compare data from consecutive editions of *The State of the World's Children*.

DEFINITIONS OF THE INDICATORS

Birth registration – Percentage of children under age 5 who were registered at the moment of the survey. The numerator of this indicator includes children reported to have a birth certificate, regardless of whether or not it was seen by the interviewer, and those without a birth certificate whose mother or caregiver says the birth has been registered.

Skilled birth attendant – Percentage of births attended by skilled health personnel (doctor, nurse or midwife).

Stunting prevalence in children under 5–Percentage of children aged 0–59 months who are below minus two standard deviations from median height-for-age of the WHO Child Growth Standards.

Stunting – Moderate and severe: Percentage of children aged 0–59 months who are below minus two standard deviations from median height-for-age of the WHO Child Growth Standards.

Diarrhoea treatment with oral rehydration salts (ORS) – Percentage of children under age 5 who had diarrhoea in the two weeks preceding the survey and who received oral rehydration salts (ORS packets or pre-packaged ORS fluids).

Primary school net attendance ratio – Number of children attending primary or secondary school who are of official primary school age, expressed as a percentage of the total number of children of official primary school age. Because of the inclusion of primary-school-aged children attending secondary school, this indicator can also be referred to as a primary adjusted net attendance ratio.

Comprehensive knowledge of HIV – Percentage of young men and women (aged 15–24) who correctly identify the two major ways of preventing the sexual transmission of HIV (using condoms and limiting sex to one faithful, uninfected partner), who reject the two most common local misconceptions about HIV transmission and who know that a healthy-looking person can be HIV-positive.

MAIN DATA SOURCES

Birth registration – Demographic and Health Surveys (DHS), Multiple Indicator Cluster Surveys (MICS), other national surveys, censuses and vital registration systems.

Skilled birth attendant – DHS, MICS and other nationally representative sources.

Stunting prevalence in children under 5 – DHS, MICS, other national household surveys, WHO and UNICEF.

Diarrhoea treatment with oral rehydration salts (ORS) – DHS, MICS and other national household surveys.

Primary school attendance ratio – DHS, MICS and other national household surveys.

Comprehensive knowledge of HIV – AIDS Indicator Surveys (AIS), DHS, MICS, and other national household surveys; DHS STATcompiler, www.statcompiler.com.

Italicized data are from different sources than the data presented for the same indicators in other tables of the report.

NOTES

– Data not available.

p Based on small denominators (typically 25–49 unweighted cases). No data based on fewer than 25 unweighted cases are displayed.

x Data refer to years or periods other than those specified in the column heading. Such data are not included in the calculation of regional and global averages, with the exception of 2005–2006 data on primary attendance from India. Estimates from data years prior to 2000 are not displayed.

y Data differ from the standard definition or refer to only part of a country. If they fall within the noted reference period, such data are included in the calculation of regional and global averages.

++ Changes in the definition of birth registration were made from the second and third rounds of MICS (MICS2 and MICS3) to the fourth round (MICS4). In order to allow for comparability with later rounds, data from MICS2 and MICS3 on birth registration were recalculated according to the MICS4 indicator definition. Therefore, the recalculated data presented here may differ from estimates included in MICS2 and MICS3 national reports.

θ Global and regional averages for stunting (moderate and severe) are estimated using statistical modelling data from the UNICEF-WHO-World Bank Group Joint Child Malnutrition Estimates, May 2017 Edition. For more information see <data.unicef.org/malnutrition>. Disaggregations for stunting (moderate and severe) are population-weighted, which means using the most recent estimate for each country with data between 2011 and 2016; therefore disaggregations may not coincide with total estimates at the global and regional level.

* Data refer to the most recent year available during the period specified in the column heading.

** Excludes China.

‡ Excludes India.

r Excludes the Russian Federation.

N Excludes Brazil.

TABLE 12. EARLY CHILDHOOD DEVELOPMENT

Countries and areas	Attendance in early childhood education 2005–2016*					Adult support for learning ++ 2005–2016*					Father's support for learning ++ 2005–2016*	Learning materials at home 2005–2016*						Children with inadequate supervision 2005–2016*				
												Children's books			Playthings ++							
	total	male	female	poorest 20%	richest 20%	total	male	female	poorest 20%	richest 20%	2005–2016*	total	poorest 20%	richest 20%	total	poorest 20%	richest 20%	total	male	female	poorest 20%	richest 20%
Afghanistan	1	1	1	0	4	73	74	73	72	80	62 y	2	1	5	53	52	57	40	42	39	43	27
Albania	40	39	42	26	60	86	85	87	68	96	53 y	32	16	52	53	57	48	13	14	11	9	16
Algeria	17	17	16	7	31	78	79	78	64	92	79 y	11	3	23	35	32	36	6	6	5	6	6
Andorra	–	–	–	–	–	–	–	–	–	–	–	–	–	–	–	–	–	–	–	–	–	–
Angola	–	–	–	–	–	–	–	–	–	–	–	–	–	–	–	–	–	–	–	–	–	–
Anguilla	–	–	–	–	–	–	–	–	–	–	–	–	–	–	–	–	–	–	–	–	–	–
Antigua and Barbuda	–	–	–	–	–	–	–	–	–	–	–	–	–	–	–	–	–	–	–	–	–	–
Argentina	63	61	66	46	85	84	83	85	73	95	57 y	61	40	83	61	58	63	8	9	8	10	5
Armenia	–	–	–	–	–	–	–	–	–	–	–	–	–	–	–	–	–	–	–	–	–	–
Australia	–	–	–	–	–	–	–	–	–	–	–	–	–	–	–	–	–	–	–	–	–	–
Austria	–	–	–	–	–	–	–	–	–	–	–	–	–	–	–	–	–	–	–	–	–	–
Azerbaijan	–	–	–	–	–	–	–	–	–	–	–	–	–	–	–	–	–	–	–	–	–	–
Bahamas	–	–	–	–	–	–	–	–	–	–	–	–	–	–	–	–	–	–	–	–	–	–
Bahrain	–	–	–	–	–	–	–	–	–	–	–	–	–	–	–	–	–	–	–	–	–	–
Bangladesh	13	13	14	12	18	78	78	78	64	94	10	9	2	23	60	57	60	12	11	12	14	12
Barbados	90	88	91	90 p	97 p	97	97	97	100 p	100 p	46 y	85	83	89	76	68	77	1	2	1	0	3
Belarus	88	86	89	75	91	96	94	97	90	99	68 y	92	83	96	79	77	79	4	4	4	4	5
Belgium	–	–	–	–	–	–	–	–	–	–	–	–	–	–	–	–	–	–	–	–	–	–
Belize	55	52	58	29	72	88	89	86	80	94	24	44	23	73	68	70	66	13	15	11	15	11
Benin	13	13	14	2	38	28	28	27	18	48	5	1	0	6	48	39	65	34	35	34	39	25
Bhutan	10	10	10	3	27	54	52	57	40	73	51 y	6	1	24	52	36	60	14	13	15	17	7
Bolivia (Plurinational State of)	–	–	–	–	–	–	–	–	–	–	–	–	–	–	–	–	–	–	–	–	–	–
Bosnia and Herzegovina	13	12	14	2	31	95	95	96	87	100	76 y	56	39	73	56	58	60	2	2	2	3	1
Botswana	18																					
Brazil	70 y	–																				
British Virgin Islands	–																					
Brunei Darussalam	–																					
Bulgaria	–																					
Burkina Faso	3 y	3 y	3 y	–	–	14	14	14	12	26	24 y											
Burundi	5	5	5	4	10	34	35	34	32	38	20 y											
Cabo Verde	–	–	–	–	–	–	–	–	–	–	–	–	–	–	–	–	–	–	–	–	–	–
Cambodia	15 y	12 y	17 y	7 y	38 y	59 y	57 y	62 y	48 y	73 y	9 y	4 y	1 y	12 y	34 y	20 y	53 y	10 y	10 y	10 y	16 y	4 y
Cameroon	28	27	29	2	66	44	45	44	50	52	4	4	0	17	53	47	65	34	34	35	52	23
Canada	–	–	–	–	–	–	–	–	–	–	–	–	–	–	–	–	–	–	–	–	–	–
Central African Republic	5	5	6	2	17	74	74	74	70	78	42 y	1	0	3	49	41	51	61	60	62	58	60
Chad	3 y	3 y	3 y	1 y	11 y	47 y	48 y	46 y	41 y	51 y	20 y	1 y	1 y	2 y	41 y	33 y	52 y	47 y	50 y	45 y	43 y	46 y
Chile	–	–	–	–	–	–	–	–	–	–	–	–	–	–	–	–	–	–	–	–	–	–
China	–																					
Colombia	37 y																					
Comoros	–																					
Congo	36	–				59	–				6	3			51	–		42	–			
Cook Islands	–										–											
Costa Rica	18	17	18	8	40	68	69	66	54	88	52 y	37	13	70	73	68	74	4	4	4	6	3
Côte d'Ivoire	5	5	5	1	15	50	50	51	55	57	40 y	5	3	13	39	44	35	59	60	58	62	51
Croatia	74 y	75 y	73 y	–	–						–											
Cuba	76	75	77	–	–	89	89	90			18	48	–	–	78	–	–	4	4	4	–	–
Cyprus	–																					
Czechia	–																					
Democratic People's Republic of Korea	98	98	97	–	–	91	88	93	–	–	75 y	79	–	–	47	–	–	17	17	16	–	–
Democratic Republic of the Congo	7 y	7 y	7 y	1 y	20 y	52 y	55 y	48 y	45 y	64 y	4 y	1 y	0 y	2 y	27 y	18 y	49 y	49 y	50 y	48 y	57 y	29 y
Denmark	–	–	–	–	–	–	–	–	–	–	–	–	–	–	–	–	–	–	–	–	–	–
Djibouti	14	12	16	–	–	37 y	38 y	35 y	–	–	28 y	15	–	–	24	–	–	8	8	8	–	–
Dominica	–	–	–	–	–	–	–	–	–	–	–	–	–	–	–	–	–	–	–	–	–	–
Dominican Republic	40	39	40	16	72	58	58	59	38	73	6	10	2	28	57	57	58	5	5	5	7	3
Ecuador	–	–	–	–	–	–	–	–	–	–	–	–	–	–	–	–	–	–	–	–	–	–
Egypt	47 y	48 y	47 y	34 y	50 y	–	–	–	–	–	–	–	–	–	–	–	–	4	4	4	7	2
El Salvador	25	24	26	19	44	59	57	62	45	78	8	18	6	44	62	62	58	4	4	3	4	4
Equatorial Guinea	–	–	–	–	–	–	–	–	–	–	–	–	–	–	–	–	–	–	–	–	–	–
Eritrea	–	–	–	–	–	–	–	–	–	–	–	–	–	–	–	–	–	–	–	–	–	–
Estonia	–	–	–	–	–	–	–	–	–	–	–	–	–	–	–	–	–	–	–	–	–	–
Ethiopia	–	–	–	–	–	–	–	–	–	–	–	–	–	–	–	–	–	–	–	–	–	–
Fiji	–	–	–	–	–	–	–	–	–	–	–	–	–	–	–	–	–	–	–	–	–	–
Finland	–	–	–	–	–	–	–	–	–	–	–	–	–	–	–	–	–	–	–	–	–	–
France	–	–	–	–	–	–	–	–	–	–	–	–	–	–	–	–	–	–	–	–	–	–

TABLE 12. EARLY CHILDHOOD DEVELOPMENT   199

Countries and areas	Attendance in early childhood education 2005–2016*					Adult support for learning ++ 2005–2016*					Father's support for learning ++ 2005–2016*	Learning materials at home 2005–2016*						Children with inadequate supervision 2005–2016*				
												Children's books			Playthings ++							
	total	male	female	poorest 20%	richest 20%	total	male	female	poorest 20%	richest 20%	2005–2016*	total	poorest 20%	richest 20%	total	poorest 20%	richest 20%	total	male	female	poorest 20%	richest 20%
Gabon	–	–	–	–	–	–	–	–	–	–	–	–	–	–	–	–	–	–	–	–	–	–
Gambia	18	17	19	12	32	48	49	47	50	55	21 y	1	0	4	42	28	50	21	22	19	25	18
Georgia	62 y	–	–	–	–	83	82	84	85	82	35 y	58 y	40 y	74 y	38	41	41	6 y	6 y	7 y	6 y	8 y
Germany	–	–	–	–	–	–	–	–	–	–	–	–	–	–	–	–	–	–	–	–	–	–
Ghana	68	65	72	42	97	40	38	42	23	78	30 y	6	1	23	41	31	51	21	21	21	27	15
Greece	–	–	–	–	–	–	–	–	–	–	–	–	–	–	–	–	–	–	–	–	–	–
Grenada	–	–	–	–	–	–	–	–	–	–	–	–	–	–	–	–	–	–	–	–	–	–
Guatemala	–	–	–	–	–	–	–	–	–	–	–	–	–	–	–	–	–	–	–	–	–	–
Guinea	–	–	–	–	–	–	–	–	–	–	–	–	–	–	–	–	–	–	–	–	–	–
Guinea-Bissau	13	13	14	3	46	34	41	28	33	51	0	1	0	3	31	24	46	31	31	31	27	38
Guyana	61	63	59	45	76	87	85	90	82	94	16	47	25	76	69	65	70	5	5	5	10	1
Haiti	–	–	–	–	–	–	–	–	–	–	–	–	–	–	–	–	–	–	–	–	–	–
Holy See	–	–	–	–	–	–	–	–	–	–	–	–	–	–	–	–	–	–	–	–	–	–
Honduras	19	17	21	13	28	48	47	49	28	75	59 y	11	1	34	78	74	81	4	5	4	8	2
Hungary	–	–	–	–	–	–	–	–	–	–	–	–	–	–	–	–	–	–	–	–	–	–
Iceland	–	–	–	–	–	–	–	–	–	–	–	–	–	–	–	–	–	–	–	–	–	–
India	–	–	–	–	–	–	–	–	–	–	–	–	–	–	–	–	–	–	–	–	–	–
Indonesia	17	16	18			–	–	–	–	–	–	–	–	–	–	–	–	–	–	–	–	–
Iran (Islamic Republic of)	20 y	19 y	22 y	–	–	70 y	69 y	70 y	–	–	60 y	36 y	–	–	67 y	–	–	15 y	15 y	15 y	–	–
Iraq	4	4	4	1	10	58	58	59	40	78	55 y	5	1	16	34	34	32	8	8	7	9	8
Ireland	–	–	–	–	–	–	–	–	–	–	–	–	–	–	–	–	–	–	–	–	–	–
Israel	–	–	–	–	–	–	–	–	–	–	–	–	–	–	–	–	–	–	–	–	–	–
Italy	–	–	–	–	–	–	–	–	–	–	–	–	–	–	–	–	–	–	–	–	–	–
Jamaica	92	92	91	88	100	88	86	90	76	86	28 y	55	34	73	61	64	56	2	2	2	2	1
Japan	–	–	–	–	–	–	–	–	–	–	–	–	–	–	–	–	–	–	–	–	–	–
Jordan	22 y	21 y	23 y	11 y	39 y	82 y	81 y	83 y	75 y	87 y	72 y	23 y	11 y	40 y	70 y	68 y	74 y	9 y	9 y	9 y	11 y	8 y
Kazakhstan	55	53	58	45	70	86	84	87	83	95	7	51	35	73	60	63	61	5	4	6	8	3
Kenya	–	–	–	–	–	–	–	–	–	–	–	–	–	–	–	–	–	–	–	–	–	–
Kiribati	–	–	–	–	–	–	–	–	–	–	–	–	–	–	–	–	–	–	–	–	–	–
Kuwait	–	–	–	–	–	–	–	–	–	–	–	–	–	–	–	–	–	–	–	–	–	–
Kyrgyzstan	23	23	23	12	50	72	74	70	63	73	3	27	15	54	59	63	54	5	5	4	6	5
Lao People's Democratic Republic	23	21	25	5	73	57	58	57	42	87	52 y	5	1	24	41	29	50	14	15	13	20	8
Latvia	–	–	–	–	–	–	–	–	–	–	–	–	–	–	–	–	–	–	–	–	–	–
Lebanon	62	63	60	–	–	56 y	58 y	54 y	–	–	74 y	29	–	–	16 y	–	–	9	8	10	–	–
Lesotho	–	–	–	–	–	–	–	–	–	–	–	–	–	–	–	–	–	–	–	–	–	–
Liberia	–	–	–	–	–	–	–	–	–	–	–	–	–	–	–	–	–	–	–	–	–	–
Libya	–	–	–	–	–	–	–	–	–	–	–	–	–	–	–	–	–	–	–	–	–	–
Liechtenstein	–	–	–	–	–	–	–	–	–	–	–	–	–	–	–	–	–	–	–	–	–	–
Lithuania	–	–	–	–	–	–	–	–	–	–	–	–	–	–	–	–	–	–	–	–	–	–
Luxembourg	–	–	–	–	–	–	–	–	–	–	–	–	–	–	–	–	–	–	–	–	–	–
Madagascar	–	–	–	–	–	–	–	–	–	–	–	–	–	–	–	–	–	–	–	–	–	–
Malawi	39	37	41	26	67	29	29	30	22	44	3	1	0	6	45	35	66	37	37	37	39	28
Malaysia	53	52	55	–	–	25	25	24	–	–	–	56	–	–	62	–	–	3	3	3	–	–
Maldives	–	–	–	–	–	–	–	–	–	–	–	–	–	–	–	–	–	–	–	–	–	–
Mali	5	6	5	1	21	55	55	55	53	65	5	0	0	2	52	42	70	32	32	32	31	27
Malta	–	–	–	–	–	–	–	–	–	–	–	–	–	–	–	–	–	–	–	–	–	–
Marshall Islands	–	–	–	–	–	–	–	–	–	–	–	–	–	–	–	–	–	–	–	–	–	–
Mauritania	12	–	–	–	–	44	–	–	–	–	5	1	–	–	33	–	–	34	–	–	–	–
Mauritius	–	–	–	–	–	–	–	–	–	–	–	–	–	–	–	–	–	–	–	–	–	–
Mexico	60	58	62	58	71	76	71	80	62	94	14	35	15	64	76	74	85	5	5	5	8	3
Micronesia (Federated States of)	–	–	–	–	–	–	–	–	–	–	–	–	–	–	–	–	–	–	–	–	–	–
Monaco	–	–	–	–	–	–	–	–	–	–	–	–	–	–	–	–	–	–	–	–	–	–
Mongolia	68	68	68	36	90	55	55	55	38	71	10	33	13	57	56	57	58	10	9	11	15	8
Montenegro	40	39	42	7	66	98	97	99	93	98	45	73	48	87	60	61	66	3	3	2	3	3
Montserrat	–	–	–	–	–	–	–	–	–	–	–	–	–	–	–	–	–	–	–	–	–	–
Morocco	39	36	41	6	78	35 y	34 y	35 y	16 y	59 y	58 y	21 y	9 y	52 y	14 y	19 y	7 y	11	–	–	–	–
Mozambique	–	–	–	–	–	47	45	48	48	50	20 y	3	2	10	–	–	–	33	33	32	–	–
Myanmar	23 y	22 y	25 y	11 y	42 y	54 y	53 y	56 y	43 y	77 y	6 y	5	1 y	15 y	72 y	64 y	76 y	13 y	14 y	13 y	21 y	5 y
Namibia	–	–	–	–	–	–	–	–	–	–	–	–	–	–	–	–	–	–	–	–	–	–
Nauru	–	–	–	–	–	–	–	–	–	–	–	–	–	–	–	–	–	–	–	–	–	–
Nepal	51	52	49	41	84	67	70	64	51	90	10	5	1	16	59	60	60	21	20	21	30	12
Netherlands	–	–	–	–	–	–	–	–	–	–	–	–	–	–	–	–	–	–	–	–	–	–
New Zealand	–	–	–	–	–	–	–	–	–	–	–	–	–	–	–	–	–	–	–	–	–	–
Nicaragua	–	–	–	–	–	–	–	–	–	–	–	–	–	–	–	–	–	–	–	–	–	–

TABLE 12. EARLY CHILDHOOD DEVELOPMENT

Countries and areas	Attendance in early childhood education 2005–2016*					Adult support for learning ++ 2005–2016*					Father's support for learning ++ 2005–2016*	Learning materials at home 2005–2016*						Children with inadequate supervision 2005–2016*				
												Children's books			Playthings ++							
	total	male	female	poorest 20%	richest 20%	total	male	female	poorest 20%	richest 20%	2005–2016*	total	poorest 20%	richest 20%	total	poorest 20%	richest 20%	total	male	female	poorest 20%	richest 20%
Niger	–	–	–	–	–	–	–	–	–	–	–	–	–	–	–	–	–	–	–	–	–	–
Nigeria	43	42	43	10	84	65	66	64	48	89	37 y	6	0	19	38	29	48	40	40	40	40	34
Niue	–	–	–	–	–	–	–	–	–	–	–	–	–	–	–	–	–	–	–	–	–	–
Norway	–	–	–	–	–	–	–	–	–	–	–	–	–	–	–	–	–	–	–	–	–	–
Oman	29	28	31	–	–	81	78	84	–	–	22	25	–	–	75	–	–	45	44	45	–	–
Pakistan	–	–	–	–	–	–	–	–	–	–	–	–	–	–	–	–	–	–	–	–	–	–
Palau	–	–	–	–	–	–	–	–	–	–	–	–	–	–	–	–	–	–	–	–	–	–
Panama	37	38	35	28	67	74	73	74	55	89	45 y	26	7	59	69	67	68	3	3	2	6	1
Papua New Guinea	–	–	–	–	–	–	–	–	–	–	–	–	–	–	–	–	–	–	–	–	–	–
Paraguay	–	–	–	–	–	–	–	–	–	–	–	–	–	–	–	–	–	–	–	–	–	–
Peru	77 y	76 y	79 y	70 y	90 y	–	–	–	–	–	–	–	–	–	–	–	–	–	–	–	–	–
Philippines	–	–	–	–	–	–	–	–	–	–	–	–	–	–	–	–	–	–	–	–	–	–
Poland	–	–	–	–	–	–	–	–	–	–	–	–	–	–	–	–	–	–	–	–	–	–
Portugal	–	–	–	–	–	–	–	–	–	–	–	–	–	–	–	–	–	–	–	–	–	–
Qatar	41	41	41	–	–	88	89	88	–	–	85 y	40	–	–	55	–	–	12	12	11	–	–
Republic of Korea	–	–	–	–	–	–	–	–	–	–	–	–	–	–	–	–	–	–	–	–	–	–
Republic of Moldova	71	74	67	50	88	89	86	92	81	95	47 y	68	33	87	68	75	69	6	6	6	9	5
Romania	82 y	82 y	83 y	–	–	–	–	–	–	–	–	–	–	–	–	–	–	–	–	–	–	–
Russian Federation	–	–	–	–	–	–	–	–	–	–	–	–	–	–	–	–	–	–	–	–	–	–
Rwanda	13 y	12 y	14 y	3 y	45 y	49 y	49 y	49 y	36 y	66 y	3 y	1 y	0 y	3 y	30 y	21 y	41 y	35 y	35 y	35 y	38 y	21 y
Saint Kitts and Nevis	–	–	–	–	–	–	–	–	–	–	–	–	–	–	–	–	–	–	–	–	–	–
Saint Lucia	85	87	84	–	–	93	89	96	–	–	50 y	68	–	–	59	–	–	5	5	5	–	–
Saint Vincent and the Grenadines	–	–	–	–	–	–	–	–	–	–	–	–	–	–	–	–	–	–	–	–	–	–
Samoa	–	–	–	–	–	–	–	–	–	–	–	–	–	–	–	–	–	–	–	–	–	–
San Marino	–	–	–	–	–	–	–	–	–	–	–	–	–	–	–	–	–	–	–	–	–	–
Sao Tome and Principe	36	34	39	21	63	63	63	63	48	74	3	6	1	20	65	65	57	16	17	14	26	8
Saudi Arabia	–	–	–	–	–	–	–	–	–	–	–	–	–	–	–	–	–	–	–	–	–	–
Senegal	35 y	35 y	34 y	12 y	68 y	–	–	–	–	–	–	–	–	–	–	–	–	–	–	–	–	–
Serbia	50	52	49	9	82	96	95	96	87	98	37	72	44	83	75	78	76	1	2	1	3	2
Seychelles	–	–	–	–	–	–	–	–	–	–	–	–	–	–	–	–	–	–	–	–	–	–
Sierra Leone	14	13	15	5	42	54	53	55	45	79	42 y	2	0	10	35	24	50	32	33	32	29	28
Singapore	–	–	–	–	–	–	–	–	–	–	–	–	–	–	–	–	–	–	–	–	–	–
Slovakia	–	–	–	–	–	–	–	–	–	–	–	–	–	–	–	–	–	–	–	–	–	–
Slovenia	–	–	–	–	–	–	–	–	–	–	–	–	–	–	–	–	–	–	–	–	–	–
Solomon Islands	–	–	–	–	–	–	–	–	–	–	–	–	–	–	–	–	–	–	–	–	–	–
Somalia	2	2	2	1	6	79	80	79	76	85	48 y	–	–	–	–	–	–	–	–	–	–	–
South Africa	48 y	–	–	–	–	–	–	–	–	–	–	–	–	–	–	–	–	–	–	–	–	–
South Sudan	6	6	6	2	13	–	–	–	–	–	–	–	–	–	–	–	–	–	–	–	–	–
Spain	–	–	–	–	–	–	–	–	–	–	–	–	–	–	–	–	–	–	–	–	–	–
Sri Lanka	–	–	–	–	–	–	–	–	–	–	–	–	–	–	–	–	–	–	–	–	–	–
State of Palestine	26	27	26	21	38	78	77	78	69	87	12	20	13	31	69	64	72	14	14	15	15	12
Sudan	22	22	23	7	59	–	–	–	–	–	–	2	0	7	46	36	55	–	–	–	–	–
Suriname	34	33	35	16	63	73	71	75	56	91	26 y	25	4	61	59	61	60	7	7	7	9	8
Swaziland	30	26	33	28	48	39	33	44	25	59	2	6	2	19	67	56	78	17	16	17	18	15
Sweden	–	–	–	–	–	–	–	–	–	–	–	–	–	–	–	–	–	–	–	–	–	–
Switzerland	–	–	–	–	–	–	–	–	–	–	–	–	–	–	–	–	–	–	–	–	–	–
Syrian Arab Republic	8	8	7	4	18	70	70	69	52	84	62 y	30	12	53	52	52	51	17	17	17	22	15
Tajikistan	6	–	–	–	–	74	73	74	56	86	23 y	17	4	33	46	43	44	13	13	12	15	11
Thailand	85	84	85	86	84	93	93	92	87	98	34	41	23	73	76	81	67	2	6	6	8	3
The former Yugoslav Republic of Macedonia	30	–	–	–	–	92	92	91	81	96	71 y	52	18	81	71	70	79	5	5	5	11	1
Timor-Leste	–	–	–	–	–	–	–	–	–	–	–	–	–	–	–	–	–	–	–	–	–	–
Togo	26 y	26 y	26 y	15 y	52 y	25 y	25 y	25 y	20 y	42 y	21 y	1 y	0 y	3 y	34 y	22 y	48 y	29 y	26 y	33 y	36 y	26 y
Tokelau	–	–	–	–	–	–	–	–	–	–	–	–	–	–	–	–	–	–	–	–	–	–
Tonga	–	–	–	–	–	–	–	–	–	–	–	–	–	–	–	–	–	–	–	–	–	–
Trinidad and Tobago	75	74	76	65	87	98	98	98	96	100	63 y	81	66	93	65	63	72	1	1	1	2	0
Tunisia	44	42	47	13	81	71	68	74	44	90	71 y	18	3	40	53	46	56	13	13	14	18	9
Turkey	–	–	–	–	–	–	–	–	–	–	–	–	–	–	–	–	–	–	–	–	–	–
Turkmenistan	43	43	43	17	81	94	94	95	92	98	15	48	30	66	53	59	56	1	0	1	1	1
Turks and Caicos Islands	–	–	–	–	–	–	–	–	–	–	–	–	–	–	–	–	–	–	–	–	–	–
Tuvalu	–	–	–	–	–	–	–	–	–	–	–	–	–	–	–	–	–	–	–	–	–	–
Uganda	–	–	–	–	–	–	–	–	–	–	–	–	–	–	–	–	–	–	–	–	–	–
Ukraine	52	54	50	30	68	98	97	98	95	99	71 y	91	92	92	52	61	51	7	6	7	11	5
United Arab Emirates	–	–	–	–	–	–	–	–	–	–	–	–	–	–	–	–	–	–	–	–	–	–
United Kingdom	–	–	–	–	–	–	–	–	–	–	–	–	–	–	–	–	–	–	–	–	–	–

TABLE 12. EARLY CHILDHOOD DEVELOPMENT

201

Countries and areas	Attendance in early childhood education 2005–2016*					Adult support for learning ++ 2005–2016*					Father's support for learning ++ 2005–2016*	Learning materials at home 2005–2016*						Children with inadequate supervision 2005–2016*				
												Children's books			Playthings ++							
	total	male	female	poorest 20%	richest 20%	total	male	female	poorest 20%	richest 20%	2005–2016*	total	poorest 20%	richest 20%	total	poorest 20%	richest 20%	total	male	female	poorest 20%	richest 20%
United Republic of Tanzania	–	–	–	–	–	–	–	–	–	–	–	–	–	–	–	–	–	–	–	–	–	–
United States	–	–	–	–	–	–	–	–	–	–	–	–	–	–	–	–	–	–	–	–	–	–
Uruguay	81	83	80	–	–	93	94	91	–	–	66 y	59	–	–	75	–	–	3	3	3	–	–
Uzbekistan	21 y	21 y	21 y	–	–	91	91	90	83	95	54 y	43	32	59	67	74	62	5	5	5	6	7
Vanuatu	–	–	–	–	–	–	–	–	–	–	–	–	–	–	–	–	–	–	–	–	–	–
Venezuela (Bolivarian Republic of)	66 y	–																				
Viet Nam	71	74	69	53	86	76	76	76	52	96	15	26	6	58	52	44	54	7	6	8	14	2
Yemen	3	3	3	0	8	33	34	32	16	56	37 y	10	4	31	49	45	49	34	36	33	46	22
Zambia	–	–	–	–	–	–	–	–	–	–	–	–	–	–	–	–	–	–	–	–	–	–
Zimbabwe	22	20	23	17	34	43	43	43	35	59	3	3	1	12	62	48	74	19	19	18	25	7
SUMMARY																						
East Asia and Pacific	37 **	37 **	37 **	–	–	–	–	–	–	–	–	–	–	–	–	–	–	–	–	–	–	–
Europe and Central Asia	–	–	–	–	–	–	–	–	–	–	–	–	–	–	–	–	–	–	–	–	–	–
Eastern Europe and Central Asia	–	–	–	–	–	–	–	–	–	–	–	–	–	–	–	–	–	–	–	–	–	–
Western Europe	–	–	–	–	–	–	–	–	–	–	–	–	–	–	–	–	–	–	–	–	–	–
Latin America and Caribbean	61	–	–	–	–	–	–	–	–	–	–	–	–	–	–	–	–	–	–	–	–	–
Middle East and North Africa	26	25	26	15	37	61	61	61	–	–	58	19	–	–	45	–	–	11	12	11	14	8
North America	–	–	–	–	–	–	–	–	–	–	–	–	–	–	–	–	–	–	–	–	–	–
South Asia	–	–	–	–	–	–	–	–	–	–	–	–	–	–	–	–	–	–	–	–	–	–
Sub-Saharan Africa	27	25	26	8	54	53	53	52	44	69	23	3	0	12	39	–	–	39	–	–	–	–
Eastern and Southern Africa	–	–	–	–	–	–	–	–	–	–	–	–	–	–	–	–	–	–	–	–	–	–
West and Central Africa	27	27	28	8	58	54	55	53	44	72	24	4	0	13	38	30	50	41	41	41	44	32
Least developed countries	13	13	14	7	29	55	56	55	47	69	17	4	1	11	47	40	57	31	–	–	–	–
World	–	–	–	–	–	–	–	–	–	–	–	–	–	–	–	–	–	–	–	–	–	–

For a complete list of countries and areas in the regions, subregions and country categories, see page 150 or visit <data.unicef.org/regionalclassifications>.
It is not advisable to compare data from consecutive editions of *The State of the World's Children*.

DEFINITIONS OF THE INDICATORS

Attendance in early childhood education – Percentage of children 36–59 months old who are attending an early childhood education programme.

Adult support for learning – Percentage of children 36–59 months old with whom an adult has engaged in four or more of the following activities to promote learning and school readiness in the past 3 days: a) reading books to the child, b) telling stories to the child, c) singing songs to the child, d) taking the child outside the home, e) playing with the child, and f) spending time with the child naming, counting or drawing things.

Father's support for learning – Percentage of children 36–59 months old whose father has engaged in four or more of the following activities to promote learning and school readiness in the past 3 days: a) reading books to the child, b) telling stories to the child, c) singing songs to the child, d) taking the child outside the home, e) playing with the child, and f) spending time with the child naming, counting or drawing things.

Learning materials at home: Children's books – Percentage of children 36–59 months old who have three or more children's books at home.

Learning materials at home: Playthings – Percentage of children 0–59 months old with two or more of the following playthings at home: household objects or objects found outside (sticks, rocks, animals, shells, leaves etc.), homemade toys or toys that came from a store.

Children with inadequate supervision – Percentage of children 0–59 months old left alone or in the care of another child younger than 10 years of age for more than one hour at least once in the past week.

NOTES

– Data not available.

p Based on small denominators (typically 25–49 unweighted cases). No data based on fewer than 25 unweighted cases are displayed.

y Data differ from the standard definition or refer to only part of a country. If they fall within the noted reference period, such data are included in the calculation of regional and global averages.

++ Changes in the definitions of several ECD indicators were made between the third and fourth round of MICS (MICS3 and MICS4). In order to allow for comparability with MICS4, data from MICS3 for the adult support for learning, father's support for learning and learning materials at home (playthings) indicators were recalculated according to MICS4 indicator definitions. Therefore, the recalculated data presented here will differ from estimates reported in MICS3 national reports.

* Data refer to the most recent year available during the period specified in the column heading.

MAIN DATA SOURCES

Attendance in early childhood education – Demographic and Health Surveys (DHS), Multiple Indicator Cluster Surveys (MICS), and other national surveys.

Adult support for learning – DHS, MICS and other national surveys.

Father's support for learning – DHS, MICS and other national surveys.

Learning materials at home: Children's books – DHS, MICS and other national surveys.

Learning materials at home: Playthings – DHS, MICS and other national surveys.

Children with inadequate supervision – DHS, MICS and other national surveys.

TABLE 13. ECONOMIC INDICATORS

Countries and areas	Population below international poverty line of US$1.90 per day (%) 2010–2014*	National monetary child poverty (%)[p] 2010–2016*	ODA inflow in millions US$ 2015	ODA inflow as a % of recipient GNI 2015	Share of household income (%, 2009–2013*) poorest 40%	Share of household income (%, 2009–2013*) richest 20%
Afghanistan	–	–	4,239	21	–	–
Albania	1	–	334	3	22	38
Algeria	–	–	88	0	–	–
Andorra	–	–	–	–	–	–
Angola	30 x	–	380	0	15 x	49 x
Anguilla	–	–	–	–	–	–
Antigua and Barbuda	–	24 x	1	0	–	–
Argentina	2	–	-23	0	15	47
Armenia	2	34	348	3	21	40
Australia	–	–	–	–	19	42
Austria	–	–	–	–	21	38
Azerbaijan	1 x	5	70	0	21 x	41 x
Bahamas	–	–	–	–	–	–
Bahrain	–	–	–	–	–	–
Bangladesh	19	–	2,570	1	21	42
Barbados	–	32	–	–	–	–
Belarus	0	9	105	0	24	36
Belgium	–	–	–	–	23	36
Belize	14 x	–	27	2	11 x	58 x
Benin	53	–	430	5	16	51
Bhutan	2	–	97	5	18	46
Bolivia (Plurinational State of)	7	–	787	2	12	52
Bosnia and Herzegovina	0	–	355	2	19	41
Botswana	18 x	26	66	0	9	65
Brazil	4	–	999	0	11	57
British Virgin Islands	–	29 x	–	–	–	–
Brunei Darussalam	–	–	–	–	–	–
Bulgaria	2	25	–	–	18	43
Burkina Faso	44	–	997	9	17	47
Burundi	78 x	55	367	12	21 x	43 x
Cabo Verde	8 x	–	153	10	14 x	53 x
Cambodia	2	–	677	4	22	40
Cameroon	24	–	664	2	15 x	49 x
Canada	–	–	–	–	20	41
Central African Republic	66 x	–	487	31	10 x	61 x
Chad	38	–	607	6	15	49
Chile	1	18	50	0	13	57
China	2	7 y	-332	0	15	48
Colombia	6	–	1,347	0	11	58
Comoros	14 x	–	66	12	11 x	61 x
Congo	37	54 x	89	1	12	54
Cook Islands	–	–	–	–	–	–
Costa Rica	2	–	109	0	12	54
Côte d'Ivoire	29 x	–	653	2	–	–
Croatia	1	21	–	–	20	40
Cuba	–	–	553	–	–	–
Cyprus	–	–	–	–	20	43
Czechia	0	–	–	–	24	36
Democratic People's Republic of Korea	–	–	131	–	–	–
Democratic Republic of the Congo	77	–	2,599	8	16	48
Denmark	–	–	–	–	23	38
Djibouti	23	–	170	–	15	50
Dominica	–	38 x	11	2	–	–
Dominican Republic	2	–	278	0	14	53
Ecuador	4	–	311	0	13	53
Egypt	–	29	2,488	1	–	–
El Salvador	3	44	88	0	15	50
Equatorial Guinea	–	–	8	0	–	–
Eritrea	–	–	92	–	–	–
Estonia	1	–	–	–	20	41
Ethiopia	34	–	3,234	5	21	42
Fiji	4 x	–	102	2	16 x	50 x
Finland	–	–	–	–	23	37

TABLE 13. ECONOMIC INDICATORS

203

Countries and areas	Population below international poverty line of US$1.90 per day (%) 2010–2014*	National monetary child poverty (%)ᴾ 2010–2016*	ODA inflow in millions US$ 2015	ODA inflow as a % of recipient GNI 2015	Share of household income (%, 2009–2013*) poorest 40%	Share of household income (%, 2009–2013*) richest 20%
France	–	–	–	–	20	41
Gabon	8 x	–	99	1	16 x	49 x
Gambia	45 x	–	108	12	14 x	53 x
Georgia	10	27	448	3	16	46
Germany	–	–	–	–	22	39
Ghana	25 x	–	1,768	5	15 x	49 x
Greece	–	–	–	–	17	42
Grenada	–	51 x	23	2	–	–
Guatemala	9	68	408	1	12	57
Guinea	35	–	538	9	20	42
Guinea-Bissau	67	–	95	9	13	57
Guyana	14 x	–	31	1	14 x	50 x
Haiti	54	–	1,043	12	8	64
Holy See	–	–	–	–	–	–
Honduras	16	74	537	3	10	58
Hungary	0	–	–	–	21	39
Iceland	–	–	–	–	23	36
India	21	–	3,163	0	20	44
Indonesia	8	17 x	-43	0	18	47
Iran (Islamic Republic of)	0	–	111	–	18	45
Iraq	–	–	1,485	1	–	–
Ireland	–	–	–	–	20	41
Israel	–	–	–	–	14	47
Italy	–	–	–	–	19	42
Jamaica	2 x	–	57	0	15 x	52 x
Japan	–	–	–	–	20 x	40 x
Jordan	–	19	2,150	6	–	–
Kazakhstan	0	45	83	0	24	36
Kenya	34 x	–	2,474	4	13 x	54 x
Kiribati	14 x	–	65	19	18 x	44 x
Kuwait	–	–	–	–	–	–
Kyrgyzstan	1	46	769	12	23	38
Lao People's Democratic Republic	17	–	471	3	18	46
Latvia	1	–	–	–	19	42
Lebanon	–	–	975	2	–	–
Lesotho	60	–	83	3	10	58
Liberia	69 x	–	1,094	62	18 x	44 x
Libya	–	–	158	–	–	–
Liechtenstein	–	–	–	–	–	–
Lithuania	1	–	–	–	19	42
Luxembourg	–	–	–	–	19	42
Madagascar	78	78	677	7	16	49
Malawi	71	–	1,049	17	15	52
Malaysia	0 x	–	-1	0	13	51
Maldives	7 x	–	27	1	17	45
Mali	49 x	–	1,200	10	20	41
Malta	–	–	–	–	–	–
Marshall Islands	–	–	57	24	–	–
Mauritania	6	–	318	7	18 x	42 x
Mauritius	1	–	77	1	19	44
Mexico	3	54	309	0	14	54
Micronesia (Federated States of)	17	–	81	22	15	48
Monaco	–	–	–	–	–	–
Mongolia	0	–	236	2	20	42
Montenegro	0	13	100	2	20	40
Montserrat	–	47 x	–	–	–	–
Morocco	3 x	–	1,369	1	17 x	48 x
Mozambique	69 x	–	1,815	12	15 x	51 x
Myanmar	–	–	1,169	2	–	–
Namibia	23 x	34	142	1	9	66
Nauru	–	–	31	25	–	–
Nepal	15	–	1,216	6	20	42
Netherlands	–	–	–	–	23	37
New Zealand	–	–	–	–	–	–

TABLE 13. ECONOMIC INDICATORS

Countries and areas	Population below international poverty line of US$1.90 per day (%) 2010–2014*	National monetary child poverty (%)[P] 2010–2016*	ODA inflow in millions US$ 2015	ODA inflow as a % of recipient GNI 2015	Share of household income (%, 2009–2013*) poorest 40%	Share of household income (%, 2009–2013*) richest 20%
Nicaragua	6	–	454	4	14	51
Niger	46	63 x	866	12	22	41
Nigeria	54 x	–	2,432	1	15	49
Niue	–	–	–	–	–	–
Norway	–	–	–	–	24	35
Oman	–	–	–	–	–	–
Pakistan	6	–	3,790	1	22	40
Palau	–	–	14	5	–	–
Panama	4	–	9	0	11	56
Papua New Guinea	39 x	–	590	–	14	49
Paraguay	3	32	56	0	13	53
Peru	3	–	332	0	14	50
Philippines	13	–	515	0	15	50
Poland	0	–	–	–	20	41
Portugal	–	–	–	–	19	43
Qatar	–	–	–	–	–	–
Republic of Korea	–	–	–	–	–	–
Republic of Moldova	0	13	313	4	–	–
Romania	0	38	–	–	23	36
Russian Federation	0	–	–	–	16	48
Rwanda	60	47	1,082	13	14	57
Saint Kitts and Nevis	–	31 x	–	–	–	–
Saint Lucia	36 x	37 x	13	1	15 x	48 x
Saint Vincent and the Grenadines	–	38 x	13	2	–	–
Samoa	1 x	–	94	12	16 x	50 x
San Marino	–	–	–	–	–	–
Sao Tome and Principe	32	–	49	15	21	40
Saudi Arabia	–	–	–	–	–	–
Senegal	38	49	879	7	17	47
Serbia	0	30	313	1	22	38
Seychelles	1	–	7	0	15	53
Sierra Leone	52	–	946	23	20	42
Singapore	–	–	–	–	–	–
Slovakia	0	–	–	–	23	35
Slovenia	0	–	–	–	24	35
Solomon Islands	46 x	–	190	17	14 x	52 x
Somalia	–	–	1,254	23	–	–
South Africa	17	56	1,421	0	7	69
South Sudan	43 x	–	1,675	21	13	51
Spain	–	–	–	–	18	42
Sri Lanka	2	–	427	1	18	47
State of Palestine	0 x	–	1,873	13	20	43
Sudan	15 x	–	900	1	19	42
Suriname	23 x	–	15	0	– x	– x
Swaziland	42 x	–	93	2	12	57
Sweden	–	–	–	–	23	36
Switzerland	–	–	–	–	21	40
Syrian Arab Republic	–	–	4,882	–	–	–
Tajikistan	20	–	426	5	22	40
Thailand	0	–	59	0	18	45
The former Yugoslav Republic of Macedonia	1 x	29	214	2	15 x	50 x
Timor-Leste	47 x	48	212	8	22 x	41 x
Togo	54	–	200	5	14	52
Tokelau	–	–	–	–	–	–
Tonga	1 x	–	68	16	18	45
Trinidad and Tobago	3 x	–	–	–	–	–
Tunisia	2	–	475	1	18	43
Turkey	0	33	2,145	0	16	47
Turkmenistan	42 x	–	24	0	16 x	48 x
Turks and Caicos Islands	–	26	–	–	–	–
Tuvalu	3	–	50	89	16	48
Uganda	35	22	1,628	6	17	48
Ukraine	0	–	1,458	2	25	35